AF286295

Journal of Cultural Management and Cultural Policy 2024
Resiliency in the Cultural Sector

Zeitschrift für Kulturmanagement und Kulturpolitik 2024
Resilienz im Kulturbereich

The *Journal of Cultural Management and Cultural Policy* is dedicated to international perspectives that address a wide range of issues in cultural management and cultural policy research and practice. We invite articles that reflect on organizational structures of creative enterprises, economic and managerial issues in the arts, cultural policy in all its dimensions, as well as creative and aesthetic processes in cultural production, distribution and perception. The journal aims to present multifaceted analysis and rich discourse on current issues in cultural management and cultural policy and to promote the development of research designs and methods relating to both new and established practices in these fields. The journal is open to any theoretical and methodological approach, as long as authors adhere to scholarly rigor.

Die *Zeitschrift für Kulturmanagement und Kulturpolitik* (Journal of Cultural Management and Cultural Policy) vertritt eine internationale Perspektive auf aktuelle Fragestellungen aus Forschung, Lehre und Praxis in den Feldern Kulturmanagement und Kulturpolitik. Das Themenspektrum umfasst nationale und internationale Kulturpolitik auf allen Ebenen (cultural policy, polity und politics); das Kunst- und Kultursystem /-feld sowie deren Institutionen, Praktiken und Angebote; Akteure in Kultur und den Künsten sowie Prozesse der Produktion, Distribution und Rezeption von Kunst und Kultur. Ebenfalls finden methodische (qualitative, quantitative, experimentelle) und theoretisch-analytische Arbeiten ein Podium, wobei eine prinzipielle interdisziplinäre Offenheit angestrebt ist.

JOURNAL OF CULTURAL MANAGEMENT AND CULTURAL POLICY

ZEITSCHRIFT FÜR KULTURMANAGEMENT UND KULTURPOLITIK

Editors-in-Chief
Constance DeVereaux, Steffen Höhne, Martin Tröndle

Volume 10 | Number 2
2024

[transcript]

Fachverband
Kulturmanagement

Editors-in-Chief
Prof. Dr. Constance DeVereaux, PhD, University of Connecticut, USA (Interim Managing Editor)
Prof. Dr. Steffen Höhne, University of Music Franz Liszt Weimar/Friedrich-Schiller-University Jena, Germany
Prof. Dr. Martin Tröndle, Würth Chair of Cultural Production, Zeppelin University Friedrichshafen, Germany

Journal Review Editor
Prof. Dr. Volker Kirchberg, Leuphana Universität Lüneburg, Germany

Book Review Editors
Prof. Dr. Karen van den Berg, Zeppelin Universität Friedrichshafen, Germany
Dr. Leticia Labaronne, ZHAW School of Management and Law, Winterthur, Switzerland
Dr. Simone Wesner University of London, United Kingdom

Editorial Board
Prof. Dr. Sigrid Bekmeier-Feuerhahn, Leuphana Universität Lüneburg, Germany
Prof. Milena Dragićević Šešić, PhD, University of Arts in Belgrade, Serbia
Dr. Tal Feder, Israel Institute of Technology, Israel
Prof. Dr. Hellen Gross, Hochschule Coburg
Prof. Dr. Michael Hutter, Prof. em. Wissenschaftszentrum Berlin für Sozialforschung, Germany
Prof. Dr. Arturo Rodriguez Morató, University of Barcelona, Spain
Prof. Dr. Tiago de Oliveira Pinto, University of Music Franz Liszt Weimar/Friedrich-Schiller-University Jena, Germ.
Prof. Dr. Martin Piber, Universität Innsbruck, Austria
Dr. Marcin Poprawski, Adam Mickiewicz University in Poznan, Poland
Prof. Dr. Dan Eugen Ratiu, Babeş-Bolyai University, Romania
Prof. Deborah Stevenson, PhD, Western Sydney University, Australia
Prof. Dr. Tasos Zembylas, Universität für Musik und darstellende Kunst Wien, Austria

The journal is available for annual subscription directly from the publisher. The subscription begins with the current issue and includes all issues of one year. Delivery of the subscribed issues occurs immediately after their appearance. Invoicing occurs with delivery of the first issue of a year. The subscription is automatically continued by one year, unless canceled with the publisher by February 1st.

The Journal of Cultural Management and Cultural Policy is available in bookstores worldwide. Further information available at: http://www.transcript-verlag.de/zkmm.

Bibliographic information published by the Deutsche Nationalbibliothek
The Deutsche Nationalbibliothek lists this publication in the Deutsche Nationalbibliografie; detailed bibliographic data are available online at http:/dnb.d-nb.de; indexed in EBSCOhost databases.

© 2024 transcript Verlag, Bielefeld
transcript Verlag | Hermannstraße 26 | D-33602 Bielefeld | live@transcript-verlag.de

All rights reserved. No part of this book may be reprinted or reproduced or utilized in any form or by any electronic, mechanical, or other means, now known or hereafter invented, including photocopying and recording, or in any information storage or retrieval system, without permission in writing from the publisher.

Cover concept: Hans-Dirk Hotzel, Kordula Röckenhaus, Bielefeld
Layout concept: Hans-Dirk Hotzel
Copy editing: Constance DeVereaux, Steffen Höhne
Typesetting: Hannah Friedrich

ISSN: 2701-8466
eISSN: 2701-9276
ISBN Print: 978-3-8376-6870-4
ISBN PDF: 978-3-8394-6870-8

https://doi.org/10.14361/zkmm-2024-frontmatter1002
Up to Volume 5, issue 2/2019 published as "Zeitschrift für Kulturmanagement: Kunst, Politik, Wirtschaft und Gesellschaft" (ISSN 2363-5562 / eISSN 2363-5533)

Printed on permanent acid-free text paper.

From vol. 11 (no. 1/2025), the magazine will be published by Sage Publications. Subscribers can contact Customer Services by visiting this page: https://uk.sagepub.com/en-gb/eur/contact-us, going to the Customer Services information at the end of the page and raising a ticket.

Contents / Inhalt 2024/2

Special Issue / Schwerpunkt

RESILIENCY IN THE CULTURAL SECTOR
RESILIENZ IM KULTURBEREICH

Reviews

Journal of Cultural Management and Cultural Policy

Review after ten years

With this issue we would like to say goodbye to transcript, with whom we have been able to publish the Journal of Cultural Management and Cultural Policy (JCMCP) for the past 10 years (since 2015). It was a very constructive collaboration, for which we would like to express our sincere thanks.

During this time, it was possible to attract not only many scientists, but also young researchers, through which the journal has been able to reach an increasingly higher level. The JCMCP is now the only academic journal for questions of cultural management and cultural policy on the European continent.

Next year we will be moving the JCMCP to SAGE, which we hope will give us a much stronger profile and visibility internationally. As before, we will continue to publish selected topics on current research questions and projects. We would like to invite you to participate in this process. We also request suggestions for topics and guest editors.

At the end of these ten years, the editors provide—in this issue—a look into our text archive and reprint some selected texts in a separate section that thematically fit the current focus. All texts from the past ten years are also available on the JCMCP website: <https://jcmcp.org>.

We would like to use this opportunity to thank all authors and our editorial board, who have contributed significantly to the success of the JCMCP during the last years. And last but not least, we would like to thank the Association for Cultural Management, which played a key role in financing the journal.

We hope to be able to continue to work together in one form or another within the framework of the JCMCP in the future.

THE EDITORS

Journal of Cultural Management and Policy, 2024/2, pp. 9
doi 10.14361/zkmm-2024-0201

RESEARCH ARTICLES

Economies of Worth: A Critical and Reflexive Perspective on EDI in the Cultural Sector

Ökonomien der Wertschätzung: Eine kritische und reflexive Perspektive auf EDI im Kultursektor

JULIE BÉRUBÉ[*], JACQUES-BERNARD GAUTHIER[**]

Université du Québec en Outaouais

Abstract

Cultural organizations must address issues related to equity, diversity, and inclusion (EDI). In this perspective, we used the critical theory *On Justification Economies of Worth* of Boltanski and Thévenot (1991; 2006) to understand the role of cultural organizations in relation to these EDI issues. We found during a reflective methodology exercise that the way researchers use this theoretical framework to code their interviews perpetuates oppositions and fosters group conflicts. We reevaluated the coding strategy for our data, leading us to adopt the compromises between worlds. Our contribution is to propose a novel coding strategy for EDI research when using this framework. With this strategy, researchers can foster collaboration in existing group dynamics to transcend internal oppositions and establish inclusive practices.

Kulturelle Organisationen müssen sich mit Fragen der Gleichberechtigung, Vielfalt und Integration (EDI) auseinandersetzen. Zugrunde gelegt wird die kritische Theorie über Rechtfertigungsökonomien von Boltanski und Thévenot (1991; 2006), um die Rolle von Kulturorganisationen in Bezug auf diese EDI-Themen zu verstehen. Im Rahmen einer methodischen Reflexion wird untersucht, wie die Forschung diesen theoretischen Rahmen zur Kodierung von Interviews verwendet, Widersprüche aufrechterhält und Gruppenkonflikte fördert. Wir haben die Kodierungsstrategie für unsere Daten neu bewertet, was uns dazu veranlasste, die Kompromisse zwischen den Welten anzunehmen. Unser Beitrag besteht darin, eine neue Kodierungsstrategie für die EDI-Forschung zu entwickeln. Mit dieser Strategie können Forscher die Zusammenarbeit in bestehenden Gruppendynamiken fördern, um interne Widersprüche zu überwinden und integrative Praktiken zu etablieren.

Keywords

Diversity/Diversität, Arts organization, cultural organization/Kulturorganisation, methods development/Methodenentwicklun, management

[*]   Julie.berube@uqo.ca
[**] Jacques-bernard.gauthier@uqo.ca

Journal of Cultural Management and Policy, 2024/2, pp. 13–31

doi 10.14361/zkmm-2024-0202

1. Introduction

Equity, diversity and inclusion (EDI) are of interest for all spheres of society, including the cultural sector (VAN EWIJK 2011). Indeed, these three concepts are represented in the literature in the cultural sector suggesting the presence of systemic discrimination (EIKHOF & WAR-HURST, 2013). Several studies focus on artists, but few address EDI issues in relation to cultural organizations. To address this gap, we used the theoretical framework of Boltanski and Thévenot (1991, 2006)—*On Justification, Economies of Worth* (henceforward, Economies of Worth) to understand the role of cultural organizations in EDI matters. We conducted 65 semi-structured interviews, including 40 with artists and 25 with individuals working in Canadian cultural organizations.

Boltanski and Thévenot's theoretical framework (2006) takes a critical perspective on the way in which theories have conceptualized how people manage to coordinate when different value systems conflict. Thus, it can be used to help grasp EDI issues such as when dominant groups oppress minority groups (hegemony). However, during the analysis of the 65 interviews, we realized that this framework created a division by establishing rigid categories rather than promoting inclusion (it maintains the dominance relationship between groups of individuals).

In this article, we present the reflective methodological exercise that we undertook to analyze and interpret our research findings in order to move beyond the categories induced by Boltanski and Thévenot's critical theory. This reflective exercise revealed that it is not the theoretical framework that creates these categories, but rather the way researchers code their data when using this framework (BÉRUBÉ/DEMERS 2019; BERUBÉ/GAUTHIER 2023; GOND et al. 2016; PATRIOTTA et al. 2011; POHLER 2020). Our contribution is thus methodological in nature, proposing a new way of analyzing interview content using the Economies of Worth framework, particularly in EDI research within the cultural sector. The next section explains this theoretical framework.

2. On Justification, Economies of Worth

According to Boltanski and Thévenot (2006), legitimacy is grounded in various *orders of worth*, in other words, higher-order normative principles. These orders of worth represent a unique interpretation of the common good. Actors justify their actions by referencing these overarching principles, a practice particularly evident in disputes, controversies, and tension. Each order of worth is underpinned by a specific value system that governs what is named a particular social common world (BOLTANSKI/THÉVENOT 2006). The common worlds arise from what Boltanski and Thévenot (2006) have termed *cités*.

> The cités refer to some core values in our Western societies, such as creativity, productivity, freedom, reputation, solidarity, among others, which, although grounding the diffuse background of our common sense, refer to certain structured conceptions of political bonds, i.e. of the common agreement. (SILVA CORRÊA/DE CASTRO DIAS 2020: 725).

Since *cités* are abstract concepts, Boltanski and Thévenot (2006) developed a grid which defines each of their six worlds (inspired, domestic, world of fame, civic, market and industrial) according to 13 characteristics. Lafaye and Thévenot (1993) proposed, as well, the green world. However, they pointed out that this world is still too abstract to be employed for justifications and tests. Boltanski and Chiapello (2007) subsequently introduced the projective world. Table 1 presents the common world analysis grid with the 13 categories, as well as each of the worlds.

Characteristics	Description	Inspired	Domestic	Of fame	Civic	Market	Industrial	Projective
Higher common principle	Allows qualifying and comparing the beings, objects, subjects. 'convention for establishing equivalence among beings' (p. 140)	Outpouring of inspiration	Engenderment according to tradition	Reality of public opinion	Pre-eminence of collectives	Competition	Efficiency	Activity, projects
State of worthiness	Represents what is important, admired, expected. 'Worthy beings are guarantors of the *higher common principle*' (p. 141)	Inexpressible and ethereal	Hierarchical superiority	Fame	Rule governed and representative	Desirable	Efficient	Engaged, engaging, mobile
Human dignity	Allows beings to rise in the common good 'must be inscribed in human nature, and they must anchor the order of worth in a particular aptitude possessed by human beings' (p. 142)	Anxiety of creation	Poise of habit	Desire to be recognized	Aspiration to civil rights	Interest	Work	The need to connect
List of subjects	'For each world, it is possible to establish a *list of subjects*, most often qualified by their state of worth' (p. 142)	Visionaries	Superiors and inferiors	Stars and their fans	Collective persons and their representatives	Competitors	Professionals	Mediator, project head
List of objects and arrangements	Can be linked to subjects and help determine their worth 'All objects can be treated as the trappings or mechanisms of worth, whether they are rules, diplomas, codes, tools, buildings, machines, or take some other form' (p. 142)	Waking dream	Rules of etiquette	Names in the media	Legal forms	Wealth	Means	All the instruments of connection

Cha-racteri-stics	Description	Inspired	Domes-tic	Of fame	Civic	Market	Indust-rial	Projec-tive
Invest-ment formula	'by tying access to the state of worthiness to a sacrifice, it constitutes an *economy of worth* in which benefits turn out to be "balanced" by burdens' (p. 142)	Escape from habits	Rejection of selfish-ness	Giving up secrets	Renun-ciation of the particular	Oppor-tunism	Progress	Adapt-ability
Relation of worth	'specifies the relation of order among *states of worth* by spelling out the way in which the state of worthiness, because it contributes to the *common good*, encompasses the state of deficiency' (p. 143)	Universal value of unique-ness	Respect and responsi-bility	Being rec-ognized and iden-tifying	Relation of delega-tion	Possess	Control	Redistri-bution of connec-tions
Natural relation among beings	Link subjects and objects together according to their worth 'Some natural rela-tions entail worths of equal importance, while others indicate a hierarchical distribution' (p. 143)	Alchemy of unex-pected encoun-ters	Company of well-brought-up people	Persua-sion	Gather-ing for collective action	Interest (to)	Function	Connec-tion
Harmo-nious figure of the natural order	'are invoked as realities that conform to the princi-ple of equity' (p. 143)	Reality of the imaginary	Soul of the home	Public image	Dem-ocratic republic	Market	Organiza-tion	The network
Model tests	Represents a strong, important moment 'whose outcome is uncertain, a test that entails a pure and particularly consistent arrangement of beings from a single world' (pp. 143-144)	Vaga-bondage of the mind	Family ceremo-nies	Presenta-tion of the event	Demon-stration for a just cause	Deal	Trial	End of a project and the begin-ning of another
Mode of expres-sion of judg-ment	'ratifies a test (...) characterizes the form in which the higher common principle is manifested' (p. 144)	Stroke of genius	Knowing how to bestow trust	Judgment of public opinion	Verdict of the vote	Price	Effective	Being called on to partici-pate
Form of evidence	'modality of knowledge appropriate to the world under consideration' (p. 144)	Certainty of intu-ition	Exem-plary anecdote	Evidence of success	Legal text	Money	Measure	Inserting, Causing to partici-pate
State of deficien-cy and decline of the polity	Negating the state of worthiness can be more difficult to qualify than the state of worthiness. Represents that which is decried, devalued. 'when beings are on the point of being denatured' (p. 144)	Temp-tation to come down to earth	Lack of inhibition	Indiffer-ence and banality	Division	Enslave-ment to money	Instru-mental action	Unem-ployable closure of the network

Table 1: Common Worlds Analysis Grid

All quotes in Table 1 are from Boltanski and Thévenot (2006)

Boltanski and Thévenot (2006) argue that an intricate entity cannot be con-fined to a single world but can be seen instead as embodying a combination of worlds. Tensions arise between the value systems coming from the higher common principle of each world, leading to a clash. In fact, when two worlds meet, a critique of one world emerges from the other, which is the source of the value tension. To avoid the clash, Boltanski and Thévenot suggest that a compromise between the worlds may be reached. "In a compromise, people agree to come to terms, that is, to suspend a clash—a dispute involving more than one world—without settling it through recourse to a test in just one of the worlds" (BOLTANSKI/THÉVENOT 2006: 277). They further propose illustrations of compromise between the worlds as presented in Table 2.

	Domestic world	World of fame	Civic world	Market world	Industrial world	Projective world
Inspired world	The initiatory relation of master to disciple	The hysteria of fans	Man in revolt, the gesture of protest, collective genius	The creative market, do something crazy, the sublime is priceless	The passion for hard work, creative techniques, inventors	Collective creation
Domestic world	–	Maintain good contacts	Behave properly toward civil servants, the extension of civil rights, the public school community	Trust in business, personalized service, alienable property	The spirit and know-how of the home, the effectiveness of good habits, the competence of the professional, traditional quality, the supervisor's responsibility, human resources	The family spirit or atmosphere in the company
World of fame	See domestic/ of fame	–	Touching public opinion, Putting one's name at the service of a cause, official sanction, campaign for support	Brand image	Methods for implanting an image, the measure of opinion, an objective opinion	Individual reputation; public memory
Civic world	See domestic/ civic	See of fame/ civic	–	Business in the service of the community	Workers' rights, effective methods of mobilization, the increased productivity of motivated workers, working in group, certifying competency, the imperative of safety, the efficiency of public service	The links between collectives
Market world	See domestic/ market	See of fame/ market	See civic/market	–	A salable product, control of demand, methods for doing business, utility between desire and need	Business trust; reputation; 'coopetition'
Industrial world	See domestic/ industrial	See of fame/ industrial	See civic/ industrial	See market/ industrial	–	Adaptable or changing work methods tailored to each situation/ organization

Table 2: Illustrations of Compromise

In Table 2, unless otherwise stated, compromises are copied from the notes presented in the margins of Boltanski and Thévenot (2006). Compromises proposed are from Bérubé (2015); they are not directly stated by Boltanski and Chiappelo (2007) or Boltanski and Thévenot (1991).

The issues surrounding EDI involve the confrontation of different value systems, and since cultural organizations coordinate many stakeholders around common projects (another theme at the heart of the Economies of Worth theory), we have chosen this theoretical framework to study the role of cultural organizations in addressing EDI issues. The next section provides an overview of research on EDI in the cultural sector, particularly those focusing on cultural organizations.

3. Literature Review

3.1 What is EDI in the Cultural Sector?

EDI concepts are polysemous because they are social constructs (VAN EWIJK, 2011). To define equity in our research, we refer to a Canadian research granting agency, the Natural Sciences and Engineering Research Council of Canada (2017); among the definitions we have reviewed to date, their definition appears to best convey the concept of equity:

> Equity means fairness; people of all identities being treated fairly. It means ensuring that the processes for allocating resources and decision-making are fair to all and do not discriminate on the basis of identity. There is a need to put measures in place to eliminate discrimination and inequalities which have been well described and reported and ensure, to the best degree possible, equal opportunities. (*Natural Sciences and Engineering Research Council of Canada* 2017: 3)

For inclusion, we turn to Dobusch who refers to it, among other things "as a process and condition where people gain access to areas from which they were formerly un/-intentionally excluded" (DOBUSCH 2014: 220). In practical terms, this means ensuring that people's input is recognized and that all have access to the same opportunities (*Social Sciences and Humanities Research Council* 2023). For diversity, some define the concept narrowly, referring to race, gender, ethnicity, age, national origins, religion and disability (VAN EWIJK 2011). We prefer a more comprehensive definition: diversity includes all the ways in which individuals differ from one another and includes the characteristics that make an individual or group of individuals different from one another (CUYLER 2013; VAN EWIJK 2011; WENTLING/PALMA-RIVAS 1997).

3.2 Cultural Organizations Facing EDI Issues

Cultural funding organizations are increasingly attentive to EDI issues when granting subsidies to artists. Most of these funding organizations have established grant programs specifically designed to include artists from underrepresented groups, but cultural organizations receive little emphasis in the granting criteria. These cultural organizations are typically non-profit entities that support artists and structure the sector. Indeed, they play an important role in shaping policies specific to the cultural sector (ACOSTA 2016). Therefore, we assumed that cultural organizations would play a central role in managing EDI. Published research that specifically addresses this role seems to be rare, if it exists at all.

Indeed, research suggests that systemic discrimination in this sector is exacerbated by the policies implemented for their promotion (OAKLEY 2006; EIKHOF/WARHURST 2013). Research also reveals gender and ethnicity-based discrimination, as well as discrimination based on physical abilities, age, and location (EIKHOF 2017; EIKHOF/YORK 2015; TANDLE/HARDY 2016). EIKHOF (2017) reports that studies on this theme in the cultural sector primarily focus on the exclusion of women and ethnic minorities (GILL 2002; RANDLE et al. 2014), implications related to hiring and working practices (EIKHOF/WARHURST 2013; RANDLE/HARDY 2016), and sexism and ageism (DEAN 2008; EIKHOF 2017; EIKHOF/YORK 2015; GILL 2002). These studies examine the specificities among workers that contribute to discrimination.

Other studies on EDI focus on consequences resulting from the structure of the sector; the majority delve into the importance of the sector's social and professional networks (GRUGULIS/STOYANOVA 2012; SIEBERT/WILSON 2013). Eikhof (2017) proposed a theoretical framework in which she examined, on one hand, individuals working in creative and cultural industries and their decisions, and on the other hand, decision-makers and the context in which they make EDI-related decisions. However, she did not consider the role of cultural organizations. Consequently, we conducted research to understand the role of cultural organizations in addressing EDI issues in the sector (BÉRUBÉ/DORIS/ POULIOT 2024). The next section presents 1) the methodology to understand the role of cultural organizations and 2) reflexive methodology to move beyond the categories induced by Boltanski and Thévenot's critical theory.

4. Methodology

To understand the role of cultural organizations in matters of EDI, we conducted a survey using semi-structured interviews with two groups of participants selected by purposive sampling (SCHWANDT 2015), conforming to the following criteria: 1) participants must work in one of the following Canadian cities: Toronto, Montreal, Vancouver, or the National Capital Region; 2) be a professional artist or have worked for at least one year for a cultural organization. In total, we recruited 40 artists and 25 cultural organization workers.

We addressed the following themes during the semi-structured interviews: the participants' identity, the policies and resources structuring EDI, the role of cultural organizations, and the participants' practices related to EDI. Drawing on authors (NYBERG/WRIGHT 2013, PATRIOTTA et al. 2011), we coded the interviews using grammar describing the worlds of Boltanski and Thévenot (2006) as presented in Table 1. We then performed comparative analyses of participants' statements, highlighting elements of convergence and divergence.

Following data analysis, we felt uncomfortable about how the theory guides the categorization of the data into opposing groups. We had the feeling that this approach was contrary to the very principles of EDI that we were studying. We wanted to probe the cause of this discomfort, and to do so, we turned to reflexive methodology.

4.1 Reflexive Methodology

In their study concerning gender—a component of EDI, Alvesson and Billing (2019) advocate for an evaluation process in the practice of social science to achieve a reflexive reorientation. According to Alvesson and Sköldberg (2018) and Alvesson and Deetz (2020), having a critical theoretical orientation does not exempt researchers from engaging in reflexive exercises about their research practices. Drawing inspiration from Alvesson (2011), Alvesson and Kärreman (2011), Alvesson and Sandberg (2013), Alvesson and Sköldberg (2018), Cunliffe (2003; 2009), Harbour and Gauthier (2017), we distinguish between two orders of reflexivity: the first order involves interpreting social researchers' practices to better understand these practices, and the second order involves interpreting the interpretations that researchers make of their practices.

To conduct reflexive exercises on our own practices of social research on EDI in the cultural sector, we adapted the frameworks proposed by the above authors. The first order of reflexivity consists of four levels of interpretation. It is important to document the interpretations made at each of these four levels.

The first level concerns our interpretations of the literature review on EDI in the cultural sector. These interpretations led us to the specific research question: what is the role of cultural organizations in matters of EDI? The second level focuses on the interpretation of the empirical context (the Canadian cultural sector including artists and cultural organizations) from which we developed the sampling strategy, interview scheme, and the way of conducting interviews to provide the most relevant response to our specific research question. With the third level of interpretation, we used Boltanski and Thévenot (2006)'s theory Economies of Worth to interpret interview transcripts to extract research results (empirical response to the research question). Finally, the fourth level involves our interpretations of the issues occurring in the field of management and organizations, to align our strategies for disseminating the results.

The second order of reflexivity is composed of five degrees of reflection. The first four degrees are intended as a retrospective examination of the four interpretations comprising the first order of reflexivity. To these four degrees of reflection, a fifth degree is added, which involves revisiting the four interpretations again, but this time from a perspective of self-critique as illustrated in Figure 1.

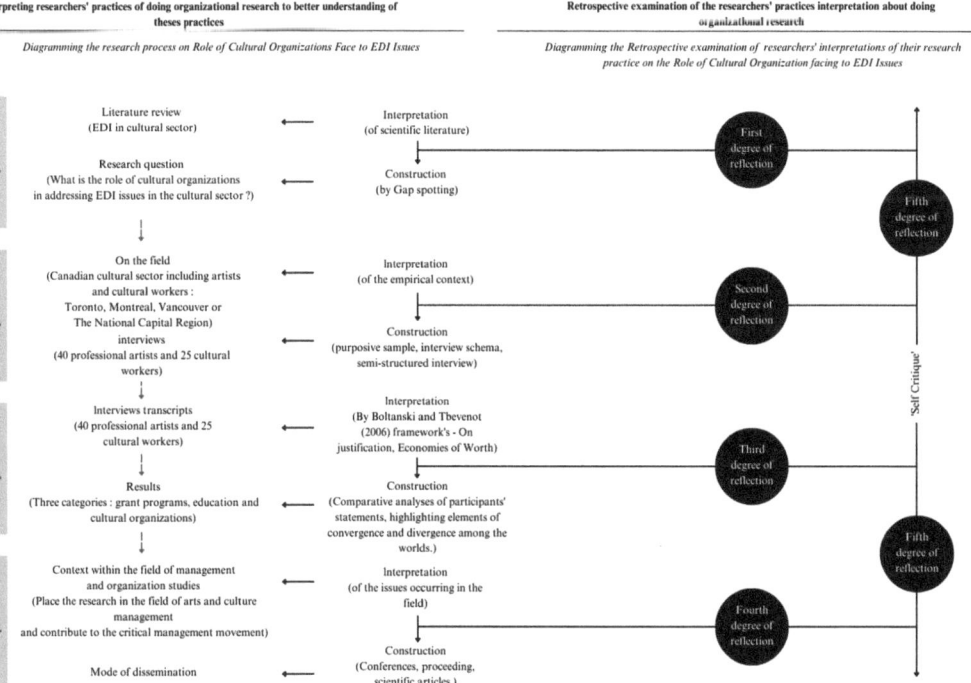

Figure 1: Reflexive Methodology Process

The present article details the third level of interpretation and its degree of reflection. We conducted a retrospective examination of the interpretations while analysing the interview transcripts based on the grammar of Boltanski and Thévenot (2006) as shown in Table 1. This review created discomfort for us because the use of this grammar to interpret the data creates a hermetic categorization of participants. For example, this pitted artists from visible minorities against artists from the dominant group. However, we initially believed that employing a critical theory, meant adopting a perspective aligned with the principles of EDI. Instead, this interpretation of data, using Boltanski and Thévenot's grammar (2006), divided participants creating opposition between them, and excluded them from each other, which inhibits an appreciation of diversity among all participants. Specific examples are given in the next section. We demonstrate how this hermetic categorization underlies interpretations when mobilizing the grammar of Boltanski and Thévenot (2006).

4.2 Second Order of Reflexivity

The second order of reflexivity is a retrospective examination of the interpretation resulting from Boltanski and Thévenot's (2006) grammar. Our goal in this section is not to review all the retrospective examinations (second order of reflexivity) that we conducted on the interpretation of data (transcripts), but rather to illustrate the process that we followed. We will engage in a third level of reflection on each of the components of EDI, namely equity, diversity, and inclusion. To do so, we present a significant citation from the transcript that illustrates the creation of hermetic categories for each component of EDI when interpreting the data according to Boltanski and Thévenot's (2006) grammar.

4.3 Reflexive Methodology on Equity

Following the Economies of Worth theory, researchers coded transcript excerpts according to a single world (GOND et al. 2016; PATRIOTTA et al. 2011).

The first transcript excerpt is from an interview with an artist who identifies as an Algonquin descendant (an Indigenous nation in Canada) but who is not recognized as an Indigenous person under Canadian law. He was responding to a question regarding his identity.

Well, I'm a Quebecer of French and Algonquin descent. The Framework Agreement on First Nation Land Management Act [a Canadian law] tells me that I'm not Indigenous because someone from the government said that after so many generations, you're no longer Indigenous. Well, that's the very technical side of the law, but they forgot people like me, who are convinced that somewhere in me, my Indigenous roots, the spirit that inhabits me, is Algonquin. That's how I see myself; I'm an Algonquin, born on Algonquin territory, and the Algonquin elders have confirmed that I'm right. When I talk with the elders from the Algonquin territories, the spiritual guides, no one can contradict that. (participant A2)

We coded this excerpt during the coding exercise of this interview with the Legal text code from the civic world (Form of evidence), given the reference to the law. Indeed, the artist is not recognized under Canadian law as an Indigenous person, so he is not eligible to apply for grants or programs intended solely for Indigenous people in Canada. However, as we reflected on this initial interpretation, we noted that the civic world does not consider the individual's identity dimension. In this case, the artist's Indigenous identity comes from deep intuition, which instead is under the inspired world. *Certainty of intuition* is the form of evidence in the inspired world.

Assigning a code from the civic world reflects the association with legal text but does not capture the equity issue. Canadian law excludes him from the group with which he identifies, thereby denying him access to programs and grants. Indeed, the civic world (Canadian law) does not recognize his Algonquin identity. Conversely, if our interpretation had focused on the artist's identity and we had coded for *certainty of intuition* from the inspired world, we would not have been able to highlight the equity issue on the legal level. In sum, neither the civic world nor the world of inspiration—taken individually—allows for consideration of this artist's dual identity as an Algonquin Canadian artist. The civic world deprives him of the rights granted to Indigenous people, while the world of inspiration ignores the Canadian law to which the artist must adhere.

4.4 Reflexive Methodology on Diversity

Similarly, we found problems with interpretations relating to individuals from invisible minorities. An individual from an invisible minority is associated with the dominant group, but possesses distinctive characteristics that are not readily visible such as sexual orientation, an invisible disability, or others. An example is the case of an artist from an invisible minority who uses social media to share his experience.

> I'm a queer, hard of hearing, Jewish person. (...) Having an invisible identity, we now have more methods of communicating with each other and communicating our own experiences to each other via social media. There's always been the need, a lot of people are more aware of things that are happening and wouldn't have necessarily had access to that before. (...) I just want everyone, especially marginalized people, to have the freedom to connect. (participant A24)

Using the Economies of Worth theory, our initial interpretation of this quote assigned it to the civic world. We coded it: *gathering for collective action*, which represents the *natural relation among beings* in the civic world. Indeed, the participant discusses how his presence on social media (collective action), enables him to share his experience as an artist who identifies as an invisible minority (queer, hard of hearing, and Jewish person).

Coding with the civic world allows us to demonstrate how social media reveal characteristics that are invisible to the public. However, the civic world only presents the various forms of diversity (visible minority, invisible minority, as examples), particularly invisible diversity in this case. On reflection, the participant's statement goes further as he explains that social media also allow him to establish connections with other individuals, especially marginalized people.

A dimension of connection between individuals is not accounted for when coding the participant's statements with the civic world. To capture the dimension of relationship-building, it would be necessary to code the excerpt according to the projective world. The code associated with the category *list of objects with arrangements* for the projective world is *all the instruments of connection*. Coding with the projective world thus demonstrates the creation of links and connections between individuals but lacks the emphasis on diversity available with the civic world. In sum, neither the civic world nor the projective world, taken individually, allow for the recognition of the full reality of this artist from the invisible minority.

4.5 Reflexive Methodology on Inclusion

For inclusion, we selected an excerpt from an interview with a non-white artist discussing his experience with grant-funding organizations.

> Of course, I feel that one of the most challenging aspects is that the impact and evaluation are done according to the terms of the funders. These terms are often very restrictive because they are based on a bureaucratic, white supremacist institution founded on specific ideas of artistic excellence that fundamentally exclude non-white individuals. It is built on peer review systems that have good intentions but, from

what I understand, often perpetuate harmful stereotypes in the assessment of grant applications and project proposals. Historically, I believe this has devalued organizations' relationships with the communities they serve. (participant A5)

According to our initial interpretation, the dominant world in this quote is the industrial world. We coded with the higher common principle in the industrial world, which is *efficiency*. Indeed, the quote highlights that to efficiently assess artistic excellence, funding organizations establish an evaluation process based on criteria of excellence and individuals who embody those criteria (peer review). The industrial world reveals the technical aspects of the evaluation process of funding organizations but does not show the exclusionary aspect of this process, as explained by participant A5.

The evaluation process is therefore based on the concept of excellence designed by the dominant group. On reflection, this implies that one collective (the dominant group) is favored over another collective (marginalized group). The *pre-eminence of the collective* of the civic world is the higher common principle. Indeed, the civic world aims at the well-being of all collectives and not of a particular collective.

Coding with the civic world would highlights the dominance of collective well-being, which is the goal of grants from funding organizations. However, the civic world does not reveal how the operation of the evaluation process excludes certain groups of artists whose work is not harmonized with criteria of excellence.

5. Discussion: Methodological Issues and Proposition

As shown in the three examples, the codification of data with the critical theory, Economies of Worth, poses a problem. Indeed, it is tempting for researchers to seek the simplest solution, to assign the most obviously relevant code to associate the speaker with a single world. For example, in our initial coding, the dominant world took precedence over the minority. And since we want to analyze for EDI solutions, this mode of coding does not give equal weight to the whole statement. Subsequently, researchers bring out tensions between the worlds, and the analysis highlights a compromise. This methodological approach creates divisions and pits groups against each other, whereas critical theories, particularly those related to EDI, aim to transcend these divisions and oppositions.

To counter our problem, the simplest solution might be to code the excerpts with more than one world. However, this approach reproduces the issue, and the worlds still end up in opposition. To move beyond dualism and strive for integration in this case, we propose coding directly with the compromise, and to compare the different compromises in the analysis. To illustrate this approach, we use the three examples presented in the previous section.

For the first example on equity, we could have coded the participant's statements with both the civic world (to represent the legal aspect related to the Framework Agreement on First Nation Land Management Act) and the inspired world (to represent the uniqueness of individual identity). This approach highlights the opposition between the artist and the legal system. Indeed, for this artist, art reflects Indigenous values and customs, but he is not legally recognized as an Indigenous person. Coding with both worlds would demonstrate that the artist's values and identity are challenged by the law. The compromise proposed by Boltanski and Thévenot between the civic world and the world of inspiration is *man in revolt, the gesture of protest*. That compromise represents the real message conveyed by the artist who senses that his identity is being violated by the law. Thus, the gesture of protest would target the law that should be amended to recognize the artist's identity. By coding with both worlds, we were challenging the identity of the artist, whereas by coding with the compromise, we challenge the law. This compromise is truly rooted in critical theories that expose the hegemony of institutions, in this case, legal institutions.

For the example on diversity, we would have coded according to the civic world (to showcase diversity on social media) and the projective world to illustrate connection instruments. By coding with both worlds, there is no integration between diversity and connection; these two concepts evolve in parallel. Boltanski and Thévenot (2006) and Boltanski and Chiapello (2007) do not present compromises between the world of projects and other worlds. As shown in Table 2, we have adopted compromises proposed by Bérubé (2015). Thus, the compromise between the civic world and the world of projects would be *the links between collectives*. The compromise better represents the participant's lived experience, his desire to expose his invisible diversity and contribute to the creation of a network of marginalized individuals through social media.

In the example for inclusion, we proposed coding using the industrial world to illustrate the evaluation process and criteria prioritizing excellence in the granting systems of funding organizations. To demonstrate that one collective is favored over another in this system, we added the civic world. By coding according to these two worlds, the duality of concepts of excellence between marginalized and dominant groups (representing the funding organizations) is exposed. This emphasizes exclusion rather than inclusion. The compromise between the industrial world and the civic world is *certifying competency*. A certification process involves recognition of the different expressions of competence in a field. In the case of arts funding organizations, it would involve acknowledging and including the competencies (represented by excellence) of artists belonging to marginalized groups. This approach reflects the participant's comments criticizing the current system based on the excellence criteria established by dominant groups.

In summary, all three examples depict situations in which a participant identifies with a marginalized group: Indigenous communities, invisible minorities, and visible minorities. We anticipated that by using the critical theory Economies of Worth we would transcend divisions and oppositions. However, the conventional coding approach with this theory places marginalized groups in opposition to dominant institutions (law, Western society, funding organizations).

Our contribution focuses on research on EDI when using Economies of Worth theory. The use of compromises to code with this theory allows for a shift in the research perspective by focusing on EDI practices that condemn injustices and suggesting ways to overcome them.

As an example, consider the work of Randle and Hardy (2016), cited earlier, which investigates systemic discrimination against women and people with disabilities in the UK film and television industry. Their article proposed a long-term solution by changing sectorial hiring practices, but it situates these marginalized groups against dominant groups. The issue concerns hiring criteria (referring to the industrial world) that favor one collective over another (civic world). Recall that the compromise between the industrial world and the civic world is *certifying competency*. If they had coded by using the compromises of the Economies of Worth theory, they would have been able to identify other potential solutions to revise current practices of project teams. This case recalls the example from our research that we provided regarding inclusion. Thus, in Randle and Hardy's case, it would be necessary to reassess current performance measurement criteria (which favored the dominant group) and acknowledge the distinctive competence of marginalized groups. This change would lead to a better appreciation of their work, resulting in more equitable and inclusive teams. In the longer term, the sector will recognize the benefit of having a broader pool of competence.

6. Conclusion

In this article, we re-examine the initial results of a study on EDI issues in the cultural sector obtained by employing the theoretical framework of *On Justification Economies of Worth*. Usually, researchers code their material using the grammar of the worlds of Boltanski and Thévenot (2006). Using this coding strategy, we observed that instead of overcoming oppositions, our analyses were creating or sustaining them. We did a reflexive exercise that prompted us to question our coding strategy, aiming to truly resolve these oppositions. We turned to the compromises proposed by Boltanski and Thévenot (2006). Our contribution is to propose a new way to use the Economies of Worth theoretical framework when conducting research on EDI in the cultural sector. This approach enables analysis to go beyond the opposition formed by the current composition of groups (marginalized versus dominant groups) to establish equitable and inclusive practices.

This research presents some limits which suggest avenues for further research. First, this exploratory exercise focused on a single study. The reflexive exercise and this new coding strategy should be replicated using data from other research on EDI, as well as address other themes within the field of the cultural sector. Additionally, we conducted this reflective exercise using only Boltanski and Thévenot's theory. It would be interesting to replicate this exercise with other critical theories to see if other theories also perpetuate issues such as the creation of hermetic groups that oppose minority groups and dominant groups.

References

ACOSTA, Javier Hernandez (2016): The Role of Arts Organizations in Cultural Policy: The "Cultural Return" Analysis. – In: *International Journal of Arts Management* (Special Edition), 56–83.

ALVESSON, Mats (2011): *Interpreting interviews*. London: SAGE.

ALVESSON, Mats/BILLING, Due Yvonne (²2009): *Understanding Gender and Organizations*. London: SAGE.

ALVESSON, Mats/DEETZ, Stanley (2020): *Doing critical research*. London: SAGE.

ALVESSON, Mats/KÄRREMAN, Dan (2011): *Qualitative research and theory development: mystery as method*. London: SAGE.

ALVESSON, Mats/SANDBERG, Jorgen (2013): *Constructing research questions : doing interesting research*. London: SAGE.

ALVESSON, Mats/SKÖLDBERG, Kaj (³2018): *Reflexive methodology : new vistas for qualitative research*. London: SAGE.

BÉRUBÉ, Julie (2015): *La gestion du travail créatif dans les petites agences de publicité situées en périphérie des grands centres urbains*. Montréal: Ph.D., HEC Montreal.

BÉRUBÉ, Julie/DEMERS, Christiane (2019): Creative organizations: when management fosters creative work. – In: *Creative Industries Journal* 12(3), 314–340 <https://doi.or g/10.1080/17510694.2019.1621619>.

BÉRUBÉ, Julie/GAUTHER, Jacques-Bernard (2023): Managing projects in creative industries: a compromise between artistic and project management values. – In: *Creative Industries Journal* 16(1), 76–95 <https://doi.org/10.1080/17510694.2021.1979278>.

BÉRUBÉ, Julie/DORIS, Julien/POULIOT, Alexis (2024): The role of cultural organisations in matters of equity, diversity, and inclusion. – In: *Cultural Trends*, 1–16 <https://doi.org/10.1080/09548963.2024.2387771>.

BOLTANSKI, Luc/CHIAPELLO, Ève (2007): *The New Spirit of Capitalism*. London: Verso.

BOLTANSKI, Luc/THÉVENOT, Laurent (1991): *De la justification : les économies de la grandeur*. Paris: Gallimard.

BOLTANSKI, Luc/THÉVENOT, Laurent (2006): *On Justification: Economies of Worth*. New Jersey: University Press.

CUNLIFFE, Ann L. (2003): Reflexive Inquiry in Organizational Research: Questions and Possibilities. – In: *Human Relations* 56(8), 983–1003 <https://doi.org/10.1177/00187267030568004>.

CUNLIFFE, Ann L. (2009): Reflexivity, learning and reflexive practice. – In Armstrong, Steven, J./Fukami Cynthia V. (Eds.), *The SAGE handbook of management learning, education and development*. London: SAGE, 405–418.

CUYLER, Antonio (2013): Affirmative Action and Diversity: Implications for Arts Management. – In: *Journal of Arts Management, Law & Society* 43(2), 98–105 <https://doi.org/10.1080/10632921.2013.786009>.

DEAN, Debora (2008): No Human Resource is an Island: Gendered, Racialized Access to Work as a Performer. – In: *Gender, Work & Organization* 15(2), 161–181 <https://doi.org/10.1111/j.1468-0432.2007.00389.x>.

DOBUSCH, Laura (2014: How exclusive are inclusive organisations? – In: *Equality, Diversity and Inclusion: An International Journal* 33(3), 220–234 <https://doi.org/http://dx.doi.org/10.1108/EDI-08-2012-0066>.

EIKHOF, Doris Ruth (2017): Analysing decisions on diversity and opportunity in the cultural and creative industries: A new framework. – In: *Organization* 24(3), 289–307 <https://doi.org/10.1177/1350508416687768>.

EIKHOF, Doris Ruth/WARHURST, Chris (2013): The promised land? Why social inequalities are systemic in the creative industries. – In: *Employee Relations* 35(5), 495–508 <https://doi.org/http://dx.doi.org/10.1108/ER-08-2012-0061>.

EIKHOF, Doris Ruth/YORK, Charlotte (2015): 'It's a Tough Drug to Kick': A Woman's Career in Broadcasting. – In: *Work, Employment and Society* 30(1), 152–161 <https://doi.org/10.1177/0950017015601859>.

GILL, Rosalind (2002): Cool, Creative and Egalitarian? Exploring Gender in Project-Based New Media Work in Euro. – In: *Information, Communication & Society* 5(1), 70–89 <https://doi.org/10.1080/13691180110117668>.

GOND, Jean-Pascal/CRUZ, Luciano Barin/RAUFFLET, Emmanuel/CHARRON, Mathieu (2016). To Frack or Not to Frack? The Interaction of Justification and Power in a Sustainability Controversy. – In: *The Journal of Management Studie*, 53(3), 330–363. < https://doi.org/10.1111/joms.12166>.

GRUGULIS, Irena/STOYANOVA, Dimitrinka (2012): Social Capital and Networks in Film and TV: Jobs for the Boys? – In: *Organization Studies* 33(10), 1311–1331 <https://doi.org/10.1177/0170840612453525>.

HARBOUR, Michelle/GAUTHIER, Jacques-Bernard (2017): *Complex polysemy and reflexivity in organizational research.* – In: H. O. Science <https://hal.science/hal-01543416>.

KÖHLER, Tine/RUMYANTSEVA, Maria/WELCH, Catherine (2023): Qualitative Restudies: Research Designs for Retheorizing. – In: *Organizational Research Methods* 0(0). <https://doi.org/10.1177/10944281231216323>.

LAFAYE, Claudette/THÉVENOT, Laurent (1993): Une justification écologique? Conflits dans l'aménagement de la nature. – In: *Revue Française de Sociologie* 34(4), 495–524.

Natural Sciences and Engineering Research Council of Canada (2017): *Guide for Applicants: Considering Equity, Diversity and Inclusion in your Application.* <https://www.nserc-crsng.gc.ca/_doc/EDI/Guide_for_Applicants_EN.pdf>.

NYBERG, Daniel/WRIGHT, Christopher (2013): Corporate corruption of the environment: sustainability as a process of compromise. – In: *The British Journal of Sociology* 64(3), 405–424 <https://doi.org/10.1111/1468-4446.12025>.

OAKLEY, Kate. (2006). Include Us Out—Economic Development and Social Policy in the Creative Industries. – In: *Cultural Trends* 15(4), 255–273 <https://doi.org/10.1080/09548960600922335>.

PATRIOTTA, Gerardo/GOND, Jean.-Pascal/SCHULTZ, Friederike (2011): Maintaining Legitimacy: Controversies, Orders of Worth, and Public Justifications. – In: *The Journal of Management Studies* 48(8), 1804–1836 <https://doi.org/10.1111/j.1467-6486.2010.00990.x>.

POHLER, Nina. (2020): Evaluation and the tension between generalization and particularity: The negotiation of supplementary child allowance in a collective firm. – In: *Ephemera: Theory & Politics in Organization* 20(3), 123–152.

RANDLE, Keith/FORSON, Cynthia/CALVELEY, Moira (2014): Towards a Bourdieusian analysis of the social composition of the UK film and television workforce. – In: *Work, Employment and Society* 29(4), 590–606. <https://doi.org/10.1177/0950017014542498>

RANDLE, Keith/HARDY, Kate. (2016): Macho, mobile and resilient? How workers with impairments are doubly disabled in project-based film and television work. – In: *Work, Employment and Society* 31(3), 447–464 <https://doi.org/10.1177/0950017016643482>

SCHWANDT, Thomas. A. (⁴2015): *The SAGE dictionary of qualitative inquiry.* London: SAGE.

SIEBERT, Sabina/WILSON, Fiona (2013): All work and no pay: consequences of unpaid work in the creative industries – In: *Work, Employment and Society* 27(4), 711–721 <https://doi.org/10.1177/0950017012474708>.

SILVA CORRÊA, Diogo/de CASTRO DIAS, Rodriogo. (2020): The critique and its critical moments: The recent pragmatic turn in French sociology. – In: *Current Sociology* 68(6), 721–737 <https://doi.org/10.1177/0011392120914702>.

Social Sciences and Humanities Research Council (2023): *Best practices in equity, diversity and inclusion in research practice and design* <https://www.sshrc-crsh.gc.ca/funding-financement/nfrf-fnfr/edi-eng.aspx>.

VAN EWIJK, Anne (2011): Diversity and diversity policy: diving into fundamental differences. – In: *Journal of Organizational Change Management* 24(5), 680–694 <https://doi.org/10.1108/09534811111158921>.

WENTLING, Rose Mary/PALMA-RIVAS, Nida (1997): *Diversity in the workforce: a literature review* (Diversity in the Workforce Series Report No.1, Issue).

„Teilen, Teil nehmen, Teil geben, Teil haben, Teil werden, Teil sein!" Zumutungen einer kulturpolitischen Zielsetzung in der Schweiz

"Share, take part, give part, have part, become part, be part!" Impositions of a Cultural Policy Objective in Switzerland

STEFAN KOSLOWSKI*

Bundesamt für Kultur, Hallwylstrasse 15, CH 3003 Bern

Abstract

Der vorliegende Essay zeichnet aus bundespolitischer Perspektive den Aufstieg der kulturpolitischen Zielsetzung ‚kulturelle Teilhabe' während der letzten zehn Jahre in der kulturföderalen Schweiz nach. Dabei geht es nicht nur um kulturelle Teilhabe im aktuellen Kunstschaffen und in den Kulturinstitutionen, sondern auch um Teilhabe am materiellen und immateriellen Kulturerbe. Der Ruf nach Teilhabe von möglichst Vielen am kulturellen Leben erscheint im Rückblick als ebenso notwendige wie alternativlose Reaktion von Kulturpolitik, Kulturschaffenden, Kulturinstitutionen, Kulturorganisationen auf die tektonischen Verschiebungen in Gesellschaft und Kultur. Denn von einem gesamtgesellschaftlichen Verständnis davon, was ‚Kultur' sei, können Kulturpolitik und Kulturförderung schon geraume Zeit nicht mehr ausgehen. Auch muss sich die Kulturförderung öffnen nicht nur zum Austausch mit anderen Politik- und Förderbereichen, sondern auch zu gemeinsamen Fördermaßnahmen. So säumen Aushandlungsprozesse und Widerstände den Weg in dieses kulturpolitische Neuland. Der Essay zieht so eine Zwischenbilanz einer kulturpolitisch wirkungsvollen Zielsetzung, hält wichtige Wegmarken und Diskussionspunkte in ihrer Etablierung fest und leistet nicht zuletzt so einen Beitrag zur – zumindest in der Schweiz – vernachlässigten Geschichtsschreibung von Kulturpolitik.

From a federal policy perspective, this essay traces the rise of the cultural policy objective of 'cultural participation' over the last ten years in culturally federalised Switzerland. It is not only about cultural participation in current artistic creation and in cultural institutions, but also about participation in tangible and intangible cultural heritage. In retrospect, the call for as many people as possible to participate in cultural life appears to be both a necessary and unavoidable reaction of cultural policy, creative artists, cultural institutions and cultural organisations to the tectonic shifts in society and culture. For some time now, cultural policy and cultural funding can no longer be based on an understanding of what 'culture' is that is shared by society as a whole. Cultural promotion must also open up not only to dialogue with other policy and funding areas, but also to joint funding measures. Negotiation processes and resistance line the path into this new cultural policy territory. The essay thus draws an interim balance of an effective cultural policy objective, records important milestones and discussion points in its establishment and, last but not least, makes a contribution to the—at least in Switzerland—neglected historiography of cultural policy.

Keywords

arts managment/Kulturverwaltung, cultural policy/Kulturpolitik, diversity/Diversität, transformation/Entwicklungsprozesse, social cohesion/sozialer Zusammenhalt

* Stefan.Koslowski@bak.admin.ch

Kulturelle Teilhabe hat sich in der Schweiz in den letzten zehn Jahren zu einem Schlüsselbegriff in der kultur- und gesellschaftlichen Debatte entwickelt. Voraussichtlich noch im laufenden Jahr 2024 werden in der Schweiz die parlamentarischen Debatten über die *Botschaft zur Förderung der Kultur in der Schweiz in den Jahren 2025–2028* (*Kulturbotschaft 2025–2028*) abgeschlossen. In ihren *Kulturbotschaften* präsentiert die eidgenössische Landesregierung (Bundesrat) die Ziele und wichtigsten Maßnahmen für jeweils vierjährige Förderperioden sowie die Finanzierung sämtlicher Förderbereiche des *Bundesamtes für Kultur BAK* ebenso wie die Bundesbeiträge an die *Schweizer Kulturstiftung Pro Helvetia* und an das *Schweizerische Nationalmuseum*. Darin spielt – wie auch schon in den beiden vorhergehenden *Kulturbotschaften* –kulturelle Teilhabe eine gewichtige Rolle im Gesamtspektrum der intendierten Kulturpolitik des Bundes. Dies zeigt sich allein in der häufigen Nennung kultureller Teilhabe in den meisten der dort ausgewiesenen Handlungsfeldern. Die grundlegende kulturpolitische Bedeutung kultureller Teilhabe wurde bei der im Sommer 2023 durchgeführten öffentlichen Vernehmlassung (Anhörung) bestätigt und in keiner Weise in Frage gestellt. (EDI Vernehmlassungsbericht 2024) Diese aktuelle politische Debatte ist Anlass für diesen Beitrag, der resümierend auf den Aufstieg der kulturpolitischen Zielsetzung von kultureller Teilhabe zurückschaut, wichtige Wegmarken und Diskussionspunkte in ihrer Etablierung festhält und nicht zuletzt so einen Beitrag zur – zumindest in der Schweiz – vernachlässigten Geschichtsschreibung von Kulturpolitik leisten möchte.

Kulturpolitische Wegweisungen

Erste Auslöser für die Debatte in der Schweiz über kulturelle Teilhabe in den 2010-er Jahren waren der bundesrätliche Entscheid für die kulturpolitische Handlungsachse Kulturelle Teilhabe im Rahmen der *Kulturbotschaft 2016–2020* sowie die Verankerung kultureller Teilhabe in Strategien oder Leitlinien einzelner Städte oder Kantone. Schon im Jahr 2014 hatte sich im Vorfeld der Verabschiedung der erwähnten *Kulturbotschaft* eine eigene Arbeitsgruppe im Rahmen des *Nationalen Kulturdialogs NKD* gebildet, dem kulturpolitischen Austauschgremium der Städte und Gemeinden, Kantone und des Bundes. Ziele der bis 2020 aktiven Arbeitsgruppe waren, begrifflich-konzeptionelle Fragen zu klären und die ins Auge gefassten Fördermaßnahmen im kulturföderalen Gefüge der Schweiz abzustimmen (KOSLOWSKI 2019). Die Mitglieder

der Arbeitsgruppe stützten sich vor allem auf ihre eigene Kulturver-
waltungserfahrung ab und agierten pragmatisch orientiert auf die Um-
setzbarkeit dieser kulturpolitischen Zielsetzung im föderalen Kultur-
verwaltungsgetriebe. Nur am Rande setzte sich die Arbeitsgruppe mit
kulturmanagerial-wissenschaftlicher Erkenntnis auseinander.

Ausgangspunkt der Diskussionen innerhalb der Arbeitsgruppe war
die Feststellung, dass eine entfesselte Globalisierung und mannigfaltige
Migrationsbewegungen, potenzierte Mobilität und explodierende Viel-
fältigkeit der Bevölkerung, ideologisch motivierte Gewalt und politische
Polarisierungen, fortschreitende Individualisierung und allgegenwärtige
Digitalisierung das Kulturleben fundamental verändert hätten. Eine wachsende Vielheit kultureller Ausdrucksformen und ihrer Organisationswei-
sen wurde konstatiert. Ebenso, dass von einem gesamtgesellschaftlich ge-
tragenen Verständnis von Kultur nicht mehr ausgegangen werden könne.
Aus kulturpolitischer Perspektive ein weiteres: In den letzten Jahrzehnten
wäre es gelungen, das Angebot insbesondere der Kulturinstitutionen zu
professionalisieren und zu erweitern. Gleichwohl wiesen die statistischen
Erhebungen in der Schweiz aus, dass die Teilhabe am kulturellen Leben
weiterhin abhängig ist von Bildung, Einkommen und Herkunft (BUN-
DESAMT FÜR STATISTIK 2014/2019a). Eine gezielte Stärkung der Teilhabe am kulturellen Leben, so die Hoffnung der Arbeitsgruppe, könnte
nicht zuletzt auch die gesellschaftspolitische Legitimation von kulturellem
Schaffen und seiner Förderung unterstützen.

Das Anliegen hinter dem Begriff 'kulturelle Teilhabe' war und ist auch
in der Schweiz nicht neu – wenn auch kulturpolitisch von anderen Diskussionen, z.B. über Kulturwirtschaft, in den Hintergrund gerückt. Eine in der
Schweiz kulturpolitisch maßgebliche Referenz stellt der 1969 vom Eidgenössischen Departement des Innern in Auftrag gegebene und erst im Jahr
1975 publizierte sogenannte *Bericht Clottu* dar (EXPERTENKOMMISSI-
ON 1975). Seine Entstehung war überschattet von heftigen persönlichen
und politischen Auseinandersetzungen über das Verständnis von Kultur.
Trotz seiner turbulenten Entstehung ist er ein erstes Dokument weiträumi-
gen Nachdenkens in der Schweiz über die Rolle der öffentlichen Hand im
Bereich der Kultur. Zu den wichtigsten Forderungen des Clottu-Berichts,
diesem „unvollkommenen Werk" (EXPERTENKOMMISSION 1975: 9), ge-
hörte die Aufnahme eines Kulturartikels in die Bundesverfassung. Dies wurde im Jahr 1999 im Rahmen der Totalrevision der Verfassung umgesetzt.
Artikel 69 der Bundesverfassung ermöglicht seither dem Bund ein stärkeres
kulturpolitisches Engagement. Neben dieser konkreten Forderung verfolg-
te dieser Klassiker schweizerischer Kulturpolitik einen in weiten Teilen

kulturdemokratischen Grundansatz und machte für die Schweiz fruchtbar, was beispielsweise der deutsche Kulturpolitiker Hilmar Hoffmann (1925–2018) oder auch André Malraux (1901–1969) als französischer Kulturminister gefordert hatten. Insbesondere klagte der *Bericht Clottu* einen „demokratischen Zugang zur Kultur" ein; Kultur solle nicht „das Privileg einer kleinen Zahl von Menschen bleiben" (EXPERTENKOMMISSION 1975: 13).

Die *Arbeitsgruppe Kulturelle Teilhabe des NKD* beauftragte zunächst den *Verband Kulturvermittlung Schweiz KVS*, einen *Bericht Stärkung kultureller Teilhabe in der Schweiz* zu erarbeiten. Dieser bot einen Überblick über die damaligen Bemühungen im Schweizer Kulturleben um kulturelle Teilhabe. Parallel zu dieser Bestandsaufnahme entwickelte die *Arbeitsgruppe Kulturelle Teilhabe* ein *Positionspapier* (NATIONALER KULTURDIALOG 2019: 355–357), um auf ein ebenso gemeinsames wie offenes und anschlussfähiges Verständnis von kultureller Teilhabe hinzuwirken.

Das *Positionspapier* hebt hervor, dass Teilhabe ein etablierter politischer Begriff sei, der in verschiedenen Politikfeldern verwendet werde. So ergänzten sich politische, wirtschaftliche, soziale und eben auch kulturelle Teilhabe am Gemeinwesen, verstärkten einander und trügen in ihrem Zusammenwirken zu gesellschaftlicher Kohäsion bei.

Dass Begriff und Konzept Kulturelle Teilhabe unscharf sind, wie verschiedentlich angemerkt wurde, darüber herrschte Einigkeit: Der Begriff teile seine Unschärfe und Auslegungsnotwendigkeit aber mit anderen Formulierungen, nicht nur solchen aus dem Feld der Kulturpolitik. Dieses vermeintliche Manko stellte im politischen Diskurs eben auch eine Stärke dar. Dies auch im Vergleich zu diskriminierungs- und machtkritischen Ideologemen wie Ableismus und Klassismus, die in der Schweiz bis heute erklärungsbedürftig und politisch schwer durchsetzbar scheinen (PIECECK 2023; STIFTUNG FÜR KULTURELLE WEITERBILDUNG UND KULTURBERATUNG 2023; DIVERSITY.ARTS.CULTURE Wörterbuch; INSTITUT NEUE SCHWEIZ 2022: PERTSCH 2023; Micossé-Aikins 2023).

Zudem bereichern und differenzieren verschiedene andere Begriffe die Diskussion um kulturelle Teilhabe, so die Meinung der Arbeitsgruppe, und dies jeweils abhängig vom Sprachraum der Schweiz und von ihren Wissenschafts-, Entstehungs- und Verwendungszusammenhängen. Man dachte an teils synonym, teils unterschiedlich verwendete Begriffe wie Inklusion, Ko-Konstruktion, Kollaboration, Kooperation, Mitwirkung, Zugang und natürlich auch an Partizipation. Die pragmatische Anerkennung, dass es mannigfaltige Begriffe, Konzepte und Erscheinungsformen von kultureller Teilhabe gibt, war der konsensorientierten *Arbeitsgruppe Kulturelle Teilhabe des NKD* wichtiger als ein handlungshemmendes Ringen um eine wissenschaftlich abgefederte, wasserdichte Definition des Begriffsschirms 'kulturelle Teilhabe'.

Utopische Setzung ohne großes Ganzes

Auch wenn sich kulturelle Teilhabe einer trennscharfen Definition entzieht, war klar, dass der Ausdruck nicht eine Maßnahme (wie Kulturvermittlung) benennt, sondern ein übergeordnetes kulturpolitisches Ziel mit einem durchaus utopischen Beiklang: Allen festgestellten ungleichen Startchancen bezüglich Bildung, Einkommen, Herkunft sowie physischen, psychischen und kognitiven Voraussetzungen zum Trotz, sollen möglichst viele Menschen die Möglichkeit haben, sich einzeln und in Gruppen auf unterschiedliche Weise mit Kultur auseinanderzusetzen und sich nach eigenen Vorstellungen kulturell auszudrücken.

Dabei gilt es aus kulturpolitischer Perspektive, das geförderte kulturelle Leben sozial durchlässiger zu machen und auch gezielt diverse Bevölkerungsgruppen zu ermächtigen, ihre ureigenen Interessen und Vorlieben zu erkennen und diese vor- und einzubringen, sichtbar- und damit verhandelbar zu machen. Die Zielsetzung kulturelle Teilhabe animiert dazu, „einerseits im kulturell diversifizierten Heute von der Differenz her zu denken und zu gestalten und andererseits zukunftsgerichtet von der Vielfalt her und vom Potenzial der Einzelnen und Gruppen her." (KOSLOW-SKI 2022a) Es geht also um das ‚eingebundene Teilsein in antwortenden Beziehungen' (ROSA 2016), die Wertschätzung der kulturellen Beiträge von Einzelnen und Gruppen, um deren Mitgestaltung des kulturellen Lebens und – das ist nicht zu vergessen – deren Mitverantwortung dafür. Aktives Gestalten ist gefragt und Teilhabe, die keiner privilegierten Position der Erkenntnis bedarf. Ohne ein homogenes Ganzes vorauszusetzen oder anzustreben meint kulturelle Teilhabe im kulturpolitischen Diskurs des Bundes, der Kantone sowie der Gemeinden und Städte, die staatspolitisch stets den 'gesellschaftlichen Zusammenhalt' der vier sprachlich-kulturell unterschiedlich organisierten Landesteile mitdenken: Teilen, Teil nehmen, Teil geben, Teil haben, Teil werden, Teil sein.

Umsetzungsherausforderungen

Kulturelle Teilhabe als kulturpolitisches Ziel zu setzen, brauchte nicht nur Mut und Gestaltungswillen: Kulturelle Teilhabe zu fördern, ist leichter gesagt als getan (NATIONALER KULTURDIALOG 2019). Auf jeden Fall bedingt sie auch für die Förderstellen selbst, einerseits die eigene Förderpraxis zu überprüfen und, wo notwendig, anzupassen oder zu ergänzen. Und andererseits über den kulturellen Tellerrand hinaus zu agieren: Kooperation und Kollaboration sind nicht nur auf Ebene der kulturellen Produktion von Projektstrukturen sowie von Institutionen und Organisationen angesagt, sondern auch zwischen verschiedenen Förderstellen, privaten und öffentlichen wie auch solchen verschiedener Politikbereiche.

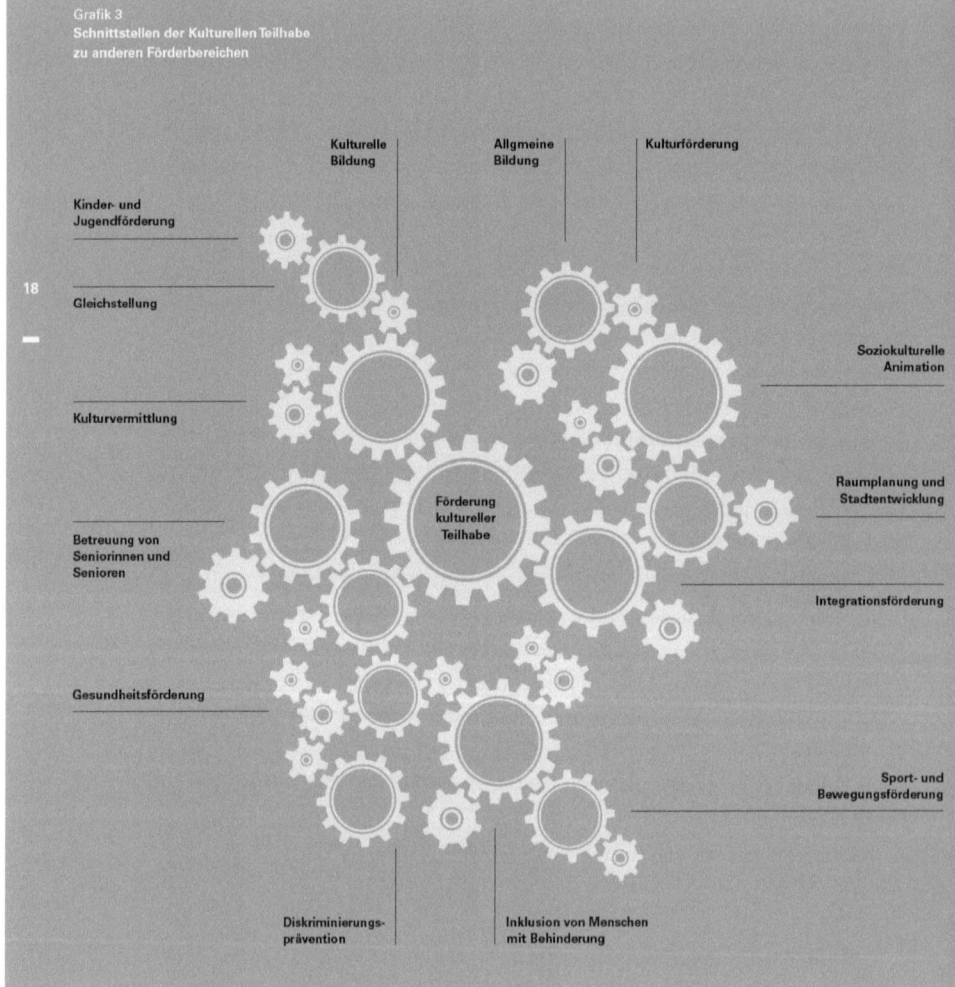

Abb. 1: *Schnittstellen der Kulturellen Teilhabe zu anderen Förderbereichen (NATIONALER KULTURDIALOG 2021: 18).*

Gleichzeitig gilt es die Besonderheiten teilhabeorientierter Kultur-produktion herauszuschälen, um überhaupt deren Zumutungen ge-recht werden zu können. Diese haben ja Folgen für die personelle und konzeptionelle Aufstellung und Vernetzung eines Projekts, aber auch für dessen Rezeption und Beurteilung durch die Öffentlichkeit und die Förderstellen. So stehen ja bei teilhabeorientierten Projekten häufig nicht ein Produkt, dessen Einmaligkeit oder dessen ästheti-sche Qualität im Vordergrund, sondern seine Prozesse, sein Ermäch-tigungspotenzial, seine gesellschaftliche Vernetztheit, seine Wieder-holbarkeit oder Übertragbarkeit. Dies im Gegensatz zur Förderung künstlerischer Avantgarde, bei der es um Exzellenz und Einmaligkeit geht.

Wenn die Akteurinnen und Akteure an der Ausrichtung und Aus-gestaltung eines Vorhabens maßgeblich beteiligt sind, wenn Ent-scheidungs-, Gestaltungs- und Deutungshoheiten zu Disposition ste-hen, sind weder der Weg noch das Ergebnis eines Projekts zwingend vorgegeben oder vorhersehbar. Die Moderation zwischen den Akteu-rinnen und Akteuren wie auch die Kommunikation nach innen und nach außen erhalten ein besonderes Gewicht. Flexibilität – und nicht selten auch Geduld und Vertrauen – sind von allen Beteiligten und Betroffenen gefragt.

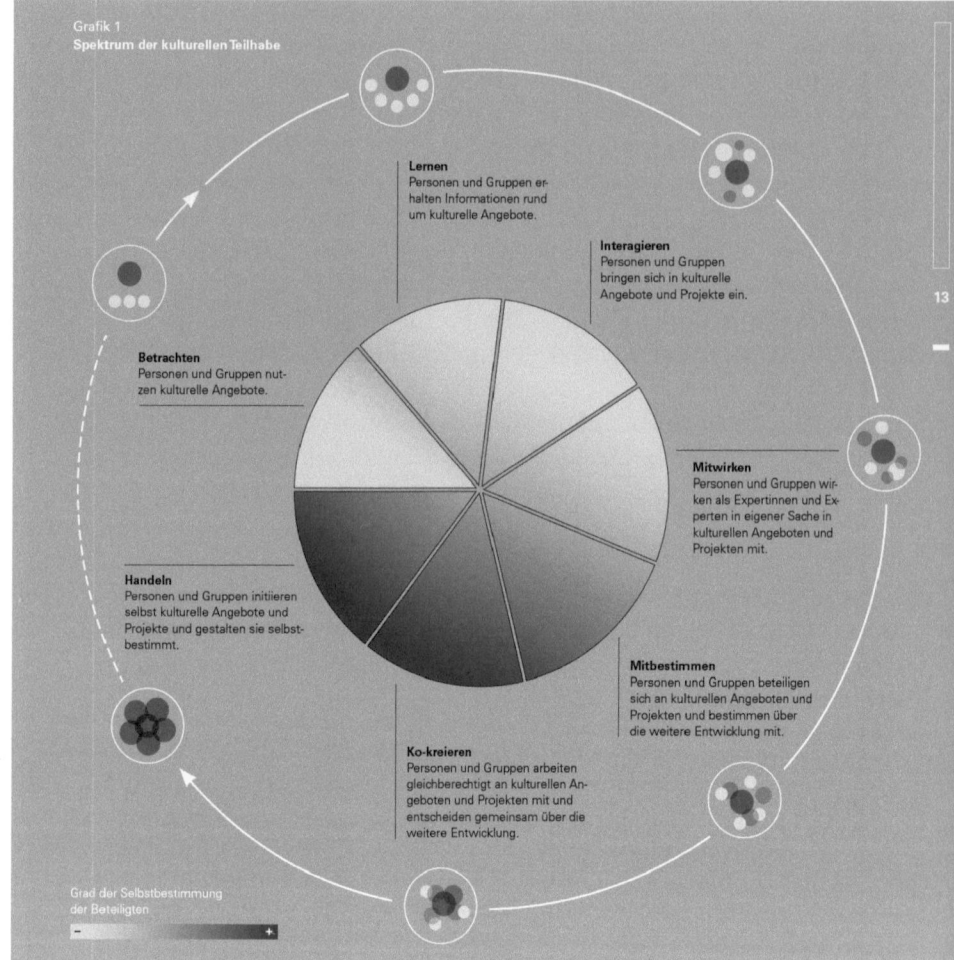

Abb. 2: *Spektrum kultureller Teilhabe (NATIONALER KULTURDIALOG 2021: 13).*

Teilhabeorientierung kommunizieren

Um diese Überlegungen zur Verfügung und zur Diskussion zu stellen, veranstaltete das *Bundesamt für Kultur* im Januar 2017 zusammen mit dem *Kanton Bern*, der *Stadt Bern*, dem *Schweizerischen Städteverband* sowie *Swissfoundations*, dem Dachverband der Vergabestiftungen der Schweiz, im Berner *Zentrum Paul Klee* die erste zweitägige nationale Fachtagung *Kulturelle Teilhabe fördern*. Zwei Jahre später folgte die nationale Fachtagung *Kulturelle Teilhabe in der Praxis* in Solothurn; auch deren Trägerschaft war breit abgestützt. Beide Tagungen richteten sich ausdrücklich an private und öffentliche Förderstellen. Vor dem Hintergrund des erwähnten *Positionspapiers* war zudem klar, auch Personen, Stellen und Institutionen einzuladen, die mit der Förderung der Teilhabe in Politik, Gesellschaftspolitik und Wirtschaft betraut sind. Kulturelle Teilhabe fördern erfordert – das machten beide Tagungen deutlich – transdisziplinäres Denken und Zusammenwirken.

Um über den Kreis der Tagungsteilnehmenden hinauszuwirken, haben der *Nationale Kulturdialog* das dreisprachige *Handbuch Kulturelle Teilhabe. Participation culturelle. Partecipazione culturale* (2019) sowie den in drei der Landessprachen, auf Deutsch, Französisch und Italienisch verfügbaren *Leitfaden Förderung kultureller Teilhabe* herausgegeben.

Insbesondere die in diesen Publikationen vorgeschlagenen Schemata haben über den Kreis der Förderstellen bei den Leitungen von teilhabeorientierten Institutionen und Projekten positive Resonanz erfahren, so etwa das Schema, das das Zusammenwirken verschiedener Politikbereiche durch ineinandergreifende Zahnräder illustriert (Abb. 1) oder jenes das verschiedene Grade der Teilhabe in einem Kuchendiagramm ausweist (Abb.2). Die Nachfrage der Förderstellen sowie der kulturellen Akteurinnen und Akteure nach umsetzungsorientierten Leitfäden, Arbeitshilfen und Vorbildern (best practice) übersteigt deutlich den Wunsch nach wissenschaftlicher Fundierung und Durchdringung der kulturpolitischen Herausforderung kultureller Teilhabe.

Angeregt durch die *Kulturbotschaften 2016–2020* bzw. *2021–2024* und die noch in der politischen Beratung stehende *Kulturbotschaft 2025–2028* sowie die erwähnten Tagungen und Publikationen des *Nationalen Kulturdialogs* haben verschiedene kulturelle Organisationen in ihren Fachkreisen Tagungen und Workshops zum Thema kulturelle Teilhabe durchgeführt und weiteres spezifisches Wissen zu kultureller Teilhabe in den jeweiligen Bereichen generiert und geteilt. So bereitet der *Verband Kulturvermittlung Schweiz* aktuell die wichtigsten Erkenntnisse des *Handbuchs kultureller Teilhabe* und des *Leitfadens Kulturelle Teilhabe fördern* für die Mitarbeitenden von Kulturinstitutionen und Kulturorganisationen sowie für frei agierende Kulturschaffende auf.

Gesetzesgrundlagen schaffen

Die *Arbeitsgruppe Kulturelle Teilhabe des NKD* beriet das *Bundesamt für Kultur* insbesondere auch bei der Ausgestaltung und Lancierung von Fördermöglichkeiten für teilhabeorientierte Vorhaben. Dazu wurde 2016 eigens das *Bundesgesetz über die Kulturförderung* (Kulturförderungsgesetz KFG, SR 441.1) um Artikel 9a ergänzt: „Der Bund kann Vorhaben zur Stärkung der Teilhabe der Bevölkerung am kulturellen Leben unterstützen." (Art. 9a KFG) Seine Spezifizierung leistet die Verordnung des Eidgenössischen Departements des Innern über das Förderungskonzept zur Stärkung der kulturellen Teilhabe (SR 442.130). Sie nennt als die Ziele der bundestaatlichen Förderung:

> „a. die Auseinandersetzung mit Kultur und die kulturelle Betätigung möglichst vieler zu fördern sowie Hindernisse in Bezug auf die Teilhabe am kulturellen Leben abzubauen,
>
> b. den Wissensaustausch, die Vernetzung und die Koordination der Akteure zu stärken
>
> c. die konzeptionellen und die statistischen Grundlagen zur Stärkung der kulturellen Teilhabe zu vertiefen." (Artikel 1 Bst a-c Verordnung)

Zunächst eröffnete das *BAK* eine Fördermöglichkeit für Projekte, die dem Ziel a der Verordnung entsprachen; seit 2022 auch für Projekte, die den Zielen b und c der Verordnung entsprechen. Ausdrücklich ausgeschlossen werden gemäß Artikel 3 Abs. 3 der Verordnung (Stand 2020) Beiträge an Infrastrukturen und an den Betriebsaufwand von Kulturinstitutionen (Strukturbeiträge). Zudem müssen die Projekte von 'nationalem Interesse' sein oder 'Modellcharakter' aufweisen (Artikel 4, 5 und 6 der Verordnung) – eine hohe Hürde, aber den Regeln der kantonalen Kulturhoheit und der bundesstaatlichen Kulturförderung entsprechend. Die geförderten Projekte werden jeweils auf der Webseite des *BAK* publiziert.

Auf spartenspezifische Ausschreibungen verzichtete das *BAK*, um auch Projekte anzusprechen, die sich kultureller Formate oder Inhalte bedienen, ohne jedoch den eingeübten und tradierten Kategorisierungen der (Hoch-)Kulturförderung wie Theater, Literatur oder bildende Kunst zu folgen. Auch von zielpublikumsspezifischen Ausschreibungen sah man ab, um der Gefahr einer positiven Diskriminierung bestimmter Bevölkerungsgruppen (affirmative action) zu entgehen. Schließlich setzte das *BAK* einen Schwerpunkt auf die „Aktivierung eigener und selbstständiger kultureller Tätigkeit" (Art. 7 Abs. 1 Bst. b der Verordnung). Gemeint ist damit kultureller Selbstausdruck, bei dem das Mitwirken, Mitbestimmen, Ko-Kreieren und Handeln gemäß Abb. 2. im Vordergrund steht. So blieb die Ausschreibung vergleichsweise allgemein, aber offen für unterschiedliche oder vorerst unerkannte Förderbedürfnisse der Akteure.

Förderung kultureller Teilhabe diversifizieren

Anfangs wurde die neue Fördermöglichkeit des *BAK* mehrheitlich nur von der Kulturszene wahrgenommen. Allen Klärungsbemühungen des *BAK* und des *NKD* zum Trotz bestand auch eine Unsicherheit darüber, was mit kultureller Teilhabe gemeint sei. Auffallend viele Fördergesuche trafen ein von kleinen, durchaus interessanten Initiativen, die bislang keine öffentlichen Gelder erhalten hatten. Das *BAK* konnte viele davon jedoch nicht unterstützten, da sie die Fördervoraussetzungen 'nationales Interesse' oder 'Modellcharakter' nicht erfüllten.

In den vergangenen Jahren ist der Ruf nach Strukturbeiträgen lauter geworden. So wird aktuell diskutiert, die Projekt- um eine Strukturförderung zu ergänzen, um den teilhabeorientierten Vorhaben eine längere Finanzierungsperspektive zu ermöglichen. Inzwischen haben sich auch andere Förderakteure, wenngleich unter anderem Titel, der Förderung kultureller Teilhabe geöffnet. Zu nennen sind auf Bundesebene beispielsweise *Pro Helvetia* oder die *Eidgenössische Kommission für Migrationsfragen EKM*. Das EKM-Integrationsförderprogramm *Neues Wir – Kultur, Migration, Teilhabe* unterstützt seit 2020 Projekte,

„die Erfahrungen und Wirklichkeiten der Migrationsgesellschaft Schweiz sichtbar machen und diese als Teil der lokalen, regionalen oder nationalen Öffentlichkeit verstehen. [...] In Projekten, die vom Programm ‚Neues Wir – Kultur, Migration, Teilhabe' unterstützt werden, sollen sich die Erfahrungen von Menschen mit Migrationshintergrund im Programmangebot, beim Personal, im Publikum sowie bei den Partnerschaften zeigen (sogenannte 4-P-Regel im Kulturbereich). Die Wirkung der Projekte ist dadurch nachhaltiger und vermag strukturelle Veränderungsprozesse anzustossen." (EIDGENÖSSISCHE MIGRATIONSKOMMISSION EKM 2020; JAIN 2019)

Ausgangspunkt für die Kulturstiftung *Pro Helvetia* für ein starkes Engagement im Bereich Diversitätsförderung war die Feststellung, dass die Schweizer Gesellschaft ausgeprägt divers sei, dass sich dieses jedoch im hiesigen Kulturbetrieb nicht ausreichend spiegele. Die Chancen, im Kulturbetrieb Fuß zu fassen, seien nicht für alle gleich. Was sich allein daran ablesen lässt, dass es für Frauen nach wie vor schwieriger ist, Leitungsfunktionen zu erlangen. Zudem verdienen Frauen im Durchschnitt 17 Prozent weniger als ihre männlichen Kollegen (ZENTRUM GENDER STUDIES 2021). Auch Kulturschaffende aus migrantischen Communities finden nur selten eine Stelle in Kulturinstitutionen; ebenso sind sie in künstlerischen Programmen und in der Förderung deutlich unterrepräsentiert. Dabei haben etwa vierzig Prozent der in der Schweiz lebenden Menschen einen Migrationshintergrund. Bei den 15- bis 34-Jährigen beträgt dieser Anteil über fünfzig Prozent (ESPAHANGAZI 2023). In Folge hat *Pro Helvetia* Kulturinstitutionen bei der Entwicklung von diversitätsorientierten Prozessen gefördert und aktiv begleitet.

Denn vielen Kulturinstitutionen fehlt es an Ressourcen und Kenntnissen, die Herausforderungen einer diversen Gesellschaft anzugehen. Oft mangelt es an Methoden und Wissen, das Potenzial der Diversität zu nutzen und die Strukturen entsprechend langfristig anzupassen. Unter dem Titel *Diversität und Chancengleichheit im Kulturbetrieb* lancierte *Pro Helvetia* 2022 die Ausschreibung *Tandem Diversität*. Damit erhalten Kulturorganisationen die Möglichkeit, ihre Strukturen zu durchleuchten und diversitätsorientiert auszurichten. Die ausgewählten Kulturorganisationen arbeiten im *Tandem* mit Diversitätsexpertinnen und -experten ihrer Wahl zusammen. Auf diese Weise erhalten sie Ressourcen, steigern ihre Kompetenzen und entwickeln Methoden, um die Diversität und Chancengleichheit in ihren Betriebsstrukturen zu verbessern – gleichzeitig können sie nachhaltige Diversitätsmaßnahmen testen.

Teilhabe am immateriellen Kulturerbe

Verschiedene internationale Abkommen, denen auch die Schweiz beigetreten ist, rütteln an einem Verständnis von Kulturförderung, das die kulturelle-gesellschaftliche Leistung des nicht-professionellen Kulturschaffens eher wenig berücksichtigt. Dazu gehören das *UNESCO-Übereinkommen über die Bewahrung des immateriellen Kulturerbes* (2003 Konvention), das *Rahmenübereinkommen des Europarats über den Wert des Kulturerbes für die Gesellschaft* (2005; Konvention von Faro) oder auch das *UNESCO-Übereinkommen über die Bewahrung und Förderung der Vielfalt kultureller Ausdrucksformen* (2005 Konvention). Diese und weitere Dokumente drängen auf eine konsequente Valorisierung vielheitlicher Vorstellungen von Kultur (DeVereaux et al. 2024).

Diese internationalen Abkommen gehen von einer Gleichwertigkeit unterschiedlicher kultureller Ausdrucksformen aus, unabhängig vom Professionalisierungsgrad der jeweiligen Akteure und ohne bestimmte Ausdrucksformen normierend hervorzuheben. Das zwingt, die eigenen Sinne und die Wahrnehmung für jegliche kulturelle Praktiken zu schärfen. Und dies eben jenseits unhaltbarer gesellschaftlicher Ausgrenzungen und

Diskriminierungen, überkommener Hierarchisierungen und Aufspaltungen von kulturellem Tun in E- und U-Kultur, Hoch- versus Alltags-, Trivial-, Unterhaltungs-, Massen-, Pop-, Laien-, Amateur- oder Volkskultur. Eine Herausforderung für eine Kulturförderung, die seit ihren Anfängen hochkulturell imprägniertes Kulturschaffen favorisiert. Die damit verbundene Wertehierarchie einer Kulturpolitik, die sich – aus der Perspektive der *UNESCO-Kulturdefinition* (Mexiko 1982) – verengend auf Kunst in einem emphatischen Sinne ausrichtet, scheint ins Wanken geraten zu sein. Der (Hoch-)Kulturbegriff wird der gewachsenen Vielfalt kultureller Ausdrucksformen in der ‚superdiversen Gesellschaft' (VERTOVEC 2023) schon lange nicht mehr gerecht. Dieses Defizit ist wohl auch dadurch nicht behoben, dass sich eine Jazz-, Rock- und Popförderung etabliert hat und dass inzwischen auch Comedy oder Game Culture gefördert werden.

Die Zumutungen kultureller Teilhabe betreffen nicht nur das zeitgenössische Kulturschaffen, deren Institutionen und Organisationen, sondern auch – und das wird gerne ausgeblendet – den Umgang mit dem Kulturerbe. So hebt die *2003 Konvention* in Artikel 15 eine möglichst weitreichende Beteiligung der Gemeinschaft, der Gruppen und gegebenenfalls Individuen hervor, die das immaterielle Kulturerbe schaffen, bewahren und weitergeben. Die Betonung des zivilgesellschaftlichen Beitrags jenseits der Fachexpertise und jenseits politisch-administrativer Entscheide ist ein Spezifikum dieses *UNESCO*-Übereinkommens, durch das es sich von anderen Konventionen abhebt. Der Prozess der Erbmachung, also der Definition und Festlegung dessen, was als ‘Kulturerbe' gilt, wird nicht mehr als Privileg von Eliten aus Kulturpolitik, Kulturverwaltung, Kulturwissenschaft oder Kulturinstitutionen verstanden. Weitere Akteure wie Medien, zivilgesellschaftliche Organisationen und sonstige Kreise, die sich der Bewahrung oder Pflege des Kulturerbes verschrieben haben, nehmen aktiv an dieser Erbmachung teil (GROSCHWITZ 2023).

Aus kulturpolitischer Perspektive geht es auch darum, die Selbstwahrnehmung, Selbstwertschätzung und Selbsttätigkeit der jeweiligen Akteurinnen und Akteure als Trägerinnen und Träger immateriellen Kulturerbes anzuregen (RIEDER 2019). Und dies nicht nur bei den ohnehin artikulationsstarken, brauchtumsorientierten Milieus, die sich ihres ‘Wir' sicher sind, sondern auch bei Gruppen, die sich durch die Konvention zunächst wenig angesprochen fühlen, wie sich beispielsweise bei den Aktualisierungen 2017 und 2023 der „Liste der lebendigen Traditionen in der Schweiz" zeigte. Zu ihnen gehören auch informell organisierte Netzwerke oder zugewanderte Bevölkerungsgruppen. Als hilfreich in den Kontaktaufnahmen und Diskussionen mit den Trägergruppen, die ihre soziale Praktik nicht auf nebulöse Wurzeln zurückführen, hat sich dazu der vom *BAK* produzierte *Nachhaltigkeitskompass* erwiesen. Dieser hebt neben anderen Bezügen des immateriellen Kulturerbes zur nachhaltigen Entwicklung ausdrücklich die Bedeutung kultureller Teilhabe hervor.

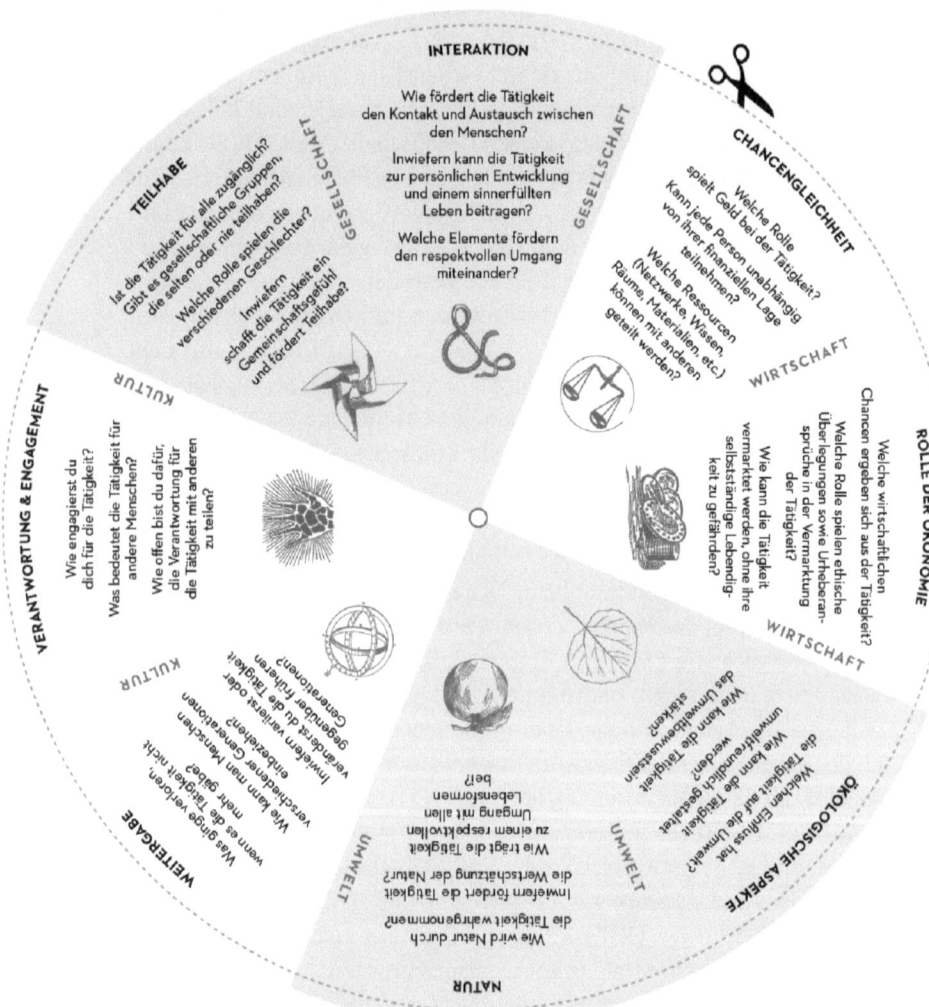

Abb. 3: *Nachhaltigkeitskompass https://www.lebendige-traditionen.ch/tradition/de/home/aktuelles/nachhaltigkeitskompass.html*

Die *2003 Konvention* setzt zivilgesellschaftliches Engagement voraus und aktiviert es gleichzeitig. Sie begrüßt ausdrücklich kulturelle Teilhabe und die Mitgestaltung des kulturellen Lebens von möglichst vielen Menschen. Immaterielles Kulturerbe kann als Musterbeispiel für kulturelle Teilhabeorientierung gelesen werden.

Teilhabe in Museen

Die Gedächtnisinstitutionen wie Museen, Archive, Bibliotheken oder Mediatheken spielen bei der Inwertsetzung von immateriellem Kulturerbe eine wichtige Rolle. Schon in der Vergangenheit haben sie, avant la lettre, immateriellem Kulturerbe eigene Ausstellungen gewidmet. Dies, weil es gesellschaftlich und kulturell eben ein unübergehbar wichtiges Thema ist und weil materielles Kulturerbe nur aus seinem immateriellen Kontext heraus verständlich ist und dadurch auch gesellschaftliche Praktiken ins Blickfeld der Museen rücken. Das hatten die Ausstellungsverantwortlichen erkannt, bevor die *UNESCO* das entsprechende Abkommen verabschiedete. Spätestens seither diskutieren die Museen vermehrt über immaterielles Kulturerbe. Dessen Schutz, Dokumentation und Vermittlung gehören seit 2004 zu den offiziellen Zielen des *Internationalen Museumsrats ICOM*. Dass Teilhabe oder Partizipation dabei eine zentrale Rolle spielt, hat sich auch in der neuen Museumsdefinition niedergeschlagen, die der *ICOM* im Jahr 2022 im Rahmen seiner 26. Generalkonferenz in Prag verabschiedet hat.

Diese Museumsdefinition ist Zeugnis eines tiefgreifenden Wandels der Institution Museum, der schon länger in der übergreifenden Debatte zur Gegenwartsorientierung von Museen, der neuen Museologie und deren partizipativen Ansätzen diskutiert wurde. In musealen Räumen werden immer häufiger Gegenwarts- und Alltagsthemen beleuchtet, welche eine retrospektive oder auf Objekte konzentrierte Betrachtung ergänzen oder ganz ersetzen. Gleichzeitig entwickelt sich das Museum weg von einem Ort der Vermittlung von Expertenwissen und hin zu einer Plattform des Austauschs und der Auseinandersetzung. Bezeichnend dabei ist das Bestreben, das Publikum auf Augenhöhe zu begrüßen, Laienmeinung und Expertenwissen gleichermaßen in die Diskussion einfließen zu lassen, betroffene Individuen, Gruppierungen und Gemeinschaften nicht nur zu Wort kommen zu lassen, sondern auch in die Entwicklung der Ausstellungen oder Sammlungen einzubeziehen (GESSER et al. 2012;

THIEL 2019; BÜCHEL 2022; REGIONALMUSEUM CHÜECHLIHUS 2023; VERBAND DER MUSEEN DER SCHWEIZ 2023).

Mit der Förderung und mit der Ausrichtung verschiedener gemeinsamer Tagungen, Veranstaltungen und Publikationen des *Verbands der Museen der Schweiz* trägt das *BAK* dazu bei, Teilhabe auch im Feld des immateriellen Kulturerbes in Museen zu positionieren und weiterzuentwickeln (BUNDESAMT FÜR KULTUR 2015; VERBAND DER MUSEEN DER SCHWEIZ 2023).

‚Teilhabe. Museen. Wirkungen'

In der Schweizer Museumslandschaft gibt es seit den 2010er Jahren ein wachsendes Interesse an der Partizipation als Methode und an ihrer Wirkung. Dies nicht zuletzt als Folge des museologischen Fachdiskurses im angelsächsischen und benachbarten deutschsprachigen Raum sowie des Nachdenkens über das erwähnte Engagement der Museen im Bereich des immateriellen Kulturerbes. Ein erster Meilenstein in der Schweiz war die Tagung *Das partizipative Museum* im *Stapferhaus Lenzburg* (GESSER et al. 2012).

Den unmittelbaren Impuls für einen runden Tisch des *BAK* mit Vertretungen von Museen, Kulturförderung und Wissenschaft zum Thema „Teilhabe. Museen. Wirkungen" gab der vom *Netzwerk P* durchgeführte *Workshop P* am 24./25. März 2022 im *Zentrum Paul Klee* in Bern. Das *Netzwerk P* ist eine lose Gruppierung von Akteurinnen und Akteuren der Schweizer Museumslandschaft, welche den Diskurs über neue Formen der Partizipation an den Schweizer Museen anregen will. Im Rahmen des Workshops entstanden neun Thesen zur Partizipation am Museum. Die These 8 „Partizipation ist Teil des Leistungsauftrags und benötigt angemessene Erfolgskriterien" wiederum nahm die *Stiftung für Kunst, Kultur und* Geschichte SKKG zum Anlass, im November 2022 Vertreterinnen und Vertreter aus Förderung und Praxis zu einem weiteren zweitägigen Workshop einzuladen. In dessen Rahmen diskutierten Fachleute über adäquate Qualitätskriterien und Evaluationsinstrumente für partizipatives Schaffen im Museum. Dabei konstatierten die Teilnehmenden ein weiteres Mal, wie relevant, aber auch wie komplex die Fragen der Wirkung von Teilhabe für sämtliche Beteiligte – sowohl für die Museumsfachleute als auch für die Förderstellen – sind, auch im Hinblick auf Fragen der Qualität. Dies bei der gleichzeitigen Feststellung, dass zu diesem Thema sowohl empirische Daten als auch praxisnahe Wirkungsmodelle fehlen.

Beim runden Tisch des BAK ‚Teilhabe. Museen. Wirkungen' stand die offene Frage im Hintergrund, ob kulturelle Teilhabe tatsächlich das einlöse, was sich Kulturpolitik und -förderung, aber auch die Museen selbst davon versprächen. Ziele des runden Tisches waren erstens eine Bestandsaufnahme bisheriger Bemühungen zur Auseinandersetzung mit den Wirkungen kultureller Teilhabe, zweitens die Formulierung allfälliger Bedarfe, Bedürfnisse, Interessen und Potenziale zur Vertiefung des Themas Wirkungen kultureller Teilhabe sowie drittens die Identifizierung möglicher Pisten, diesen Bedarfen, Bedürfnissen und Interessen nachzukommen.

Inzwischen hat die *Universität Zürich (Institut für Sozialanthropologie und Empirische Kulturwissenschaft – Populäre Kulturen ISEK)* zur Veranstaltung *Museen und Teilhabe: Wirkungen gemeinsam erforschen* im März 2024 eingeladen. Sie knüpft direkt an den vom *BAK* organisierten runden Tisch an:

> „Ausgangspunkt ist der gemeinsame Befund, dass Forschung zu Partizipation auch eine partizipative Neuausrichtung erfordert: Sie sollte nicht länger über, sondern mit Museen, d.h. stärker im Verbund zwischen Museen und Wissenschaft gestaltet werden."

All die hier erwähnten kleineren oder größeren Veranstaltungen tragen dazu bei, das Thema kulturelle Teilhabe im Museumsbereich präsent zu halten und weiterzuentwickeln.

Teilhabe am materiellen Kulturerbe

„In der schweizerischen Denkmalpflege gibt es heute durchaus aktive Teilhabe und Bürgerbeteiligung. Allerdings steht sie nur einem kleinen, ausgewählten Segment der Gesellschaft in ganz bestimmten Teilbereichen offen. Den meisten Menschen bleibt der aktive Zugang verwehrt. Sie werden nicht als potenzielle Partnerinnen und Partner erkannt, sondern ausschliesslich als Konsumierende angesprochen. Methoden, Instrumente und theoretische Grundlagen werden den kulturellen Werten der heterogenen Gesellschaft nicht mehr gerecht. Es besteht also Handlungsbedarf und zwar auf mehreren Ebenen." (MEKACHER 2019a: 161; MEKACHER 2019b)

Der Herausforderung Teilhabe am materiellen Kulturerbe hat sich in der Schweiz insbesondere die *Nationale Informationsstelle zum*

Kulturerbe NIKE angenommen. Der für alle offene Ideen- und Projekt-wettbewerb *Kulturerbe für alle*, ausgeschrieben vom *BAK* im Rahmen des *Europäischen Jahres des Kulturerbes 2018*, ermöglichte neben anderen Gewinnerprojekten die Unterstützung des *NIKE*-Vorhabens *Teilhabe am Kulturerbe – ein Leitfaden*. Dieser regt Kulturerbe-Fachleute mit theoretischen Überlegungen und Praxisbeispielen dazu an, teilhabeorientiertes Denken und Handeln auch im Bereich des materiellen Kulturerbes stärker zu berücksichtigen. Der Teilhabe widmete *NIKE* auch ihre Jahrestagung 2022 und veröffentlichte die Tagungsakten *PARTICIPATIO – Teilhabe am Kulturerbe* noch in demselben Jahr. Dem Sog kultureller Teilhabe können sich, so scheint es, auch die Akteure im Feld des materiellen Kulturerbes nicht entziehen.

Zusammenarbeit von Kultur- und Integrationsförderstellen

Es war dem BAK stets ein Anliegen, die eigene Förderung nicht nur mit den Kantonen, Städten und Gemeinden sowie privaten Förderstiftungen abzustimmen, sondern auch mit *Pro Helvetia* und innerhalb der Bundesverwaltung u.a. mit dem *Bundesamt für Sozialversicherung BSV*, das insbesondere in der Jugendförderung eine wichtige Rolle spielt, mit dem *Eidgenössischen Büro für die Gleichstellung behinderter Menschen EBGB*, mit der *Fachstelle Rassismusbekämpfung FRB*, mit dem *Staatssekretariat für Migration SEM* und mit der *Eidgenössischen Kommission für Migrationsfragen EKM*. Diese unter Bundesstellen verschiedener Departemente nicht immer übliche enge Abstimmung hat den Boden bereitet für die intensivierte Kooperation zwischen dem *BAK*, der *EKM*, *Pro Helvetia* und dem *SEM* im Rahmen des Projekts *Förderpraxis Kultur und Integration*. Dies geht auf eine Initiative der *EKM* im Rahmen ihres schon oben erwähnten Projekts *Neues Wir* zurück. Die beteiligten Stellen setzen sich darin das Ziel, über die Grenzen der jeweiligen Politikfelder hinaus und die föderalen Ebenen vernetzend einen Beitrag zur Stärkung der kulturellen Teilhabe in einer vielfältigen Schweiz zu leisten.

In der Regel haben die kultur- und die integrationspolitischen Diskurse wenig Berührungspunkte und Austausch. Das spiegelt sich auch in den Verwaltungsstrukturen. Integrations- und Kulturstellen gehören selten derselben Verwaltungseinheit an, unterliegen anderen politischen Vorgaben und gesetzlichen Grundlagen ohne Querbezüge. Deshalb kommt es nicht selten vor, dass vielversprechende Vorhaben daran scheitern, dass sich weder die Integrations- noch die Kulturstellen dafür verantwortlich fühlen und die Gesuchstellenden gegenseitig aufeinander verweisen. So fällt manches förderungswürdiges Vorhaben 'zwischen Stuhl und Bank'. Dem könnten Entsäulung, Vernetzung und Zusammenarbeit der betroffenen Politikbereiche und Verwaltungsstellen entgegenwirken im Sinne einer Sensibilisierung, einer erweiterten Kenntnis der jeweils anderen Politik- und Verwaltungsbereiche sowie einer kontinuierlichen Zusammenarbeit bei der Entwicklung von Strategien und deren operativer Umsetzung. Neben einer abgestimmten Förderung von Projekten zur kulturellen Teilhabe, insbesondere von Migrantinnen und Migranten sowie ihren Nachkommen, sind auch Prozesse anzuregen der institutionellen Öffnung von Kulturinstitutionen und Kulturorganisationen für migrantische Kulturschaffende sowie der Öffnung der Förderstellen selbst hin zu einer diversitätsorientierten Personal- und Programmpolitik.

Für den Kulturbereich stellen sich – das haben die bisherigen Analysen und Diskussionen in den Projekt-Arbeitsgruppen *Projekte der kulturellen Teilhabe, Förderstrategien und Finanzierung* und *Statistische Grundlagen und Monitoring* gezeigt – beispielsweise die Herausforderungen Kulturföderalismus und Kulturbegriff.

Wie andere föderalistisch organisierte Staaten und anders als zentralistisch aufgebaute Staatsgebilde kennt die Schweiz keine flächendeckend einheitliche Kulturpolitik. Grund ist das im schweizerischen Staatsföderalismus angelegte doppelte Subsidiaritätsprinzip. Dieses stellt ab auf die Entfaltung der individuellen Fähigkeiten, die Selbstbestimmung und Selbstverantwortung der Einzelnen. Nur dort, wo die Möglichkeiten von Einzelnen bzw. einer kleinen Gruppe nicht ausreichen, greifen staatliche Institutionen in föderaler Stufung ein: Gemeinde-Kantone-Bund. Die in Artikel 69 der *Schweizerischen Bundesverfassung* festgelegte kantonale Kulturhoheit führt zu deutlich begrenzten Kompetenzen, Lenkungsmöglichkeiten und Verantwortlichkeiten des Bundes. Sich vermehrt der Förderung kultureller Teilhabe zu widmen, konnte deswegen nicht mehr als ein Vorschlag der Bundesbehörden an die kantonalen und städtischen Förderstellen sein. Einige haben diese Anregung aufgegriffen und sich zu eigen gemacht; andere verfolgen weiterhin andere kulturpolitische Ziele. Zudem haben die Kantone und häufig auch die Städte und Gemeinden je eigene rechtliche Grundlagen entwickelt, die neben der Kunstförderung auch andere Bereiche wie Archäologie, Denkmalpflege oder Bibliothekswesen umfassen, aber nicht zwingend von derselben Behörde umgesetzt werden. Ein Beispiel sind die unterschiedlichen Fördermöglichkeiten von professionellem bzw. nicht professionellem Kulturschaffen in ländlichen Gemeinden oder Kantonen gegenüber solchen in Städten oder Stadtkantonen.

Der Politik- und Verwaltungsbereich Kultur ist also stark segmentiert, basiert auf unterschiedlichen rechtlichen Grundlagen und Verwaltungsstrukturen. Hinzu kommen unzählige private Kulturförderinstitutionen – etwa Stiftungen, Unternehmen oder Privatpersonen – mit jeweils unterschiedlichen Schwerpunkten und Zielsetzungen. So ergibt sich eine buntscheckige Förderlandschaft, die nicht nur für Außenstehende schwer zu überblicken ist. Bei der Koordination einer teilhabeorientierten Strategieentwicklung und deren Umsetzung sind also in der Regel mehrere Stellen aus dem Bereich Kultur einzubeziehen, was die Komplexität einer Zusammenarbeit weiter erhöht.

Eine zweite große Herausforderung der Förderung kultureller Teilhabe sind unterschiedliche Vorstellungen von Kultur selbst. Während sich die staatliche Kulturförderung zumeist entlang der Kriterien Einmaligkeit, Innovation, Exzellenz auf die Förderung des professionellen Kunstschaffens fokussiert, geht die Integrationsförderung in ihren Verlautbarungen nicht von einem engen, kunstorientierten Kultur-Begriff aus, sondern von einem im Vergleich zur Kulturförderung sehr breiten, oft unreflektierten Kultur-Verständnis. Inzwischen haben die bundesstaatlichen Trägerschaften des Projekts Förderpraxis Kultur und Integration acht Empfehlungen für Kultur- und Integrationsstellen erarbeitet, die sie im Mai 2024 auf einer nationalen Tagung vorstellten und debattierten. Diese demnächst veröffentlichten Empfehlungen legen den Kultur- und Integrationsförderstellen eine vermehrte Zusammenarbeit und Abstimmung nahe sowie eine konsequente strukturelle Öffnung der Förderstellen, der Kulturinstitutionen und -organisationen.

Blick zurück nach vorne

Der Ruf nach Teilhabe von möglichst Vielen erscheint in der Schweiz auch nach zehn Jahren der Bemühungen und Diskussionen um eine teilhabeorientierte Kulturpolitik und -förderung als eine folgerichtige Reaktion von Kulturpolitik, Kulturschaffenden, Kulturinstitutionen, Kulturorganisationen auf die tektonischen Verschiebungen in der Kulturlandschaft. Dass sich in der Schweiz Kulturpolitik und Kulturszene kultureller Teilhabe angenommen haben, davon zeugen u.a. die erwähnten Tagungen, Publikationen und Initiativen. Wie die

Wirkungen teilhabeorientierter Kulturförderung zu messen sind. Wie kultureller Selbstausdruck unter den Bedingungen sich überlagernder, intersektionaler Hindernisse zu fördern ist. Welche neue Formen und Wege Teilhabe in der digital aufgeheizten Alltagswelt finden wird. Wie kulturpolitisches Denken und Handeln mit einem breit ausgelegten Nachhaltigkeitsverständnis zu verbinden ist. Das sind einige der offenen Fragen, zu deren Beantwortung eine stärkere Zusammenarbeit dringend geboten wäre von Wissenschaft, staatlichen und privaten Förderstellen sowie kulturellen Akteuren. Dabei werden Kompetenzen verschiedenster Fachdisziplinen gebraucht, die die kulturellen, politischen, sozialen und ökonomischen Wechselwirkungen analysieren und kulturpolitisch handhabbar machen können. Gleichzeitig sind eine Offenheit und der Wille - nicht nur der kulturpolitischen - Akteure gefragt, Förderpolitiken zu entwickeln, die der Fülle des kulturellen Lebens gerecht werden.

Literatur

BÜCHEL, Julia (2022): *Repräsentation Partizipation Zugänglichkeit. Theorie und Praxis gesellschaftlicher Einbindung in Museen und Ausstellungen.* Bielefeld: transcript.

BUNDESAMT FÜR KULTUR/VERBAND DER MUSEEN DER SCHWEIZ/MUSEUM FÜR KOMMUNIKATION/ALPINES MUSEUM DER SCHWEIZ (Hgg.) (2015): *Lebendige Traditionen ausstellen. Exposer les traditions vivantes.* Baden Hier und Jetzt.

BUNDESAMT FÜR KULTUR BAK (Hg.) (2022): *Nachhaltigkeitskompass Immaterielles Kulturerbe.* Bern <www.lebendige-traditionen.ch/tradition/de/home/aktuelles/nachhaltigkeitskompass.html> [22.01.2024].

BUNDESAMT FÜR STATISTIK BFS (Hg.) (2014/2019a): *Kulturverhalten – Besuch von Kultureinrichtungen und -anlässen, nach soziodemografischen Merkmalen.* Neuenburg <www.bfs.admin.ch/bfs/de/home/statistiken/kultur-medien-informationsgesellschaft-sport/kultur/kulturverhalten.assetdetail.17464015.html> [22.01.2024].

Diversity.Arts.Culture: Wörterbuch <https://diversity-arts-culture.berlin/diversity-arts-culture/woerterbuch> [22.01.2024].

EIDGENÖSSISCHES DEPARTEMENT DES INNERN EDI (2024): *Botschaft zur Förderung der Kultur in den Jahren 2025–2028 (Kulturbotschaft) Bericht über die Ergebnisse der Vernehmlassung* <fedlex-data-admin-ch-eli-dl-proj-2023-17-cons_1-doc_20-de-pdf-a.pdf> [22.01.2024].

EIDGENÖSSISCHE MIGRATIONSKOMMISSION EKM (2020): *Grundlagendokument des Programms ‚Neues Wir – Kultur, Migration, Teilhabe'.* Bern <www.ekm.admin.ch/ekm/de/home/projekte/neues-wir.html> [22.01.2024]).

ESPAHANGIZI, Kijan (2023): *Der Migrations-Integrations-Komplex. Wissenschaft und Politik in einem (Nicht-)Einwanderungsland, 1960–2010.* Konstanz: University Press.

EXPERTENKOMMISSION FÜR FRAGEN EINER SCHWEIZERISCHEN KULTURPOLITIK (1975): *Beiträge für eine Kulturpolitik in der Schweiz.* Bern.

FACHSTELLE FÜR RASSISMUSBEKÄMPFUNG FRB (2021): *Roadmap Institutionelle Öffnung*. Bern <www.edi.admin.ch/dam/edi/de/dokumente/FRB/Neue%20Website%20 FRB/T%C3%A4tigkeitsfelder/%C3%96ffnung_Institutionen/roadmap.pdf.download. pdf/Roadmap_%C3%96ffnung%20der%20Institutionen_d_Web.pdf> [22.01.2024].

GESSER, Susanna/HANDSCHIN, Martin/JANELLI, Angela/LICHTENSTEIGER, Sibylle (Hgg.) (2012): *Das partizipative Museum. Zwischen Teilhabe und User Generated Content. Neue Anforderungen an kulturhistorische Ausstellungen*. Bielefeld: transcript.

GROSCHWITZ, Helmut (2022): Kulturerbe vermitteln. Strategien, Loyalitäten und Ambivalenzen in Beratung und Forschung. – In: Drascek, Daniel/Ders./Wolf, Gabriele (Hgg.), *Bayerische Schriften zur Volkskunde, 12: Kulturerbe als kulturelle Praxis – Kulturerbe in der Beratungspraxis*. München, 25–48.

INSTITUT NEUE SCHWEIZ INES (Hg.) (2021): *Handbuch Neue Schweiz*. Zürich: Diaphanes.

JAIN, Rohit (2019): Die kulturelle Arbeit an einem neuen Wir. Teilhabe und Ausschluss in der postmigrantischen Schweiz. – In: Nationaler Kulturdialog (Hg.), *Kulturelle Teilhabe. Ein Handbuch*. Zürich, Genf: Seismo, 94–103 <www.seismoverlag.ch/de/daten/ kulturelle-teilhabe-participation-culturelle-partecipazione-culturale/> [22.01.2024].

KELLER, Barbara/KOSLOWSKI, Stefan/MEYER, Cornelia/SCHENK, Ulrich (2015): Editorial. – In: Bundesamt für Kultur/Verband der Museen Schweiz/Museum für Kommunikation/Alpines Museum der Schweiz (Hgg.), *Lebendige Traditionen ausstellen*. Baden: Hier und Jetzt, 16–20.

KOSLOWSKI, Stefan (2015a): Warum und wozu ‚Lebendige Traditionen' ausstellen und vermitteln. Zur Umsetzung des UNESCO-Übereinkommens zur Bewahrung des immateriellen Kulturerbes. – In: Bundesamt für Kultur/Verband der Museen Schweiz/Museum für Kommunikation/Alpines Museum der Schweiz (Hgg.), *Lebendige Traditionen ausstellen*. Baden: Hier und Jetzt, 34–45.

KOSLOWSKI, Stefan (2015b): Kulturpolitik betritt Neuland. – In: Heimberg, Liliana/ Schmidt, Yvonne/Siegfried, Kathrin (Hgg.), *Freilichttheater – eine Tradition auf neuen Wegen*. Baden: Hier und Jetzt, 217–233.

KOSLOWSKI, Stefan (2019): Einleitung. - In: Nationaler Kulturdialog (Hg.), *Kulturelle Teilhabe. Ein Handbuch*. Zürich, Genf: Seismo, 13–30. <www.seismoverlag.ch/de/daten/ kulturelle-teilhabe-participation-culturelle-partecipazione-culturale/> [22.01.2024].

KOSLOWSKI, Stefan (2022a): Teilen, Teil nehmen, Teil geben, Teil haben, Teil werden, Teil sein. – In: Nationale Informationsstelle zum Kulturerbe NIKE (Hg.), *Participatio*. Basel, Berlin: Schwabe, 6f. <www.schwabeonline.ch/schwabe-xaveropp/elibrary/media. xav/9783796547379.pdf?SID=&iid=40403&sinst=F8294FF6&ssinst=&_csrf=051C-7BAC0868EA0BD511FB000D5571D8CD83FB66> [22.01.2024].

KOSLOWSKI, Stefan (2022b): Immaterielles Kulturerbe und Teilhabe. – In: Drascek, Daniel/Groschwitz, Helmut/Wolf, Gabriele (Hgg.), *Kulturerbe als kulturelle Praxis – Kulturerbe in der Beratungspraxis*. München. Bayerische Schriften zur Volkskunde 12, 233–244.

KULTURVERMITTLUNG SCHWEIZ (2015a): *Stärkung kultureller Teilhabe in der Schweiz. Ein Bericht im Auftrag der Arbeitsgruppe Kulturelle Teilhabe des Nationalen Kulturdialogs*. Bern <www.bak.admin.ch/bak/de/home/sprachen-und-gesellschaft/ kulturelle-teilhabe/grundlagen.html> [22.01.2024].

KULTURVERMITTLUNG SCHWEIZ KVS (2015b): *Stärkung kultureller Teilhabe in der Schweiz. Anhang zum Bericht vom 18. November 2015* <www.bak.admin.ch/dam/bak/de/dokumente/kulturelle_teilhabe/berichte/anhang_zum_berichtstaerkungkulturellerteilhabeinderschweiz.pdf.download.pdf/anhang_zum_berichtstaerkungkulturellerteilhabeinderschweiz.pdf> [22.01.2024].

MEKACHER, Nina (2019a): Denkmalpflege braucht Menschen. Wege zu einer partizipativen Denkmalpflege. – In: Nationaler Kulturdialog (Hg.), *Kulturelle Teilhabe. Ein Handbuch*. Zürich, Genf: Seismo, 156–163.

MEKACHER, Nina (2019b): Kulturerbe für alle! Perspektiven für eine zukunftsfähige Denkmalpflege. – In: Nationale Informationsstelle zum Kulturerbe NIKE/Bundesamt für Kultur BAK/ICOMOS Suisse (Hgg.), *Kulturerbe. Ein gemeinsames Gut. Für wen und warum?* Basel, Berlin: Schwabe.

MICOSSÉ-AIKINS, Sandrine (2023): Diversität und Antidiskriminierung im Kulturbetrieb. Eine Zwischenbilanz. – In: Kulturpolitische Gesellschaft /Landschaftsverband Westfalen-Lippe (Hgg.), *Diversität*. Bonn, Münster, 12–17 <file://adb.intra.admin.ch/Userhome$/BAK-01/U80754336/config/Desktop/Brosch%C3%BCre%20Diversit%C3%A4t%20IfTeilhabeforschung.pdf> [22.01.2024].

NATIONALE INFORMATIONSSTELLE ZUM KULTURERBE NIKE (Hg.) (2021): *Teilhabe am Kulturerbe. Ein Leitfaden*. Bern <www.nike-kulturerbe.ch/de/publikationen/teilhabe-am-kulturerbe/ [22.01.2024].

NATIONALE INFORMATIONSSTELLE ZUM KULTURERBE NIKE (Hg.) (2022): *Participatio*. Basel, Berlin: Schwabe <www.schwabeonline.ch/schwabe-xaveropp/elibrary/media.xav/9783796547379.pdf?SID=&iid=10403&sinst=F8294FF6&ssinst=&_cs-rf=051C7BAC0868EA0BD511FB000D5571D8CD83FB66> [22.01.2024].

NATIONALER KULTURDIALOG (Hg.) (2019): *Kulturelle Teilhabe. Ein Handbuch*. Zürich, Genf: Seismo <www.seismoverlag.ch/de/daten/kulturelle-teilhabe-participation-culturelle-partecipazione-culturale/> [22.01.2024].

NATIONALER KULTURDIALOG (Hg.) (2021): *Förderung Kultureller Teilhabe. Ein Leitfaden für Förderstellen*. Bern <www.bak.admin.ch/dam/bak/de/dokumente/kulturelle_teilhabe/publikationen/leitfaden-foerderung-kulturelle-teilhabe.pdf.download.pdf/Leitfaden%20F%C3%B6rderung%20kultureller%20Teilhabe.pdf> [22.01.2024].

PERTSCH, Sebastian (Hg.) (2023): *Vielfalt. Das andere Wörterbuch*. Mannheim: Duden.

PIECECK, Monika (2023): Was ist Ableismus? <https://agile.ch/artikel/was-ist-ableismus/> [22.1.2024].

REGIONALMUSEUM CHÜECHLIHUS (2023): ~~Deakzession~~ Entsammeln. *10 Gründe dafür – und einer dagegen. Erkenntnisse und Einblicke aus dem partizipativen Entsammlungsprojekt*. Langnau i. E. <https://entsammeln.ch/wp-content/uploads/2024/01/Entsammeln-10-gute-Gruende-dafuer_-RMC-2023-D.pdf> [22.1.2024].

RIEDER, Kathrin (2019): Was die Gemeinschaft zusammenhält. Teilhabe als Merkmal des immateriellen Kulturerbes. – In: Nationaler Kulturdialog (Hg.), *Kulturelle Teilhabe. Ein Handbuch*. Zürich, Genf: Seismo, 142–154 <www.seismoverlag.ch/de/daten/kulturelle-teilhabe-participation-culturelle-partecipazione-culturale/> [22.01.2024].

ROSA, Hartmut (2016): *Resonanz. Eine Soziologie der Weltbeziehung*. Berlin: Suhrkamp.

STIFTUNG FÜR KULTURELLE WEITERBILDUNG UND KULTURBERATUNG (Hg.) (2023): *Kunst kommt von Können?! Klassismus im Kulturbetrieb*. Berlin <https://diversity-arts-culture.berlin/sites/default/files/2023-08/kunstkoennengesamt-web.pdf> [22.1.2024].

THIEL, Sonja (2019): Das partizipative Museum. – In: Nationaler Kulturdialog (Hg.), *Kulturelle Teilhabe. Ein Handbuch*. Zürich, Genf: Seismo, 164–172 <www.seismoverlag. ch/de/daten/kulturelle-teilhabe-participation-culturelle-partecipazione-culturale/> [22.01.2024].

VERBAND DER MUSEEN DER SCHWEIZ (HG.) (2023): *Museen und immaterielles Kulturerbe. Im Dialog mit Traditionsträgern*. Zürich <www.museums.ch/admin/data/ files/media/file/509/vms_immaterielles_kulturerbe_de_web.pdf?lm=1703162866> [22.1.2024].

VERTOVEC, Steven (2023): *Superdiversity. Migration and Social Complexity*. London, New York: Routledge.

ZENTRUM GENDER STUDIES DER UNIVERSITÄT BASEL (Hg.) (2021): Geschlechterverhältnisse im Schweizer Kulturbetrieb. Eine qualitative und quantitative Analyse mit Fokus auf Kulturschaffende, Kulturbetriebe und Verbände. Ergebnisse der Vorstudie. Basel   <https://genderstudies.philhist.unibas.ch/de/forschung/aktuelle-forschungs-projekte/geschlechterverhaeltnisse-im-schweizer-kulturbetrieb/> [22.01.2024].

Potentiale für die Weiterentwicklung des Lebensstilansatzes für die Kulturpraxis

Potential for the Further Development of the Lifestyle Approach for Cultural Practice

OLIVER TEWES-SCHÜNZEL[*]

Institut für Kulturelle Teilhabeforschung

Abstracts

Die Entwicklung erfolgreicher Maßnahmen im Bereich Kultureller Teilhabe erfordert ein detailliertes Verständnis der (Nicht-)Besuchern von Kultureinrichtungen. Besonders geeignet dafür ist die Erhebung von Lebensstilen und sozialen Milieus. Gunnar Ottes Lebensführungstypologie ermöglicht ihre kostengünstige Erhebung mithilfe eines Kurzfragebogens. Hinsichtlich der Lebensstilbeschreibungen und der Trennschärfe der Typologie weist sie jedoch noch Verbesserungspotentiale auf. Durch die Wahl einer anderen Berechnungsmethode, der sog. Latenten Klassenanalyse, kann die Typologie inhaltlich aufgefrischt und weiterentwickelt werden. Auf der Grundlage des Fragebogeninstrument Ottes wurde mit repräsentativen Daten für Berlin ein neues Modell berechnet, das als „Kulturmilieumodell" bezeichnet werden soll. Abschließend werden neun aktualisierte Milieubeschreibungen vorgestellt sowie Desiderata diskutiert.

The development of successful measures in the area of cultural participation requires a detailed understanding of the (non-)visitors to cultural institutions. The survey of lifestyles and social milieus is particularly suitable for this purpose. Gunnar Otte's lifestyle typology makes it possible to conduct a cost-effective survey using a short questionnaire. However, there is still room for improvement with regard to the lifestyle descriptions and the selectivity of the typology. By choosing a different calculation method, the so-called latent class analysis, the content of the typology can be refreshed and further developed. On the basis of Otte's questionnaire instrument, a new model was calculated using representative data for Berlin, which will be referred to as the "cultural milieu model". Finally, nine updated milieu descriptions are presented and desiderata are discussed.

Keywords

Besucherforschung/Visitor research, Diversität/diversity, Kultursoziologie/cultural sociology, Methodenentwicklung/method development

[*] O.Tewes-Schuenzel@iktf.berlin

Journal of Cultural Management and Policy, 2024/2, pp. 57–87

doi 10.14361/zkmm-2024-0204

Für die Entwicklung erfolgreicher Maßnahmen im Bereich Kultureller Teilhabe ist ein möglichst gutes Verständnis davon, wer zu den typischen Besuchern bzw. Besucherinnen einer Kultureinrichtungen zählt – und wer nicht –, eine zentrale Voraussetzung.[1]

Es ist aus diesem Grund sehr erfreulich, dass in jüngster Zeit Bevölkerungs- und Besucherbefragungen auf verstärktes Interesse stoßen (LIZ MOHN CENTER 2023; BRÜGGEMANN 2023). In der Praxis des Kulturmanagements geht es dann darum, Konsequenzen aus diesem Wissen für Marketing, Programmplanung und Vermittlungsarbeit von Kultureinrichtungen zu ziehen. Häufig werden bislang sowohl bei Publikumsbefragungen als auch bei (Nicht-)Besucherstudien vor allem soziodemografische Merkmale, wie Alter oder formale Bildung, erhoben, um unterschiedliche (Ziel-)Gruppen zu differenzieren. Sie können schnell und kostengünstig erhoben werden, stellen jedoch in der Praxis oftmals zu grobe Kategorien dar, um eine präzise Zielgruppenansprache entwickeln zu können (RENZ/ TEWES-SCHÜNZEL 2022). Erfolgversprechender ist es daher auf Segmentierungsinstrumente zu setzen, die ein detaillierteres Bild über den spezifischen Geschmack und die Bedürfnisse unterschiedlicher (Nicht-) Besuchergruppen zeichnen können. In Hinblick auf Kulturbesuche zeigten dabei insbesondere die Arbeiten von Kirchberg (2005), aber auch Allmanritter und Kollegen (2020), dass Lebensstilinstrumente sich als deutlich erklärungskräftiger erwiesen haben als soziodemografische oder sozioökonomische Faktoren. Ein solches Instrument ist die soziologische Lebensführungstypologie von Gunnar Otte, die 2004 publiziert wurde (OTTE 2004; 2005) und in aktualisierter Form (OTTE 2019) seit 2019 bei der „Kulturelle Teilhabe in Berlin"-Studienreihe und den Publikumsbefragungen des Berliner Kulturmonitoring (KulMon®) zum Einsatz kommt (ALLMANRITTER et al. 2020; ALLMANRITTER/TEWES-SCHÜNZEL 2022; TEWES-SCHÜNZEL/ALLMANRITTER/RENZ 2024). Statt Personen über äußere Merkmale wie Alter oder formale Bildung zu gruppieren, gruppiert dieses Erhebungsinstrument aus dem Bereich der soziologischen Ungleichheitsforschung auf der Grundlage von Merkmalen, die das Freizeitverhalten, Werte, aber auch (materielle) Konsumpräferenzen und nicht zuletzt das kulturelle Vorwissen und Interesse (kulturelles Kapital) beinhalten. Anders als andere Segmentierungsinstrumente, die sich auf den Kulturbereich fokussieren und unterschiedliche Kulturbesuchertypen differenzieren, zielt die Lebensführungstypologie darauf ab, gesellschaftliche Strukturen

1   Mein ausdrücklicher Dank gilt Werner Georg (†), Peter Schmidt, Steffen Lepa, Vera Allmanritter und den Gutachter/innen für ihre äußerst anregenden und hilfreichen Anmerkungen und methodischen Hinweise.

abzubilden und unterschiedliche Alltagskulturen möglichst zielgenau zu erfassen. Sie ist damit nicht auf den Kulturbereich beschränkt, sondern hat den Anspruch, bereichsübergreifend soziales Verhalten erklären zu können. Dies hat den Vorteil, ein deutlich facettenreicheres Verständnis der Mentalitäten, Bedürfnisse und Geschmäcker unterschiedlicher Zielgruppen zu fördern, die nicht unbedingt zu den regelmäßigen Besuchern uns Besucherinnen von (klassischen) Kulturangeboten zählen. Um dieses Versprechen für die Kulturpraktiker/innen einzulösen, bedarf es jedoch zunächst möglichst aktueller, dichter und eingängiger Typ-Beschreibungen, die die Entwicklung einer geeigneten Publikumsansprache, etwa durch Personas, auch für empirisch interessierte Laien anleiten können. Solche ausformulierten Beschreibungen wurden von Otte letztmals 2004 vorgelegt und wurden auch bei der Überarbeitung des Fragebogeninstruments nicht mehr aktualisiert (OTTE 2019).

Dieser Text verfolgt vor allem drei Ziele: Erstens soll der interessierten Leser ein kurzer Einblick in (ausgewählte) grundlegende Ideen der Lebensstil- und Milieusoziologie gegeben werden. Zweitens soll eine Weiterentwicklung von Ottes Lebensführungstypologie vorgeschlagen werden, die im Folgenden als „Kulturmilieumodell" bezeichnet wird. Die Weiterentwicklung bezieht sich dabei insbesondere auf eine neue Berechnungsmethode, die klarer abgegrenzte Typen („soziale Milieus") generiert, und einen stärkeren theoretischen Rückbezug auf die Werke von Pierre Bourdieu und Gerhard Schulze. Drittens sollen auf Grundlage der neuen Berechnungen und repräsentativer Umfragedaten der Berliner Bevölkerung neun ausformulierte Beschreibungen der Kulturmilieus vorgestellt werden.

1. Theoretische Grundlagen von sozialen Milieus und Lebensstilen

Die soziale Milieu- und Lebensstilforschung entstand an der Schnittstelle von sozialer Ungleichheitsforschung und Kultursoziologie und erfährt in letzter Zeit wieder vermehrt Aufmerksamkeit (GROH-SAMBERG/ SCHRÖDER/SPEER 2023; TEWES-SCHÜNZEL 2023; ALLMANRITTER/TEWES-SCHÜNZEL 2022; ALLMANRITTER 2017). Sie gewann insbesondere seit den frühen 1980er Jahren in Deutschland an Bedeutung (RÖSSEL/OTTE 2012b). Streng genommen handelt es sich nicht um einen einheitlichen Ansatz, vielmehr werden unter diesem Begriff methodisch, theoretisch und nicht zuletzt gesellschaftsdiagnostisch eine Vielzahl konkurrierender Ansätze zusammengefasst, die an dieser Stelle aus Platzgründen nicht dargestellt werden können. Sich gut ergänzende Überblicke über die enorme Pluralität des Feldes liefern der Überblickstext von Burzan (2011: 89–124), die Sammelbände von Rössel und Otte (2012a) sowie Isenböck, Nell und Renn (2014).

Im Folgenden sollen jedoch einige zentrale Ideen des Lebensstil- und Milieuansatzes vorgestellt werden, die von Otte, aber insbesondere auch von zwei zentralen Autoren des Ansatzes, Pierre Bourdieu und Gerhard Schulze, geteilt werden. Die Werke von Bourdieu (1982) und Schulze (1992) stellen dabei zentrale Bezugspunkte für Ottes Lebensführungstypologie dar. Ottes theoretische Herleitung seiner Typologie kann mit einigem Recht als eine handlungstheoretische (im Sinne von Rational Choice) Synthese von Elementen aus Bourdieus praxeologisch-strukturalistischer Klassensoziologie und Schulzes wissenssoziologischer Milieusoziologie gedeutet werden. Seine Typologie kann daher über den Bezug auf die einschlägigeren Theorien von Bourdieu und Schulze erschlossen werden. Auf eine Darstellung der handlungstheoretischen Besonderheiten von Ottes Ansatz wird hier aus Platzgründen verzichtet. Für einen ausführlicheren Vergleich von Bourdieus und Schulzes Theorien verweise ich auf Tewes-Schünzel (2023: 20–46).

Eine Begriffsklärung vorab: Für Schulze verknüpft der Lebensstil konzeptuell die pragmatische Ebene der Handlungen und Zeichen (bspw. *Kleidung, Aussprache, Haltung, Gang, Umgangsformen*) mit ihrer Bedeutungsebene. Diese werden in Stilen übersituativ (also relativ dauerhaft) miteinander verknüpft. Lebensstile werden demnach als Ausdruck einer gewissen Lebensphilosophie aufgefasst, aber auch als Ausdruck der sozialen Stellung. Eine Lederjacke ist demnach nicht nur eine Lederjacke, sondern auch der Ausdruck von Individualismus etc. (SCHULZE 1992: 96, TEWES-SCHÜNZEL 2023: 37). Otte verwendet demgegenüber den Begriff der Lebensführung, da er Lebensstil nur als manifestes und beobachtbares Verhalten versteht. In seine Typologie fließen jedoch ebenfalls Einstellungen und Orientierungen ein, die er nicht zum Lebensstil im engen Sinne zählt. Deshalb präferiert er stattdessen den Begriff der Lebensführung (OTTE 2004: 90). Im Sinne Schulzes sind Orientierungen und Einstellungen jedoch Teil der Bedeutungsebene von Lebensstilen, weshalb im Folgenden der Begriff des Lebensstils verwendet wird.

Die Grundidee des Lebensstil- und Milieuansatzes lassen sich darüber hinaus in einigen Worten skizzieren: Menschen bewerten sich gegenseitig in ihrem Alltag, ob sie wollen oder nicht.

„Der soziale Instinkt spürt seine Anhaltspunkte in dem System von Zeichen auf, die
[...] jeder Körper an sich hat: Kleidung, Aussprache, Haltung, Gang, Umgangsformen.
Unbewußt registriert, begründen sie „Antipathien" und „Sympathien" [...]. Der Geschmack paart die Dinge und Menschen, die zueinander passen, die aufeinander abgestimmt sind, und macht sie einander verwandt." (BOURDIEU 1982: 374)

Auch wenn sie nicht immer und in allen Belangen identisch sein mögen, gleichen sich Freund, aber auch Partner, daher zumeist in lebens-
stilistischen Belangen. Denn einerseits suchen sich Menschen meistens
Freunde und Freundinnen aus, die ihnen bereits ähnlich sind (BOUR-
DIEU 1982: 114, 377), andererseits beeinflussen sie ihren Lebensstil gegenseitig und ähneln sich im Laufe der Zeit häufig an: Man verhält sich
in der Regel so, dass man von seinen eigenen Freunde und Freundinnen
dafür Wertschätzung erfährt (OTTE 2004: 100). Welcher Kommentar
oder welche Kleidung in einer Situation als „unmöglich", „unbedarft",
„angemessen", „normal" oder aber „schick" bewertet wird, hängt dabei
entscheidend vom sozialen Umfeld ab (BOURDIEU 1982: 114; OTTE
2004: 106ff.). Lebensstile sind also keine individuelle Angelegenheit,
sondern sozial vermittelt. Da sich Personen mit ähnlichen Lebensstilen
häufig ein ähnliches Umfeld (franz. „Milieu") teilen, werden in der Soziologie gesellschaftliche Gruppen mit ähnlichen Lebensstilen als soziale
Milieus bezeichnet (SCHULZE 1992; VESTER et al. 2001). Tatsächlich
wird der Begriff des „sozialen Milieus" von einem der zentralen Bezugspunkte des Ansatzes, dem Werk von Pierre Bourdieu, kaum verwendet.
Bourdieu spricht stattdessen konsequent von „sozialen Klassen". In der
deutschsprachigen Rezeption Bourdieus wurde der Begriff der sozialen
Klasse oftmals durch den Begriff des sozialen (Klassen-)Milieus (VES-
TER ET AL. 2001) oder Bildungsmilieus ersetzt (GRUNDMANN et al.
2003). Der Milieuansatz verdeutlicht dabei, dass die Gesellschaft keinen
uniformen Block darstellt, sondern aus unterschiedlichen Alltagskulturen besteht.

Lebensstil- oder Milieumodelle visualisieren die Gesellschaft analog
einer sozialen Landkarte, in der die unterschiedlichen sozialen Milieus
bzw. Lebensstile entlang zweier Dimensionen angeordnet sind. Im Werk
Bourdieus ist diese soziale Landkarte, die er als sozialen Raum bezeichnet, entlang unterschiedlicher Ressourcen, sog. Kapitalformen, struktu-
riert. Die vertikale Dimension beschreibt dabei das Gesamtvolumen von
ökonomischem und kulturellem Kapital. Das ökonomische Kapital beschreibt für Bourdieu vor allem Eigentum und Vermögen. Das kulturelle
Kapital wird von Bourdieu in inkorporiertes kulturelles Kapital (Wissen,
Geschmack), objektiviertes kulturelles Kapital (z.B. Bücher, Musikin-
strumente) und institutionalisiertes kulturelles Kapital (z.B. formale

Bildungsabschlüsse) differenziert (BOURDIEU 1983). Unterschieden werden hier die oberen Klassen, mittleren Klassen und die Volksklassen. Zusätzlich verfügt das Modell jedoch auch über eine horizontale Dimension, die das relative Verhältnis von ökonomischem und kulturellem Kapital zum Ausdruck bringt und unterschiedliche Klassenfraktionen voneinander abhebt. Innerhalb der oberen Klassen erlaubt das Modell somit eine Differenzierung zwischen Besitz- und Bildungsbürgertum, die jeweils über einen relativen „Überschuss" an ökonomischen bzw. kulturellem Kapital verfügen. Die Mittelklassen werden von Bourdieu analog in absteigende, exekutive und neue Mittelklasse(nfraktion) differenziert. Eine Differenzierung der Unterklasse wurde von Bourdieu nicht weiter vorgenommen (BURZAN 2011: 125-138; BOURDIEU 1982).

Diese dimensionale Grobstruktur des sozialen Raumes konnte wiederholt für viele europäische Länder repliziert werden (ATKINSON 2020).

Der bourdieusche Ansatz betont gegenüber anderen Lebensstil- und Milieuansätzen insbesondere den gesellschaftlichen Machtaspekt in Bezug auf Kulturkonsum und Lebensstile. Nicht nur gelingt es statushöheren Klassen zu definieren, was als legitim und (u.a. künstlerisch) wertvoll zu gelten hat, auch gelingt es ihnen sich über ihren distinktiven Lebensstil gegenüber niedrigeren Klassen abzugrenzen und damit den eigenen, höheren Status abzusichern. Die französischen Oberklassen der 1960er und 1970er Jahre zeichnen sich in Bourdieus Analysen dabei durch einen selbstsicheren Umgang mit Kulturgütern aus (sei es Esskultur oder höherer Kultur), den sie in ihren privilegierten Herkunftsfamilien wie selbstverständlich erlernt haben (BOURDIEU 1982: 405ff.), während der Lebensstil mittlerer Klassen von verkrampfter Prätention und Bildungsbeflissenheit geprägt ist (BOURDIEU 1982: 500ff.). Den unteren Volksklassen attestiert Bourdieu demgegenüber einen einfachen „Geschmack der Notwendigkeit" (BOURDIEU 1982: 585ff.).

Der konsequent ungleichheitstheoretische Ansatz von Bourdieu zählt zu den am häufigsten rezipierten Ansätzen der gewärtigen (Kultur-) Soziologie. Er ist jedoch nicht unwidersprochen geblieben. Bourdieu wurde insbesondere von Vertretern der Individualisierungstheorie kritisiert. Entgegen der von Bourdieu vertretenen engen Verknüpfung (sog. „Homologie") von sozialer Klasse und Lebensstil (bzw. Kulturkonsum) argumentieren die Vertreter/innen dieses Ansatzes, dass auf der Grundlage historischer Wohlstandsgewinne in spätmodernen Staaten die Prägekraft traditioneller Sozialstrukturen wie Familie oder sozialer Klasse an Bedeutung verloren hätte. Das spätmoderne Subjekt müsse demnach selbst als reflexiver Gestalter seiner Biografie in Erscheinung treten, was auch als krisenhaft erlebte, zu bewältigende Aufgabe gedeutet wird. Neben der Soziologie Bourdieus findet die Lebensstil- und Milieusoziologie hier ihren zweiten theoretischen Bezugspunkt. Lebensstile werden in diesem Ansatz nicht mehr als Stabilisatoren sozialer Ungleichheit wie bei Bourdieu gedeutet, vielmehr bilden sie entlastende Orientierungspunkte, derer sich das spätmoderne Subjekt stilistisch bewusst bedienen kann (BECK 1983; 1986, 206).

An diesem Kritikpunkt setzt Gerhard Schulze mit seinem Werk *Die Erlebnisgesellschaft* (1992) an, das sich als prägender Bezugspunkt für die Milieusoziologie erwiesen hat. Aus seinem Werk sollen insbesondere drei Aspekte in Abgrenzung zu Bourdieu hervorgehoben werden (ausführlicher Vergleich bei Tewes-Schünzel 2023): Dies betrifft (1) die stärkere Ausrichtung des Ansatzes auf die unterschiedlichen kulturellen (Lebens-)Stile („alltagsästhetische Schemata"). Anders als Bourdieu, der sich vorranging auf den Bereich der Hochkultur fokussierte, beleuchtet Schulze ebenfalls die Bereiche der Popkultur („Spannungsschema") und der Volkskultur („Trivialschema"). Seine wissenssoziologischen Lebensstilanalysen jenseits formal höhergebildeter Milieus fallen gegenüber Bourdieu daher deutlich detailreicher aus. Dies führt (2) zu einer konzeptuellen Abschwächung des klassenspezifischen Ungleichheitsmoments: Bildung spielt als einzig betrachtete „Kapitalsorte" anders als für Bourdieu nur als Erkennungszeichen unterschiedlicher Milieus und als Ort des Erlernens des Genusses komplexer Kulturgüter eine Rolle. Die materielle Ungleichheit selbst und dessen symbolische Reproduktion sind für Schulze jedoch nicht (mehr) der zentrale Gegenstand der Analyse, sondern vielmehr soziale Beziehungswahlen im Kontext der individualisierten Spätmoderne (SCHULZE 1992: 396ff.). Mit der Öffnung der Frage, welche gesellschaftlichen Kategorien von besonderer Tragweite für Beziehungswahlen sind, tritt (3) zusätzlich zu den Lebensstilen und der formalen Bildung (die bereits bei Bourdieu zentral waren) nun die Kategorie des Alters stärker in den Vordergrund. Sie markiert den Unterschied zwischen jüngeren Generationen, für die die actionbetonte Popkultur (Spannungsschema) mitsamt „narzisstischer" Lebensphilosophie (SCHULZE 1992: 156) an die Stelle der traditionellen Volkskultur (Harmonieschema) mit ihrer Lebensphilosophie der „Gemütlichkeit" getreten ist, die von älteren Generationen vertreten wird (SCHULZE 1992: 153). Schulze ging zum Zeitpunkt der Veröffentlichung der Erlebnisgesellschaft davon aus, dass die altersspezifische Milieugrenze bei etwa 40 Jahren liegt (SCHULZE 1992: 366 ff.). Diese Altersgrenze ist für Schulze dabei sowohl das Resultat von generationsspezifischen Sozialisationseffekten als auch genuiner Alterseffekte. Während Bildung bei Schulze die vertikale Differenzierungsachse beschreibt, wird die horizontale Achse nun durch das Merkmal Alter geprägt, dass an die Stelle des relativen Verhältnisses von ökonomischem und kulturellem Kapital bei Bourdieu tritt. Die sozialen Milieus von Schulze stellen dabei spezifische Kombinationen von Alter, Bildung und Lebensstilen dar.

	Alter: unter 40 Jahre	Alter über 40 Jahre
Formale Bildung: hoch	Selbstverwirklichungsmilieu: Hochkulturschema + Spannungsschema	Niveaumilieu: Hochkulturschema
Formale Bildung: mittel		Integrationsmilieu: Hochkulturschema + Trivialschema
	Unterhaltungsmilieu: Spannungsschema	
Formale Bildung: niedrig		Harmoniemilieu: Trivialschema

Tabelle 1: Erlebnismilieus nach Gerhard Schulze (1992) nach Bildung, Alter und alltagsästhetischen Schemata (Lebensstil)

In der Auseinandersetzung mit der Individualisierungstheorie und der bourdieuschen Klassentheorie wurden in den 1980er und 1990er Jahren im deutschsprachigen Raum weitere Lebensstilanalysen durchgeführt (BLASIUS/WINKLER 1989; VESTER ET AL. 2001; MÜLLER-SCHNEIDER 1994; SPELLERBERG 1996; GEORG 1998; HARTMANN 1999; OTTE 2004). Dabei lag der zentrale Streitpunkt darin, ob die Klassen- oder Schichtzugehörigkeit den Lebensstil determiniert oder ob der gestiegene Lebensstandard in der Spätmoderne zu einer Individualisierung und Entkoppelung von der Klassenlage geführt hat. Die Metaanalyse von Otte (2005) zeigte für den deutschen Raum, dass sich die Alters- und Bildungsdimensionen, wie von Schulze postuliert, weitgehend bewährt haben. Die Hypothese der Auflösung der vertikalen Ungleichheit im Bereich der Lebensstile wird demnach von den meisten Autor/innen zurückgewiesen. Das Gros der Lebensstil- und Milieutypologien enthält weiterhin eine vertikale Dimension (z.B. Bildung, Ausstattungsniveau, Klasse) und eine horizontale Dimension (biografische Perspektive oder Modernitätsdimension). Letztere korreliert stark mit dem Alter (OTTE 2005: 73ff.). Dies widerspricht dem bourdieuschen Klassenmodell nicht unbedingt, wie etwa Vester und Kolleg/innen argumentieren. Demnach korrespondiert ein „kulturkapitallastiger" Habitus mit modernen, individualisierten Einstellungen, die vor allem in jüngeren Milieus vorkommen. Dieser Zusammenhang von Alter, kulturellem Kapital und Modernität sei der Bildungsexpansion und dem Wandel zur Dienstleistungsgesellschaft geschuldet, durch die jüngere, individualisierte Jahrgänge höhere Bildungsabschlüsse erreichen (VESTER et al. 2001: 79).

2. Lebensstile empirisch messen: Die Lebensführungstypologie von Gunnar Otte

Quantitative Milieu- und Lebensstilanalysen sind häufig ressourcenintensiv, da sie zumeist über eine große Anzahl erhobener Merkmale gebildet werden müssen (Otte 2005: 443). Dies stellt eine Hürde insbesondere für den praktischen Einsatz bei Besucherbefragung dar, bei denen oftmals nur wenige Fragen gestellt werden können. Eine praktikable Möglichkeit das Milieu bzw. den Lebensstil einer Person empirisch zu bestimmen, liegt aber im Kurzinstrument der Lebensführungstypologie von Gunnar Otte. Sie wurde in ihrer ursprünglichen Fassung 2004 veröffentlicht und der zugrundeliegende Fragebogen 2019 aktualisiert (OTTE 2004; 2019). Sie weist einige Vorteile auf, die sie besonders für Besucherbefragungen geeignet erscheinen lässt. Diese liegen zunächst in dem vergleichsweise überschaubaren Erhebungsaufwand und der Möglichkeit der unabhängigen Berechnung für Einzelpersonen. Beides ist Voraussetzung für den Einsatz des Instrumentes in Besucherbefragungen mit kleinen Stichproben und kurzen Befragungsdauern. Darüber hinaus hat sie gegenüber kommerziellen, proprietären Segmentierungsinstrumenten die Vorteile, frei von Lizenzgebühren einsetzbar und vollständig inhaltlich transparent zu sein.

Ottes Lebensführungstypologie basiert auf der Metaanalyse von über 30 Milieu- und Lebensstiluntersuchungen, die für die deutsche Gesellschaft bis 2004 publiziert wurden. Es handelt sich um ein Fragebogenkurzinstrument, mit dem Lebensstile anhand von 10 Fragen (2004) bzw. 12 Fragen (2019) erfasst werden können. Vorherige Lebensstiluntersuchungen waren demgegenüber auf sehr ausführliche Frageinstrumente mit teils über 100 Fragen angewiesen (OTTE 2005: 443). Im Folgenden wird die aktuelle Version von 2019 genauer vorgestellt (OTTE 2019) (Tabellen 2 und 3).[2]

---

2 Aus Gründen des Umfangs und der Leserlichkeit wird der teils abweichende (fachsprachliche) Begriffsapparat Ottes hier nicht vollständig übernommen.

		← Modernitätsgrad →		
		Traditional/ biografische Schließung	Teilmodern/ biografische Konsolidierung	Modern/biografische Offenheit
↑ Ausstattungsniveau ↓	Gehoben	Konservativ Gehobene	Liberal Gehobene	Innovativ Gehobene
	Mittel	Konventionalisten	Mittelständische	Hedonisten
	Niedrig	Bodenständig Traditionelle	Heimzentrierte	Unterhaltungssuchende

Tabelle 2: Die Lebensführungstypologie in der Version von 2019 (OTTE 2019)

Konservativ Gehobene	„Tradition des Besitzbürgertums, Konservatismus, Distinktion durch „Rang", Exklusivität im Lebensstandard, klassische Hochkultur, Leistungs- und Führungsbereitschaft, Religiosität"
Konventionalisten	„Tradition des Kleinbürgertums, Pflicht- und Akzeptanzwerte, Sicherheitsorientierung, Hochkulturkonsum mit volkstümlichem Einschlag, konservativ-religiöse Moral, häusliche Idylle"
Traditionelle Arbeiter (2004) (Bodenständig Traditionelle (2019))	„Tradition der Facharbeit, Bescheidenheit, Orientierung am Praktischen, Bedeutung sozialer Sicherheit, gewerkschaftliche Nähe, deutsches Liedgut, Vereinsleben"
Liberal Gehobene	„Tradition des Bildungsbürgertums, Liberalität, berufliche Selbstverwirklichung, Hochkulturkonsum mit „alternativem" Einschlag, Sinn für Authentizität, Kennerschaft im Konsum"
Aufstiegsorientierte (2004) (Mittelständische (2019))	„Zentriertheit um solide Berufskarriere, Familie und Partizipation am Mainstream der modernen Freizeitkultur, „Durchschnittlichkeit" und interne Heterogenität des Typus durch Mittelposition"
Heimzentrierte	„Familienzentriertheit und Häuslichkeit durch Kinder und geringe Ressourcenverfügbarkeit, traditionelle Volksfestszene und moderne Massenkultur wie Popmusik und Fernsehen"
Reflexive (2004) (Innovativ Gehobene (2019))	„Kulturelle, akademisch geprägte Avantgarde, Reflexivität, Kreativität und Experimentierfreude, Suche nach eigenverantwortlicher Persönlichkeitsentfaltung, globales Lebensgefühl"
Hedonisten	„Jugendkultureller Stilprotest durch Mode und Musik, Innovationsfreude, gegenwartsbezogene Genuss- und Konsumorientierung, Extraversion, städtische Spektakel- und Clubkultur"
Unterhaltungssuchende	„Erlebniskonsum, materialistische Statussymbolik und außerhäusliche Unterhaltungsorientierung vor dem Hintergrund einer Deklassierungsbedrohung, Depolitisiertheit"

Tabelle 3: Kurzbeschreibungen („hypothetische Handlungslogiken") der Lebensführungstypen (Otte 2004: 454).[3]

3   Die Tabelle wurde sofern zutreffend durch neuen Typenbezeichnungen von 2019 ergänzt. Für die Version von 2019 liegt keine Aktualisierung der Beschreibungen vor.

Im 2019er Erhebungsinstrument von Otte werden einer Person insgesamt 12 Aussagen vorgelegt, die sie auf eine Skala von vier Ausprägungen bewerten kann (trifft voll und ganz zu/trifft eher zu/trifft eher nicht zu/trifft gar nicht zu). Diese Aussagen decken dabei unterschiedliche Teilaspekte des Lebensstils ab, von denen aus der empirischen Sozialforschung bekannt ist, dass sie die zwei Dimensionen (vertikal: Ausstattungsniveau, horizontal: Modernitätsgrad/biografische Perspektive) der deutschen Milieustruktur gut abbilden.

Betrachten wir zunächst die vertikale Ungleichheitsdimension, die einen kulturellen und einen materiellen Aspekt des Lebensstils beinhaltet. Der kulturelle Aspekt entspricht dabei dem inkorporierten kulturellen Kapital bei Bourdieu, bzw. die Nähe oder Distanz zum Hochkulturschema im Sinne Schulzes. Der materielle Aspekt misst demgegenüber Merkmale, die mit der ökonomischen Kapitalausstattung bei Bourdieu assoziiert sind und bei Schulze keine direkte Entsprechung haben.

Der kulturelle Aspekt des Lebensstils wird von den folgenden Items erfasst:

- „In Kunst und Kultur kenne ich mich allgemein sehr gut aus."
- „Ich lese gern anspruchsvolle Bücher."
- „Ich informiere mich umfassend über Politik und Zeitgeschehen."

Der materielle Aspekt wird mit den folgenden drei Statements erfasst:

- „Ich pflege einen gehobenen Lebensstandard."
- „Ich leiste mir manchmal ein richtig teures Menü im Restaurant."
- „Es ist mir zu teuer, regelmäßig große Urlaube im Ausland zu machen."

Diese beiden Teildimensionen werden von Otte zur übergeordneten Dimension des sog. „Ausstattungsniveaus" zusammengefasst. Er unterscheidet dabei zwischen niedrig, mittel und gehoben ausgestatteten Lebensstilen.

Die zweite, horizontale Dimension wird von Otte als „biografische Perspektive" bzw. „Modernitätsgrad" bezeichnet. Die Teildimension der biografischen Perspektive bezeichnet dabei Merkmale die typisch für unterschiedliche Lebensphasen sind. So zeichnen sich jüngere Leute häufiger durch eine Offenheit gegenüber Neuem, aber auch durch eine höhere Unternehmungslust aus, während ältere Personen es (in der Tendenz) etwas ruhiger oder häuslicher mögen, wichtige Lebensentscheidungen (wie die Berufs- oder Partnerwahl) bereits getroffen haben und neuen Stilen gegenüber etwas verhaltener sind (OTTE 2005: 452; SCHULZE 1992: 188). Dass es jüngere „geschlossene" oder ältere „offene" Personen gibt, ist dabei explizit mitgedacht: Einige Personen neigen früh zu einer biografischen Schließung, andere gar nicht. Nicht zuletzt können kritische Lebensereignisse zu einer tendenziellen Öffnung oder Schließung von Lebensstilen beitragen, wie Familiengründungen oder Trennungen (OTTE 2004: 115). Die Teildimension des Modernitätsgrades hebt demgegenüber auf Werteunterschiede zwischen Generationen ab. Kurz gesagt, werden dabei Werte wie die Orientierung an Sicherheit oder Beständigkeit oder auch die Befürwortung familiärer Traditionen einem traditionalen Pol zugeordnet, während Werte wie Selbstverwirklichung dem stärker modernen Pol zugerechnet werden (OTTE 2005: 459; VESTER et al. 2001: 311; KLAGES 1984).

In der überarbeiteten Variante der Lebensführungstypologie wurde die analytische Differenzierung zwischen biografischer Perspektive und Modernitätsgrad von Otte ein Stück weit aufgeweicht und ihr Fokus in Richtung der biografischen Perspektive verschoben. So wurde nur ein Statement ins neue Fragebogeninstrument übernommen, das primär den Modernitätsgrad erfasst („halte an familiären Traditionen fest"), während fünf Items der biografischen Perspektive zuzuordnen sind. Die Zustimmung zu drei Items wird nun dem biografisch offenen und modernen Pol zugerechnet, die Zustimmung zu drei weiteren Items dem biografisch geschlossenen und traditionalen Werteabschnitt der Gesellschaft (OTTE 2019: 7–11):

Biografisch Offen/Modern:

- „Mein Leben gefällt mir dann besonders gut, wenn ständig etwas los ist."
- „Ich suche immer wieder nach neuen Herausforderungen und Erfahrungen."
- „Selbstverwirklichung ist mir in meinem Leben sehr wichtig."

Biografisch Geschossen/Traditional:

- „Es gibt für mich nichts Schöneres, als mich in Haus und Heim zu betätigen."
- „Sicherheit und Beständigkeit sind das oberste Gebot in meinem Leben."
- „Ich halte an Traditionen und Bräuchen meiner Familie fest."

Wie die Berechnung des Lebensstiltypus erfolgt, soll am Beispiel des Ausstattungsniveaus verdeutlicht werden. Dafür wird ein sog. additiver Index auf der Grundlage der Zustimmungswerte (4 = trifft voll und ganz zu, ..., 1 = trifft gar nicht zu) gebildet. Damit die Werte inhaltlich zueinander passen, muss dafür zuerst ein Statement („große Urlaube zu teuer") umgekehrt werden, sodass hohe nummerische Werte immer für ein hohes Ausstattungsniveau stehen. Anschließend werden die Werte miteinander addiert und durch die Anzahl der beantworteten Fragen geteilt. Dieser Durchschnittswert gibt Auskunft über die Dimension des Ausstattungsniveaus. Dasselbe Verfahren wird auf die sechs Statements des Modernitätsgrades/der biografischen Perspektive angewendet. Die Positionierung entlang dieser beiden Dimensionen entscheidet dann, welchem Lebensstil eine Person zugeordnet wird (OTTE 2019: 14).

Das Lebensstilinstrument ist dabei aus zweierlei Sicht auch für die Publikumssegmentierung günstig: Erstens wurden die zugrundliegenden Merkmale so gewählt, dass sie die Gesamtbevölkerung in ihrer Unterschiedlichkeit möglichst gut erfassen. Es handelt sich bei den gebildeten Typen also tatsächlich um allgemeine Lebensstile, die auch Selten- oder Niebesucher/innen in ihrer Vielschichtigkeit beschreiben. Denn der Anspruch dieser Typologie liegt darin begründet, in möglichst *vielen* Lebensbereichen soziokulturelle Differenzen aufdecken zu können, sei es bei unterschiedlichen Formen des Konzertbesuchs, bei der Wahl des Wohnortes oder Urlaubsziels oder auch dem zivilgesellschaftlichen Engagement (OTTE 2004). Bei der Überarbeitung des Fragenkataloges 2019 wurde das Instrument in Hinblick auf die Eignung für Erhebungen im Kulturbereich auf Anregung von Vera Allmanritter optimiert (OTTE 2019: 2). Dies spiegelt sich auch bei der Auswahl der Items wider, die wichtige Informationen für die Besucherforschung erheben: Für die Untersuchung des kulturellen Besuchsverhaltens bieten sie einen Einblick in das (hoch-)kulturelle und diskursive Vorwissen der Besucher/innen. Der zentrale Fortschritt gegenüber der 2004er Version liegt darin begründet, dass nicht mehr die Besuchshäufigkeit von Kunstausstellungen und Galerien zur Erfassung des kulturellen Lebensstils herangezogen wird (OTTE 2005: 456). Bei der Analyse der Besuchshäufigkeit von Kunstausstellungen hätte dies jedoch eine Tautologie zu Folge gehabt: Besuche würden mit Besuchen erklärt werden. Die Version von 2019 umgeht diese Problematik.

Die Items für den materiellen Aspekt wiederum geben Hinweise auf die Zahlungsbereitschaft und die (materielle) Anspruchshaltung, etwa in Bezug auf Gastronomiebesuche. Die biografische Offenheit und der

Modernitätsgrad können als Hinweise auf das bevorzugte außerhäusliche (und körperliche) Aktivitätsniveau sowie die Experimentierfreudigkeit oder eben Traditionalität des Publikums gelesen werden.

Für die Kulturelle Teilhabeforschung, aber auch das Kulturmarketing ist dabei auch von besonderem Interesse, dass idealtypische Kulturpublika mit den unterschiedlichen Dimensionen verknüpft sind. Idealtypisch lassen sich folgende Tendenzen formulieren: Mit steigendem Ausstattungsniveau steigt grundsätzlich das Interesse für klassische Kulturangebote, d.h. etwa für klassische Musik oder den Besuch von Museen. Differenzierter nach Lebensstilen betrachtet, interessieren sich Innovativ Gehobene stärker für experimentelle Angebote, Konservativ Gehobene für klassische Inszenierungen und Ausstellungsarten. Mit steigendem Modernitätsgrad bzw. offenerer biografischer Perspektive werden hingegen jugendkulturelle Kulturangebote wichtiger. (Gangster-)Rap, Techno, Punkrock-Konzerte und Clubs werden am stärksten von den drei modernen Lebensstilen (Innovativ Gehobene, Hedonisten, Unterhaltungssuchende) besucht. Zu guter Letzt kann den traditionalen und weniger gehobenen Lebensstilen (insbesondere den Konventionalisten und den Bodenständig Traditionellen) eine Vorliebe für Schlager, volkstümliche Hitparade und Volksfeste (Schützenfeste etc.) zugeordnet werden (OTTE 2004: 174ff.; ALLMANRITTER et al. 2020: 76–86; ALLMANRITTER/TEWES-SCHÜNZEL 2022: 72–90).

3. Potentiale für die Weiterentwicklung

Die Lebensführungstypologie von Otte bietet darüber hinaus aufgrund ihres wissenschaftlichen Ursprungs – im Gegensatz zu kommerziellen Segmentierungsinstrumenten (DIAZ-BONE 2004) – die Möglichkeit der Weiterentwicklung und Aktualisierung. Eine Reihe von Weiterentwicklungen sind aus Sicht der Kulturellen Teilhabeforschung und des empirischen Kulturmarketing besonders relevant.

Hierzu zählt zunächst eine Aktualisierung der Typologie insgesamt, da die oben dargestellte Zuordnung von unterschiedlichen Kulturpublika und Lebensstilen im Kern etwas veraltet ist. Die dafür wegweisenden Untersuchungen von Gerhard Schulze basieren auf Erhebungen in Nürnberg aus dem Jahre 1985 (SCHULZE 1992: 593), das Modell von Gunnar Otte auf Daten, die zwischen 1999 und 2001 in Mannheim erhoben wurden (OTTE 2004: 143). Analysen des Instituts für Kulturelle Teilhabeforschung (IKTf) aus den Jahren 2019 bis 2023 für Berlin zeigen, dass die Typologie grundsätzlich noch immer Geltung hat, sich jedoch einige Zuordnungen verschoben haben. So mag Rockmusik etwa vor 30 Jahren insgesamt noch als Ausweis von lebensstilistischer Modernität und Jugendkultur ein aussagekräftiges Merkmal für die Milieuzugehörigkeit gewesen sein. Dem ist jedoch nicht mehr so, wie den tabellarischen Lebensstil-Steckbriefen der „Kulturelle Teilhabe in Berlin"-Studien entnommen werden kann. Musik, die unter die übergeordnete Kategorie „Rock" fällt, wird inzwischen milieuübergreifend gehört (ALLMANRITTER et al. 2020: 76-86; ALLMANRITTER/TEWES-SCHÜNZEL 2022: 72−90). Anders als der Fragebogen, wurden die ausformulierten inhaltlichen Lebensstilbeschreibungen 2019 jedoch (noch) nicht überarbeitet, sodass das Modell von einer Aktualisierung deutlich profitieren würde.

Neben ihrer mangelnden Aktualität bergen die Verfügbarkeit, Detailliertheit und Eingängigkeit der Lebensstilbeschreibungen aber auch ohnehin erhebliches Potential für eine Weiterentwicklung der Typologie mit dem Ziel einer praktischen Anwendung im Kulturbereich. Denn bereits die Kurzbeschreibungen von Otte von 2004 waren deutlich weniger ausführlich und pointiert als etwa die Milieubeschreibungen von Gerhard Schulzes Erlebnismilieus (SCHULZE 1992: 277−330). Zudem liegen die Lebensstilbeschreibungen von 2004 hinter der Bezahlschranke eines wissenschaftlichen Verlags. Für die aktualisierte Version von 2019 hat das IKTf auf der Grundlage der repräsentativen „Kulturelle Teilhabe in Berlin"-Studien von 2019 und 2021 bereits tabellarische Steckbriefe veröffentlicht, mit relevanten Informationen für Praktiker/innen im Kulturbereich (ALLMANRITTER/TEWES-SCHÜNZEL 2022: 72−90). Ausformulierte, lebensnahe Beschreibungen lagen bislang jedoch noch nicht vor. Sie würden eine Nutzbarkeit des Instrumentes in (unter anderem) der kulturmanagerialen Praxis deutlich erhöhen. Beispielsweise würde dies die Erstellung von Personas als Basis für die Erarbeitung von Kulturelle Teilhabe Maßnahmen deutlich vereinfachen.

Eine Herausforderung für die praktische Anwendbarkeit von Ottes Typologie besteht zudem in deren sehr fachsprachlichen und wenig eingängigen Begriffsapparat aus der Sozialwissenschaft. So spricht Otte strenggenommen etwa von Lebensführungstypen, anstatt der einschlägigeren Begriffe des Lebensstils oder des sozialen Milieus (siehe oben). Auch etwa Ottes Definition des „Ausstattungsniveaus", welche hochkulturelles Wissen und Interessen gemeinsam mit Aspekten des materiellen Lebensstandards zusammenfasst, weicht vom alltagssprachlichen Verständnis des Wortes ab und kann in der praktischen Vermittlung des Modells zu Missverständnissen führen. Im Sinne einer stärkeren praktischen Anwendbarkeit wäre es daher sinnvoll, bei der Weiterentwicklung einen anderen Begriffsapparat zu wählen, der sowohl wissenschaftlichen Bedürfnissen Rechnung trägt, aber auch von interessierten Praktiker/innen gut nachvollzogen werden kann. Statt von Lebensführungstypen oder Lebensstiltypen zu sprechen, soll bei der Weiterentwicklung dieses Ansatzes von sozialen Milieus als Trägergruppen von Lebensstilen gesprochen werden – so wie es im allgemeinen Sprachgebrauch auch üblich ist. Tatsächlich stellt diese veränderte Wortwahl dabei keinen Kompromiss in Bezug auf die Wissenschaftlichkeit des Instrumentes dar, da sie in der sozialwissenschaftlichen Literatur von vielen Autoren so verwendet wird (SCHULZE 1992; VESTER et al. 2001; BAUR/KULKE 2023). Otte hat zudem in seiner Dissertation den empirischen Nachweis geführt, dass sich die Netzwerke von Personen in Bezug auf den Lebensstil ähneln (OTTE 2004: 225–254). Wichtig ist jedoch hervorzuheben, dass die Grenzen zwischen den Lebensstilen bzw. Milieus solch makrosoziologischer Milieumodelle willkürlich gesetzt und in der Realität fließend sind.

Daneben birgt auch die Berechnungsmethode des Instruments noch Potential für die Weiterentwicklung. In ihrer bisherigen Form führt sie nämlich zu einem höheren Maß an typeninterner Heterogenität als notwendig, was insbesondere einer prägnanteren Ausarbeitung der Milieubeschreibungen im Wege steht. Hintergrund hierbei ist, dass die Berechnungsmethode den beiden Dimensionen (Ausstattungsniveau und Modernitätsgrades/biografische Perspektive) Vorrang vor der Eigenlogik der unterschiedlichen Milieutypen gibt. Die Berechnung der Dimensionen baut dabei auf der recht starken Vorannahme auf, dass die jeweiligen Subdimensionen in einem engen statistischen Zusammenhang stehen: Im Fall der Dimension des Ausstattungsniveaus bedeutet dies, dass sie auf der Summe aus dem ökonomischen Ausstattungsniveau und dem kulturellen Ausstattungsniveau basieren kann. Im Zweifelsfall heißt dies jedoch, dass Personen mit einem begüterten Lebensstil, die aber kulturell desinteressiert sind, in dieselbe mittlere Kategorie einsortiert werden, wie Personen mit sehr hohem kulturellem Interesse, aber in materieller Hinsicht bescheidenem Lebensstil. Dass sich diese Personen ähnlich und mit erhöhter Wahrscheinlichkeit befreundet sind, erscheint jedoch nicht plausibel. Die mittlere Kategorie des Ausstattungsniveaus ist daher relativ heterogen besetzt.

Dasselbe Problem gilt auch für den Modernitätsgrad bzw. die biografische Perspektive. Hier gilt die Vorannahme, dass Personen, die traditional eingestellt sind, ein weniger aktives Leben in Bezug auf außerhäusliche Aktivitäten bevorzugen und ein geringes Maß an

Selbstverwirklichung anstreben. Auch dies ist eine Annahme, die nicht für alle Personen zutrifft. Tatsächlich, so zeigt eine Faktorenanalyse bereits von Otte selbst, liegt hier ein entscheidendes Problem der horizontalen Dimension vor. So sind die Items, deren Zustimmung den offenen biografischen/modernen Abschnitt markieren sollen („Leben gefällt, wenn ständig etwas los." „Suche neue Herausforderungen und Erfahrungen." „Selbstverwirklichung sehr wichtig.") statistisch stärker mit der Dimension des Ausstattungsniveau assoziiert als jene Items, die den traditionalen Abschnitt der Typologie bestimmen (OTTE 2019: 13).

Allein die an den Ecken der Typologie positionierten Typen (Konservativ Gehobene, Innovativ Gehobene, Bodenständig Traditionelle, Unterhaltungssuchende) sind von dieser Problematik weniger stark betroffen, während die anderen fünf Typen (Konventionalisten, Liberal Gehobene, Mittelständische, Heimzentrierte, Hedonisten) durch die Berechnungsmethode eher etwas unspezifische Mischtypen darstellen. Für die Ausarbeitung charakteristischer und dichter Beschreibungen eigenen sich diese Mischtypen daher nicht besonders gut. Insbesondere der Mitteltypus der „Mittelständischen" ist dabei schwierig zu deuten, da er die unscharfe Mitte sowohl der Modernitätsdimension als auch des Ausstattungsniveaus repräsentiert. Nicht zuletzt nährt dieser Sachverhalt doch etwas den Verdacht, dass die Lebensstilbeschreibungen von 2004 (vgl. Abb. 1) für diese Mischtypen ein höheres Maß an Präzision und inhaltlicher Spezifik suggerieren, als empirisch begründet sein dürfte.

3.1 Eine neue Berechnungsmethode

Die logische Weiterentwicklung des Modells lag daher in der Wahl einer neuen Berechnungsmethode, die einerseits eine neue, aktualisierte Typologie mit charakteristischen Typen erstellt und andererseits die Vorzüge von Gunnar Ottes Instrument beibehält: Wissenschaftlichkeit, Transparenz, Lizenzkostenfreiheit und die Möglichkeit der einfachen Typenzuweisung für einzelne Befragte.

Daneben sollten für die Weiterentwicklung zentrale Merkmale des Instrumentes beibehalten werden: Dies betrifft insbesondere den Fragenkatalog, der bereits 2019 aktualisiert wurde und für den durch die „Kulturelle Teilhabe in Berlin"-Studien des IKTf (ALLMANRITTER et al. 2020; ALLMANRITTER/TEWES-SCHÜNZEL 2022) und die Berliner Befragungsreihe KulMon® seit 2019 fortlaufende Datenreihen zur Verfügung stehen. Die Beibehaltung des Erhebungsinstruments erlaubt es, die Typologie auch rückwirkend zu berechnen, sodass Zeitreihenanalysen mit diesen Daten weiterhin möglich sind und die Kontinuität gewährleistet bleibt. Neben dem Fragenkatalog sollte sowohl die Zahl von neun Lebensstiltypen als auch die tabellarisch-dimensionale Darstellung wie bei der ursprünglichen Typologie beibehalten werden.

Die Neuberechnung der unterschiedlichen Typen hat jedoch zur Folge, dass alte und neue Typen, selbst bei teils ähnlichem Zuschnitt und Bezeichnung nicht direkt miteinander vergleichbar sind. Obwohl sich die Bezeichnung der neuen Typen teils an die bereits bekannten Typen anlehnt, unterscheiden sie sich im Einzelnen, um die Zugehörigkeit zur jeweiligen Typologie eindeutig zu markieren.

Der Auswahl des neuen Berechnungsverfahren liegt eine Reihe von Überlegungen zugrunde. Zunächst sollte ein Verfahren gewählt werden, dass im Sinne dichter Typenbeschreibungen die Eigenlogik der Milieus stärker herausarbeitet als ein dimensionales Vorgehen (bspw. Faktorenanalysen oder multiple Korrespondenzanalyse). Dies ist vor allem bei clusteranalytischen Verfahren gegeben, aber auch bei der sog. latenten Klassenanalyse (LCA). Als statistische Methode für die Neuberechnung der Typologie wurde letztlich die latente Klassenanalyse gewählt. Es handelt sich um ein statistisches Verfahren, mit dem Personen probabilistisch in intern homogene Subgruppen („latente Klassen") eingeteilt werden. Die Zugehörigkeit einer Person zu den unterschiedlichen Klassen wird mit klassenspezifischen Antwortprofilen erklärt (HAGENAARS/McCUTCHEON 2009; GEISER 2011: 235). Ausschlaggebend für die Wahl der LCA war, dass sie als parametrisches Verfahren besser als die Clusteranalyse in der Lage ist, eine eindeutige, optimale Klassenlösung replizierbar zu berechnen. Diese ist unabhängig von Merkmalen wie unterschiedlichen Startwerten oder der Reihenfolge der Fälle im Datensatz, die bei Clusteranalysen die Ergebnisse erheblich beeinflussen (HARTMANN 2012: 73). Eine Limitierung auf verhältnismäßig wenige Variablen, wie sie die LCA gegenüber Clusteranalysen aufweist, spielte für den gegeben Fall keine Rolle. Ein weiterer Vorteil der LCA liegt darin, dass die Validität der Klassenlösung in anderen Datensätzen und Grundgesamtheiten inferenzstatistisch geprüft werden kann (ebd.) (siehe unten). Die so gewonnene Typologie kann auf ihre Übertragbarkeit auf andere Grundgesamtheiten getestet werden, was tatsächlich einen höchst interessanten Ausgangspunkt für zukünftige komparative Lebensstilanalysen ermöglicht.

Die latente Klassenanalyse erlaubt zudem, auch nachträglich Personen latenten Klassen (also sozialen Milieus) zuzuordnen (sog. posterior probabilities). Diese nachträgliche Zuordnung auf Grundlage des neuen

Modells kann auch bei anderen Datensätzen erfolgen. Einzelnen Personen wird dabei auf der Grundlage ihres Antwortverhaltens für jeden Typus eine Zugehörigkeitswahrscheinlichkeit berechnet. Anschließend wird sie jenem Milieu zugeordnet, für das sie die höchste Zugehörigkeitswahrscheinlichkeit besitzt (sog. „modale Zuordnung"). Die für die Zuordnung benötigten Informationen und der Algorithmus werden vom IKTf im Laufe des Jahres 2024 veröffentlicht. Diese werden das Einspielen der Typologie bei Datensätzen, die das vollständige Befragungsinstrument enthalten bei allen gängigen Statistikprogrammen ermöglichen.

Als Datengrundlage für die Neuberechnung der Typologie wurden die Studien „Kulturelle Teilhabe in Berlin" von 2019 und 2021 herangezogen. Dabei handelt es sich um postalische Befragungen auf der Grundlage einer Zufallsstichprobe des Einwohnermeldeamts des Landes Berlin. Die Grundgesamtheit besteht aus der in Berlin gemeldeten Wohnbevölkerung ab einem Alter von 15 Jahren. Es wurden jeweils 13.000 Personen angeschrieben, mit einem bereinigten Rücklauf von 3.402 (2019) bzw. 3.629 (2021) Personen (Rücklaufquote 27% bzw. 28%). Bei der Berechnung der Typen wurde eine Poststratifizierungsgewichtung verwendet, die den Datensatz in Hinblick auf Alter, Geschlecht, Haushaltsgröße, Bezirk und formalen Bildungsgrad an Referenzdaten des Amts für Statistik Berlin-Brandenburg anpasste.

Es steht zu vermuten, dass die Berliner Bevölkerung kulturaffiner und möglicherweise biografisch offener ist als etwa ländliche Gebiete der Bundesrepublik. Das für Berlin berechnete Modell dürfte damit einen etwas größeren Schwerpunkt auf kulturaffine Milieus legen, als dies bei einer bundesweiten Datengrundlage der Fall wäre. Die Unterschiede dürften jedoch eher graduell sein, d.h. in der unterschiedlichen Besetzungsstärke der Typen liegen und weniger in ihrem inhaltlichen Zuschnitt. Die weitgehende inhaltliche Übertragbarkeit der Typologie und der Berechnungsmethode auch auf andere Bundesländer sollte grundsätzlich gut möglich sein. Dies sollte in Zukunft jedoch empirisch überprüft werden.

Für die vorliegenden Berliner Datensätze wurden Validierungstests in Bezug auf die zeitliche Stabilität der Typologie durchgeführt. Dafür wurde eine sogenannte Multigruppenanalyse durchgeführt, bei der die unterschiedlichen Erhebungszeiträume in Bezug auf qualitative Veränderungen der Typologie (sog. „Strukturinvarianz") oder quantitative Veränderung der relativen Besetzungsstärke (sog. „Messinvarianz") statistisch geprüft werden (EID/LANGEHEINE/DIENER 2003). Bei den Analysen wurde festgestellt, dass der inhaltliche Zuschnitt der unterschiedlichen Milieus 2019, 2021 und 2023 unverändert blieb. Lediglich marginale Verschiebungen gab es bei der Besetzungsstärke der Typen, was in Anbetracht des starken alltäglichen Einflusses der Corona-Pandemie 2021 ein mehr als zufriedenstellendes Ergebnis darstellt.

4. Die Berliner Kulturmilieus

Das Ergebnis der Neuberechnung ist eine neue Typologie, die in Abgrenzung zur Lebensführungstypologie Ottes als „Kulturmilieumodell" bezeichnet werden soll.

Für die Formulierung der detaillierten Milieubeschreibungen wurden nicht nur die 12 Items herangezogen, sondern auch zusätzliche Daten, die in der Studie erhoben worden sind, wie Einkommen, Alter, Bildungsabschlüsse, Wohnort, Beruf, kulturelle Interessen und Freizeitgestaltung (Musik- und Filmgeschmack, Hobbies) sowie auch soweit erfasst weitere Werte und Einstellungen. Die Formulierung der Typen folgt dem Konzept der Hermeneutik der Massendaten von Schulze (SCHULZE 1992: 141): Die Daten allein sprechen nicht für sich, sie müssen vergleichend interpretiert werden, um zu idealtypischen Milieubeschreibungen verdichtet zu werden.

Die Bezeichnungen der Milieus orientiert sich dabei einerseits an Ottes Lebensführungstypologie, um einen Wiedererkennungseffekt insbesondere bei ähnlichen Typen zu ermöglichen. Andererseits wurde jedoch darauf geachtet, jedem Milieu einen neuen Namen zu geben, um Verwechselungen vorzubeugen.

Analog zur ursprünglichen Typologie werden die Milieus entlang zweier Dimensionen bestimmt: Statt über das Ausstattungsniveaus und den Modernitätsgrad bzw. die biografische Perspektive werden die Milieus nun entlang ihrer Schwerpunkte beim formalen Bildungsgrad (vertikal) und dem Altersschwerpunkt (horizontal) angeordnet (Tabelle 4). Dies ist einerseits der neuen Berechnungsmethode geschuldet, welche die Dimensionalität der Eigenlogik der Typen unterordnet, andererseits orientiert sich diese Anordnung an den Erlebnismilieus von Gerhard Schulze (1992). Wie bei der ursprünglichen Typologie von Otte gilt jedoch auch hier (anders als bei Schulze): Die Milieuzugehörigkeit ist keinesfalls vollständig durch das Alter oder den formalen Bildungsgrad determiniert. Sie gehen nicht in die Berechnung der Typen mit ein, für die lediglich das Fragebogeninstrument von Otte herangezogen wurde. Inhaltlich ergeben sich jedoch viele Analogien zu den Erlebnismilieus

Schulze. Analog zu Schulze wächst näherungsweise entlang der formalen Bildungsdimension die Wahrscheinlichkeit klassische Kulturangebote zu besuchen (Hochkulturschema). Jugendkulturelle Stile und actionbetonte Freizeitgestaltung hingegen werden bei Milieus mit jüngerem Altersschwerpunkt bevorzugt („Modern Gehobene", „Prekäre Avantgarde", „Unterhaltungsmilieu", „Konservatives Unterhaltungsmilieu").

Beim neuen Zuschnitt der Typen ist zudem der Bezug zu Bourdieu stärker ausgeprägt als bei der Lebensführungstypologie Ottes. Hier kommt zum Tragen, dass Lebensstilmerkmale mit ökonomischem Kapitalbezug bei der Berechnung der Typen nicht mehr mit kulturellem Kapital vermischt werden. So können nun Milieus rekonstruiert werden, die sich durch ein hohes inkorporiertes Kapital bei niedrigem ökonomischen Kapital auszeichnen („prekäre Avantgarde", „Bescheiden-Bürgerliche"), aber auch Milieus, deren Lebensstil stärker über ökonomische Merkmale definiert wird und sich durch eine Distanz zu klassischen Kulturangeboten auszeichnet („Unterhaltungsmilieu", „Bodenständige"). Dies entspricht der horizontalen Achse von Bourdieus sozialem Raum. Daneben wird auch deutlich, dass mit den „Modern Gehobenen" ein soziales Milieu identifiziert wird, das sich ökonomisch deutlich von den anderen Milieus nach oben hin absetzt (3000 € im Median[4], Median Gesamtbevölkerung Berlins: 1833 €).

Daneben lässt sich mit dem „Konservativen Unterhaltungsmilieu" aber auch mindestens ein Milieu rekonstruieren, dessen Lebensstil analog in der postmigrantischen Milieuforschung beschrieben wurde. Tatsächlich weist dieses Milieu einen Anteil von 55 % Personen mit Migrationsgeschichte auf. S. z. B. die Beschreibung der konservativen Position und des juvenil-materialistischen Luxusstils bei türkeistämmigen Aufsteigern (TEWES-SCHÜNZEL 2023: 129ff.). Inwieweit das Konservative Unterhaltungsmilieus tatsächlich Schnittmengen mit konservativen migrantisch-geprägten Milieus aufweist, kann jedoch nur vermutet werden und sollte Anlass für weitere Studien sein. Dieses altersübergreifende Milieu ist in der Mitte des Milieutableaus angeordnet, wobei es jedoch keine vermeintliche „Mitte der Gesellschaft" repräsentiert, wie es bei Otte die vormaligen Typen der „Aufstiegsorientierten" (2004) bzw. „Mittelständischen" (2019) gewissermaßen taten. Das „Konservative Unterhaltungsmilieu" zeichnet sich durch die Kombination einer offenen biografischen Perspektive und sehr traditionalen Einstellungen aus, die zuvor nicht sinnvoll verortet werden konnte. Bei diesem Milieutypus

---

4   Angegeben ist hier das Nettoäquivalenzeinkommen.

wird deutlich, dass die typischen Antwortmuster, die die Grundlage für die Milieutypologie darstellen, nun in sehr prägnanter Weise mit weiteren Merkmalen im Zusammenhang stehen, die nicht in die Berechnung eingegangen sind, wie etwa dem Haushaltseinkommen. So schätzt das konservative Unterhaltungsmilieu sein materielles Ausstattungsniveau als sehr hoch ein, obwohl es mit dem zweitgeringsten pro-Kopf-Einkommen auskommen muss. Diese Kombination kann vermutlich als ein Ausweis einer überdurchschnittlichen Statusorientierung gedeutet werden (siehe Milieubeschreibung unten).

(← älter) Altersschwerpunkt (jünger →)

	Gehoben-Konservative (10%)	Obere Mitte (17 %)	Gehoben-Moderne (10 %)
(← geringer) Formaler Bildungsgrad (höher →)	Alter: 57 Akademiker*innen: 37 % Pro-Kopf-HH-EK: 2157 € Theater: 25 % Klass. Konzerte.: 28 % Pop/Rock-Konz: 26 %	Alter: 51 Akademiker*innen: 43 % Pro-Kopf-HH-EK: 2250 € Theater: 30 % Klass. Konzerte: 27 % Pop/Rock-Konz: 33 %	Alter: 44 Akademiker*innen: 47 % Pro-Kopf-HH-EK: 3071 € Theater: 34 % Klass. Konzerte: 35 % Pop/Rock-Konz: 41%
	Bescheiden-Bürgerliche (9 %) Alter: 57 Akademiker*innen: 26 % Pro-Kopf-HH-EK: 1719 € Theater: 21 % Klass. Konzerte: 20 % Pop/Rock-Konz: 22 %	Konservatives Unterhaltungsmilieu (5 %) Alter: 45 Akademiker*innen: 28 % Pro-Kopf-HH-EK: 1540 € Theater: 14 % Klass. Konzerte: 16 % Pop/Rock-Konz: 28 %	Prekäre Avantgarde (13 %) Alter: 39 Akademiker*innen: 30 % Pro-Kopf-HH-EK: 1775 € Theater: 35 % Klass. Konzerte: 31 % Pop/Rock-Konz: 41 %
	Bodenständige (16 %) Alter: 55 Akademiker*innen: 17 % Pro-Kopf-HH-EK: 1929 € Theater: 13 % Klass. Konzerte: 10 % Pop/Rock-Konz: 28 %	Zurückgezogene (8 %) Alter: 46 Akademiker*innen: 11 % Pro-Kopf-HH-EK: 1486 € Theater: 6 % Klass. Konzerte: 3 % Pop/Rock-Konz: 20 %	Unterhaltungsmilieu (13 %) Alter: 37 Akademiker*innen: 22 % Pro-Kopf-HH-EK: 1830 € Theater: 15 % Klass. Konzerte: 11 % Pop/Rock-Konz: 36 %

Tabelle 4: Das Kulturmilieumodell (eigene Darstellung)[5]

Die folgenden Milieubeschreibungen stellen leicht gekürzte Versionen jener Beschreibungen dar, die bereits in der Studie Kulturelle Teilhabe in Berlin 2023 im Anhang publiziert wurden. Dort sind ebenfalls die Tabellen dokumentiert, die für die Interpretation der Typen herangezogen wurden und vertiefte Informationen insbesondere für das Kulturmarketing

---

5   Die Prozentangaben bei den Kulturangeboten beziehen sich auf die mindestens einmalige Besuchswahrscheinlichkeit in den letzten 12 Monaten. Datenbasis: Berlin 2023

enthalten (z.B. genutzte Medien für die Freizeitplanung). Die Prozentangaben hinter der Milieubezeichnung beziehen sich auf den jeweiligen Bevölkerungsanteil in Berlin (2019-2023). (TEWES-SCHÜNZEL/ALLMANRITTER/RENZ 2024: 70-88).

Gehoben-Konservative (10 %)
Traditionelle Bildungsbürger/innen mit gehobenem Lebensstandard in der zweiten Lebenshälfte, oft Pensionär/innen, Beamt in höheren Laufbahnen und Freiberufler mit Angestellten. Trotz eines hohen Anteils beruflich nicht mehr aktiver Personen verfügen sie über überdurchschnittliche finanzielle Mittel. Bei den sozialen Milieus mit höherem Altersschwerpunkt handelt es sich um das formal am höchsten gebildete soziale Milieu. Gehoben-Konservative leben in Berlin häufig in gehobenen, ruhigen Stadtrandgebieten mit vielen Einfamilienhäusern (z. B. Zehlendorf, Gatow, Biesdorf). Luxus und Statussymbole, wie Besuche exklusiver Restaurants, sind bei ihnen Normalität. Werte wie Ordnung, Sicherheit und Beständigkeit sowie die Orientierung an Familientraditionen prägen ihre Lebensphilosophie. Gartenpflege ist eine ihrer typischen Interessen. Daneben verbringen sie ihre Freizeit gern in der Natur. Kulturell sind sie traditional-bildungsbürgerlich, gut informiert, lesen anspruchsvolle Bücher, und bevorzugen klassische Kulturangebote wie Oper und Theater. Sie schätzen klassische Musik und ältere Unterhaltungsmusik, interessieren sich jedoch wenig für aktuelle Pop- oder Jugendkultur. Im Kino bevorzugen sie ruhigere Genres wie Familienfilme, Drama oder Dokumentationen.

Bescheiden-Bürgerliche (9 %)
Klassisch orientierte Bildungsbürger/innen mit bescheidenem Lebensstil. Dieses Milieu hat den höchsten Anteil an Personen im Ruhestand, viele Akademiker/innen sowie Beamt oder qualifizierte Angestellte. Sie verfügen jedoch nur über ein unterdurchschnittliches Einkommen, das mit einer sparsamen Lebensführung einhergeht: seltene, preiswerte Restaurantbesuche und Urlaub im Inland. In Berlin wohnen oft in Stadtteilen abseits des Zentrums, wie Steglitz, Mariendorf oder Zehlendorf. Ihre Lebensphilosophie ist asketisch, mit Fokus auf körperliche Aktivität, Inspiration und Kreativität, aber wenig Interesse an Luxus oder Selbstverwirklichung. Bescheiden-Bürgerliche sind gut informiert, lesen gern anspruchsvolle Bücher und haben einen klassischen, bildungsbürgerlichen Kulturgeschmack, jedoch kaum Interesse an Pop- oder Jugendkultur.

Sie bevorzugen Dokumentationen im Kino und meiden Actionfilme, mit einer insgesamt geringeren Besuchshäufigkeit von Kulturangeboten.

Bodenständige (16 %)

Konservatives Milieu in der zweiten Lebenshälfte, mit hohem Anteil nicht-akademischer Fachkräfte und mittlerem Einkommen. Sie pflegen einen heimzentrierten Lebensstil, typische Hobbies sind Gärtnern oder Heimwerken. In Berlin leben sie eher am Stadtrand, wie in Neukölln (außer Nord-Neukölln), Marienfelde/Lichtenrade oder Biesdorf. Ihre konservativ-bodenständige Lebensphilosophie betont Familientraditionen, Sicherheit und Beständigkeit, während Selbstverwirklichung, Gender- und Klimagerechtigkeit weniger wichtig sind. Sie bevorzugen ruhige Erholung und Gemütlichkeit in ihrer Freizeit. Kunst, Kultur, anspruchsvolle Bücher sowie Politik interessieren sie wenig. Sie hören gern Popklassiker, aktuelle Charts oder Schlager und besuchen selten klassische Kulturangebote. Freizeitangebote wie Fußballstadien, Volksfeste oder Popkonzerte sind beliebter. In Filmen bevorzugen sie Krimis und Familienfilme, haben jedoch wenig Interesse an Arthouse-Filmen.

Obere Mitte (17 %)

Die akademische geprägte Mittelklasse mittleren Alters mit innerer Distanz zu allen Extremen. Bei der „oberen Mitte" ist der Name lebensphilosophisches Programm: Nicht traditional, aber auch nicht zu wild, nicht abgehoben, aber doch angekommen. Ein Milieu, das sich in seiner Selbsteinschätzung Bescheidenheit und Mäßigung auferlegt hat und sich selbst einen eher mittleren Lebensstandard attestiert, obwohl es überdurchschnittlich finanzstark ist. Typische Berufe beinhalten Beamtenpositionen im höheren Dienst oder Angestellte mit eigenständigen Tätigkeiten. In Berlin wohnen sie gediegenen innerstädtischen Lagen (z.B. Pankow, Wilmersdorf, Charlottenburg). Ihre Werte betonen eine Balance zwischen Sicherheit, Beständigkeit und neuen Herausforderungen. Freizeitgestaltung umfasst sowohl intellektuelle Stimulation als auch Entspannung, z.B. Lesen, Gärtnern und häufige Restaurantbesuche. Sie interessieren sich für Politik und Zeitgeschehen, ebenso wie anspruchsvolle Bücher. Kulturell geben sie sich bescheiden, besuchen klassische Kulturangebote jedoch durchaus häufig. Ihre vielfältigen Interessen schließen Jazz, Soul, klassische Musik und anspruchsvolle Filme (Arthouse, Dramen, Dokumentationen) ein, während sie volkstümliche Musik, Schlager und Horrorfilme ablehnen.

Konservatives Unterhaltungsmilieu (5 %)
Ein altersübergreifendes Milieu, das traditionelle Werte, Statusorientierung, Hedonismus und Offenheit für Neues miteinander vereint. Es ist kulturell interessiert und durchaus versiert, zeichnet sich jedoch durch nicht durch einen hohen Anteil von Akademiker/innen aus. Sie schätzen Luxus und attestieren sich einen hohen Lebensstandard, verfügen jedoch nur über unterdurchschnittliche Einkommen. Viele von ihnen sind Arbeiter/innen und wohnen in Berlin in einfachen Wohnlagen in Innenstadtnähe, wie Schöneberg (Nord), Kreuzberg (Nord) oder Gesundbrunnen. Sie vereinen Werte, die sonst selten zusammen auftreten, wie etwa der Wunsch nach Selbstverwirklichung und neuen Erfahrungen einerseits und eine starke Orientierung an Häuslichkeit und Familientraditionen andererseits. Das Milieu priorisiert in seiner Freizeit familientaugliche Angebote mit einem guten Preis-Leistungs-Verhältnis, wobei es stärker als etwa das Milieu der Bodenständigen Wert auf Kreativität legt. Sowohl klassische Kulturangebote als auch kulturelle Freizeitangebote werden von ihnen durchschnittlich häufig besucht. Ihr kultureller Geschmack ist breit gefächert: Klassische Musik, Gangster-Rap, Volksmusik, Familienfilme, Dramen, Action-, Science-Fiction- und Horrorfilme sind beliebt, während Rockmusik (Punk, Indie, Heavy Metal) weniger gehört wird.

Zurückgezogene (8 %)
Ein sozioökonomisch vulnerables Milieu mittleren Alters mit geringem außerhäuslichen Aktivitätsniveau und hohem Anteil armutsgefährdeter Personen. Sie führen einen einfachen Lebensstandard, machen selten teure Urlaube oder Restaurantbesuche und arbeiten oft als angelernte Arbeiter/innen oder einfache Angestellte. Sie wohnen in Berlin meist in einfachen Stadtrandlagen wie Hellersdorf oder Reinickendorf und sind gebürtige Berliner/innen. Ihre Lebensphilosophie konzentriert sich auf Alltagsbewältigung, Sicherheit und Ruhe. Selbstverwirklichung und Familientraditionen spielen kaum eine Rolle. Politisches Interesse und Vorkenntnisse im Bereich Kunst und Kultur sind eher gering ausgeprägt. Ihre Freizeitgestaltung findet vor allem zu Hause statt, wobei Fernsehen, Audio-/Videostreaming und Computerspiele bevorzugt werden. Sie besuchen selten Kulturangebote, Kneipen, Cafés oder Restaurants. Bücher und Podcasts sind wenig beliebt. Musikgeschmack umfasst Pop-Klassiker, aktuelle Charts und Schlager. Bei Filmen bevorzugen sie Horror, Action und Animation/Zeichentrick, während Arthouse-Produktionen und Dramen wenig Interesse finden.

Gehoben-Moderne (10 %)

Dieses privilegierte, einkommensstarke Milieu mittleren Alters steht an der Spitze der Berliner Sozialstruktur mit dem höchsten Durchschnittseinkommen und Qualifikationsniveau. Führungskräfte sind überproportional vertreten. Sie schätzen gehobene Kulinarik und häufige Auslandsreisen, bevorzugen dabei einen authentischen, modernen und individuellen Stil. Typische Wohngebiete in Berlin sind gehobene Innenstadtlagen wie Prenzlauer Berg und Mitte sowie der Südwesten (Wannsee, Gatow/Kladow). Viele von ihnen sind nach Berlin Zugezogene. Selbstverwirklichung durch beruflichen Erfolg steht im Mittelpunkt ihrer Lebensphilosophie. Familientraditionen sind nicht besonders wichtig, werden von ihnen aber auch nicht abgelehnt. Sie sind offen für Veränderungen und haben keine Zukunftsängste. Ihre Freizeitgestaltung ist anspruchsvoll und außerhäuslich orientiert, mit starkem Bedürfnis nach intellektueller Stimulation und körperlicher Aktivität (Fitness, Yoga). Sie priorisieren Qualität und Originalität in ihrem Konsum und sind kulturell versiert, lesen viel und nutzen Podcasts und Streaming-Dienste. Ihr Musikgeschmack reicht von Heavy Metal, Indie-Rock und elektronischer Musik bis hin zu Jazz und klassischer Musik. Volkstümliche Musik und Schlager sind selten. Sie besuchen häufig klassische Kulturangebote und interessieren sich überdurchschnittlich für Kino, besonders für Arthouse-Produktionen und Dramen.

Prekäre Avantgarde (13 %)

Ein junges Milieu kosmopolitischer Kulturbegeisterter, formal hoch gebildet, aber mit geringem Einkommen. Viele sind Studierende oder pflegen einen studentischen Lebensstil im Erwerbsleben, oft als Solo-Selbstständige oder Freelancer. Sie wohnen in Szenevierteln wie Kreuzberg, Nord-Neukölln, Friedrichshain oder Wedding und sind häufig Zugezogene. Ihre Lebensphilosophie ist von der Suche nach Stimulation und neuen Erfahrungen geprägt, mit starkem Fokus auf Selbstverwirklichung und einem erlebnisreichen Leben. Konservative Werte und Sicherheit lehnen sie ab, ihr Lebensstil ist stärker ethisch-politisch motiviert (gendergerechte Sprache, Antirassismus, Klimaschutz, vegane Ernährung) als in anderen Milieus. Sie leben sparsam, aber sind sehr aktiv in ihrer Freizeit, oft in Cafés und Bars in Szenevierteln. Kreativität, Inspiration und das Knüpfen neuer Kontakte sind zentral. Sie treiben oft Fitnesstraining, Yoga oder Pilates. Sie sind das kulturell aktivste Milieu, besuchen häufig klassische Kulturangebote und engagieren sich künstlerisch oder ehrenamtlich. Ihr Musikgeschmack ist vielseitig, von

Indie-Rock, Hip-Hop, Elektro bis zu klassischer Musik und Jazz, aber sie meiden volkstümliche Musik, Musicals und Schlager. Im Kino bevorzugen sie anspruchsvolle Filmkunst, mit breitem Genreinteresse außer Familienfilmen.

Unterhaltungsmilieu (13 %)
Ein junges, pragmatisches Milieu mit Fokus auf Spaß und Action. Dieses Milieu hat ein höheres Einkommen als die Prekäre Avantgarde, ist jedoch weniger akademisch geprägt und umfasst viele junge Familien. Typische Wohnlagen in Berlin liegen außerhalb des Stadtzentrums, wie Weißensee, Gesundbrunnen, Marienfelde, Lichtenrade oder Hellersdorf. Lebensphilosophisch zeichnen sie sich durch Unternehmungslust aus, wobei ihnen Spaß und Spannung wichtig sind. Sie sind pragmatisch eingestellt und für ihr Alter etwas konservativ, schätzen Sicherheit und Beständigkeit sowie familiäre Traditionen. Individualismus zeigt sich eher in ästhetischen Präferenzen und Hobbys wie Tattoos, Piercings und leistungsstarken Fahrzeugen. Häufig besuchen sie Fitnessstudios, eher selten Entspannungssportarten wie Yoga. In ihrer Freizeit bevorzugen sie niedrigschwellige, familientaugliche Angebote wie Volksfeste, Weihnachtsmärkte, Freizeitparks, Stadionbesuche und Pop- sowie Rockkonzerte. Anspruchsvolle Kulturangebote werden weniger präferiert. Ihr Musikgeschmack umfasst aktuelle Charts, Gangster-Rap, Hip-Hop, R'n'B, Schlager und einige Rockarten, weniger klassische Musik oder Jazz. Sie sind große Fans von Horror-, Action-, Fantasy- und Animationsfilmen und weniger interessiert an Arthouse-Produktionen.

5. Ausblick und Desiderata

Dieser Artikel macht einen Vorschlag für die Weiterentwicklung der Lebensführungstypologie nach Gunnar Otte, die hier als Kulturmilieumodell bezeichnet wird. Begonnen wird mit einer kurzen Einleitung in die Grundlagen der Milieusoziologie, die sich aus Gründen des Umfangs auf eine Vorstellung einiger zentraler Ideen der Lebensstil- und Milieuforschung und der bisherigen Lebensführungstypologie von Gunnar Otte beschränkt. Darauffolgend wird ein programmatischer Vorschlag zur Überarbeitung der Lebensführungstypologie unterbreitet, der mit der Vorstellung einer überarbeiteten Milieutypologie mitsamt ausformulierter Typbeschreibungen abschließt. Nicht mehr berücksichtigt werden konnte an dieser Stelle, ebenfalls aus Gründen des Umfangs, die ausführliche statische Beschreibung der typologischen Berechnung (die für eine wissenschaftlich-methodische Kritik notwendig wäre), noch wurde in diesem Beitrag die Methode zum Einspielen der Typologie in dritte Datensätze erläutert. Beides wird in nachfolgenden Veröffentlichungen thematisiert werden müssen. Insofern handelt es sich bei dieser Veröffentlichung eher um eine Forschungsnotiz, denn um eine vollständige Dokumentation des Milieuinstrumentes.

Das neue Kulturmilieumodell wird sich darüber hinaus bei zukünftigen Analysen gegenüber der ursprünglichen Typologie von Otte in Hinblick auf Erklärungskraft und Deutungsplausibilität bewähren müssen. Einen ersten Schritt hierbei stellt die „Kulturelle Teilhabe in Berlin 2023"-Studie dar, bei der das neue Instrument bereits zum Einsatz gekommen ist (TEWES-SCHÜNZEL/ALLMANRITTER/RENZ 2024).

Es wäre es darüber hinaus geboten, die Typologie auch qualitativ zu validieren. So könnte das Milieuinstrument entweder das Sampling einer qualitativen Milieustudie anleiten oder bei einer solchen Untersuchung nachgeschaltet werden. Qualitative Daten würden helfen, einerseits die Milieubeschreibungen abzusichern, die bislang nur auf quantitativer Grundlage formuliert wurden. Andererseits könnten qualitative Daten die vorhandenen Milieubeschreibungen weiter anreichern und so zu noch dichteren oder themenspezifischen Beschreibungen führen.

Wie bereits erläutert, ermöglicht die latente Klassenanalyse die Typologie in ihrem inhaltlichen Zuschnitt und ihrer Besetzungsstärke komparativ mit anderen Datensätzen zu vergleichen. Gerade auch signifikante Abweichungen bei Datensätzen anderer Herkunft (also gewissermaßen ein Scheitern der Validierung) würden dabei äußerst gewinnbringende Erkenntnisse für die soziologische Lebensstil- und Milieuforschung in sich bergen. Interessant wären hier sowohl Vergleiche mit Daten aus Publikumsbefragungen als auch aus anderen Regionen. Insofern wäre es geboten, den Fragebogen von Otte in möglichst vielen (über-)regionalen Surveys einzubinden, um für ein solches Forschungsvorhaben eine breite Datengrundlage zu schaffen.

In Hinblick für die Nutzbarkeit im Kulturmarketing erscheinen diese soziologischen Potentiale vermutlich weniger relevant. Hier ist vor allem wichtig, dass das neue Kulturmilieumodell frei verfügbar und nachvollziehbar ist, sich die Milieubeschreibungen gut für die fundierte Erstellung von Personas eignen und die neue Typologie das eigene Publikum trennscharf erfasst. Etwaige „Berlinismen", die der Datengrundlage entstammen (etwa der hohe Anteil an Zugezogenen, die vermutlich überdurchschnittlich Besetzungsstärke der „prekären Avantgarde" oder die Zuordnung der Milieus zu Stadtteilen in den Milieubeschreibungen) dürften dabei einer Nutzung in anderen Teilen der BRD weniger entgegenstehen, als lediglich tabellarisch vorliegende Steckbriefe oder veraltete Milieubeschreibungen. Zu diesem Optimismus trägt die Rückbindung an Schulze und Bourdieu bei, die sich als Klassen- bzw. Milieumodelle bereits in unterschiedlichen Kontexten bewährt haben.

Literatur

ALLMANRITTER, Vera (2017): *Audience Development in der Migrationsgesellschaft. Neue Strategien für Kulturinstitutionen*. Bielefeld: transcript.

ALLMANRITTER, Vera/RENZ, Thomas/TEWES-SCHÜNZEL, Oliver/ JUHNKE, Sebastian (2020): *Kulturelle Teilhabe in Berlin 2019. Soziodemografie und Lebensstile. Ergebnisse einer repräsentativen Bevölkerungsbefragung, gefördert von der Berliner Senatsverwaltung für Kultur und Europa*. < https://www.iktf.berlin/publications/kulturelle-teilhabe-in-berlin-2019/> [27.02.2024].

ALLMANRITTER, Vera/TEWES-SCHÜNZEL, Oliver (2022): *Kulturelle Teilhabe in Berlin 2021: Kulturbesuche, Freizeitaktivitäten und digitale Angebote in Zeiten von COVID-19. Ergebnisse einer repräsentativen Bevölkerungsbefragung, gefördert von der Berliner Senatsverwaltung für Kultur und Europa*. < https://www.iktf.berlin/publications/kulturelle-teilhabe-in-berlin-2021/> [27.02.2024].

ATKINSON, Will (2020): *The Class Structure of Capitalist Societies. Volume 1: A Space of Bounded Variety*. London: Routledge.

BAUR, Nina/KULKE, Elmar (2023): Social milieus in urban space. – In: Barth, Alice/Leßke, Felix/Atakan, Rebekka/Schmidt, Manuela/Scheit, Yvonne (Hgg.): *Multivariate scaling methods and the reconstruction of social spaces. Paper in honor of Jörg Blasius*. Opladen, Berlin, Toronto: Barbara Budrich, 164-194. <https://shop.budrich.de/wp-content/uploads/2023/09/9783847418566.pdf> [21.02.2024].

BECK, Ulrich (1983): Jenseits von Klasse und Stand? Soziale Ungleichheiten, gesellschaftliche Individualisierungsprozesse und die Entstehung neuer sozialer Formationen und Identitäten. – In: Kreckel, Reinhard (Hrsg.): *Soziale Ungleichheiten*. Göttingen: Schwartz. 35–74.

BECK, Ulrich (1986): *Risikogesellschaft. Auf dem Weg in eine andere Moderne*. Frankfurt am Main: Suhrkamp.

BLASIUS, Jörg/WINKLER, Joachim (1989): Gibt es die ›feinen Unterschiede‹? Eine empirische Überprüfung der Bourdieuschen Theorie. – In: *KZfSS* Kölner Zeitschrift für Soziologie und Sozialpsychologie 41(1), 72–94.

BOURDIEU, Pierre (1982): *Die feinen Unterschiede. Kritik der gesellschaftlichen Urteilskraft*. Frankfurt/M.: Suhrkamp.

BOURDIEU, Pierre (1983): Ökonomisches Kapital, kulturelles Kapital, soziales Kapital. – In: Kreckel, Reinhard (Hrsg.): *Soziale Ungleichheiten*. Göttingen: Schwartz. 183–198.

BRÜGGEMANN, Axel (2023): *Kommentar: Relevanzmonitor Kultur: Mehr Neues in der Klassik wagen!* SWR Kultur. <https://www.swr.de/swr2/musik-klassik/relevanzmonitor-kultur-mehr-neues-wagen-100.html> [27.02.2024].

BURZAN, Nicole (2011): Soziale Ungleichheit. Eine Einführung in die zentralen Theorien. Wiesbaden: VS Verlag.

DIAZ-BONE, Rainer (2004): Milieumodelle und Milieuinstrumente in der Marktforschung. – In: *Forum Qualitative Sozialforschung*, 5(2). <https://www.qualitative-research.net/index.php/fqs/article/download/595/1291?inline=1> [31.08.2024]

EDELSTEIN, Benjamin (2023): Welcher Anteil der Jungen und Mädchen erlangt das Abitur? (1950-2018). <https://www.bpb.de/themen/bildung/dossier-bildung/520286/welcher-anteil-der-jungen-und-maedchen-erlangt-das-abitur-1950-2018/> [23.02.2024].

EID, Michael/LANGEHEINE, Rolf/DIENER, Ed (2003): Comparing Typological Structures Across Cultures By Multigroup Latent Class Analysis: A Primer. – In: *Journal of Cross-Cultural Psychology*, 34(2), 195-210. <https://doi.org/10.1177/0022022102250427> [27.02.2024].

GEISER, Christian (2011*): Datenanalyse mit Mplus. Eine anwendungsorientierte Einführung*. Wiesbaden: VS Verlag.

GEORG, Werner (1998): *Soziale Lage und Lebensstil*. Wiesbaden: VS Verlag für Sozialwissenschaften.

GROH-SAMBERG, Olaf/SCHRÖDER, Tim/SPEER, Anne (2023): Social Milieus and Social Integration. From Theoretical Considerations to an Empirical Model. – In: *Kölner Zeitschrift für Soziologie und Sozialpsychologie*, Online First, 1-25. <https://doi.org/10.1007/s11577-023-00892-5> [27.02.2024].

HAGENAARS, Jacques A./MCCUTCHEON, Allan L. (2009): *Applied Latent Class Analysis*. Cambridge: Cambridge University Press.

HARTMANN, Peter H. (1999): *Lebensstilforschung. Darstellung, Kritik und Weiterentwicklung*. Opladen: Leske + Budrich.

HARTMANN, Peter H. (2012): Methodische und methodologische Probleme der Lebensstilforschung. – In: RÖSSEL, Jörg/OTTE, Gunnar (Hrsg.): *Lebensstilforschung*. Wiesbaden: VS Verlag.

ISENBÖCK, Peter/NELL, Linda/RENN, Joachim (Hrsg.) (2014): *Die Form des Milieus. Zum Verhältnis von gesellschaftlicher Differenzierung und Formen der Vergemeinschaftung*. Weinheim: Beltz Juventa.

KIRCHBERG, Volker (2005): *Gesellschaftliche Funktionen von Museen. Makro-, meso- und mikrosoziologische Perspektiven*. Wiesbaden: VS.

KIRCHBERG, Volker/KUCHAR, Robin (2014): Mixed Methods and Mixed Theories. Theorie und Methodik einer geplanten Bevölkerungsbefragung in Deutschland zur Kultur(nicht)partizipation. – In: Bekmeier-Feuerhahn, Sigrid/Höhne, Steffen/Keller, Rolf/Mandel, Birgit/Tröndle, Martin/van den Berg, Karen/Zembylas, Tasos (Hrsg.), *Zukunft Publikum. Jahrbuch für Kulturmanagement 2012*.Bielefeld: transcript, 153-170. <https://doi.org/10.1515/transcript.9783839422854.toc> [27.02.2024],

KLAGES, Helmut (1984): *Wertorientierung im Wandel. Rückblick, Gegenwartsanalyse, Prognosen*. Frankfurt/M.: Campus.

LIZ MOHN CENTER (Hrsg.) (2023): *Relevanzmonitor Kultur. Stellenwert von Kulturangeboten in Deutschland 2023*. <https://liz-mohn-stiftung.de/wp-content/uploads/2023/06/2023_05_31_RelevanzmonitorKultur2023_LizMohnCenter_BertelsmannStiftung-1.pdf> [27.02.2024].

MÜLLER-SCHNEIDER, Thomas (1994): *Schichten und Erlebnismilieus. Der Wandel der Milieustruktur in der Bundesrepublik Deutschland*. Wiesbaden: Deutscher Universitäts-Verlag.

OTTE, Gunnar (2004): *Sozialstrukturanalysen mit Lebensstilen. Eine Studie zur theoretischen und methodischen Neuorientierung der Lebensstilforschung.* Wiesbaden: VS Verlag.

OTTE, Gunnar (2005): Entwicklung und Test einer integrativen Typologie der Lebensführung für die Bundesrepublik Deutschland. – In: *Zeitschrift für Soziologie*, 34(6), 442-467. <https://doi.org/10.1515/zfsoz-2005-0606> [27.02.2024].

OTTE, Gunnar (2019): *Weiterentwicklung der Lebensführungstypologie, Version 2019.* <https://sozialstruktur.soziologie.uni-mainz.de/files/2019/12/Otte2019-Weiterentwicklung-der-Lebensführungstypologie-Version-2019.pdf> [27.02.2024].

OTTE, Gunnar/BAUR, Nina (2008): Urbanism as a Way of Life? Räumliche Variationen der Lebensführung in Deutschland. – In: *Zeitschrift für Soziologie* 37(2), 93–116. <https://doi.org/10.1515/zfsoz-2008-0201> [20.02.2024].

OTTE, Gunnar/RÖSSEL, Jörg (Hrsg.) (2012a): *Lebensstilforschung.* Wiesbaden: VS Verlag.

OTTE, Gunnar/RÖSSEL, Jörg (2012b): Lebensstile in der Soziologie. – In: Dies., (Hgg.), *Lebensstilforschung.* Wiesbaden: VS.

RENZ, Thomas/TEWES-SCHÜNZEL (2022): Nicht-Besucher:innenforschung revolutionieren? Lebensstile als neuer Zugang zur Erklärung von Kultureller Teilhabe. – In: *kulturmangement.net* <https://www.kulturmanagement.net/Themen/Lebensstile-als-neuer-Zugang-zur-Erklaerung-von-Kultureller-Teilhabe-Nicht-Besucherinnenforschung-revolutionieren,4418> [30.08.2024]

REUBAND, Karl-Heinz (2018a): Kulturelle Partizipation in Deutschland. Verbreitung und soziale Differenzierung. – In: Institut für Kulturpolitik der Kulturpolitischen Gesellschaft (Hgg.), *Jahrbuch für Kulturpolitik 2017/18. Thema: Welt. Kultur. Politik. Kulturpolitik in Zeiten der Globalisierung.* Bielefeld: Transcript, 377-393 <https://www.transcript-verlag.de/978-3-8376-4252-0/jahrbuch-fuer-kulturpolitik-2017/18/> [12.02.2024].

REUBAND, Karl-Heinz (2018b): *Oper, Publikum und Gesellschaft.* Wiesbaden: Springer VS.

REUBAND, Karl-Heinz (2021): *Kulturelle Partizipation im Langzeitvergleich. Eine Analyse auf der Basis der AWA-Zeitreihen des Instituts für Demoskopie.* < https://www.mkw.nrw/system/files/media/document/file/prof._reuband_kulturelle_partizipation_im_langzeitvergleich_awa_.pdf> [29.02.2024]

RÖSSEL, Jörg/OTTE, Gunnar (Hrsg.): *Lebensstilforschung.* Wiesbaden: VS.

SCHULZE, Gerhard (1992): *Die Erlebnisgesellschaft. Kultursoziologie der Gegenwart.* Frankfurt am Main, New York, N.Y.: Campus Verlag.

Spellerberg, Annette (1996): *Soziale Differenzierung durch Lebensstile. Eine empirische Untersuchung zur Lebensqualität in West- und Ostdeutschland.* Berlin: Ed. Sigma.

TEWES-SCHÜNZEL, Oliver (2023): *Milieus und Lebensstile in der postmigrantischen Gesellschaft.* Weinheim: Beltz Juventa. <https://www.beltz.de/fachmedien/soziologie/produkte/details/51554-milieus-und-lebensstile-in-der-postmigrantischen-gesellschaft.html> [12.02.2024].

TEWES-SCHÜNZEL, Oliver/ALLMANRITTER, Vera/RENZ, Thomas (2024): *Kulturelle Teilhabe in Berlin 2023. Alles wieder beim Alten? Kulturbesuche und künstlerisch-kreative Freizeitaktivitäten im Nachgang von COVID-19. Ergebnisse einer repräsentativen Bevölkerungsbefragung, gefördert von der Berliner Senatsverwaltung für Kultur und Europa.* < https://www.iktf.berlin/publications/studie-kulturelle-teilhabe-berlin-2023/ > [02.09.2024].

VESTER, Michael/OERTZEN, Peter von/GEILING, Heiko/HERRMANN, Thomas/MÜLLER, Dagmar (2001): *Soziale Milieus im gesellschaftlichen Strukturwandel. Zwischen Integration und Ausgrenzung.* Frankfurt am Main: Suhrkamp.

ESSAYS

Teilhaben am Tun Anderer?
Plädoyer für eine Veränderung der Perspektive

Participating in the Actions of Others? A Plea for a Change of Perspective

CORINNA VOSSE* UND DIETER HASELBACH**

Zentrum für Kulturforschung, Berlin

Abstract

In der öffentlich geförderten Kultur ist der Begriff der Teilhabe regelmäßig von den Akteuren her gedacht, die Angebote zum Publikum bringen möchten. Oftmals beinhaltet so verstandene Teilhabe kaum mehr als die Rezeption des Kunstprodukts. Der Essay kritisiert diesen Ansatz und geht der Frage nach, was ein angemessenes Verständnis von Teilhabe ist, angesichts der virulenten gesellschaftlichen Herausforderungen. Dass kulturelle Teilhabe ein wertebasiertes Miteinander fördern und so Demokratie stabilisieren und zudem gesellschaftliche Handlungsfähigkeit aktivieren helfen kann, ist eine Hoffnung vieler und dies beflügelt die Diskussion um Teilhabe. Wie Teilhabe in öffentlich geförderten Kultureinrichtungen, ausgestaltet sein kann, um hierzu beizutragen, wird im Beitrag diskutiert.

In publicly funded culture, the concept of participation is regularly considered from the perspective of those actors who want to bring offers to the audience. Participation understood in this way often involves little more than the reception of the art product. The essay criticizes this approach and examines the question of what an appropriate understanding of participation is in view of the virulent social challenges. It is the hope of many that cultural participation can promote value-based coexistence and thus stabilize democracy and help activate social action, and this stimulates the discussion about participation. The article discusses how participation in publicly funded cultural institutions can be designed to contribute to this.

Keywords

Diversität/diversity, Entwicklungsprozesse/development, transformation, Kulturvermittlung/audience development, art education, Sozialer Zusammenhalt/social cohesion

Einführung

Die einen machen Kunst, präsentieren eine Ausstellung, zeigen eine Aufführung, die anderen sollen teilhaben. In Kunst und Kultur ist der Begriff der Teilhabe regelmäßig von den Akteuren her gedacht, die ihre – meist öffentlich geförderten – Angebote zum Publikum bringen

* vosse@kulturforschung.de
** haselbach@kulturforschung.de

Journal of Cultural Management and Policy, 2024/2, pp. 91–105
doi 10.14361/zkmm-2024-0205

möchten. Oftmals beinhaltet so verstandene Teilhabe kaum mehr als die Rezeption des Kunstprodukts. Auch, wo Teilhabe interaktiv verstanden wird, setzten die Kunstschaffenden als Experten den Rahmen dafür, was mit welchem Ziel geteilt wird, und welche Voraussetzungen erfüllt werden müssen, um teilhaben zu können.

So verstandene, von den institutionellen Strukturen der Kunst- und Kulturproduktion her gedachte Teilhabe ist das Programm von Audience Development, bei dem es um die Rekrutierung von (zahlendem) Publikum geht. Nimmt man hingegen den im Wort Teilhabe liegenden Anspruch ernst, dann soll es hier um die gemeinsame Produktion von Bedeutung, um die Ko-Produktion von Sinn durch die Anwesenden gehen. Erst dann fällt die entscheidende Schranke zwischen der kulturellen Institution, die teilhaben lässt, und einem Publikum, das dann zum Ko-Produzenten wird.

Im Beitrag argumentieren wir, dass die geförderte Kunst und Kultur mit von der Institution her gestalteten Teilhabekonzepten hinter den Möglichkeiten und auch entstehenden Standards von Teilhabe als offenem Ko-Kreationsprozess zurückbleibt. In Teilhabe liegen Chancen, sie kann einen Beitrag zur Bewältigung oder wenigstens Fokussierung und vielleicht schrittweisen Bearbeitung der multiplen Krisen leisten, in denen wir uns als Gesellschaft befinden. Immer braucht die Krisenbewältigung andere Strategien als die, aus deren Verfolgung die Problemlagen entstanden sind, sie müssen gefunden werden. Zudem werden zunehmend Probleme mit der demokratischen Verfasstheit unserer Gesellschaft spürbar, immer mehr Menschen wenden sich von demokratischen Institutionen ab. Schließlich bietet kulturelle Teilhabe Raum für Selbstwirksamkeit und stärkt so gesellschaftliche Handlungsressourcen in einer von Fremdversorgung geprägten Konsumgesellschaft.

Der Ansatz einer passiven Quasi-Teilhabe als Publikum ist angesichts dieser Gemengelage und vor der unübersehbaren Notwendigkeit, gemeinschaftlich zu veränderten Werten und Praktiken zu kommen, obsolet, was im Folgenden argumentiert und begründet wird. Dass kulturelle Teilhabe ein wertebasiertes Miteinander fördern und so Demokratie stabilisieren und zudem gesellschaftliche Handlungsfähigkeit aktivieren helfen kann, ist eine Hoffnung vieler und dies beflügelt die Diskussion um Teilhabe. Ob die Teilhabe, wie sie in geförderten Kultureinrichtungen oft betrieben wird, solches schon leisten kann, wird folgend diskutiert.

Teilhabe in der Angebots-Kultur

Die Programmplanung in öffentlich geförderten Kultureinrichtungen folgt in der Regel vier Einflussgrößen: Erstens ist ein öffentliches Mandat zu erfüllen, das sich aus den Konditionen der Förderung ergibt. Zweitens gibt es im Betrieb Erfahrungswerte und Einschätzungen dazu, was ein Ziel-Publikum interessiert. Drittens erfolgt die Programmierung top down nach den Präferenzen der Entscheidungsbefugten und viertens ist sie von den Kapazitäten des Betriebs beeinflusst. Diese Einflussgrößen können in Widerspruch zueinander geraten, woraus sich unintendierte Effekte für die Programmierung ergeben können. In Bezug auf das hier fokussierte Thema Teilhabe stellt sich die Frage nach der Beziehung von Programm-Auftrag, wie er in der Kultureinrichtungen verstanden und umgesetzt wird, und den diversen Publikumsinteressen.

Wo Programmplanung in diesem Bezugsfeld verläuft, ist Beteiligung nicht per se vorgesehen. Die Planungsprozesse sind nicht nur wie beschrieben stark determiniert, sondern auch langfristig festgelegt. In den Leitungsebenen von öffentlichen Kultureinrichtungen sind Prinzipien teilhabeorientierter Planung nicht strukturell verankert, entsprechende Prozesse stehen meist noch am Anfang, wenn sie überhaupt im Blick sind. Hinzu kommt, dass sich in den Leitungspositionen die sich verändernde Demographie des Publikums in Deutschland noch kaum niederschlägt, so dass zu Interessen, Bedarf oder Wünschen jenseits des klassischen Kulturpublikums kaum Erfahrungen bei den Entscheidenden abrufbar sind. Es herrscht, wie in anderen gesellschaftlichen Führungsstrukturen, ein Gender Gap; Menschen mit Migrationsgeschichte sind im Vergleich zu ihrem Anteil an der Bevölkerung ebenfalls stark unterrepräsentiert (SCHMIDT 2019).

Der ganz überwiegende Teil der öffentlichen Kulturförderung fließt in große, traditionelle Kulturinstitutionen, die an einem klassischen oder auch bildungsbürgerlichem Kulturverständnis orientiert sind. Projektförderungen, die naturgemäß weniger stark dieser Tradition verpflichtet sind, liegen im unteren einstelligen Prozentbereich der Kulturförderung. Zwar ist dieser Anteil in den letzten Jahren als Reaktion auf Kritik an der Engführung in der Förderpolitik gewachsen, er bleibt jedoch relativ gesehen verschwindend. Das ist umso erstaunlicher, da das Interesse an klassischen Kulturangeboten in der Bevölkerung gering ist, wie der Relevanzmonitor Kultur (RELEVANZMONITOR 2023) nachdrücklich belegt.

Laut Relevanzmonitor interessieren sich 1/5 bis gut 2/5 der Bevölkerung nicht für Theater (21%), Oper & Tanz (44%) oder klassische Konzerte (37%). 1/3 der Befragten gab an, sich von den Angeboten nicht angesprochen zu fühlen. Diese Zahlen machen unübersehbar, was in der Kulturforschung bereits bekannt ist, aber kein politisches Gehör findet: Das klassische Kulturangebot interessiert weite Teile der Bevölkerung nicht, solche Angebote treffen nur bei bestimmten Gruppen auf Interesse, vor allem bei älteren Personen mit hohem Bildungsstand, ein Merkmal, das oft mit überdurchschnittlichem Einkommen korreliert.

Der Relevanzmonitor hat auch gezeigt, dass eine große Anzahl Menschen in Deutschland eine Zugangsbarriere zu traditionellen Kultureinrichtungen erleben, 1/4 fühlen sich fehl am Platz, 2/3 wissen nicht, oder glauben nicht zu wissen, wie man sich an solchen Kulturorten angemessen verhalten soll. Hohe und die soziale Schichtung übergreifende Zustimmungswerte für das öffentliche Engagement in der Kulturförderung widersprechen diesen Befunden nicht. Solche Zustimmung reflektiert nicht zwingend Interesse an aktivem Kulturverhalten, sondern teils sozial gewünschtes Antwortverhalten, teils den Optionsnutzen, also das Interesse an der Verfügbarkeit von kulturellen Angeboten, auch wenn man sie derzeit nicht nutzen möchte – und dies womöglich auch nicht tun wird. So haben 45 Prozent der im Relevanzmonitor Befragten angegeben, dass sie noch nie oder zuletzt vor fünf Jahren eine Theateraufführung besucht haben. Gleichzeitig stimmen 76 Prozent eher bzw. voll und ganz zu, dass Theaterhäuser mit öffentlichen Geldern gefördert werden sollen.

Mangelndes Interesse an kulturellen Angeboten wird in der Kulturpolitik traditionell auf externe, nicht in der Kultur liegende Zugangshürden zurückgeführt, immer wieder werden diese vor allem in den Eintrittspreisen gesehen. Hier ansetzende Maßnahmen sind einfach umzusetzen und erfordern keine grundsätzlichen Veränderungen. Wo an den Preisen angesetzt wird, kommt es allerdings nicht zwangsläufig zu einem Anstieg der Kulturnachfrage. Jüngst hat die Stadt Leipzig mit einem Programm „pay what you can" diese Erfahrung machen müssen.

Förderungen für die Kulturarbeit von freien Trägern und Kunstschaffenden erfolgen zu weiten Teilen projektförmig. Publikumsinteressen oder Teilhabekonzepte sind auch hier bei der Beurteilung der Förderfähigkeit von Antragsvorhaben kein strukturell verankertes Kriterium. Vielmehr werden meist kunstinterne Kriterien für die kulturelle Projektförderung angelegt, daneben sollen Projekte immer wieder neu, innovativ sein, dieses Kriterium wird in der Regel nicht qualitativ beschrieben, bezieht sich somit implizit ebenfalls auf die systemeigenen Qualitätskriterien. Viele Geldgeber erwarten darüber hinaus, dass Projekte nach der Förderung wirtschaftlich eigenständig weitergeführt werden – in einer durch Förderung geprägten Kulturlandschaft mit entsprechend geringer Zahlungsbereitschaft ist dies meist eine Illusion, die Antragstellende notgedrungen bedienen, die aber für alle Beteiligten kaum glaubhaft ist.

Viele soziale Projekte entstehen im Austausch mit Adressaten, nehmen Bedürfnisse oder Interessen Dritter in den Blick. Aber zwischen Kultur und Sozialem besteht eine Zuständigkeitsbarriere, die institutionell nur in der Soziokultur nicht besteht. Hier und in der Kulturproduktion von freien Trägern und Kunstschaffenden wird teilweise in öffentlichen Räumen gearbeitet, also Räumen, die weniger Zugangsbarrieren aufweisen und in denen sich Publika auch zufällig einfinden. Zwar kann dies auch schlicht aus dem Mangel an erschwinglichen Räumen heraus entstehen, zweifellos ist jedoch, dass eine solch niedrigschwellige Teilhabemöglichkeit in diesen Produktionsstrukturen häufiger als in der Arbeit von Kultureinrichtungen hergestellt wird. Trotzdem ist es auch im Bereich der Soziokulturförderung bisher nicht systematisch gelungen, Grade der Teilhabe zu definieren und in die Bewertungskriterien zu heben.

Zusammenfassend lässt sich sagen: In der geförderten Kultur wird Teilhabe verbreitet umgesetzt als Audience-Development und setzt nicht konsequent bei der Schaffung von Teilhabemöglichkeiten an, sondern bei der Ansprache von potentiellem Publikum für top-down definierte kulturelle Inhalte. Die Frage, ob sich das Publikum für diese Angebote interessiert, liegt nicht im Fokus der Angebotsformulierung. Institutionelle Kulturförderung setzt keine Publikumsbeziehungen voraus, Anreize durch die Förderpolitik werden nicht gesetzt. Vielmehr wird in der Förderung meist stillschweigend akzeptiert, dass z.B. in den darstellenden Künsten das Publikumsinteresse immer weiter abnimmt, trotz aller Bemühungen. Um dies zu sehen, muss man nur die Theaterstatistik des Deutschen Bühnenvereins (DBV jährlich) über einen längeren Zeitraum betrachten. Probleme für die Kulturbetriebe entstehen hierdurch nicht: Abnehmende Ticketeinnahmen werden durch zunehmende Förderung kompensiert.

Teilhabewünsche und -standards im Wandel

In den letzten Jahrzehnten haben sich Wünsche und Erwartungen an Teilhabe stark verändert, nicht nur im Kulturbereich, sondern auch in der Stadtentwicklung, im Gesundheitswesen, im Bildungsbereich (DIEHL 2017). Top-Down angelegte Verfahren sind zunehmend nicht akzeptiert, was Politik unter Druck setzt. Die Entwicklung des Internets zu einem Medium, was, neben Information und Unterhaltung zu bieten, allen Menschen mit Zugang auch ermöglicht, selbst Content zu teilen, hat diese Verschiebung von Teilhabewünschen und Standards stark angetrieben.

Im Web 2.0, namentlich in Chat-Foren, Blogs und Sozialen Medien, gibt es sehr niedrigschwellige Teilhabemöglichkeiten. Menschen können hier ihre Sicht auf Entwicklungen und Problemlagen formulieren, ihr Wissen teilen, für andere sichtbar machen und in den Austausch treten. Direkte öffentliche Meinungsäußerung ist auf Basis dieser Technik zu einer verbreiteten Normalität geworden, auch die Content-Produktion ist hierdurch demokratisiert. Manchmal bleibt solche Teilhabe im digitalen Raum Meinungsäußerung, führt nicht zu Interaktion und Erleben. Zudem begünstigt dieser Raum in besonderer Weise die Entstehung von Filterblasen, Radikalisierung, Verschwörungstheorien. Die Abschließung in je eigene Echoräume sind eine Gefahr, die bei der Betrachtung der Teilhabemöglichkeiten digitaler Medien nicht außer Acht gelassen werden kann (PAAL/HENNEMANN 2017).

Das Internet hat auch neue Möglichkeiten der Einflussnahme von Konsumenten auf die Produktgestaltung hervorgebracht, eine Form der Teilhabe, die bis dahin in wenigen personenbezogenen Leistungen üblich war, wie Haarschnitt oder Maßschneiderei. Jedoch bleibt das so genannte Prosuming, also die definierte Einflussnahme an bestimmten Produktionsschritten bei z.B. Turnschuhen oder Autos, in einer kapitalistischen Logik verhaftet und dient eher der Kundenbindung durch Angebote für eine vermeintliche Individualisierung von Produkten, nicht aber der Ermächtigung und Befähigung.

Teilhabe ist ein meritorisches Gut, konstitutiv für das Entstehen demokratischer Gesellschaften und demokratiestabilisierend in gesellschaftlichen Entwicklungs- und Aushandlungsprozessen. Wie unverzichtbar es ist, dass Teilhabe gelernt wird, wird an den andauernden Auswirkungen von undemokratischen Politiksystemen auf das zivilgesellschaftliche Gefüge einer Gesellschaft sichtbar. Zu beobachten ist dies u.a. an der unterschiedlichen Entwicklung von Strukturen des Dritten Sektors in West- und Ostdeutschland (GENSICKE et al. o.J.: 17 ff.).

Eine weitere Entwicklung, die großen Einfluss auf gesellschaftliches Verständnis und Praxis von Teilhabe hat, ist die beschleunigte Verbreitung von identitätspolitischen Strömungen. Das zeigt sich im rechten wie im linken politischen Spektrum. In rechts verorteten politischen Milieus sind Abgrenzungen gegen vermeintlich Fremde ein altes Thema, Identität ist hier mit Herkunft verknüpft und mit ethnisch konnotierten Zeichen verbunden. Die sich verbreitende Angst vor Migration, die bis ins Wählerverhalten hineinwirkt, zeigt, dass dieses Thema soziale Kraft gewinnt. Im linken Spektrum herrscht die Betonung sexueller und sozialkultureller Identitäten vor. Sie wird dann für den sozialen Zusammenhalt problematisch, wenn solche Identität als ein exklusiver Zugang zu besonderen Wirklichkeiten und Wirklichkeitswahrnehmungen verstanden wird, wenn es also nicht mehr um Anerkennung, sondern um Abgrenzung geht (EL-MAFAALANI 2019: 45). Das so genannte Othering, also die Distanzierung von anderen Gruppen, um die eigene Normalität zu bestätigen, kennzeichnet einen solchen identitären Übergang.

Von beiden Seiten führt identitätspolitische Radikalisierung zu einem Auseinanderfallen in Kulturen, die ihre je eigenen symbolischen Ausdrucksformen verlangen. So entstehen immer mehr Subkulturen, auch in der Mitte der Gesellschaft; ein verbindendes Wertefundament wird aus solcher Perspektive negiert, verliert an Haltekraft. Pluralität, die Koexistenz von Orientierungen erscheint aus dieser Perspektive als Gefährdung von Identität. Wokeness, von der Aufmerksamkeit für Diskriminierung zu einem Mittel der Darstellung moralischer Überlegenheit verkehrt, trägt, als eine identitätspolitische Gestimmtheit vor allem in der Linken, mittlerweile zu solchen Abschließungs- und Abgrenzungstendenzen bei. Da, wo Teilhabe dem Skandalisierungspotential sozialer Medien ausgesetzt ist, wird sie unter diesem Druck zum Risiko: Wer eine Position vertritt oder sich öffentlich exponiert, läuft Gefahr, einen Shitstorm abzubekommen.

Derweil ermutigen Diskurse des Postkolonialismus marginalisierte Gruppen, eigene Themen und kulturelle Ausdrucksformen zu erarbeiten und sichtbar zu machen. Hierin kann man die andere Seite der Wokeness sehen, in der ein Feingefühl entsteht, einmal mehr zu überlegen, bevor eine Erscheinung oder Praxis zur gesellschaftlichen Normalität ausgerufen wird, an die es sich anzugleichen gilt (DYK 2019: 28). Derweil ist in diesen Entwicklungen, in der Entstehung künstlerischen Ausdrucks aus identitätspolitischen Impulsen, auch angelegt, dass sich die potentiellen Teilhabegruppen verkleinern. So gibt es zunehmend auch im analogen Raum Filterblasen, die durch Kultur nicht verbunden, sondern erzeugt werden.

Kulturinstitutionen könnten hier einen Unterschied machen, zumindest wenn sie Wünsche und Erwartungen des Publikums aufnehmen. Der schon zitierte Relevanzmonitor Kultur zeigt: 80 Prozent der Befragten erwarten, dass Theaterhäuser ein Treffpunkt für Menschen sind. Das ist im eigentlichen Sinn nichts Neues, ist doch die Entstehung der bürgerlichen Kulturinstitutionen auch von dem Impuls geprägt, sich in Gesellschaft zu zeigen und zu spiegeln. Überraschend, ist, dass aus einer repräsentativen Bevölkerungsgruppe ein so großer Anteil diese Erwartung an klassische Kultureinrichtungen hat, derweil sie – wie oben dargestellt – von dieser Gruppe kaum oder nicht genutzt werden.

Die gute Nachricht ist also: Es gibt noch Wünsche an Kultureinrichtungen. Menschen wollen sich treffen und sich über ein gemeinsames kulturelles Erleben austauschen. Jedoch passiert dieser Austausch der Anwesenden nicht automatisch, es muss dafür ein Raum geschaffen werden, als Teil der kulturellen Teilhabe. Auch stellt sich die Frage, ob die von den Befragten bestätigte Vorstellung von Kulturorten als Treffpunkte der sozialen Realität standhält – oder ob der Austausch über das Kulturerleben eher im Nachgang mit Dritten aus dem eigenen Lebensumfeld stattfindet und der Distinktion dient. So erklärt die so genannte Super Star Theorie, warum so viele Menschen die selben Stücke, Musikgruppen, Filme präferieren: Dies diene der Vergewisserung einer positiven Gruppenidentität (CRAIN / TOLLISON 2002).

Sozialer Austausch zwischen Menschen scheint nicht ohne weiteres zu entstehen, davon zeugen der – mit Corona nochmals gestiegene – Mangel an Kontakt und die entstehenden psychischen Belastungen. Auch die oben angesprochenen politischen Verwerfungen rufen nach Austausch, nach menschlicher Begegnung, die die Kraft entfalten kann, jene durch identitätspolitischen Populismus entstandene Schranken abzubauen. Schließlich braucht es Kommunikation zwischen Menschen, um neues Wissen zu verbreiten und zur Anwendung zu bringen. Angesichts multipler gesellschaftlicher Krisen geht die Bedeutung von sozialem Austausch mehr denn je über Fragen der Sozialhygiene hinaus und wird zu einer Überlebensfrage. Die gesellschaftliche Verbreitung von Informationen betreffend hat Mark Granovetter die Bedeutung von so genannten weak ties erkannt und beschrieben (GRANOVETTER 1973). Seine Theorie verdeutlicht einmal mehr, dass der Austausch zwischen Menschen mit wenigen sozialkulturellen Gemeinsamkeiten fruchtbarer für den Informationsaustausch ist, da sie über maximal unterschiedliche Wissensbestände verfügen.

Ansätze der Weiterentwicklung von Publikumsbeziehungen / Teilhabe in der Kultur

Kunst und Kultur sind weder Therapieersatz noch Substitut für Politik. Sie haben eine gesellschaftliche Rolle, und diese wandelt sich mit sich verändernden sozialen, ökonomischen und ökologischen Bedingungen. Welche Konzeptionen und Praktiken der Teilhabe angesichts der dargestellten Veränderungen entstehen, was das bedeutet und wo es Transformationswiderstände gibt, ist Gegenstand der folgenden Überlegungen.

Um Teilhabe (besser) zu verankern, sind zwei Ansatzebenen möglich. Es kann in der Kultureinrichtung gehandelt werden, das ist eine Frage des Managements. Es kann teilhabeorientiertes Handeln durch Vorgaben, Förderentscheidungen oder Förderbedingungen unterstützt oder zum Standard gemacht werden, das ist eine Aufgabe von Kulturpolitik.

Auf managerialer Ebene erfordert die Orientierung auf Teilhabe eine Umkehrung: Frage ist nicht mehr, was aus der Sicht der Organisation das Angebot sein soll, sondern ein Angebot muss konsequent vom Publikum her gestaltet werden. Das ist ein tiefgreifender Eingriff in die Organisationspraxis, der auch von Fördermittelgebern unterstützt werden muss, um zu funktionieren. Denn erforderlich ist dafür, Interessen und Bedürfnisse des Publikums zu kennen, und diese Kenntnis muss schrittweise aufgebaut werden, was Ressourcen bindet. Erforderlich ist auch, dem Publikum nicht nur die Wahl zwischen verschiedenen Programmoptionen einzuräumen, denn ein Kulturbesuch ist noch nicht Teilhabe. Hier startet die Reise erst und an welchen Stellen Entscheidungsmacht abgegeben, wo und wie die Basis für Entscheidungen über das, was im jeweiligen Kulturbetrieb passiert, verbreitert wird, lässt sich nicht mit einem Standardrezept lösen.

In einigen Theatern werden Bemühungen sichtbar, sich dieser Herausforderung zu stellen. Immer mehr Theater arbeiten punktuell mit dem Format der Bürgerbühne, in dem Bewohner zusammen mit dem ganzen Theaterapparat Geschichten und Erfahrungen zur Aufführung bringen können. In der Schweiz gibt es Experimente mit Teamleitungen am Theater, um auf der Ebene von Organisationsstrukturen Vielfalt zu stärken und Theater für diverse gesellschaftliche Realitäten zu öffnen. Im Thalie Theater in Hamburg wurden Stellen für Diversitätsreferenten eingerichtet als Instrument, das Teilhabe als Querschnittsthema im Theater verankern soll.

Der Wandel von Organisationsstrukturen berührt zwangsläufig Interessen und Privilegien und ist somit ein herausfordernder Prozess, der oftmals auch viel Widerstand hervorruft. Er kann jedoch nicht übersprungen werden, denn solange sich in Kulturinstitutionen die Vielfalt einer durch Migration und soziale Differenzierung geprägten Gesellschaft nicht auch in den Personal- und Führungsstrukturen abbildet, so lange ist es auch nicht möglich, den Kreis der Teilhabe über einen traditionellen Besuchskreis hinaus auszuweiten. Positiv gesagt: Gesellschaftliche Vielfalt muss sich in den institutionellen Strukturen der Kultureinrichtungen abbilden. In der Kultureinrichtung, ihrem Personal und ihren Entscheidungsgremien müssen Erfahrungswelten unterschiedlicher sozialer Kreise vertreten sein (EL-MAFAALANI 2019: 43). Erst dann sind Kompetenzen verfügbar und können abgerufen werden, um unterschiedliche gesellschaftliche Gruppen zu erreichen, ihre Angebotswünsche als legitim anzuerkennen und kommunikative Wege zu ihnen und von ihnen zur Kultureinrichtung zu ebnen. Erst dann also kann sich eine nachhaltige Teilhabepraxis entwickeln.

Ein weiterer möglicher Schritt zu mehr Teilhabe liegt für Kultureinrichtung darin, laienkulturelle Praktiken in der jeweiligen Kunstsparte in die Aufmerksamkeit zu nehmen. Laienkultur geht über den Kulturbesuch hinaus, ist kulturelles Handeln. Sie entsteht nicht als Produkt für Dritte, für Kulturbesucher, sondern als eigener kultureller Ausdruck davon, was Menschen selbst künstlerisch und kulturell tun, ausdrücken wollen, zunächst unabhängig von gesellschaftlicher Herkunft. Natürlich kann auch laienkulturelle Praxis ihre eigenen Abschließungstendenzen haben, aber als kreatives Tun in Gemeinschaft und als kulturelle Ermächtigung ist sie unzweifelhaft.

Die Potentiale von Laienkultur für Teilhabe lassen sich anhand von Beispielen verdeutlichen. Laienchöre sind weit verbreitet, es gibt sie in unterschiedlichen Organisationstiefen in einem weiten Praxisfeld. Solche Chöre gibt es auch in migrantischen Communities, als Verbindung zur eigenen Musiktradition. Es gibt auch sehr erfolgreiche Projekte, die Chöre unterschiedlicher kultureller Traditionen zusammenbringen, sie eröffnen eine weitere Ebene der Teilhabe und des kulturellen Lernens voneinander, die sich potentiell auf Publika ausdehnt. Auftritte der Laienkultur finden an ganz unterschiedlichen Orten statt, zu denen es weniger oder zumindest andere Zugangsschwellen gibt als zur traditionellen Kultureinrichtung. Umgekehrt kann ein solcher Auftritt in einem

Theater natürlich auch ein Anlass sein, Menschen für einen Erstbesuch zu gewinnen – dann ist die Ansprache gelungen und es kann etwas daraus folgen.

Allgemeiner gesprochen ist die Emanzipation der Rezipienten und Rezipientinnen ein Ziel von Teilhabe in der Kultur. Die Legitimität ihrer Bedürfnisse muss anerkannt werden und diese Haltung muss Movens von Kulturmanagement werden. Laienkultur kann als ein Einstieg in die Welt symbolischer Bedeutungen und ästhetischer Praxen verstanden werden. Aufgabe einer Kultureinrichtung kann nicht sein, exklusive und vielleicht elitäre Räume zu schaffen und zu erhalten, sondern Menschen auch im Alltag, im beruflichen Kontext, in ihren ästhetischen und kulturellen Selbstverständnissen abzuholen. Abzuholen zu einem ko-kreativen Prozess, denn in ihm realisiert sich Teilhabe.

Ein solches Herangehen steht im Gegensatz zum Selbstverständnis vieler Einrichtungen der geförderten Kultur, somit zum kulturpolitischen Paradigma. Immer noch wird in manchem Kulturdiskurs der Künstler als genialer Schöpfer gefeiert. Der gesellschaftliche Kontext, in dem Kunst entsteht, und der konkrete Beitrag von Infrastruktur, Materialinnovation oder technischer Entwicklung als Voraussetzung und Inspiration für Kunstschaffen, fällt aus diesem Bild heraus In solchem Verständnis kann Publikum keine andere als eine passive Rolle einnehmen. Es wird nicht das Subjekt wahrgenommen, es nimmt nicht Teil, sondern empfängt, akzeptiert – allerdings nur, wenn es auch kommt.

Dass es auch anders geht, verdeutlichen derweil viele künstlerische Projekte, bisher meist solche, die außerhalb traditioneller Kultureinrichtungen entstehen. Das soziokulturelle Zentrum Kulturfabrik in Hoyerswerda hat nach der Wende zusammen mit vielen städtischen Akteuren den Prozess der städtischen Schrumpfung und die damit verbundenen Abrisse von Häusern mit einer Reihe von künstlerischen Projekten begleitet. Sie setzten im Kern auf die Initiative der Bewohner und regten ihre Auseinandersetzung mit den Umbrüchen der eigenen Lebensumgebung an. Nicht für sie, sondern durch sie entstand die künstlerische Praxis und entstand das künstlerische Produkt. Als sehr bekannt gewordenes Beispiel dafür sei ‚Eine Stadt tanzt' genannt. Auch in den sich entleerenden ländlichen Räumen, meist im Osten des Landes gelegen, gibt es beeindruckende Beispiele von teilhabeorientierten künstlerischen Projekten, wie das Projekt ‚Dorf macht Oper' im Brandenburgischen Klein Leppin. Unmittelbar entsteht durch solche Praxis eine andere Sicht auf Kunst, die scharfe Trennung zur Laienkunst wird in Frage gestellt, mittelbar wird der Diskurs um den gesellschaftlichen Kunstbegriff befruchtet. Ein Erfolgsfaktor dieser beiden Kunstprojekte ist die Befähigung der Mitwirkenden durch gut ausgebildete Kunstschaffende.

Hier liegt einer der Übergänge zu kulturpolitischen Aufgaben, die Ausbildung von Kunstschaffenden ist eine Aufgabe, die kaum ohne öffentliche Gelder zu bewerkstelligen ist, wenn sie nach Begabung zugänglich bleiben, also teilhabeoffen sein soll. Wenn es jedoch um öffentliche Kulturförderung im engeren Sinne geht, ist diese ganz überwiegend nicht am Ziel der Teilhabe ausgerichtet, bzw. macht sie die Beförderung von Teilhabe in der Kultur nicht zum Förderkriterium. Ohne eine Änderung von Förderbedingungen und Anreizen fördert sie somit tendenziell den Status quo und setzt zumindest dem traditionellen Verständnis von Teilhabe als passiver Rezeption nichts entgegen. Expliziten Raum für Teilhabe schaffen Förderstrukturen der Soziokultur. In den letzten Jahren sind weitere Programme entstanden, in denen kulturelle Befähigung und eigener kultureller Ausdruck gefördert werden, dies zumeist im Kontext von ländlicher Entwicklung. Die hier eingesetzten Fördergelder jedoch sind in der Regel Projektförderungen und können so nur selten Strukturen schaffen oder unterhalten.

Mangelnde Teilhabemöglichkeiten tragen dazu bei, dass mit Kulturmitteln immer noch vor allem Besserverdienende subventioniert werden. Das ist bekannt und in der Literatur zum Kulturmanagement auch immer wieder kritisiert worden, es ändert sich bisher aber nicht. Denn solche Kritik trifft auf mächtige Gegner in der Lobby der traditionellen Kultureinrichtungen, auch wenn ‚Kultur für alle' seit Jahrzehnten ein nie bezweifelter, aber ebenso wenig zur Realität gewordener Grundsatz kulturpolitischer Programmatik ist. Das könnte anders sein: Förderung empfangende Kultureinrichtungen müssen stärker gefordert werden, Teilhabe zu ermöglichen. In einem ersten Schritt könnte dies in Zielvereinbarungen verankert werden. Die Verwendung öffentlicher Mittel hat generell das Ziel, zur Wohlfahrtsproduktion beizutragen, das sollte auch für Kulturförderung anhand geeigneter, messbarer Indikatoren vereinbart und nachvollzogen werden. Zu solchen Indikatoren darf auch gehören, die gesellschaftliche Vielfalt in der Personal-, wichtiger noch: der Führungsstruktur zu spiegeln.

Neben den Zugangsbarrieren für Publika gibt es ebensolche Barrieren und Exklusionsmechanismen für Kunstschaffende. In Ausschreibungen und den Auswahlprozessen sind die ausschlaggebenden Kriterien in der Regel das anhand formeller Ausbildung dargestellte Expertentum und ein auf die Kunstwelt bezogener Referenzrahmen. Eine Anonymisierung von Bewerbungen und Anträgen, wie in anderen Disziplinen üblich, gibt es hier noch kaum. Diese institutionellen Strukturen insbesondere der projektbezogenen Kulturförderung verhindern bzw. erschweren so Vielfalt und sind wenig durchlässig.

Fazit

Das gesellschaftliche Verständnis von Teilhabe ist im Wandel, in vielen öffentlich geförderten Kultureinrichtungen ist eine Entwicklung mit diesem Wandel noch nicht vollzogen, es überwiegt die Produktion von kulturellen Angeboten, für die Publika geworben werden. Hinzu kommt, dass viele Bevölkerungsgruppen kaum erreicht werden, Angebote häufig nur von einem gesellschaftlichen Ausschnitt wahrgenommen werden. Zugespitzt: Kulturförderung bringt weniger Teilhabe sondern mehr die Musealisierung eines bildungsbürgerlichen Kanons hervor.

Dies hat zum einen personelle Gründe, die auch mit der Fortführung – um nicht zu sagen: Verteidigung – von Interessen und Privilegien zusammenhängen. Es wirkt auch die Trägheit der Organisation, deren eingespielte Routinen zu ändern zusätzlicher Energie und auch neuer Kompetenzen bedarf; beides muss erstmal mobilisiert werden. Und es wirkt das Fördersystem selbst, das weder konsequent Anreize setzt, um Teilhabe zu fördern, noch Sanktionen ausspricht, wenn Teilhabestandards nicht umgesetzt werden.

Dieser Zustand ist nicht hinnehmbar. Offensichtlich ist die innewohnende soziale Ungerechtigkeit, wenn in der öffentlich geförderten Kultur der kulturelle Kanon mancher Gruppierungen kaum als Referenzpunkt auftaucht und somit kaum Anschlussstellen für kulturelle Teilhabe angelegt sind. Das konservative Audience Development scheitert hier.

Ein weiterer Grund, dies zu ändern, liegt in der gesellschaftlichen Brisanz, mit der aktuell Wertedebatten geführt werden, in der sich die Erosion eines geteilten demokratischen Wertegerüsts abzeichnet. Rödder spricht von einem bevorstehenden „politisch-kulturellen Paradigmenwechsel" (RÖDDER 2024), also einer Verschiebung dessen, was sagbar und folglich auch politisch machbar ist. Seiner Analyse nach geht diese Verschiebung auch darauf zurück, dass die geltende Hegemonie ‚ideologisch überzogen' und ‚den Rahmen des Sagbaren immer enger gezogen' hat – cancel culture statt Teilhabe-Kultur. Seine Szenarien für eine neue Hegemonie gehen davon aus, dass populistische, libertäre und undemokratische Strömungen weiter an Definitionsmacht gewinnen. In dieser zugespitzten Situation sind die großen Demonstrationen im Januar

2024, die sich gegen Positionen und Pläne von rechts artikulieren, ebenso ein Ausdruck der Polarisierung der Gesellschaft, wie sie die Position von Menschen in den öffentlichen Raum tragen, die sich sonst nicht wahrnehmbar artikulieren. Die lange gewachsene Unzufriedenheit einer rechts wählenden Minderheit mit der politischen und sozialen Ordnung wird auf diesem Weg leider nicht anerkannt und bearbeitet, sondern die Feindschaft erklärt – Teilhabe ausgeschlossen.

Derweil nimmt die ökologische Krise weiter Fahrt auf, woraus sich ein drittes Argument für eine Kultur der Teilhabe ableitet. Die ökologische Krise erfordert grundlegende Veränderungen unserer Lebens- und Wirtschaftsweise, und die soziale Grundlage für eine solche sozial-ökologische Transformation sind gemeinsam gewandelte Vorstellungen vom guten Leben. Nur auf Basis von gewandelten und geteilten Vorstellungen kommen wir voran bei der dringend benötigten Entwicklung und Verbreitung zukunftsfähiger Praxen. Damit diese entstehen, braucht es Anlässe und Räume für die Teilhabe an der Definition von Bedeutung und Sinn. Die erforderliche gesellschaftliche Transformation braucht die Mitwirkung aller: Menschen müssen Gestaltungsmacht und Selbstwirksamkeit erfahren, um sich diesem Prozess nicht ausgeliefert zu fühlen, sondern die Gestaltung tragen zu helfen. Kulturelle Teilhabe kann gesellschaftliche Handlungsfähigkeit aktivieren helfen, als Form der wechselseitigen Anerkennung, aber auch als Prozess der Selbstversicherung.

Angesichts der Krisen und ihrer absehbaren Zuspitzungen überschätzen sich öffentliche geförderte Kultureinrichtungen, wenn sie sich als Sinngeber sehen und anpreisen. Nicht Kultureinrichtungen zeigen mögliche Wege aus den multiplen Krisen auf, sondern diese müssen sich, wenn sie soziale Akzeptanz finden wollen, im Zusammenwirken verschiedener gesellschaftlicher Kräfte entwickeln. Auch auf Krisenbewältigung gerichtetes staatliches Handeln kann nur erfolgreich sein, wenn es aus der Zivilgesellschaft akzeptiert und gestützt wird. Wenn aus der geförderten Kultur Impulse für die Krisenbearbeitung hervorgehen, sind sie kaum wahrnehmbar; reichlich aber hört man die Forderung nach mehr Förderung für die Institutionen. Dass auch in der Kultur und in der Kulturförderung die problematischen Mechanismen des Wachstums verstanden und überwunden werden müssen, diese Erkenntnis steht noch aus. Erst eine Verabschiedung der Wachstumslogik macht den Blick frei, um mögliche Wege in eine sozial gerechte und ökologisch tragfähige Lebensweise innerhalb planetarer Grenzen zu suchen.

Was Kultureinrichtungen in dieser Situation können, und darauf sollten sie sich besinnen, ist Räume und Gelegenheiten zu organisieren, wo ein gemeinsames Suchen nach solchen Wegen stattfinden kann. Wobei Teilhabe nicht die Aufgabe von Kunst und Kultur ist, sondern vielmehr Teil ihrer Bedingungen: Kultur braucht gesellschaftlich getragene demokratische Strukturen und sie wird angewiesen sein auf ökologisch dauerhaft tragfähige Praxen, welche nur kollektiv entwickelt werden können. Beginnen kann dieser Umbau von Kultureinrichtungen jetzt. Denn nicht ein Mangel an Geld verhindert Teilhabe, sondern die kulturpolitische Zementierung der Verhältnisse und Machtbeziehungen in Kunst und Kultur.

Literatur

CRAIN, Mark/TOLLISON, Robert D. (2002): Consumer Choice and the Popular Music Industry: A Test of the Superstar Theory. – In: *Empirica* 29(1), 1–9.

DBV (Hg.) (jährlich): *Theaterstatistik des Deutschen Bühnenvereins.*

DIEHL, Elke (Hg.) (2017): *Teilhabe für alle?! Lebensrealitäten zwischen Diskriminierung und Partizipation.* Bonn: BpB.

DYK, Silke van (2019): Identitätspolitik gegen ihre Kritik gelesen. Für einen rebellischen Universalismus. – In: *Aus Politik und Zeitgeschichte* 69(9–11), 25–32.

EL-MAFALAANI, Aladin (2019): Alle an einen Tisch. Identitätspolitik und die paradoxen Verhältnisse zwischen Teilhabe und Diskriminierung. – In: *Aus Politik und Zeitgeschichte* 69(9–11), 41–45.

GENSICKE, Thomas et. al (o. J.): *Entwicklung der Zivilgesellschaft in Ostdeutschland. Quantitative und qualitative Befunde.* In Auftrag gegeben und hrsg. vom Bundesministerium für Verkehr, Bau und Stadtentwicklung.

GRANOVETTER, Mark S. (1973): The Strength of Weak Ties. – In: *American Journal of Sociology* 78, 1360–1380.

PAAL, Boris P./HENNEMANN, Moritz (2017): Meinungsbildung im digitalen Zeitalter. Regulierungsinstrumente für einen gefährdungsadäquaten Rechtsrahmen. – In: *JuristenZeitung* 72, 641–52.

RELEVANZMONITOR Kultur (2023): <liz-mohn-center.de/wp-content/uploads/2023/05/2023_05_31_RelevanzmonitorKultur2023_LizMohnCenter_BertelsmannStiftung-1.pdf> [24.1.2024].

RÖDDER, Andreas (2024): Das Ende der grünen Harmonie. – In: *Frankfurter Allgemeine Zeitung* (12.1.24).

SCHMIDT, Thomas (2019): Macht als Struktur- und Organisationsbildendes Konzept des Theaterbetriebes. – In: *Zeitschrift für Kulturmanagement* 5(2), 93–134.

Covid-19 and Ballet Production in Japan: The Impact of the Crisis

Covid-19 und die Ballettproduktion in Japan: Die Auswirkungen der Krise

ANNEGRET BERGMANN[*]

Freie Universität Berlin

Abstract

This article delves into the repercussions of the COVID-19 pandemic in the landscape of ballet production in Japan, with a particular focus on the experiences of the Japan Performing Arts Foundation (NBS). The paper examines the challenges faced by the NBS and other cultural organizations, shedding light on their efforts to adapt to the crisis. It explores the response of the Japanese government, particularly the financial aid programs introduced by the Agency for Cultural Affairs, and the response of artists, and argues that both government support for ballet and artist advocacy increased because of and during the COVID crisis and further describes the innovation and temporization of both.

Dieser Artikel befasst sich mit den Auswirkungen der COVID-19-Pandemie auf die Ballettproduktion in Japan, insbesondere mit den Erfahrungen der Japan Performing Arts Foundation (NBS) liegt. Der Beitrag untersucht die Herausforderungen, mit denen die NBS und andere kulturelle Organisationen angesichts der Pandemie konfrontiert waren, beleuchtet ihre Bemühungen, die Krise zu meistern und untersucht die Maßnahmen der japanischen Regierung, mit dem Fokus auf die finanziellen Hilfsprogramme des Amts für kulturelle Angelegenheiten sowie die Reaktion der Künstler darauf. Er zeigt, dass die staatliche Unterstützung für das Ballett sowie das Engagement der Künstler für mehr staatliche Unterstützung wegen und während der COVID-Krise zugenommen haben.

Keywords
cultural production, cultural organizations, cultural policy, social change, arts organizations

Introduction

In Japan, engagement in arts and culture, whether by creation or consumption, is often regarded as a private, and not a state matter, and as having little significance for society at large (KAWASHIMA 2020). Despite being declared a cultural state (*bunka kokka*) in its constitution of

[*]   a.bergmann@fu-berlin.de

1947, most people and policymakers in Japan lack the perception that culture should be actively promoted by the state (IKEDA 2010). However, in 2020, for the first time in its history, Japan allocated a substantial amount of public funds to cultural activities and institutions, revising and doubling the initial cultural budget of 2020. Nonetheless, artists' associations criticized the cultural budget and the programs it supported (BUNKA GEIJUTSU SUISHIN FŌRAMU 2021; GEIDANKYŌ 2022) demanding "structural changes in policy and an expansion of state cultural support" (LEE ET AL. 2021: 2).

This article elucidates the reasons behind this demand, its cultural and economic contexts, and its outcome, focusing on the impact of the COVID-19 pandemic and the supportive measures implemented by the Japanese government on the performing arts sector in Japan. The article argues that the Japanese government became more supportive of ballet due to COVID 19; that artists in Japan were galvanized by COVID 19 to make demands; and that the results were improvements in cultural policy, and insights into the need for more effective government support for ballet and arts in general.

My particular focus is the Japan Performing Arts Foundation, referred to here as NBS, an acronym derived from the Foundation's Japanese name, *Nihon butai geijutsu shinkōkai*, and widely known in Japan. The selection of NBS as a focus is motivated by its status as the foremost private non-profit producer of ballet and opera, on an international scale, in Japan. Further, the Tokyo Ballet was one of the most active companies during the COVID-19 pandemic. Specifically, this article explores the impact of the COVID-19 pandemic on ballet productions by NBS, alongside an examination of relief programs instituted by the Japanese government and specific implications for NBS in 2020 and 2021. It also sheds light on the characteristics of ballet productions in Japan in general, which have enjoyed little governmental financial support. Ballet in Japan is traditionally commercially produced, a situation that is generally true for the production of all art and culture in Japan. In the midst of the crisis, it became clear how little the governmental measures were tailored to the situations of artists, and that without long-term governmental support, cultural enterprises could no longer be maintained. The non-profit sector, which includes NBS as well as other small organizations and individuals with a weak financial base, play the central role in supporting culture. As these cultural organizations are dependent on admission fee revenue, diminishing audiences due to the COVID-19 restrictions, cancellations of performances, and uncertainty as to how to overcome the crisis, led to louder demands for long-term financial support tailored to the situation of cultural organizations. Demands such as these, brought about advocacy by NBS for structural changes in cultural policy in this essay, as well as advocacy by other artists and artists groups as well as expansions in state cultural financial support.

The Context and Import of the Question

The Covid crisis as a phenomenon and its impact across the arts and culture has been widely studied at a general level (DE PEUTER et al. 2023), at the level of the performing arts (CHATZICHRISTODOULOU et al. 2022; AEBISCHER/GRAY 2024), with regard to dance production outside Japan (BAYBUTT et al. 2021), and with regard to ballet production specifically, outside Japan (KAHN 2021; BATISTA et al. 2022). Japan, however, stands out in three key areas with regard to the arts before the COVID crisis. It had an especially low budget for the arts, it was characterized by extreme privatization of the sector, and in its capacity for artist advocacy was very limited. Responses to the crisis at the governmental level and at the level of the artists and their organizations in Japan in the context of one particular art form and in one organization, as represented in this essay, thus presents a specific examination of the effects of the crisis, including the opportunities it created in an especially limited and disinterested political, economic, and cultural framework. The article thus provides insights into possibilities for increased cultural funding in one sector, as well as insights into artists' responses in a particular geopolitical cultural situation. Such insights are especially valuable since government valuation of the arts has declined in many places, including the United States and German-speaking countries (KIRCHBERG/ZEMBYLAS 2022). It remains to be seen which of the changes and opportunities will survive long past COVID, but the close examination provided here can provide clues at the meso- and macro-levels of analysis for future points of relevance. This example is also noteworthy because it marks the first significant increase in financial support for artists in the history of Japanese cultural policy, which previously focused two thirds of its cultural budget on the preservation of cultural properties.

Cultural Policy in Japan

Following World War II, Japan's domestic policy primarily prioritized economic development, and it was not until 1959 that the Ministry of Education commenced subsidizing the arts. The lack of proactive measures in promoting performing arts is an enduring characteristic of Japanese cultural policy since the establishment of the modern nation-state in the latter half of the 19th century. Japanese cultural policies have stipulated that the promotion of arts and culture should only be actively pursued when stable economic conditions have been achieved. In fact, up until the 1980s, Japan did not have a true national cultural policy. Instead, professionals in the performing arts sector took the initiative to organize on their own (KAWASHIMA 2012). Private enterprises and production companies produced opera and ballet performances and engaged in the production by artists and companies from abroad, as exemplified by NBS. Government cultural policy measures, in contrast, focused support on the preservation of cultural artifacts; policymakers were seemingly reluctant to promote the performing arts at all. This is also reflected in the fact that none of the six Japanese National Theatres finance a resident company to promote the performing arts, as national theatres in other countries generally do (WILMER 2008). Against this backdrop, and with significantly less government financial support than in European countries, ballet is nonetheless produced and performed in Japan. In the next section, I take a closer look at ballet production in Japan to provide context for looking at cultural policy issues.

Ballet Production in Japan

Japanese ballet productions are predominantly characterized as semi-professional, primarily showcasing the accomplishments of ballet school pupils. Only a few, such as the Tokyo Ballet Company, manage to achieve economic viability. The ballet world is largely organized under the Japan Ballet Association (*Nihon barē kyōkai*) which was established in 1957, and which comprises more than 2500 members, including ballet dancers, choreographers, and ballet masters and mistresses (JAPAN BALLET ASSOCIATION n.d.). However, no professional qualification system, no qualifying exams or grades, nor any licensing system for ballet teachers or ballet schools and companies exists. Japan lacks official records documenting either the number of ballet studios or the percentage of the population engaged in learning ballet (ONO 2016). The ballet training program at the New National Theatre established in 2001, featuring a comprehensive two-year professional program designed for an average cohort of six young dancers, typically aged between 17 and 19 at enrollment, was the first of its kind after the establishment of the New National Theatre in 1997. Additionally, a two-year pre-professional program is offered to a maximum of six dancers, with a minimum age requirement of 15 (NEW NATIONAL THEATRE 2022). As the New National Theatre does not maintain a permanent ballet company, graduates of this program face an uncertain future similar to those who complete training at private ballet schools. This situation also highlights the government's lack of interest in providing long-term support for ballet dancers. The absence of professional qualifications and the lack of opportunities for long-term contracts with a government-funded company further illustrate the government's minimal interest in ballet.

Consistent with prevailing practices in other ballet companies like the Tokyo Ballet Company, the New National Theatre ballet company contracts dancers for one year only, rather than housing a resident *corps de ballet*, as most of the National Theatres in Europe do. The support policy for ballet adopted by the Japanese government reflects its inclination towards limited financial backing for performing arts and leaves the responsibility for productions predominantly to the private sector. Regarding subsidies, ballet companies and other performing arts groups may apply for grants from the Agency for Cultural Affairs (ACA) on an annual basis. Established in 1968, the ACA operates as an extra-ministerial bureau under the purview of the Ministry for Education, Culture, Sports, Science, and Technology. Its grant allocations are decided by a commission of experts and include decisions on the extent of financial support and its recipients. These grant programs have faced criticism for their perceived lack of clear criteria and overarching visions, with concerns raised regarding their perceived arbitrariness and dependence on the personal preferences of reviewers (KAWASHIMA 2012). Therefore, the framework for ballet productions, as defined by the above-mentioned cultural policy, primarily relies on private initiatives. Project-based funding requires new applications to be repeatedly submitted to the ACA, resulting in producers like NBS having no reliable financial support from the government. In this context, the restrictions and cancellations of performances—and thus income—due to COVID-19 measures posed significant challenges for ballet producers (TAKAHASHI 2021). The following section briefly introduces the history and production structure of NBS, situating the foundation within Japan's ballet landscape to illustrate the conditions under which the government's financial support programs could be implemented.

The Japan Performing Arts Foundation (Nihon butai geijutsu shinkokai, NBS)

In 1957, Sasaki Tadatsugu (1933–2016), the manager and impresario of the Tokyo Ballet Company founded the opera stage management organization called Japan Art Staff Inc., the predecessor of NBS. In 1960 he established the Tokyo Ballet Company to perpetuate the legacy of the Tchaikovsky Memorial Tokyo Ballet School, which had been inaugurated with the support of the Ministry of Culture of the Soviet Union in 1960 but had failed financially one year later. Sasaki aimed at institutionalizing a professional ballet ensemble in Japan and at elevating the social status of ballet dancers within the Japanese performing arts scene. Notably, in the 1960s, ballet in Japan predominantly existed more as a hobby than a professional performing art (SASAKI 2001). Consequently, most ballet troupes operated as semi-professional entities, often resulting in precarious living conditions for performers due to uncertain and irregular income, a situation that persists in the 21st century, as evidenced by a survey conducted by the Japan Council of Performers Rights and Performing Arts Organizations (*Geidankyō*) in 2021(TAKAHASHI K. 2021; Geidankyō 2022).

Before the foundation of the NBS in 1981, the Tokyo Ballet, under the management of Sasaki, had firmly established itself as a leading professional ballet company in Japan, and had also gained international acclaim. As one of the professional companies with stable, regular performances at home and abroad, the Tokyo Ballet played a central role in the Japanese ballet world. Up until the onset of the COVID-19 pandemic, the ballet company had an annual repertoire of six to ten productions, and its soloists made notable appearances on stages across the globe (NBS 2014). In 1980, due to disagreements about performances by foreign opera companies, Sasaki terminated a collaboration with Association for Music for All (*Minshu ongaku kyōkai*), an audience organization that had provided the Tokyo Ballet Company with performance opportunities and facilitated international opera productions under his management. The same year, the formerly favorable relations with the Soviet Union, which had facilitated close ties to esteemed Russian instructors for the

Tokyo Ballet and performances in Russia, turned unfavorable. In 1980, Sasaki faced suspicion of supporting the defection of Sulamith Messerer to Great Britain. Messerer had been a prominent Russian ballerina, choreographer, and primary instructor of the Tokyo Ballet (SASAKI 2001). These developments made it necessary for Sasaki to reorganize his performing arts productions, resulting in the foundation of the Japan Performing Arts Foundation, or NBS, in 1981. In 2003, operational responsibilities for NBS were transferred from Sasaki to Takahashi Norio as the new executive director.

NBS is based on three pillars: The production of ballet performances by the Tokyo Ballet Company, the presentation of performances by foreign ballet and opera companies in Japan, and the operation of the Tokyo Ballet School (NBS 2022a). In 2005, the NBS became a Designated Organization for the Promotion of Public Interest (*tokutei kōeki zōshin hōjin*), a function bestowed by the Japan's Minister of Education, Culture, Sports, Science, and Technology. As of April 1, 2011, aligning with the government's initiative to reform incorporated public interest foundations, the NBS became a Public Interest Incorporated Foundation (*kōeki zaidan hōjin*) (NBS 2022). This development facilitated solicitation of donations from both individuals and corporations.

Domestic performances of the Tokyo Ballet did and do receive financial support by the government. In 2012, however, these subsidies amounted to only 4% of its budget (TAKAHASHI 2012). According to the management of NBS, the subsidies received from the Agency of Cultural Affairs for the fiscal year 2019, which predates the onset of COVID-19, constituted 10% of its total income. In contrast, the financial support extended by the government in fiscal 2021 increased to 35% of NBS's annual income. This notable shift can be attributed to a consistent absolute subsidy amount, with the observed increase arising from reduced expenditures incurred by NBS. The inability to host international opera productions in the wake of OVID-19 led to decreased spending, thereby raising the proportion of government support to the institution, but the increase did not compensate for opera and ballet productions from overseas that had to be cancelled due to pandemic measures (TAKAHASHI 2022). When assessing changes in support for the arts in relation to COVID, one must be careful not to interpret accidental increases, which are nominal only, as real changes. It should be noted that the financial aid programs could only be applied to domestic productions. Guest performances abroad, such as those regularly given by the Tokyo Ballet and managed by NBS, as well as performances by foreign troupes and artists, were excluded from the aid packages. This shows that, although the significant increase in the cultural budget had a positive impact, it was not tailored to all areas. Nevertheless, definite positive changes in support did come about. The following section deals with NBS's experiences during the initial two years of the Covid-19 pandemic and the corresponding relief measures implemented by the government.

Governmental support programs and the Japan Performing Arts Foundation (NBS)

The PIA Research Institute annually releases data on the dimensions of the music and stage entertainment market in Japan, showing a consistent and incremental growth in this commercially driven sector since the inception of its survey in 2000. In 2019, preceding the onset of the COVID-19 pandemic, the aggregate value of the stage and music entertainment market reached 629.5 billion yen, with 205.8 billion yen attributed to the music sector and 423.7 billion yen to stage entertainment. This marked a noteworthy 7.4% increase compared to the preceding year (PIA RESEARCH INSTITUTE 2021) signifying a flourishing state commercial entertainment domain when the initial anti-coronavirus measures were implemented. In contrast, a 2021 study conducted by the Forum for the Promotion of Culture and the Arts revealed a stark decline of 58% in operating revenues in the ballet sector during fiscal year 2020 in comparison to 2019 (BUNKA GEIJUTSU SUISHIN FŌRAMU 2021). This stark contrast underscores the profound and adverse impact of COVID-19 on ballet in Japan.

On February 26, 2020, former Prime Minister Abe Shinzō issued a directive urging all theatres to voluntarily suspend performances, declaring in a press conference that these were "nonessential" (fuyō fukyū) activities (PRIME MINISTER'S OFFICE OF JAPAN n.d.). Originally intended to last for a two-week period, the situation evolved, and on April 7, a state of emergency was officially declared in Tokyo and six additional prefectures. Subsequently, on April 16, these restrictions were extended nationwide. The state of emergency persisted until May 25. 50 percent admission restrictions, which had been imposed on theatres were not lifted until September 19, 2020.

In the first month of the COVID-19 crisis, artists, dispirited by the characterization of their work by the government as nonessential, began to unite. Despite the competitive nature of the performing arts scene, collaborative efforts emerged with groups of artists submitting joint applications for Corona grants, such as ballet companies for the Art Caravan program, described below. Further, and significantly, the organization Japan Performing Arts Solidarity Network (JPASN) was established in 2020 and comprises 100 participating organizations and 20 endorsing organizations. JPASN was formed to look at ways to continue performances under pandemic restrictions, and described its mission in this way:

> Beyond our differences, we are coming together in solidarity, working together and sharing information to fight for the survival of the profession and to make sure we can safely reopen and rebuild our industry. Our goal is not just to protect the economy of the industry and the survival of individual groups, but to protect the profession as a whole and ultimately to safeguard the future of Japanese culture. (JPASN n.d.)

This clearly shows how much artists had seen themselves as being on their own, and that they had hardly expected any substantial help from the public sector to overcome the crisis. Yet now, probably for the first time, the Japanese cultural scene resonated with a unified voice, asserting that in a democratic society, socially relevant art and culture necessitate clear and fair guidelines for financial aid and, most importantly, reliable support. At the same time, the Agency for Cultural Affairs expanded the scope of its support programs aiming to reach a broader range of artists and cultural institutions than ever before.

Despite such galvanization and concomitant changes, the crisis also brought acute problems for the ballet sector. Following the late Prime Minister Abe Shinzō's call to refrain from performances on a voluntary basis, and the nationwide proclamation of a state of emergency in April, live performances became impossible for the Tokyo Ballet. In total, eight productions by the NBS had to be either canceled or postponed due to government-imposed restrictions aimed at curbing the spread of COVID-19. The canceled events were mainly productions invited from abroad, for which most of the tickets had already been sold, and for which concert halls and opera houses had already been rented by NBS. Likewise, due to travelling restrictions at home and worldwide, the ballet company had to cancel all performances abroad. Nevertheless, during the first year of the pandemic, the Tokyo Ballet Company was able to realize eight programs, canceling only two. Paradoxically, in 2021, amid the ongoing pandemic, the number of domestic performances the company produced actually increased. This unexpected increase can be attributed to the unique conditions stipulated by governmental support programs created in reaction to the crisis. Specifically, compliance with the terms of financial support programs necessitated the production of additional performances. This presented the company with other problems however, as financial aid was only granted for new programs, a requirement that was almost impossible to meet under the restrictive conditions. How NBS dealt with this situation is exemplified by the ARTS for the Future and the Art Caravan programs.

ARTS for the Future

The ARTS for the Future program received funding from the government's third supplementary budget, which was approved in fiscal year 2020 spanning from April 2020 through March 2021. This initiative consisted of subsidies aimed at fostering culture and the arts under the category of "support for the enhancement of cultural and artistic activities to overcome the Corona pandemic" (ARTS FOR THE FUTURE 2022). Projects eligible for subsidies, including performances and exhibitions, had to be executed between January 8, and December 31 of 2021. The grants were designed to bolster organizations actively involved in public performances, exhibitions, and other activities accessible to the general public, with the intention of generating ticket revenues and additional income.

The subsidy was accessible to domestic arts and culture-related organizations, as well as to the proprietors or operators of cultural facilities in Japan, excluding local public organizations. The maximum subsidy amount per organization was 25 million yen, and specific subsidy categories ranging from 6 million to 25 million yen were determined based on factors such as the number of individuals involved in performances, and the organizational size. Throughout 2021, two application periods were designated, one from the end of April to the end of May and another during September. Out of a total of 11,200 applications received, financial support was granted to 7,024 projects (ARTS FOR THE FUTURE 2022).

The primary challenge associated with this program stemmed from its restriction on using funds to finance ballet performances that had already been planned or which had necessitated postponement. A prerequisite for eligibility for this subsidy was the initiation of new projects or the introduction of innovations in performance practices. Faced with these conditions, producers and organizations, including NBS, found themselves compelled to devise creative solutions, given the impracti-cality of launching entirely new productions amidst the challenges posed by the COVID-19 pandemic. To address these seemingly incongruous additional requirements, NBS and other relevant entities adopted inno-vative measures and strategic responses. For instance, the Tokyo Ballet Company squeezed in an extra performance of The Pirate with an added behind-the-scenes tour, in order to meet the previously planned or post-poned requirement. The grant provided by the program covered 15% of the extra production's costs, and thus rendered it profitable (TAKA-HASHI 2021; YONEZU 2022).

In summary, the ARTS for the Future program diverged from pro-viding support for existing or pre-scheduled performances, which was previously deemed desirable by Takahashi Norio (TAKAHASHI 2021). Instead, the program exclusively focused on co-financing new and sup-plementary performances. Consequently, this emphasis resulted in an increased number of performances and, correspondingly, more stage opportunities for the 76 company dancers. The impact was positive for individual dancers, many of whom held side jobs such as teaching posi-tions that had been canceled during the pandemic (TAKAHASHI 2021). This showed that increased government funding for professional ballet productions could relieve dancers of the need to finance themselves with part-time jobs, which are particularly burdensome for the artists. More reliable long-term financial security for dancers and production compa-nies, by the government, could thus foster greater creativity given that artists would not have to worry as much about earning a living, but could concentrate more fully on their art instead.

In regard to governmental support for individual dancers, the second supplementary budget provided a distinct financial subsidy for freelanc-er artists with a maximum allocation of 200,000 yen. Criticisms were directed towards the program for its perceived lack of user-friendliness, primarily stemming from its nature as a subsidy intended to cover costs of artistic activities rather than a versatile financial support for such things as living expenses. Moreover, a stipulation was that the incurred expenses must exceed the maximum amount by fifty percent, compel-ling artists to expend 300,000 yen in artistic activities to qualify for the 200,000-yen financial aid. Such a requirement was particularly onerous in light of the decrease in working opportunities due to the pandemic. Notably, though members of the Tokyo Ballet company did utilize this program to procure ballet shoes and related equipment, they neverthe-less expressed a strong preference for receiving support directed towards their livelihoods (TAKAHASHI 2021). Here again the limitations of a simple formula of more government support creating better performance conditions and more public support are evident, demonstrating the need for thoughtful planning of support programs and the input of artists. Such uninformed support was attributed to the expedited development of programs coupled with a limited understanding of the scale of the arts and culture industry, as acknowledged by the Agency for Cultural Affairs itself (ACA 2022). As a consequence of the crisis, the Agency for Cultural Affairs took initiative in fiscal year 2021 by establishing the Office for Strengthening Infrastructure for Cultural and Artistic Activities (*Bunka geijutsu katsudō kiban kyōkashitsu*). This office embarked on surveys and analyses to comprehend the situation effectively, with the goal of creating opportunities for artists operating within a flexible employment system and their supporters. Despite the Agency's recognition of the imperative to address the highly volatile and precarious conditions in the production of arts and culture, concrete initiatives for implementation did not yet materialize.

Art Caravan Program

The impact of the Japanese government's support program on ballet production in Japan can also be exemplified by the Art Caravan Program. In the initial supplementary budget for fiscal year 2020, this program allocated 1.3 billion yen with the aim of revitalizing the arts sector by joining together art organizations, artists, performers, and local public organizations to organize cultural events throughout Japan (ACA 2021).

The program provided subsidies for two distinct project categories:

1. nationwide implementation of high-quality performances (large-scale performance category)
2. implementation of artistic activities in collaboration with local organizations and artists (community collaboration category)

Subsidies under the first type were contingent upon the orchestration of large-scale, high-quality performing arts performances by umbrella organizations actively advancing Japan's arts and culture. These umbrella organizations had specific prerequisites, including establishing status-of-legal-person, a documented constitution, a formal act of endowment, and internal rules setting out the organizational framework as well as an accounting infrastructure and official place of business. Projects had to be executed across a spectrum of six to twenty regions with a stipulated upper limit of 650 million yen allocated per project, as outlined in the Art Caravan guidelines of 2022 (ART CARAVAN 2022). The Association of Japanese Ballet Companies (*Nihon barē renmei*) is the umbrella organization of Japanese ballet companies. It was established in 2014 as Japan's first national organization of ballet companies and has eight members and one associate member. On behalf of its eight regular member companies, the association applied for aid under the first category of the Art Caravan Program, that is, large scale performance, and was successful in securing a comprehensive support package of 962.8 million yen for its project Ballet Brings Hope to the Nation. Recovering from the Corona Pandemic Project (HOPE JAPAN 2021). Executing a special tour called Hope Japan 2021, seven association ballet companies conducted a total of 31 performances. In fiscal 2022 the Association of Japanese Ballet Companies received 63.5 million yen from the Art Caravan program for its project Ballet Brings Hope to the Nation: Art Caravan Project by the Association of Japanese Ballet Companies. Within this framework the Tokyo Ballet again organized Hope Japan 2022 Japan National Tour and also a Nutcracker National Tour. The focus was on regions not visited on the previous tour with twelve performances in eleven cities (ART CARAVAN n.d.). Like NBS however, all members of the Association of Japanese Ballet Companies rent performance venues and work in collaboration with venue staff. In other words, the rather limited financial support for the performing arts, from the public sector, remains clear.

In response to the challenges faced by local authorities operating theatre and concert houses, including the lack of resident companies, a designated management system (*shitei kanri seido*) was instituted in 2003. The system enables local authorities to delegate management of their cultural facilities to private organizations (NISHIMATSU 2014). Private entrepreneurs and organizations contribute either full or partial financing, thereby assuming complete responsibility for ensuring profitability. This business model then signifies a partial privatization of the performing arts in public venues in Japan. The primary aim was reduction of personnel costs and outsourcing of personnel in cultural facilities (KOBAYASHI 2013). Implementation did not ensure that theatres and music halls would flourish, particularly in instances where establishments lacked adequate prior, or other funding and business expertise. The frequent turnover of management personnel, occurring every three to five years, added challenges. A substantial portion of the annual budget is allocated to venue maintenance, making it increasingly challenging, with a limited budget and increasing production costs, to produce performances that attract a sizable audience. Productions deemed less appealing result in financial losses, perpetuating a detrimental cycle characterized by insufficient funds, less attractive programs, and a diminishing audience. Further, a 2018 survey conducted by the Association of Public Theatres and Halls revealed that, in terms of professional human resources, 72.2% of respondents acknowledged inadequate reliability of qualified persons (ZENKOKU KŌRITSU BUNKA SHISETSU KYŌKAI 2020).

Despite the imposition of the *shitei kanri seido*, the Art Caravan program has demonstrated a positive impact on theatres struggling to produce high quality performances, particularly in the context of NBS. The Tokyo Ballet's performances under the Art Caravan program, spanning various locations across Japan, served to establish connections between regional theatres and halls with a highly skilled and renowned production and marketing entity, namely NBS. This combination of professional production with business knowledge and regional theatre venues resulted in more adept marketing for the performances and thus in sold-out programs at these regional venues. Testimonials from the management of these regional theatres further corroborate the success and efficacy of this initiative. For instance, Amanuma Hikaru, the Deputy Director and Director of Operations at the Yokosuka Arts Theatre, conveyed that, thanks to Art Caravan, the theatre successfully executed an expansive promotional campaign for its December 2021 Nutcracker production that would have been unfeasible under normal budget constraints. Consequently, they achieved nearly full audience capacity for the production. Similarly, the management of the Fukuyama Hall of Arts and Culture in Hiroshima Prefecture provided commendation for another 2021 Nutcracker production highlighting the program's facilitation of a comprehensive and high-level ballet performance accompanied by a full orchestra. Despite the challenges posed by the ongoing pandemic, this combination of national level expertise with local production, within the frame of Art Caravan allowed the production to attract a substantial audience, underscoring the effectiveness of Art Caravan in enhancing the cultural offerings of regional theatres.

In fact however, not all initiatives pursued by NBS in collaboration with the Association of Japanese Ballet Companies secured approval from the Art Caravan selection committees. Specifically, the envisioned All Japan Ballet Revival Gala, slated for August 2020, faced insurmountable

challenges primarily attributable to protracted decision-making processes within the administration. The intricate and multifaceted nature
of ballet productions rendered the lengthy decision timelines incompatible with the exigencies of ballet production. This example implies a mis-
alignment between administrative funding programs and the practical
needs of ballet companies.

Nonetheless, in 2020, the NBS successfully executed the triennial
event World Ballet Festival, initiated by its forerunner Arts Staff, despite
the challenging circumstances during the state of emergency in August
2021. However, leveraging the unique circumstances that permitted the
entry of foreign athletes for the Tokyo Summer Olympics, the NBS successfully navigated through various restrictions, including the closure of
Japan's borders. A total of 23 esteemed dancers from prominent foreign ballet companies participated in eight performances held in 2021
between August 13 and 22. NBS persevered, and with adaptation and
innovation, organized its triennial gala event. Despite significant economic challenges, NBS ensured continuity and maintained audiences,
which were crucial for the continued existence of the Foundation itself
(TAKAHASHI 2021).

Conclusion

This article has explored the impact of the coronavirus pandemic on the
performing arts in Japan, focusing on the years 2020 and 2021, as well
as the government's relief measures to support cultural workers. It is
worth noting that performances in 2023 have returned to pre-Corona
crisis levels. The Tokyo Ballet Company hosted a total of 97 ballet performances, including eleven overseas performances. Additionally, 24 performances featured ballet troupes from abroad, and seven showcased invited opera performances, along with three concerts. According to NBS,
their commitment to maintaining performances during the coronavirus
pandemic has paid off, allowing them to at least retain part of their core
audience. The overall structure of governmental grants and support programs has remained largely unchanged. Throughout the pandemic, the
government's policy aimed to offer broad support to individual artists
extending financial aid to both professionals and amateur artists. After
the COVID-19 period, the Japanese government reverted to supporting
professional artists and organizations. Some subsidies that proved effective during the pandemic have been extended with a modified structure.

The Art Caravan program of subsidies to umbrella organizations is one example. The system has transitioned from a handout model to a subsidy-for-deficit financial aid model, and the eligibility criteria for the subsidy has become more stringent. The positive impact of the program, established during the pandemic, is evidenced in part by the fact that NBS currently intends to leverage the subsidy system in collaboration with selected local theatres to establish cultural hubs in various regions. Nevertheless, a persistent challenge remains: the government's support is limited to specific projects and performances that require organizations to submit repeated applications. However, while the annual budget for the Agency of Cultural Affairs for the fiscal years 2020 to 2023 ranged from 106.7 to 106.1 billion yen, the budget for 2024 will be 135 billion yen, reflecting a 27.2 percent increase. Still, the prospect of sustained, dependable, and stable support for cultural production organizations like NBS remains uncertain. The voices of artists' organizations for long-term structural change might not have gotten through to the politicians in charge and might yet fade out as the days of the pandemic recede.

References

AEBISCHER, Pascale/GRAY, Karen (2024): *Pandemic Preparedness in the Live Performing Arts: Lessons to Learn from COVID-19.* The British Academy <https://ore.exeter.ac.uk/repository/bitstream/handle/10871/136395/tBA_Summary_report_published260324.pdf?sequence=1> [August 14, 2024].

ACA Agency for Cultural Affairs (2021): *Art kyaraban daikibo katsu shitsu no takai bunka geijutsu katsudō o kaku to shita āto kyaraban jigyō: saitaku jigyō* [Art Caravan Project with large-scale, high-quality cultural and artistic activities at its core list of adopted projects] <www.bunka.go.jp/shinsei_boshu/kobo/pdf/93117601_01.pdf> [June 10, 2023].

ACA Agency for Cultural Affairs (2022): *Shingata korona uirusu kansenshō no eikyō ni tomonau shogaikoku no bunka seisaku ni kan suru kenkyū: (Hōkokusho samarīban)* [Research on Structural Changes in Cultural Policies in Other Countries in Relation to the Impact of New Coronavirus Infections: (Report, Summary Version)]. Tokyo: Agency for Cultural Affairs.

ART CARAVAN (n.d.): Art kyaraban daikibō katsu shitsu no takai bunka geijutsu katsudō o kaku to shita āto kyaraban jigyō [Art Caravan project with large-scale, high-quality cultural and artistic activities at its core]. *Agency for Cultural Affairs* <www.bunka.go.jp/shinsei_boshu/kobo/92908201.html> [June 15, 2022].

ARTS FOR THE FUTURE! (n.d.): *Agency for Cultural Affairs, The Government of Japan.* <https://www.bunka.go.jp/shinsei_boshu/kobo/20210326_01.html> [May 30, 2022].

BAYBUTT, Alexandra/LEON,Anna/HAITZINGER, Nicole/KOLB, Alexandra (2021): *Dancing Through the Crisis: The Impact of Brexit Anmd Covid-19 on the UK Freelance Dance Scene.* London <https://dancingthroughcrises.wordpress.com/research-insights/> [August 15, 2024].

BATISTA, Amanda/NETO, Elmiro/BRANQUINHO, Luís/FERRAZ, Joana/ /RIBEIRO, Ricardo/FORTE, Pedro/ÁVILA-CARVALHO, Lurdes (2022): Flexibility of Ballet Dancers in COVID-19 Pandemic: A Prospective Observational Study in Portugal. – In: *International Journal of Environmental Research and Public Health* 19(15), 9235 <https://doi.org/10.3390/ijerph19159235> [August 15, 2024].

BUNKA GEIJUTSU SUISHIN FŌRAMU (2021): *Shingata korona uirusu kansenshō kakudai ni yoru bunka geijutsukai he no jindai na dageki, soshite saisei ni mukete: Chōsa hōkoku to teigen* [The devastating impact of the spread of the New Corona virus infection on the arts and culture industry, and toward Revitalization: Research Report and Recommendations]. Tokyo: Arts and Culture Forum.

CHATZICHRISTODOULOU, Maria, BROWN, Kevin/HUNT, Nick/KULING, Peter/SANT, Toni (2022): Covid-19: theatre goes digital – provocations. – In: *International Journal of Performance Arts and Digital Media* 18(1), 1–6 <https://doi.org/10.1080/14794713.2022.2040095> [August 16, 2024].

GEIDANKYŌ (2022): *Jitsuen geijutsu no saisei ni muketa teigen n ikan suru ankēto chōsa: bunseki kekka* [Survey on proposals for the revitalization of the performing arts: Analysis results]. Tokyo: Geidankyō <https://geidankyo.or.jp/archives/1856> [May 30, 2022].

DE PEUTER, Greig/OAKLEY, Kate/ TRUSOLINO, Madison (2023): The Pandemic Politics of Cultural Work: Collective Responses to the COVID-19 Crisis. – In: *International Journal of Cultural Policy* 29 (3), 377–392 <https://doi.org/10.1080/10286632.2022.2064459> [August 16, 2024].

IKEDA, Masayoshi (2010): *Bunka kokka no saisei: Bokyaku sareta rinen no fukken o motome* [Revitalization of the cultural nation: Seeking the restoration of forgotten ideals]. Tokyo: Jichitai Kenkyūsha.

JAPAN BALLET ASSOCIATION (n.d.): Japan Ballet Association. <http://www.j-b-a.or.jp/o/english_whatisjba.html> [June 9, 2022].

JPASN Japan Performing Arts Solidarity Network (n.d.) <https://www.jpasn.net/)> [June 9, 2022].

KAHN, Eva (2021): An Identity Crisis: Classical Ballet in COVID. – In: *The Texas Orator Academic-Ish* [April 26, 2021] <https://thetexasorator.com/2021/04/26/an-identity-crisis-classical-ballet-in-covid/> [August 14, 2024].

KAWASHIMA, Nobuko (2012): Corporate Support for the Arts in Japan: Beyond Emulation of the Western Models. – In: *International Journal of Cultural Policy* 18, 295–307 <https://doi.org/10.1080/10286632.2011.651132> [August 10, 2022].

KAWASHIMA, Nobuko (2020): The Development of Art Projects in Japan: Policy and Economic Perspectives. – In: *Field: A Journal of Socially Engaged Art Criticism* 15 (Winter) <http://field-journal.com/issue-8/the-development-of-art-projects-in-japan-policy-and-economic-perspectives> [August 1, 2022].

KIRCHBERG, Volker/ZEMBYLAS, Tasos (2022): Die Pandemie als Anlass: Künste und Kulturen als „gesellschaftlich irrelevanter Bereich. – In: *Journal of Cultural Management and Cultural Policy / Zeitschrift für Kulturmanagement und Kulturpolitik* 8(1), 125–142 <https://doi.org/10.14361/zkmm-2022-0106> [August 14, 2024].

KOBAYASHI, Mari (2013): Wakamono to gekijō—gekijōhō no kōzō to kadai: Dare ga ikasu hōritsu ka [Young people and the theatre: the structure and challenges of the Theatre Act and who can make use of it?]. *Bunka Keizaigaku (Cultural Economics)* 10, 1–15.

LEE, Hye-Kyung/CHAU, Karin Ling-Fung/TERUI Takao (2021): The Covid-19 crisis and 'critical juncture' in cultural policy: A comparative analysis of cultural policy responses in South Korea, Japan and China. – In: *International Journal of Cultural Policy* (June), 1–21 <https://doi.org/10.1080/10286632.2021.1938561> [May 20, 2022].

NEW NATIONAL THEATRE (2022): Barē kenshūsho gaiyō [Overview of the Ballet Training Institute]. *New National Theatre Ballet School*. <https://www.nntt.jac.go.jp/balletschool/outline/> [June 30, 2023].

NBS NIHON BUNKA GEIJUTSU SHINKŌKAI (2014): *Tōkyō Barēdan 50nen no ayumi* (Tokyo Ballet 50 Years of History). Tokyo: Nihon bunka geijutsu shinkōkai.

NISHIMATSU, Teruo (2014): Kōkyō bunka kasetsu no kanri un'ei to shitei kanrisha seido [Management and administration of public cultural facilities and the designated management system]. – In: *Geidai RAM: General Administration Course* 4, 1–15 <http://geidai-ram.jp/wp/wp content/uploads/2016/04/ram_somu_vol.4_2014.pdf> [June 25, 2023]

ONO, Sayako (2016): Ballet in Japan: Reconsidering the Westernisation of Japanese Ballet. – In: *Journal of Glocal Studies* 3, 1–24 <https://seijo.repo.nii.ac.jp/record/4036/files/glo_03_01.pdf> [August 30, 2022].

PIA RESEARCH INSTITUTE (2021): 2020nen 1gatsu no raibu entateinmento (ongaku sutēji) shijō kibo [The size of the live entertainment market in iecent years (music and stage) January–December 2020] <https://corporate.pia.jp/news/detail_live_enta20210513.html> [August 30, 2021].

PRIME MINISTER'S OFFICE OF JAPAN (n.d.): Reiwa 2nen 3 gatsu 28 nichi Abe naikaku sōri daijin kisha kaiken. [Prime Minister Abe press conference March 28, 2020] <https://www.kantei.go.jp/jp/98_abe/statement/2020/0327kaiken.html> [August 21, 2023].

SASAKI, Tadatsugu (2001): *Tatakau barē. Sugao no sutā to kanpanī no monogatari* [Fighting Ballet. The unvarnished story of a company and its stars]. Tokyo: Shinshokan.

TAKAHASHI, Kaori (2021): Geijutsuka teigi no tayōsei o fumaeta chōsa no katsuyō to keizoku (The Application and Sustainability of Artist's Survey Based on Pluralism). – In: *Bunka Seisaku Kenkyū (Cultural Policy Research)* 15, 53–63.

TAKAHASHI, Norio (2012), Executive Director of NBS. Interview with the author of this article [March 27, 2012].

TAKAHASHI, Norio (2020): Sabaibaru gēmu [Survival game]. – In: *Shin "kishō tenten" hyōryūhen* [New "Stories of ups and downs" adrift] 43 [September 2, 2020] <www.nbs.or.jp/webmagazine/series/takahashi-column/20200902-04.html> [June 10, 2023].

TAKAHASHI, Norio (2021), Executive Director of NBS. Interview with the author of this article [21 December 2021].

TAKAHASHI, Norio (2022), Executive Director of NBS. Interview with the author of this article [June 1, 2022].

YONEZU, Takayuki (2022), Production and Planning Manager, NBS. Interview with the author of this article [June 1, 2022].

ZENKOKU KŌRITSU BUNKA SHISETSU KYŌKAI (2020): *Reiwa gannendo gekijō, ongakudō nado no katsudō jōkyō ni kan suru chōsa hōkokusho* [Survey report on the activities of theatres, music halls, etc. in fiscal year 2018] <www.zenkoubun.jp/publication/survey.html> [June 10, 2023].

WILMER, Stephen E. (2008): *National Theatres in a Changing Europe*. New York: Palgrave.

CASE STUDIES

Kartographie einer Kunst- und Kulturlandschaft

Cartography of an Artistic and Cultural Landscape

SARAH KÜHNE*, THOMAS ZABRODSKY**

Forschungsgruppe Empirische Sozialwissenschaften, Fachhochschule Vorarlberg

Abstract

Ziel war es, eine Entscheidungsgrundlage für politische Maßnahmen und ggf. Anpassungen der Förderstrukturen in Vorarlberg zu schaffen. Im Fokus standen Lebens- und Einkommensverhältnisse der Kunstschaffenden, Bewertungen der Förderstrukturen sowie die Kunstrezeption durch die Bevölkerung. Die Datenerhebung umfasste sieben Interviews mit Leitungspersonen, 15 Interviews, drei Fokusgruppeninterviews und eine standardisierte Onlinebefragung mit Kunstschaffenden sowie eine Bevölkerungsbefragung. Die Ergebnisse zeigen, dass die Kunst- und Kulturszene eine systemrelevante Rolle in der Gesellschaft spielt. Eine adäquate Förderung wird von der Bevölkerung unterstützt und von Kunstschaffenden gefordert, um (exzellente) Kunst für das (anspruchsvolle) Publikum anbieten zu können. Die Ausgestaltung der Förderungslandschaft nimmt direkten und indirekten Einfluss auf die Kunstproduktion und damit auf die Fähigkeit einer Gesellschaft sich selbst im gegenseitigen Austausch reflektieren zu können.

This project aimed to create a foundation for decision-making regarding measures and potential adjustments to the funding structures in Vorarlberg. This involved socio-economic indicators, descriptions of the artists' living conditions, evaluations of funding structures and reception of art by the population. The empirical study comprised seven interviews with management personnel, 15 semi-structured interviews, three focus group interviews and one standardized online survey of artists as well as a survey of the population. The results suggest that the arts and culture scene plays a crucial role in society. Adequate funding is supported by the population and demanded by artists to offer (excellent) art to the (demanding) audience. The structure of funding landscape directly and indirectly impacts art production and thus the ability of a society to reflect on itself through mutual exchange.

Keywords

Beruf, Rolle/career, professional role; Kulturfinanzierung/fincancing the arts; Kulturproduktion/cultural production; Kulturpolitik/cultural policy; Künstler und Künstlerinnen/artists

*   sarah.kuehne@fhv.at
** thomas.zabrodsky@fhv.at

Einleitung

Die Freiheit von Kunst und Kultur ist der Wegweiser unserer Kulturpolitik. Wir verfolgen das Ziel einer aktivierenden Kulturpolitik, die den Künstlerinnen und Künstlern aus allen Sparten ebenso wie allen Bevölkerungsgruppen die Teilhabe am Kulturleben ermöglicht. Die Förderung von Kunst und Kultur sehen wir als langfristige Investition in die Gemeinschaft, denn kulturelles Leben und künstlerisches Schaffen sind wichtig für die Lebensqualität unserer Gesellschaft. (LANDESREGIERUNG VORARLBERG 2019: 75)

Dieses Zitat verdeutlicht das Ziel der Landesregierung Vorarlberg, adäquate Rahmenbedingungen für Kunstschaffende zu etablieren, um künstlerisch-schöpferisch tätig sein zu können. Dies impliziert auch die seit Jahrzehnten unveränderten prekären Einkommensverhältnisse der Kunst- und Kulturschaffenden in Vorarlberg zu verbessern (LANDES-REGIERUNG VORARLBERG 2019: 75). Als prekär wird in den Sozialwissenschaften die soziale Lage von Menschen, die Gefahr laufen, in die Armut und die damit verbundene soziale Ausgrenzung abzugleiten, betrachtet (GEIẞLER 2014). Besonders kunstschaffende Personen gehen laut Knittel (2011) einer Profession nach, die als prekär bezeichnet werden kann, *„weil sie [...] eine – nach ihrem Status – wirtschaftlich ungesicherte und – nach ihrem Habitus – „antibürgerliche" ist, [und] folglich eine Ausnahmestellung im Ensemble der bürgerlichen Professionen einnimmt"* (MÜLLER-JENTSCH 2005).

Der Ausgangspunkt des vorliegenden Beitrages ist die von der Vorarlberger Landesregierung beauftragte Studie *Lebens- und Einkommensverhältnisse Kunstschaffender in Vorarlberg* (REBITZER et al. 2023), welche zum Ziel hatte, eine theoretisch und empirisch begründete Entscheidungsgrundlage für politische Maßnahmen und ggf. Anpassungen der Kunstförderungsstrukturen zu erarbeiten. Im Zuge dieser Studie wurden acht Erkenntnisinteressen (REBITZER et al. 2023: 12f.) untersucht, wobei in diesem vorliegenden Beitrag der Fokus auf das wechselhafte Zusammenspiel aus Kunstschaffenden, Förderstrukturen und der Kunstrezeption durch die Bevölkerung eingeengt werden soll und somit die Konzentration auf folgenden vier Erkenntnisinteressen liegt:

- Erhebung von Daten, um eine Datengrundlage zur sozioökonomischen Situation bzw. Existenzsicherung Kunstschaffender in Vorarlberg auf Basis von Kennzahlen zu erhalten.
- Abbildung des subjektiven Erlebens und der Bewertung der sozioökonomischen Lebenssituation Kunstschaffender aus deren Sicht, mit Berücksichtigung der Auswirkungen dieser Lebenslagen auf ihr

künstlerisches Schaffen sowie ihrer Beurteilung der bestehenden Rahmenbedingungen.

- Erfassung der Bedeutung und (gesellschaftliche, kulturelle und ggf. identitätsstiftende) Funktion der Kunst und den diese kunstvermittelnden Institutionen für die Vorarlberger Gesellschaft
- Ermittlung des Konsumverhaltens und der Rezeption in Bezug auf die Kunstangebote in Vorarlberg aus Sicht der Vorarlberger Bevölkerung.

Um die sozioökonomische Lebenssituation der Kunstschaffenden mit Blick auf die Förderungslandschaft abbilden zu können, empfiehlt es sich einen multiperspektivischen Ansatz zu verwenden, da es gilt die verschiedenen Sichtweisen und Wahrnehmungen der verschiedenen Akteurinnen und Akteure einzubeziehen. Dies schließt branchenübergreifend die Kunstschaffenden und Schlüsselpersonen der Vorarlberger Kunst- und Kulturszene mit ein. Das Handlungsfeld und die Lebenssituation dieser handelnden Personen wird durch die etablierten Förderstrukturen und deren Mechanismen mitgeprägt und hat dadurch einen entscheidenden Einfluss auf die Kunstproduktion. Ebenfalls zu betrachten ist die Bevölkerung mit ihrer Wahrnehmung von Kunst und Kultur, da sich zum einen neue Kunstschaffende aus ihr rekrutieren und zum anderen wesentliche Einblicke in ihr Konsumverhalten und ihre Kunstrezeption gewonnen werden können.

Um diesen Erkenntnisinteressen möglichst umfänglich entsprechen zu können, ist die Studie in einem Mixed-Methods-Design angelegt. Die Erfahrungen, Wahrnehmungen und Meinungen zu den angesprochenen Themen können unter Einsatz von qualitativen Methoden ausführlich erfasst und verstanden werden. Der Einsatz von quantitativen Methoden ermöglicht einen Blick in die Breite, folglich kann das Zahlenmaterial zum Verständnis allgemeiner Eigenschaften und Meinungen einer bestimmten Gruppe (hier: Kunstschaffende und Gesamtbevölkerung) zu diesen erkenntnisinteressierenden Sachverhalten beitragen.

Mit Beginn der Erhebungen wurde deutlich, dass die Kunst- und Kulturlandschaft ein vielschichtiges System ist, welches keine stabilen Grenzen kennt, sondern sich in einem ständigen „Werden" befindet, wobei sich die Handlungen und die Beziehungen der verschiedenen Beteiligten wechselseitig bedingen. Die Beschreibung der Kunst- und Kulturlandschaft im Ergebnisteil erfolgt aufgrund dieser rhizomatischen Natur des Beziehungsgeflecht im deleuzeianischen Sinne in Form einer Kartographie, welche die Lesenden auf eine Reise mitnehmen will.

(DELEUZE/GUATTARI 1992) An verschiedenen Weggablungen werden wir Halt machen, um zuerst den einen und dann den anderen Pfad
zu erkunden und im Zuge dessen wiederkehrende Themen und Schnittmengen sichtbar zu machen. Die Befragten haben im Rahmen der Erhebung unterschiedliche Bereiche ausgeleuchtet, die am Ende zusam-
mengeführt eine Momentaufnahme, eines sich ständig wandeln System,
darstellen. Es konnte damit nicht in jeden Kapillarbereich vorgedrungen
werden, dies würde jeden Rahmen sprengen, aber es konnten die hand-
lungsleitenden Muster der Involvierten sichtbar gemacht werden und
wie sie sich im bestehenden Gefüge bevorzugt bewegen. Diese agieren
nicht im luftleeren Raum und ihre Handlungen sind nicht singulär er-
klärbar, sondern nur im Wissen um ihre reziproken Beziehungen inter-
pretierbar (STAUBMANN 2001).

Die Kartographie will am Ende das Wechselspiel aus Kunstschaffenden, Förderstrukturen und Rezeption durch die Bevölkerung nach-
gezeichnet haben und aufzeigen, welche Bilder von Kunst und Kultur
im gewärtigen Echoraum der Kunst- und Kulturlandschaft prominent
verhandelt werden. Auf Basis dessen sollen in der Schlussfolgerung
mögliche Ansatzpunkte offeriert werden, welche für öffentliche Körper-
schaften geneigt sein können, um positiv auf das bestehende Gefüge ein-
zuwirken.

Methodik

Der Mixed-Methods-Ansatz kombiniert mehrere Methoden aus qualitativer und quantitativer Forschung. Dieses multimethodische Verfahren
trägt zu einem besseren Verständnis für soziale Prozesse und Strukturen
bei, da monomethodische Ansätze dazu tendieren unvollständige oder
unzureichende Erklärungen zu liefern (KELLE 2008). Der multimethodische Ansatz verfolgt das Ziel, das zu untersuchendes Phänomen
breiter zu erfassen und bevorzugt die Sammlung und Analyse von qualitativen und quantitativen Daten innerhalb einer Studie. Hierfür gibt es
jedoch unterschiedliche Verfahren, was die Reihenfolge der qualitativen
und quantitativen Datenerhebung (sequentiell, gleichzeitig und trans-
formativ) und den Schwerpunkt der Erhebungsarten betrifft (ausgewo-
gen oder übergeordnet) (HUSSY/SCHREIER/ECHTERHOFF 2010).
Die mittels Mixed-Methods-Ansatzes erzielten Ergebnisse können kon-
vergieren, sich widersprechen oder sich ergänzen. Folglich bietet uns
dieser Ansatz die Möglichkeit, überraschende und unnachvollziehbare

Befunde mit der jeweils anderen Methode zu erklären oder fehlerhafte Interpretationen von Erkenntnissen zu korrigieren (CRESWELL 2013). In der vorliegenden Studie erfolgte neben der quantitativen Datenerhebung in Form einer Bevölkerungsbefragung bzw. einer onlinegestützten Künstlerbefragung eine qualitative Erhebung mittels Interviews und Fokusgruppen. Die qualitativen und quantitativen Datenerhebungen erfolgten in dieser Reihung aufeinanderfolgend, die verschiedenen methodischen Zugänge innerhalb dieser Studie erfuhren den gleichen Stellenwert.

Im Forschungsprozess wesentlich ist die Berücksichtigung der ethischen Aspekte und des Datenschutzes bei der Durchführung der qualitativen und quantitativen Befragung. Es wurde vorab eine Einverständniserklärung der Studienteilnehmenden eingeholt. Sie erhielten in schriftlicher Form detaillierte Informationen über diese Studie, und wurden darüber in Kenntnis gesetzt, dass alle gesammelten Daten anonym behandelt werden und die Ergebnisse nicht auf Einzelpersonen rückschließbar sind. Auch im qualitativen Teil werden die Ergebnisse nicht auf Einzelpersonen zuordbar sein, da anstelle der Namen bereits im Zuge der Transkription Pseudonyme/Codes verwendet wurden. Die Studienteilnehmende wurden auch darüber informiert, dass sie hinsichtlich der Teilnahme frei entscheiden und diese jederzeit nachteilsfrei beenden können.

Qualitative Forschung

Der qualitative Forschungsansatz mit seinem explorativen Charakter ist geeignet, um die subjektiven Lebenslagen der Kunstschaffenden sowie ggf. die Auswirkungen der Lage auf ihr künstlerisches Schaffen und ihre Einschätzung der bestehenden Rahmenbedingungen verstehen zu können. Die Daten wurden mittels leitfadengestützter Interviews und Fokusgruppen sowie einem Validierungsworkshop gesammelt. Die Rekrutierung der Personen erfolgte in Abstimmung mit der Kulturabteilung des Landes und dem für das Projekt eingesetzten Beirat:

• Sieben Interviews mit den Schlüsselpersonen der Vorarlberger Kunst- und Kulturlandschaft dienten dazu, eine Metaperspektive auf die aktuelle Kunst- und Kultursituation, in der sich die Kunstschaffenden bewegen, zu erhalten. Neben den Lebens- und Einkommenssituationen sowie Rahmenbedingungen der Kunstschaffenden liegen die Erkenntnisinteressen auch auf der Wertbeimessung für Kunst in der Bandbreite von ideellem Outcome und ökonomischer Verwertung und welche Funktionen und Bedeutungen Kunst in Vorarlberg einnimmt sowie welche Practice-Beispiele von außerhalb Vorarlbergs als mögliche Vorbilder dienen können.

- Interviews mit 17 Kunstschaffenden, die mit der Vorarlberger Kunst- und Kulturszene vertraut sind bzw. verbunden sind, konzentrierten sich auf deren individuelle Lebens- und Einkommenssituation und wie diese durch das herrschende Umfeld der Kunst- und Kulturlandschaft geprägt wird.

- Drei leitfadengestützte Fokusgruppen mit Kunstschaffenden wurden mit jeweils zwei bis drei Kunstschaffenden realisiert (angefragt wurden sechs bis sieben Personen pro Fokusgruppe; kleine Gruppen ergaben sich aufgrund von Erkrankungen und kurzfristigen Absagen). Ziel war es, relevante Themen, die aus den zuvor geführten Interviews mit Kunstschaffenden hervorgegangen waren, weiter zu vertiefen und in den Gruppen detailliert zu diskutieren. Der Fokus lag dabei auf den Förderstrukturen und Rahmenbedingungen unter denen Kunst und Kultur in Vorarlberg stattfinden.

- Der Validierungsworkshop mit elf Teilnehmenden (Kunstschaffende, Schlüsselpersonen der Vorarlberger Kunst- und Kulturszene, Kulturabteilung) beendete die Erhebungsphase. Es wurden alle Personen eingeladen, die bereits in vorherigen Interviews oder Fokusgruppen partizipiert hatten, sowie eine Reihe weiterer Schlüsselpersonen für die Vorarlberger Kunst- und Kulturszene. Zweck des Workshops war es, die erhobenen Daten und Ergebnisse einzuordnen, auf ihre Plausibilität hin zu prüfen und zu reflektieren.

Im Verlauf der qualitativen Erhebungen und der Analyse wurde ein Punkt erreicht, an dem durch weitere Erhebungen keine weiteren Ergebniskategorien mehr aufgebracht wurden und folglich eine theoretische Sättigung angenommen werden konnte, welche uns in Bezug auf die gewonnenen Daten ein adäquates Bild der Kunst- und Kulturszene Vorarlbergs zeigt. Die Interviews wurden mit Einverständnis der Befragten als mp3-Mitschnitt aufgenommen, transkribiert und mehrstufig reduziert. Das Datenmaterial wurde anschließend mit dem Programm MAXQDA codiert und entlang der sich deduktiv aus dem Leitfaden bzw. ergänzend induktiv aus den Interviews ergebenden Kategorien ausgewertet.

Quantitative Erhebungen

Der quantitative Teil der vorliegenden Studie besteht aus einer standardisierten Onlinebefragung mit Kunstschaffenden sowie einer Befragung der Vorarlberger Gesamtbevölkerung, die in einem anderen Projekt verankert ist, jedoch wertvolle Erkenntnisse auch für die Kontextualisierung der vorliegenden Thematik bietet. Die Bevölkerungsbefragung bildet ein wesentliches Element in der Interreg--ABH-V Studie *Neue Museumswelten – Eine explorative Annäherung an (Nicht-)Besucherbeziehungen zur Aktivierung der Teilhabe diverserer Publikumsgruppen durch neue Angebotsformate*, die von der Forschungsgruppe Empirische Sozialwissenschaften der FHV u.a. in Kooperation mit der Zürcher Hochschule für Angewandte Wissenschaften zeitgleich durchgeführt wurde.

Die *standardisierte Onlinebefragung der Kunstschaffenden* hatte zum Ziel, ein Verständnis für die Lebens- und Einkommenssituation in der Breite der Vorarlberger Kunstschaffenden zu erhalten, und auch mittels quantitativer Kennzahlen zu eruieren, wie es ihnen wirtschaftlich geht. So bildeten diese mit einem Bezug zu Vorarlberg die Grundgesamtheit dieser Befragung, wobei unter Vorarlbergbezug hier zu verstehen war, dass die Kunstschaffenden entweder aus Vorarlberg stammen, in Vorarlberg ihren Lebensmittelpunkt haben oder Vorarlberg als das Zentrum ihres künstlerischen Schaffens definieren.

Der Fragebogen wurde inhaltlich überwiegend auf Basis der Literatur- und Studienarbeit (ECOPLAN 2021; WEIGL/WIMMER/EHM 2018; WETZEL et al. 2018) entwickelt und der Vorarlberger Kunst- und Kulturlandschaft entsprechend angepasst. Einige Fragen wurden vom Projektteam selbst entwickelt, da in der Literatur hierzu keine passenden Fragestellungen eruiert werden konnten. Anschließend wurde er mit Projektbeirat inhaltlich abgestimmt sowie abschließend geprüft, getestet und optimiert (MICHEEL 2010). Folgende Dimensionen, die uns einen breiten Blick auf die ökonomische und soziale Lage der befragten Kunstschaffenden verschaffen sollen, bildeten den Inhalt der Befragung:

Künstlerische Berufstätigkeit; Einkommenssituation und Ausgaben; Copingstrategien zur Überbrückung finanzieller Schwierigkeiten; Soziale Absicherung; Förderungen; Soziodemografie

Die Aussendung des Onlinefragebogens an die Kunstschaffenden erfolgte im Dezember 2022 über die Verteiler der Abteilung Kultur der Vorarlberger Landesverwaltung, jener der Mitglieder des Projektbeirats und weiterer kunst- und kulturbezogener Multiplikatorinnen und Multiplikatoren. Die Einladung zur Teilnahme mit dem Link zum

Onlinefragebogen – angelegt in der Umfragesoftware EFS Survey (Unipark/TIVIAN) – wurde ausschließlich per E-Mail versandt. Dieses Vorgehen ist mit Limitationen verbunden, unter den gegebenen Umständen war dies jedoch die einzige Möglichkeit, Vorarlberger Kunstschaffende zielgerichtet zu erreichen, ohne breite Aufrufe mit einer vollständigen Veröffentlichung des Teilnahmelinks umsetzen zu müssen. Da auf diese Weise weder eine Stichprobenziehung noch eine Vollerhebung einer zwar definitorisch abgrenzbaren, jedoch nicht real quantifizier- und erreichbaren Grundgesamtheit möglich war, kann die Befragung keinen Repräsentativitätsanspruch erheben, d.h. die vorliegenden Ergebnisse müssen für einen etwaigen Rückschluss auf die Kunstschaffende mit Vorarlbergbezug insgesamt mit großer Vorsicht interpretiert werden. Sie geben eine verlässliche Auskunft nur über jene Personen, die durch das geschilderte Vorgehen erreicht wurden und teilgenommen haben.

Das Ausfüllen der Befragung wurde von 259 Personen begonnen und von 131 vollständig abgeschlossen. Nach Bereinigungen und der Prüfung einer Befüllung des Fragebogens bis zum Cut-off konnten schließlich 198 Fälle für die statistische Analyse berücksichtigt werden. In der Befragung war die Möglichkeit geboten, Fragen auszulassen bzw. diese bei Wunsch nicht beantworten zu müssen. Aus diesem Grund variiert die Zahl der gültigen Antworten je Frage und wird bei den Ergebnissen mit ausgewiesen.

Im Analyseprozess wurden neben Häufigkeitsverteilungen und deskriptiver Statistik zudem Unterschiedstests nach Kunstsparten, Geschlecht, Bildungsstand und Alter berechnet, je nach Skalenniveau und Erfüllung der für die Tests notwendigen statistischen Voraussetzungen mittels Chi-Quadrat, Mann-Whitney-U-Tests oder t-Tests.

Die *standardisierte Bevölkerungsbefragung* hatte zum Ziel das Nutzungsverhalten der Vorarlberger Bevölkerung hinsichtlich der Kunst- und Kulturangebote im Land sowie den Stellenwert von Kunst und Kultur im Allgemeinen abzufragen. Für die Fragebogenkonstruktion wurden vergleichbare Studien und Erhebungsinstrumente recherchiert, sowie Literatur zum Thema Kulturverhalten und sozialem Kulturgeschmack gesichtet (siehe Gesamtbericht REBITZER et al. 2023). Die gewählten Items wurden zum Teil an das regionale Angebot in Vorarlberg bzw. an die Vorarlberger Bevölkerung angepasst. Der Pretest wurde innerhalb des Konsortiums durchgeführt.

Der endgültige Fragebogen, welcher als Onlinebefragung in der Erhebungssoftware Unipark (TIVIAN) umgesetzt wurde, beinhaltet folgende Dimensionen: Kultur- und Freizeitverhalten der Bevölkerung;

Außenbild und Einstellung zu Kunst und Kultur; Sozialer Hintergrund, Soziodemografie und Lebensstile.

Die Einladung zur Bevölkerungsbefragung erging an 10.000 Personen ab 16 Jahren mit Hauptwohnsitz in Vorarlberg, die geschichtet nach Altersverteilung und Region entsprechend der Verteilung der Vorarlberger Grundgesamtheit per Zufallsziehung aus dem Zentralen Melderegister (ZMR) gezogen worden waren und somit eine für die Gesamtpopulation Vorarlbergs repräsentative Stichprobe darstellte. Die Einladung erfolgte, da das ZMR lediglich postalische Kontaktdaten enthält, mittels eines einseitigen postalischen Anschreibens und beinhaltete eine Vorstellung der Projektziele, eine Darlegung des öffentlichen Interesses an den Ergebnissen der Befragung sowie die Zugangsmöglichkeiten zur Onlinebefragung. Die Teilnahme an der Befragung erfolgte via Link oder QR-Code. Für Personen ohne digitalen Zugang wurde angeboten eine Teilnahme an der Befragung in telefonischer oder schriftlicher Form zu ermöglichen.

Die Teilnahme an der Befragung war im Dezember 2022 möglich. Nach der Bereinigung des Datensatzes konnten Daten von 1.377 Personen (Rücklaufquote: 13,8 %) für die Analyse herangezogen werden. Der Rücklauf der Bevölkerungsbefragung weist eine näherungsweise Repräsentativität für die Grundgesamtheit auf. Die gesammelten Daten wurden nach Abschluss der Befragung heruntergeladen und bereinigt (dokumentierte Löschung von Fällen, die nicht mindestens 50 Prozent der Befragung ausgefüllt hatten; Durchführung einer deskriptiven Analyse zur Erfassung logisch unplausibler und unmöglicher Antworten). Daran anschließend wurde eine vertiefte deskriptive Analyse erstellt. Bei Angaben, die erst im Vergleich zur Gesamtbevölkerung Aussagekraft entwickeln, wurden Sekundärdaten herangezogen und Unterschiede in den Häufigkeitsverteilungen mittels Chi-Quadrat-Test ermittelt.

Ergebnisse

Der Kunst- und Kulturraum Vorarlberg stellt ein komplexes System mit unterschiedlichen Abhängigkeiten und Ambiguitäten dar, welches sich in einem ständigen „Werden" befindet. Die Lebenssituation der Kunstschaffenden, die Förderstrukturen sowie die Rezeption von Kunst und Kultur durch die Bevölkerung bedingen sich dabei ständig gegenseitig. Um dieser rhizomatischen Natur, die keine vollständige bzw. abschließende Darstellung zulässt, gerecht zu werden, ist die vorliegende Beschreibung im deleuzeianischen Sinne als Kartographie angelegt, welche die Lesenden auf eine Reise mitnimmt, diese Welt zu erkunden. Die Beschreibung der Ergebnisse hangelt sich dabei von Kontenpunkt zu Knotenpunkt, um peu à peu einen Einblick in die Kunst- und Kulturlandschaft zu gewinnen (DELEUZE/GUATTARI 1992). Zunächst liegt der Fokus auf den drei Schwerpunkten 1) Lebens- und Arbeitsverhältnisse von Kunstschaffenden, 2) Kunstförderung und 3) Konsum und Rezeption der Bevölkerung, um abschließend die Interkonnektivität und ihre diskursiven Implikationen herauszuarbeiten.

Lebens- und Arbeitsverhältnisse von Kunstschaffenden

Bei Betrachtung der künstlerischen Berufserfahrung, zeigen die Ergebnisse der Onlinebefragung, dass die befragten Kunstschaffenden im Durchschnitt 22,4 Jahre die künstlerische Tätigkeit professionell ausüben (Median = 20,5 Jahre). Die meisten der Befragten (43,4 %) verorten ihren künstlerischen Schwerpunkt in der Bildenden Kunst, gefolgt von Musik mit 20,2 % und Darstellender Kunst mit 16,7 %. Schwerpunktmäßig in den Bereichen Literatur und Film arbeiten 8,1 % bzw. 5,6 % der Kunstschaffenden. Keiner dieser künstlerischen Schwerpunkte zuordnen wollten oder konnten 6,1 % der befragten Kunstschaffenden. Einige sehen sich nicht ausschließlich in einen dieser Schwerpunkte verhaftet, sondern folgen in der Kunstproduktionen einem interdisziplinären Ansatz und kombinieren mehrere Kunstformen. Je nach Branche bewerten sich die Kunstschaffenden zu ca. 60 % bis 85 % als gut oder eher gut etabliert.

Die Selbsteinschätzung der Etablierung innerhalb der Branchen divergiert, dies versucht Wetzel et al. (2018) folgendermaßen zu begründen: Jüngere Kunstschaffende, die am Beginn ihrer Karriere stehen und noch wenig Berufserfahrung vorweisen, sehen sich erwartungsgemäß seltener als „gut etabliert". Der Faktor Geschlecht mag für die subjektive Einschätzung der Etablierung im eigenen künstlerischen Schwerpunkt eine ebenfalls eine Rolle spielen, denn Frauen sind häufiger selbstkritischer und beurteilen sich im Vergleich zu den Männern zurückhaltender. Ein wesentliches Merkmal der Etablierung scheint die Nachfrage nach der künstlerischen Arbeit zu sein, beeinflusst von unterschiedlichsten Faktoren und mitgestaltet durch kunst- und kulturpolitische Angebote. Eine gelungene Etablierung bedeutet allerdings nicht immer ein kontinuierliche Arbeitssituation, die ein dauerhafte Existenzsicherung möglich machen würden (ebd. 2018). Wie nun die finanzielle Situation der Kunstschaffenden gestaltet ist, zeigen die folgenden statistischen Ergebnisse der Onlinebefragung.

Das jährliche Nettoeinkommen wurde für die Jahre 2019, 2020, 2021 und 2022 erhoben, so dass mit 2019 das letzte Jahr vor Corona, dann die beiden Krisenjahre sowie mit 2022 das erste Jahr nach den Einschränkungen betrachtet werden können. Spezielle Corona-Überbrückungsleistungen für entfallene Einkommen aus coronabedingt verhinderten Tätigkeiten sollten dabei berücksichtigt werden, nicht aber corona-unabhängige Transferleistungen wie Arbeitslosengeld. Die Bereinigung des Datensatzes, die Möglichkeit zum Überspringen der Fragen zum Einkommen und der Abbruch der Studienteilnahme erklären die niedrigeren Werte an berücksichtigten Fällen; die je nach Frage und Bezugsjahr zwischen n=81 Befragten und n=84 liegen.

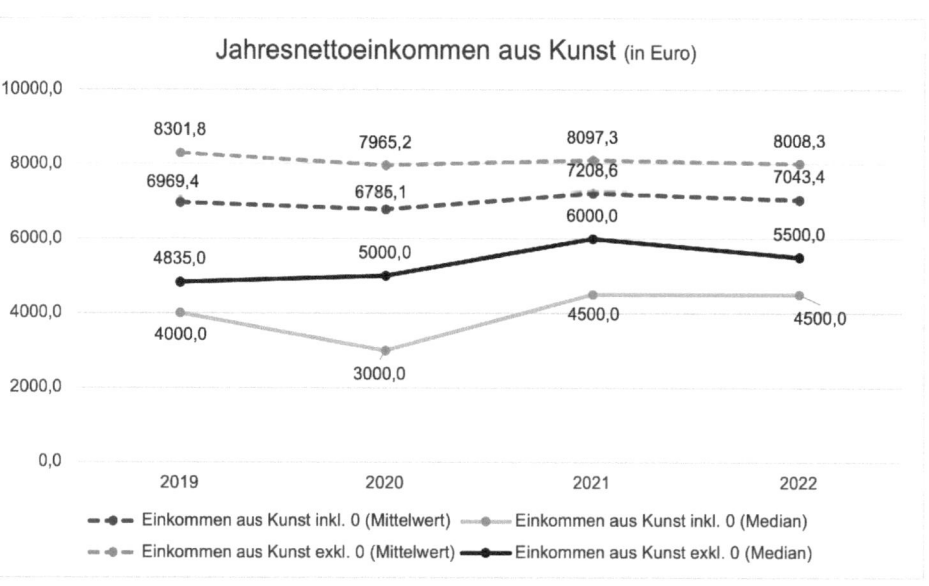

Abb. 1: *Jahresnettoeinkommen aus Kunst (inkl. und exkl. Einkommen von € 0,–)*

Abbildung 1 illustriert, dass das mittlere Jahreseinkommen aus rein künstlerischer Arbeit mit einem Medianwert von EUR 4.000,- (2019) bis EUR 4.500,- (2022) auf einem sehr niedrigen Niveau liegt. Am Medianwert teilt sich die Verteilung in zwei gleich große Hälften und lässt sich so interpretieren, dass die Hälfte der Befragten im Jahr 2019 bis zu EUR 4.000,- und die andere Hälfte der Befragten mehr als EUR 4.000,- eingenommen haben. Zu einem ähnlichen Ergebnis kamen auch Wetzel et al. (2018) in ihrer Studie, bei der das mittlere Einkommen für Österreich bei EUR 5.000,- (Medianwert) lag, was als nicht existenzsichernd betrachtet werden kann.

Die Befragten haben beim mittleren Einkommen aus künstlerischer Tätigkeit einen Betrag von EUR 0,- angegeben, in den einzelnen Jahren also kein Einkommen aus Kunst generiert. Der Anteil schwankt über die Jahre zwischen 16 Prozent im Jahr 2019 und 11 Prozent im Jahr 2021. Im nächsten Berechnungsschritt wurden diese Fälle daher ausgeschlossen, um festzustellen zu können, wie hoch das Einkommen bei den befragten Kunstschaffenden mit einem tatsächlichen Jahresnettoeinkommen aus Kunst war. Durch den Ausschluss des Jahresnettoeinkommens aus Kunst von EUR 0,- erhöhten sich die Medianwerte, blieben aber bei maximal 6.000 Euro und sind somit weiterhin auf niedrigem Niveau. Coronabedingte Einbrüche der Einkommen aus Kunst sind somit kaum feststellbar, was indiziert, dass die entsprechenden Ausgleichsleistungen, die hier mitberücksichtigt sind, entsprechende Verluste weitgehend abgefedert haben.

Beim Vergleich des mittleren Einkommens aus Kunst (inklusive und exklusive Einkommen von EUR 0,-) nach Kunstsparten, Geschlecht, Alter und Bildungsstand zeigen sich signifikante Unterschiede nur beim Bildungsstand in den Jahren 2019, 2020 und 2022. Überraschenderweise ist das Einkommen von Kunstschaffenden mit akademischer Ausbildung in diesen Jahren signifikant geringer als das von Kunstschaffenden ohne akademische Ausbildung, insbesondere wenn Fälle ohne Einkommen aus Kunst berücksichtigt werden. Eine mögliche Erklärung könnte sein, dass unter Akademikerinnen und Akademiker ein höherer Anteil existenziell auf andere Einkommensquellen zurückgreifen und daher weniger Einkommen aus der Kunst generieren (müssen).

Das mittlere individuelle Jahresnettoeinkommen (aus allen Einkommensquellen inkl. Kunst zusammengenommen) fällt aufgrund von weiteren Einkommensquellen mit einem Medianwert von € 15.000,- höher aus, bleibt jedoch auf einem niedrigen Niveau (Abb. 2). Bei Wetzel et al. (2018) lag der Wert österreichweit für Kunstschaffende vergleichsweise bei € 17.500,- (Medianwert), was damals ebenfalls deutlich unter dem österreichischen gesamtwirtschaftlichen Referenzwert von € 26.000,- lag. Beim individuellen Jahresnettoeinkommen wurde lediglich von zwischen einer und drei Personen ein Einkommen von € 0,– angegeben, was zu keinem relevanten Einfluss auf die Gesamtverteilung führt. Bei der Betrachtung des mittleren individuellen Jahresnettoeinkommen sowohl inklusive als auch exklusive dem Einkommen von € 0,– konnten keine signifikanten Unterschiede zwischen den Kunstsparten, in Bezug auf Geschlecht, Alter und Bildungsstand festgestellt werden.

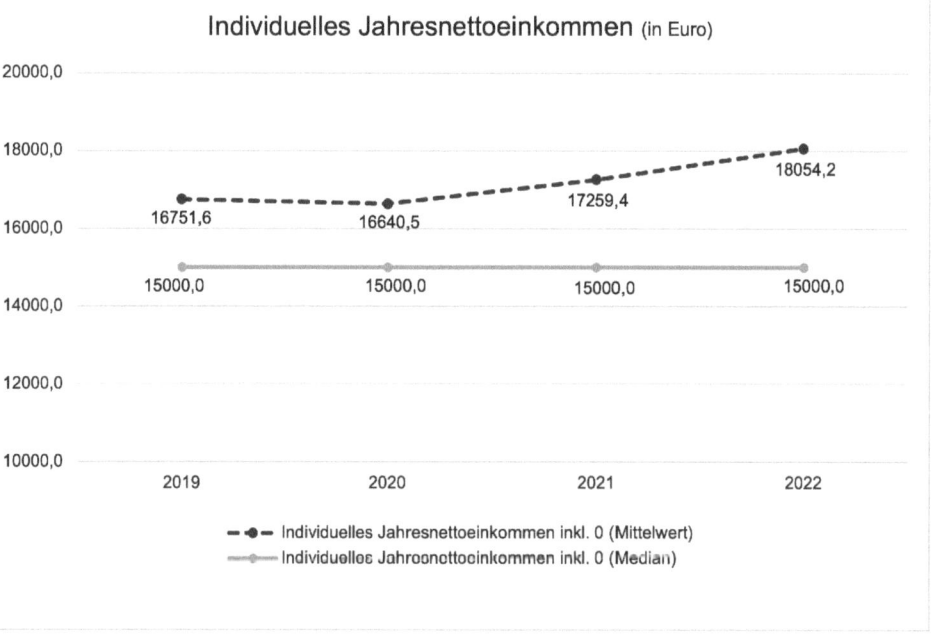

Abb. 2: Individuelles *Jahresnettoeinkommen (inkl. und exkl. Einkommen von € 0,–)*

Da viele Kunstschaffende allein von Kunst nicht leben können und Einkommen aus anderen kunstnahen oder kunstfernen Beschäftigungen beziehen, wurde in einem weiteren Schritt ermittelt, bei wie vielen Kunstschaffenden das Jahresnettoeinkommen aus Kunst zu 100 % dem individuellen Jahresnettoeinkommen (alle Einkünfte inkl. aus Kunst) entsprach. Diese Situation traf auf knapp 50 % der befragten Kunstschaffenden zu (2019: 47,4 %; 2020: 47,4 %; 2021: 46,9 %; 2022: 46,3 %.), was bedeutet, dass mehr als die Hälfte der Befragten Einkommen aus anderen Beschäftigungen bezogen haben. Diese kombinierte Erwerbstätigkeit ist die Arbeitsrealität vieler Kunstschaffender und soll das Defizit – bedingt durch die geringen Einkünfte aus Kunst – kompensieren (ECOPLAN 2021; HENNING/ SCHULTHEIS/THOMÄ 2019; PRILLER 2006; WEIGL/WILLER/EHM 2018; WETZEL et al 2018; FUCHS 2015; IBERT et al 2012).

Der Umstand, dass sich die Einnahmen der Kunstschaffenden aus unterschiedlichen Quellen speisen, konnte in den qualitativen Befragungen repliziert werden. Die Einnahmen aus Kunst stellen sich häufig aus einem unterschiedlichen Mix zusammen. Jene in den qualitativen Interviews befragten Kunstschaffende, die zu 100 % künstlerisch tätig sind, haben häufig einen Einnahmenmix, der sich aus Projekten, Förderungen, Honoraren, Stipendien, Verkäufen, Auftragsarbeiten, Werksverträgen, Arbeitslosengeld und Unterstützung durch Angehörigen oder deren Bekanntenkreis zusammensetzen kann. Jene Kunstschaffende, die sich mit kunstnahen oder kunstfernen Tätigkeiten teilweise oder voll querfinanzieren, beziehen als Kunstschaffende denselben Einnahmenmix aus der Kunstproduktion, es kommen aber unter der Bedingung des Fokus- und Ressourcensplittings Einkünfte aus Lehrtätigkeiten, Workshopleitungen, Kunstvermittlungen oder anderer Erwerbsarbeiten hinzu.

Zu beachten ist zum einen, dass kunstnahe Tätigkeiten gegenüber kunstfernen Tätigkeiten überwiegen und zum anderen, dass die unterschiedlichen Tätigkeiten ein sehr unterschiedliches Skillset voraussetzen (können). Zum Beispiel muss man als Lehrkraft handwerklich gut sein, Freude an der Vermittlung haben und den Stress der Unterrichtssituation handhaben können. Bei der kunstschaffenden Tätigkeit muss man handwerklich sehr gut sein, Selbstvermarktung (Eigenwerbung, Positionierung) betreiben und den Stress vor Publikum/Interessierten austarieren können. Kunstferne Tätigkeiten (Gastronomie, Betreuung) werden von Kunstschaffenden möglichst vermieden, da diese die eigene Marke/Image als erfolgreiche Person beschädigen könnten und damit die Chancen auf die ökonomische Verwertung der eigenen Kunst bzw. das Generieren weiterer Förderoptionen schmälern könnten.

In der Literatur finden sich hinsichtlich Kunstberuf, kunstnahe und -ferne Beschäftigung auch teils normative Zuschreibungen und Generalisierungen zum Thema, die sich so sicherlich nicht für alle Kunstschaffenden bestätigen lassen, aber ein Grunddilemma anzeigen. Demnach fordere die Kunst in hohem Maße den Menschen als Ganzes („Gibt dich ganz der Kunst hin, opfere dich für die Kunst"). Kunstschaffende sollen sich ihr Leben nicht mit außerkünstlerischen Tätigkeiten finanzieren, sondern das Leben mit Kunst verknüpfen. Allerdings steht diesem Anspruch die existenzielle Realität gegenüber (FUCHS 2015). Nebenjobs und Brotjobs bzw. die Mischwirtschaft werden zur Querfinanzierung als temporäre Lösungen gesehen. Sie verweigerten sich jedoch, so Henning, Schultheis und Thomä (2019), der Normalität des bürgerlichen Berufslebens, da sie nicht für nine-to-five geschaffen seien. Ein Kunstdasein bedeute demnach Freiheit, auch wenn sie prekär ist. Kunst sei mehr als nur Unterhaltssicherung, mehr als ein Beruf. Es gehe um Status, und noch wichtiger um ein Modell der Lebensführung, das für die Interviewten einen hohen persönlichen Wert besitzt. Das freie Arbeiten in selbstbestimmten Strukturen sei ein Selbstverständnis und bedeute für Kunstschaffende einen Gewinn an Lebensqualität. Darin finde sich auch die Begründung, warum sie trotz der schwierigen sozialen Lage motiviert seien in der freien Kunst tätig zu sein. Frei zu arbeiten sei jedoch, nicht bei allen Kunstschaffenden gleichermaßen der Wunsch (HENNING/ SCHULTHEIS/THOMÄ 2019). Ein Fünftel der in der Studie von Speicher und Haunschild (2012) befragten darstellenden Kunstschaffenden gab an, nur notgedrungen frei zu arbeiten und eigentlich ein festes Engagement vorzuziehen.

Es zeigt sich in den Beschreibungen der qualitativ befragten Vorarlberger Kunstschaffenden vor allem auch eine zunehmende Extensivierung von Arbeit. Die meisten Kunstschaffenden beschreiben Situationen, in denen die Grenze zwischen Privatleben und Arbeit verschwimmt. Das Jonglieren zwischen verschiedenen Bereichen erfordert beträchtliche Ausdauer und Energie, und alle Kunstschaffenden betonen in den qualitativen Interviews, dass dies nur mit der notwendigen Leidenschaft möglich sei. Die Vereinbarkeit von Beruf und Familie wird thematisiert, wobei die Hälfte der qualitativ Befragten kinderlos ist. Einige Kunstschaffende haben bewusst auf Kinder verzichtet, entweder aus finanziellen Gründen oder um sich auf ihre Kunst zu konzentrieren. Speicher und Haunschild (2022) konstatieren in ihrer Studie, dass aufgrund der prekären finanziellen und sozialen Lage – sofern kein anderweitiges Vermögen existiert (Erbe von Immobilien, Geld, das eine finanzielle Absicherung ermöglicht) kaum Sicherheit für die Lebensplanung gibt und Familiengründung daher verschoben oder gar ausgesetzt wird.

Von den qualitativ befragten Kunstschaffenden mit Kindern ziehen die meisten ihre Kinder in Partnerschaften auf. Bei Eltern, insbesondere Alleinerziehenden, wird deutlich, dass Kinder und Familie Zeit und Ressourcen beanspruchen, die nicht in die Kunstproduktion oder die Vernetzung mit Kunst-Stakeholdern fließen. Kunstschaffende mit Partnerin oder Partner können die Erziehungsarbeit und Kosten teilen, wobei Frauen oft den größeren Teil der Care-Arbeit leisten. Der Wiedereinstieg für Frauen nach der Karenz kann sich schwierig gestalten, wenn während dieser Zeit keine Kunst „produziert" wurde und sie somit für relevante Adressaten weniger sichtbar waren. Die Entscheidung für Kinder bringt in vielerlei Hinsicht zusätzliche Belastungen für den Haushalt mit sich.

In den Gesprächen mit den Schlüsselpersonen wurde die Lebensspanne zwischen dem 20. und 40. Lebensjahr als entscheidend herausgestellt.

In diesem Zeitraum treffen Kunstschaffende verschiedene lebenswegrelevante Entscheidungen, wie etwa bezüglich Familie und Kinder, und es wird deutlich, ob sie über die notwendige Resilienz verfügen, um in der Kunst erfolgreich reüssieren zu können. Mit zunehmendem Alter wird es schwieriger, die vielfältigen Belastungen durch Familie und Nebenjobs auszugleichen, und Fragen nach der Absicherung bei Krankheit, Unfall und im Alter werden dringlicher.

Die meisten befragten Kunstschaffenden gaben an, keine entsprechenden Sicherungssysteme für die Pension zu haben (siehe auch Studie Wetzel et al. 2018) Mehrere Kunstschaffende über 55 Jahre äußerten Unsicherheit bzgl. ihrer Zukunft, was das Risiko auf eine Altersarmut birgt. Abhängig von der Kunstsparte erfordert die Ausübung der Kunst auch eine gewisse körperliche Fitness (z. B. Tanz, Bildhauerei), die im Alter abnehmen kann. Zudem können auch junge Kunstschaffende durch Unfälle oder Krankheiten kurz- bis langfristig arbeitsunfähig werden, was für Selbstständige ohne private Unterstützung existenzbedrohend sein kann. In der quantitativen Befragung zeigte sich, dass die große Mehrheit gesetzlich krankenversichert (93,5 %), pensionsversichert (81,3 %) und unfallversichert (74,0 %) ist. Der Anteil an privaten Versicherungen fällt eher gering aus und bewegt sich zwischen 8,9 % (Pensionsversicherung) und 21,2 % (Unfallversicherung). 12,2 % sind (ggf. zusätzlich) privat krankenversichert. Der hohe Anteil an gesetzlichen Versicherungen resultiert möglicherweise aus den Beschäftigungsverhältnissen als angestellte Kunstschaffende oder aus sekundären beruflichen Tätigkeiten im Bereich der Kunst oder außerhalb des Sektors. Dennoch kann als problematisch betrachtet werden, dass mehr als jede zehnte befragte Person angibt, weder über eine gesetzliche noch eine private Altersvorsorge zu verfügen. Diese drängenden Fragen im Hinblick auf die soziale Absicherung bestätigen auch Wetzel et al (2018) und Christl und Griesser (2017). Durch die häufig aufkommende Kombination von (gleichzeitigen) unselbständigen und/oder selbstständigen Beschäftigungsverhältnissen im Verlauf eines Jahres ergeben sich durchaus komplexe sozialversicherungsrechtliche Situationen. Hier stößt die Sozialversicherungsstruktur an ihre Grenzen. Die mangelnde Kompatibilität von selbständiger und unselbstständiger künstlerischer Tätigkeit führt zudem zu einer lückenhaften Absicherung gegenüber sozialen Risiken wie Arbeitslosigkeit, erhöhte Armutsgefahr, soziale Ausgrenzung (CHRISTL/GRIESSER 2017).

Materielle Knappheit, der Zwang unzureichende Einkünfte aus dem Kunstschaffen mit anderen Tätigkeiten im Sinne einer Mischwirtschaft zu kompensieren sowie die dadurch bedingte komplexe soziale Absicherung, wird als Prekarität empfunden. Die Lebensführung ist geprägt von kontinuierlicher Unsicherheit bedingt durch die mangelnde mittel- und langfristige Vorhersehbarkeit und Planbarkeit. Daraus resultiert zudem auch die Notwendigkeit sich ständig wechselnden Konstellationen flexibel anpassen zu müssen (HENNING/SCHULTHEIS/THOMÄ 2019). Die prekäre Lebenssituation steht somit in Zusammenhang mit mannigfaltigen, Belastungsfaktoren und Vulnerabilität.

Die in den qualitativen Interviews mit Vorarlberger Kunstschaffenden herauskristallisierten Herausforderungen und Belastungen lassen sich in sieben Bereiche einteilen:

1. Zwang zur Zersplitterung des eigenen Fokus: Die Kunstschaffenden werden gezwungen ihre Aufmerksamkeit auf verschiedene Bereiche – Job, Kunst, Familie, Management, Antragstellung – aufzusplitten. Dieser Umstand erhöht häufig den Stresslevel und erfordert Kompromissbereitschaft bzgl. der zur Verfügung stehenden Zeit und Ressourcen, und reduziert häufig den Fokus für die künstlerischen Tätigkeiten und kann sich negativ auf die Qualität der Kunst auswirken.

2. Planungsunsicherheiten (Instabilität Zukunftsaussichten): Das Leben und die Arbeit von Kunstschaffenden sind häufig durch Unsicherheiten geprägt, was eine langfristige Planung erschwert. Besonders die diskontinuierlichen Engagements/Projekte/Aufträge erfordern einen hohen Energieeinsatz, wobei häufig das Gefühl keinen Fortschritt zu erzielen bleibt. Mehrere Kunstschaffende berichten in diesem Zusammenhang von Existenzängsten und einer ständigen Müdigkeit.

3. Unsichere finanzielle und versicherungstechnische Situation (Instabilität Gegenwart): Die angespannte wirtschaftliche Situation durch die häufig als prekär umschriebenen Lebenssituationen sowie durch den Umstand, dass Kunstschaffende bei der Erstellung ihrer Kunst häufig in Vorleistung (Material-, Personalkosten) gehen müssen, erzeuge nicht nur Druck, sondern zwinge zu Tätigkeiten, die nicht uneingeschränkt unterstützt werden könnten. Dies sei häufig ein Treiber von Frustration.

4. Wettbewerbssituation: Der ständige Wettbewerb um Aufmerksamkeit, Aufträge, Förderungen, etc. erzeugt einen ständigen Druck, der ein kontinuierliches Eigenmarketing erfordert, um sich gegenüber Publikum und Fördergebenden zu positionieren. Der Wert der eigenen Leistung steht dabei nicht für sich, sondern unterliegt dem permanenten Abgleich mit anderen Angeboten (Märkten).

5. Unternehmertum: Einige Kunstschaffende sehen die unternehmerischen Aspekte als Bürde, andere als Bereicherung. Die kaufmännischen Aufgaben (Kalkulationen, Anträge) konkurrieren um die Zeit für den künstlerischen Schaffensprozess und benötigen ein anderes Skillset. Zudem wird die Verpflichtung eine „Marke" zu werden als 24/7 Aufgabe empfunden, die in die anderen Lebensbereiche hineinwirkt.

6. Rechtfertigung der künstlerischen Tätigkeit nach außen: Viele Kunstschaffende nehmen eine fehlende Wertschätzung für ihre Arbeit durch die Gesellschaft wahr und würden einem ständigen Rechtfertigungsdruck unterliegen. Über Gehälter und Honorare zu sprechen, wird von Kunstschaffenden oft mit Scham verbunden. Einige berichten von einem zunehmenden Druck, sich präsentieren und die Qualität ständig steigern zu müssen. Beide Aspekte unterliegen einer regelmäßigen kritischen Prüfung von außen.

7. Rechtfertigung der künstlerischen Tätigkeit nach innen: Neben dem äußeren Druck, thematisieren viele Kunstschaffende auch eine innere Dimension. Sie setzen sich selbstkritisch mit dem eigenen Wert auseinander und subjektiveren sich dabei an Bewertungsmaßstäben, die von außen an sie herangetragen werden. Dies kann dann zu einer gesteigerten Nervosität und Selbstzweifeln führen.

Einige Kunstschaffende erleben psychische Belastungen, die in einigen Fällen von ihnen als Anzeichen für Burnouts und Erschöpfungszustände beschrieben werden. Körperliche Belastungen wurden weniger oft in den Gesprächen behandelt und betreffen hauptsächlich Personen, die für ihre Kunst eine bestimmte körperliche Leistungsfähigkeit (z.B. Tanz, Herstellung von Skulpturen) benötigen. Auch die Einsatzfähigkeit ihres eigenen Körpers im Alter wurde thematisiert.

Konfrontiert mit diesen Herausforderungen und Belastungen haben die qualitativ befragten Kunstschaffende in Vorarlberg unterschiedliche Taktiken entwickelt, um diesen zu begegnen. An erster Stelle stand für alle Befragten, dass man sich trotz aller Unsicherheiten bewusst für die Kunst entscheiden müsse. Die gängigen angewendeten Strategien können in folgende Handlungsbereiche unterteilt werden.

• Wissen aufbauen, Vernetzung und Kooperation: neue Erfahrungen sammeln, Reflexion, Kooperationen, Austausch, Weiterbildung, Vermittlungsbüros
• Künstlerische Weiterentwicklung: Weiterentwicklung von Konzepten, Handwerk und eigenen Techniken

- Geografische Ausweitung oder Veränderung: Verlassen des Heimatortes, internationales Agieren
- Ausblenden der Herausforderungen/Belastungen: Verdrängung von Problemen und Risiken, Resignation
- Anpassung an die Situation: Sparsame Lebensweise, positive Lebenseinstellung, Einnahmendiversifizierung, Work-Life-Balance, Entwicklung von Alternativen Plänen
- Managen und Ökonomisierung der eigenen Lebensführung: Aneignung von betriebswirtschaftlichen Kenntnissen, Selbstmarketing, Erhöhung der eigenen Sichtbarkeit, Auftreten als Veranstaltende, Beziehungspflege mit relevanten Stakeholdern, Nutzung von Steuer- und Finanzberatung.

In der Onlinebefragung der Kunstschaffenden wurden ebenfalls potenzielle Strategien zur Bewältigung der finanziellen Situation abgefragt. Als Antworten wurden Einschränkungen im täglichen Leben, Unterstützung durch Angehörige, Rückgriff auf finanzielle Rücklagen, Überziehung des Kontos, Überbrückung durch nicht-künstlerische Arbeit, Beantragung von Beihilfen, Förderimpulsen zur Krisenbewältigung oder öffentlichen Sozialleistungen, sowie die Aufnahme von Krediten genannt.

Kunstschaffende entwickeln laut Ibert et al. (2012) in jenen Bereichen Resilienzstrategien, die für sie leichter zugänglich sind. Sie beziehen sich ihrer Studie über Musicaldarstellende auf die Arbeit an der eigenen Identität und das soziale Netzwerk, welche sich nach der Logik der „bi-partite" nach Uzzi und Spiro aufbaut. In dieser Netzwerkstruktur spielen auch Peers eine bedeutende Rolle, da der Aufwand sowie die Kosten für das strategisch-professionelle Netzwerkmanagement untereinander aufgeteilt werden können (IBERT et al. 2012). Henning, Schultheis und Thomä (2019) Das sogenannte kreative Milieu ist dabei nicht nur eine Ressource für die wechselseitige Anerkennung, sondern auch ein privilegierter Markt für die Zirkulation der produzierten Güter. Speicher und Haunschild (2022) versuchen im Bereich der freien darstellenden Kunst die verschiedenen Bewältigungsstrategien mit dem Konzept *exit, voice, loyalty* zu erklären (in Anlehnung an Hirschmans soziologischen Klassiker: Exit, Voice, and Loyalty).

Bis zu einem gewissen Grad schaffen es die Kunstschaffenden mit vulnerablen Situationen umzugehen und eignen sich Resilienz und Bewältigungsstrategien an, nichtsdestotrotz können diese schwierigen Lebensbedingungen das kreative Schöpfen bzw. das Schaffen von Kunst im negativen Sinne beeinflussen. Eine wesentliche Rahmenbedingung für das künstlerische Schaffen könnten Förderungen darstellen.

Kunstförderung

Eine ausreichende Kunstförderung würde die Planungssicherheit für zukünftige Projekte und die Absicherung der Kunstschaffenden erhöhen. Eine stabilisierend wirkende Rahmung würde nach den Aussagen der Kunstschaffenden eine verstärkte Fokussierung der Kunstschaffenden auf ihre Kunstproduktion und deren Qualität ermöglichen. Die Bedeutung von Kunstförderung durch das Land Vorarlberg lässt sich damit durch die vorliegende Untersuchung bekräftigen. Eine Bewertung der Kunstförderung des Landes Vorarlberg unter den online befragten Kunstschaffenden zeichnet ein überwiegend positives Bild (Abbildung 3).

Trotz der gut ausfallenden Bewertung der Kunstförderung des Landes Vorarlberg auf Basis der quantitativen Daten wurden in den qualitativen Interviews auch Kritikpunkte angesprochen. Der Zugang zu den Förderangeboten von den dort befragten Kunstschaffenden wird sehr unterschiedlich interpretiert, und zwar von wenig kompliziert bis sehr aufwendig. Die online befragten Kunstschaffenden positionieren sich hier eindeutiger und beurteilen den Aufwand für die Antragsstellung weit überwiegend mit 82,2 % („sehr gut", „gut") als positiv.

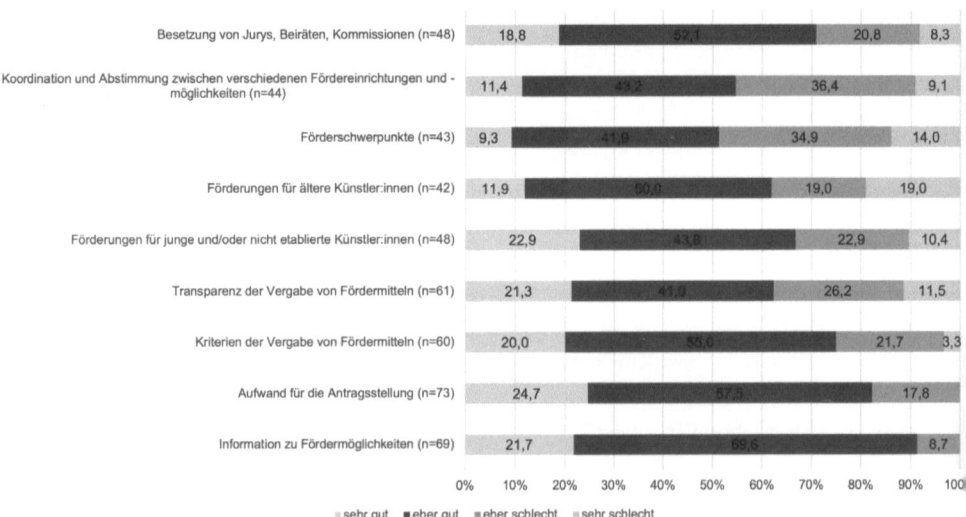

Abb. 3: *Bewertung der Kunstförderung des Landes Vorarlberg*

In den qualitativen Interviews gaben zumeist erfahrene Kunstschaffende an, vor jedem Förderantrag im Kopf die Rechnung aufzumachen, ob der Aufwand (Zeit, Arbeit, Ressourcen, Geld) für den Antrag und die mögliche Fördersumme in einer sinnvollen Relation zueinanderstehen. Gewisse Größen werden von ihnen gar nicht mehr angegangen, da sie sich nicht rechneten oder die ausgeschriebenen Fördermittel für eine ordentliche Umsetzung zu gering seien.

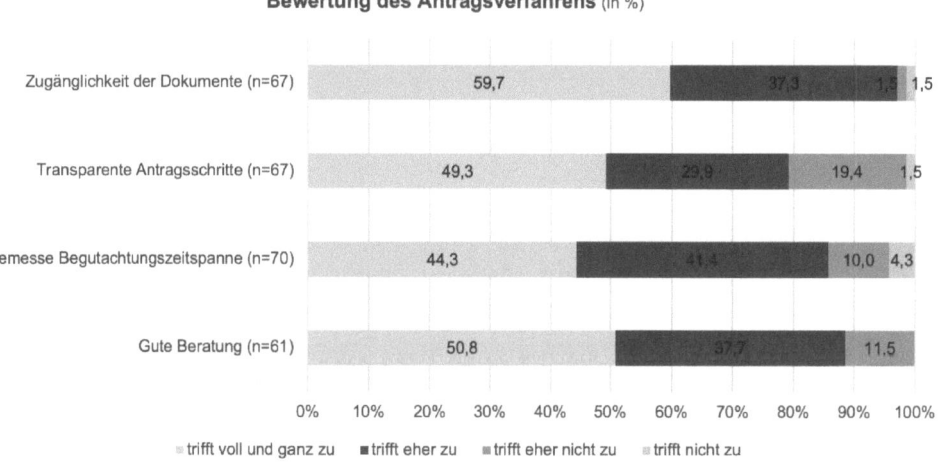

Abb. 4: *Bewertung des Antragsverfahrens*

Grundsätzlich werden die Antragsverfahren auf Kunstförderung des Landes Vorarlberg aus Sicht der online befragten Kunstschaffenden überwiegend positiv bewertet. So sind fast alle der Ansicht, dass die Dokumente für das Antragsverfahren gut zugänglich seien. Die Mehrheit der Kunstschaffenden, die dies beurteilen konnte und wollte, empfand die Beratung im Zuge der Förderansuchen als positiv ebenso die Begutachtungszeitspanne. Dass die Antragsschritte von Transparenz gekennzeichnet sind, wurde ebenfalls von vier von fünf Befragten als zutreffend bewertet (Abb. 4).

Dennoch gibt es vereinzelt auch Kritik an den Antragsstellungsverfahren oder Gründe, aus denen Befragte auf die Stellung von Anträgen generell verzichteten. In den qualitativen Interviews wurde von Kunstschaffenden berichtet, die nach einem abgelehnten Antrag aufgrund des wahrgenommenen Aufwands keinen weiteren Antrag mehr hätten stellen wollen oder sich nicht, mit Bezug auf die Corona-Beihilfen, noch einmal so „nackig" hätten machen wollen. Manchen Kunstschaffenden mit viel Potential fehle auch der Mut, da sie Angst vor einer Absage hätten. Allerdings gab kaum jemand an, gar keine Anträge mehr zu stellen. Von den wenigen Fällen wurde dies damit begründet, sich mehr Freiheit sichern zu wollen bzw. generell unabhängig sein zu wollen. Gründe gegen Ansuchen um Förderungen, die von Kunstschaffenden im Zuge der Onlinebefragung in eigenen Worten vorgebracht wurden, decken sich zum Teil mit denen aus den qualitativen Interviews. Auch hier wurden Angst vor einer Absage, der Zeitbedarf bzw. Aufwand für die Antragsstellung, die fehlende Notwendigkeit oder auch einfach das eigene Selbstverständnis (Stolz auf Unabhängigkeit) angeführt.

Förderungen besitzen einen wichtigen Stellenwert für die künstlerische Produktion. Auch wenn öffentliche Förderungen für Kunst und Kultur, für Kunstschaffende in der Kunstproduktion und in ihrer sozioökonomischen Lage eine unterstützende Wirkung haben, werden sie an Grenzen stoßen. Auch bei einer künftigen Erhöhung des Engagements der öffentlichen Förderstellen könne nach Wetzel et al. (2018) letztlich keine ausreichende und kontinuierliche Finanzierung des Kunst- und Kulturschaffens bewirkt werden. Die niedrigen Einkommen bei Kulturschaffenden werden andererseits auch als Konsequenz der Unterfinanzierung des Fördersystems betrachtet. Speicher und Haunschild (2002) sehen hier die Politik in der Pflicht, Kriterien von Förderung zu verhandeln. Darüber hinaus betonen sie, dass sie bei den Förderungen keinen sozialpolitischen Auftrag sehen, was so viel bedeutet, dass sie nicht die Kunstschaffenden per se, sondern ihre Kunst fördern (SPEICHER/HAUNSCHILD 2022).

Konsumverhalten und Kunstrezeption aus Sicht der Bevölkerung

Das Kulturbudget des Landes Vorarlberg wird unter anderem durch Steuereinnahmen finanziert. Daher ist es von erheblicher Bedeutung, wie die Bevölkerung die bereitgestellten und geförderten Kunst- und Kulturangebote beurteilt und in Anspruch nimmt. Ebenso relevant ist die generelle Einstellung der Bevölkerung zur Kunst- und Kulturförderung. Die Perspektiven in dieser Hinsicht können mithilfe der Ergebnisse der Bevölkerungsbefragung verdeutlicht werden (Abb. 5 & 6).

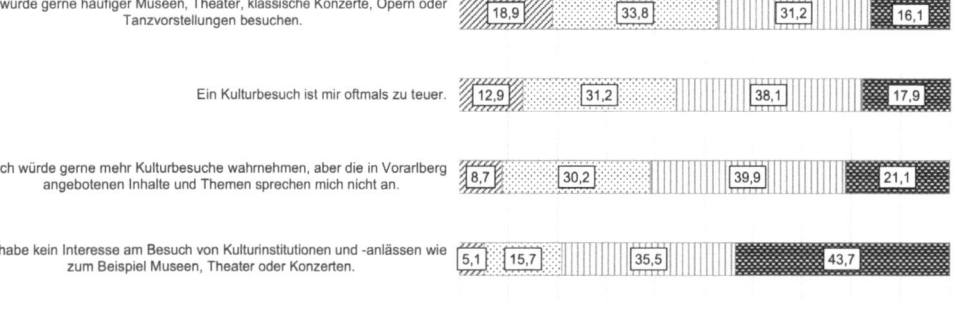

Abb. 5: *Einschätzung des Kulturverhaltens durch die Befragten*

Mehr als die Hälfte (52,7 %) der Befragten würde demnach grundsätzlich gerne häufiger Museen, Theater, klassische Konzerte, Opern oder
Tanzvorstellungen besuchen (Abb. 5). Inwieweit für die Umsetzungs-
wahrscheinlichkeit dieser grundsätzlichen Absicht ökonomische Gründe ausschlaggebend sein können, lässt sich mit dem nachfolgenden
Ergebnis abschätzen, denn knapp die Hälfte (44,1 %) befand, dass der
Kulturbesuch oftmals zu teuer sei. Allerdings stimmen nur 12,9 % dieser Einschätzung auch „voll und ganz" zu. Die verfügbaren Inhalte und
Themen des Kulturangebots in Vorarlberg scheinen für mehr als 50 %
der Vorarlberger Bevölkerung ansprechend zu sein. Weiters berichten
nur 20,8 % vom generellen Desinteresse am Besuch von Kulturinstitutionen und -anlässen wie zum Beispiel Museen, Theater oder Konzerten.
Umgekehrt kann dies so interpretiert werden, dass vier von fünf der Befragten sich selbst dem Besuch von Kulturangeboten zumindest nicht als
abgeneigt bezeichnen.

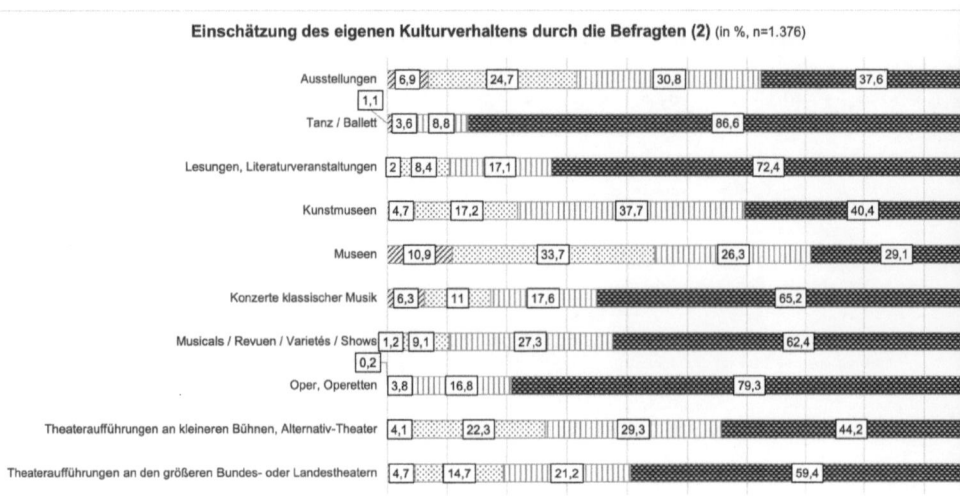

Abb. 6: *Kulturverhalten der Befragten in den letzten 12 Monaten*

Die Ergebnisse in Abbildung 6 liefern uns ein Bild über das Kulturverhalten der Vorarlberger Bevölkerung. Gefragt wurde, wie häufig die Befragten in den letzten 12 Monaten die angegebenen Kulturangebote in oder auch außerhalb Vorarlbergs (bspw. im Urlaub) besucht haben. Es geht bei der Frage also nicht um die Wahrnehmung speziell der Kulturangebote in Vorarlberg, sondern das grundsätzliche, potenzielle Interesse der Vorarlberger Bevölkerung an entsprechenden Angeboten anhand ihres tatsächlichen Verhaltens. Augenscheinlich ist, dass bestimmte Arten von insbesondere gemeinhin als eher hochkulturelle Angebote gelesene Veranstaltungen deutlich seltener besucht werden. Dies betrifft Tanz und Ballett („nie" 86,6 %), Oper, Operetten („nie" 79,3 %) und Lesungen und Literaturveranstaltungen („nie" 72,4 %). Konzerte klassischer Musik („nie" 65,2 %), Musicals, Revuen, Varietès, Shows („nie" 62,4 %) und Theateraufführungen an den größeren Bundes- oder Landestheatern („nie" 59,4 %) wurden von rund vier von zehn Befragten mindestens einmal besucht. Eher genießen die Vorarlbergerinnen und Vorarlberger Theateraufführungen an kleineren Bühnen oder Alternativtheatern (55,8 % mindestens einmal), den Besuch von Kunstmuseen (59,6 % mindestens einmal), Ausstellungen (62,4 % mindestens einmal) oder Museen allgemein (70,9 % mindestens einmal).

In Bezug auf die subjektiv wahrgenommene Wertschätzung der Vorarlberger Kunstszene durch das Land waren die Einschätzungen unter den befragten Kunstschaffenden geteilt. Einige der qualitativ befragten Kunstschaffenden und Schlüsselpersonen der Vorarlberger Kunst- und Kulturszene gaben an, sich gut durch das Land unterstützt zu fühlen, dankbar für die Angebote und Möglichkeiten zu sein und die Situation auch im Vergleich bspw. zu anderen Bundesländern positiv wahrzunehmen. Auch sei das Commitment des Landes für Kunst generell spürbar. Eine andere, unter den qualitativ Befragten etwas größere Gruppe war der entgegengesetzten Ansicht, dass zu wenig getan werde. Nahezu Einigkeit bestand hingegen darin, dass das Kulturbudget des Landes und das, was den Kunstschaffenden daraus zukäme, (viel) zu niedrig sei. Dazu wurde das Kulturbudget häufig in Vergleich zu anderen Budgetposten (z.B. Wirtschaftsförderung, Landwirtschaftssubventionen) gesetzt. Hervorgehoben wurde auch von einigen, dass man in anderen Bereichen zumeist von Investitionen spreche, im Kunst- und Kulturbereich jedoch von Förderungen oder Unterstützungen. Die im Diskurs verwendete Sprache verweise somit bereits auf die dahinterliegenden Wertzumessungen, da eine Investition einen zukünftig zu erwartenden Return on Investment impliziere, der bei einer Förderung oder Unterstützung im Wortsinne nicht enthalten sei.

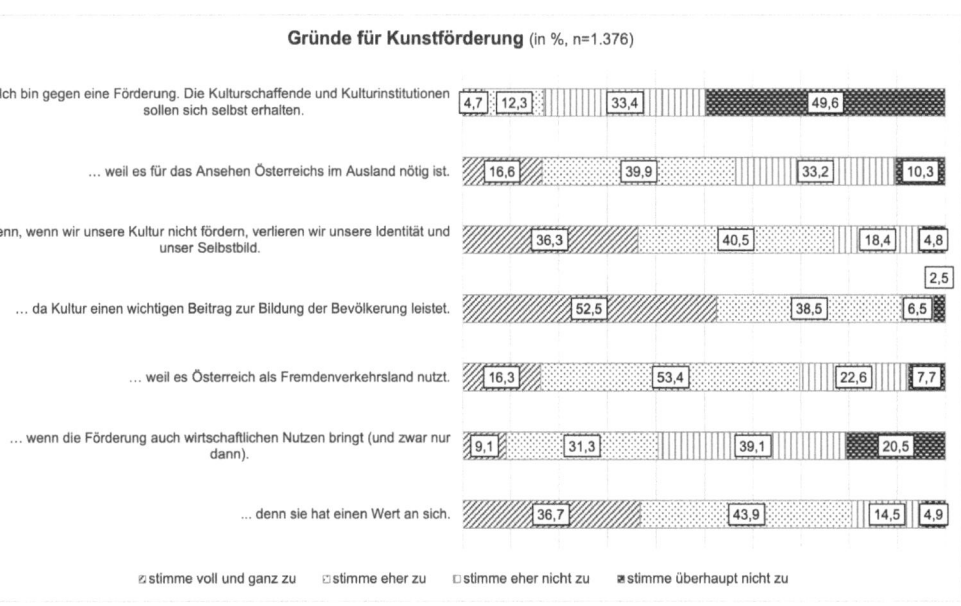

Abb. 7: *Gründe für die Kunstförderung aus Sicht der Bevölkerung*

In Abbildung 7 zeigt sich, dass sich mit 83 % eine klare Mehrheit der befragten Vorarlberger und Vorarlbergerinnen dafür ausspricht, Kulturschaffende und Kulturinstitutionen zu fördern. Sie sehen die Kulturschaffenden nicht in der Pflicht, sich selbst erhalten zu müssen. Die Gründe dafür sehen sie darin, dass Kulturschaffende und Kulturinstitutionen einen wichtigen Beitrag zur Bildung der Bevölkerung leisten (91,0 %), einen Wert an sich haben (80,6 %), wesentlich zur Identität und zum Selbstbild der Vorarlberger Gesellschaft beitragen (76,8 %), Österreich als Fremdenverkehrsland nutzen (69,7 %) und für das Ansehen Österreichs im Ausland notwendig seien (56,5 %). Die Ansicht, dass Kulturschaffende nur dann gefördert werden sollten, wenn die Förderung auch wieder einen wirtschaftlichen Nutzen bringe, lehnen die meisten der Befragten (59,6 %) hingegen (eher) ab.

Eine Kartographie einer Kunst- und Kulturlandschaft

Die beschriebenen Ergebnisse deuten darauf hin, dass die Kunst- und Kulturszene eine systemrelevante Rolle in der Gesellschaft innehat. Eine adäquate Förderung von Kunst und Kultur wird von Seiten der Bevölkerung unterstützt und von Kunstschaffenden gefordert, um weiterhin (exzellente) Kunst für das (anspruchsvolle) Publikum anbieten zu können. Die Ausgestaltung der Förderlandschaft nimmt direkten und indirekten Einfluss auf die Rahmenbedingungen, in denen eine Kunstproduktion durch die Kunstschaffenden erfolgen kann, und folglich auf die Fähigkeit einer Gesellschaft sich selbst im gegenseitigen Austausch reflektieren zu können. Die empirischen Daten gewähren uns einen Einblick in das wechselseitige Zusammenspiel von Strukturen, Beziehungsverhältnissen und den unterschiedlichen Akteurinnen und Akteuren, die daran beteiligt sind und wie sie sich dabei gegenseitig bedingen.

Ein Ausdruck dieser Interkonnektivität sind zwei Bilder von Kunst und Kultur, die im herrschenden Diskurs prominent verhandelt werden (FOUCAULT 1974, 1981). Im ersten Bild wird Kunst als essenzieller Bestandteil betrachtet, der das menschliche Zusammenleben ermöglicht und bereichert. In dieser Perspektive äußerten viele Interviewte Unverständnis darüber, warum Kunst aus ihrer Sicht während der Coronapandemie nicht sofort oder erst spät als systemrelevant anerkannt wurde. Kunst solle den gleichen Stellenwert in der öffentlichen Wahrnehmung wie beispielsweise Soziales und Bildung haben.

Kunst sei ein Indikator für die Lebensqualität bzw. für das Wohlbefinden der Gesellschaft. Eine Vernachlässigung der Kunst könnte die Grundlagen der Demokratie gefährden, da Kunst, der Gesellschaft stets einen Spiegel vorhalte, der zur Reflexion einlädt. Eine Investition in Kunst ist in dieser Dimension eine Investition in die gesellschaftliche Kohäsion (ANHEIER et al. 2016).

Im zweiten Bild wird Kunst im Kontext ihrer ökonomischen Implikationen betrachtet. Hierbei steht die Frage nach dem Marktwert und der generierten Wertschöpfung durch Kunst und Kultur im Mittelpunkt. Dies beinhaltet eine positive Außenwahrnehmung des Landes als lebendige und weltoffene Region, die attraktiv für Investitionen und Fachkräfte ist. In dieser Perspektive wird auf den monetären Nutzen hingewiesen, den Kunst und Kultur generieren. Eine Investition in Kunst bringt durch die Umwegrentabilität wirtschaftliche Vorteile mit sich. Die Produktion von Kunst und Kultur beeinflusst nicht nur die Lebensgrundlagen der Kunstschaffenden selbst, sondern auch der Tourismus und die Gastronomie profitieren davon. Darüber hinaus haben sich um die Kunst herum weitere Branchen, wie die Kunstvermittlung, etabliert. Kunst und Kultur werden in diesem Kontext als bedeutender Wirtschaftsfaktor betrachtet. Eine Investition in Kunst ist in dieser Dimension eine Investition in die ökonomische Leistungsfähigkeit einer Gesellschaft.

Während die Antworten der Befragten zwischen diesen beiden Bildern oszillierten, wird Kunst und Kultur eine inhärente Bedeutung für die Gesellschaft zugeschrieben, was die Frage nach der Finanzierung aufwirft. Einerseits wird Kunst und Kultur als ein öffentliches Gut betrachtet, das, ähnlich wie Bildung, als systemrelevant gilt und vom Staat in einem gewissen Maße bereitgestellt werden sollte. Ohne Förderungen oder Zuschüsse wären verschiedene kulturelle Angebote im Land nicht realisierbar oder müssten reduziert werden. Die Frage, in welchem Umfang der Staat fördern sollte, variiert, jedoch besteht weitgehende Einigkeit darin, dass eine reine Marktlösung nicht wünschenswert ist. Es wurde betont, dass eine Situation, in der der Staat sämtliche Kosten allein trägt, ebenfalls nicht möglich und nicht erstrebenswert sei. Einige Befragte sehen einen gewissen Wettbewerb als notwendig an, um die Kunst voranzutreiben. Dabei müsse unabhängig vom Wettbewerb von allen Kunstschaffenden immer ein gewisses Maß an Qualität gewährleistet sein, damit etwas als Kunst (und somit förderungswürdig) gelten könne. Speicher und Haunschild (2022) sehen hier die Politik in der Pflicht, Kriterien von Förderung zeitgemäß zu verhandeln. Eine präzise Definition der Förderkriterien und deren obligatorische Erfüllung war aus den verschiedenen Antworten der befragten Kunstschaffenden sowie Schlüsselpersonen der Vorarlberger Kunst- und Kulturszene kaum abzuleiten. Die Mehrheit sieht die Notwendigkeit, dies im Einzelfall zu prüfen, wie es bereits durch Kunstkommissionen geschieht. In diesem Zusammenhang besteht weitgehend Konsens darüber, dass es Unterschiede in der Qualität gibt und nicht alle Kunstproduktionen als gleichwertig angesehen werden sollten.

Schlussfolgerungen

Dieser kurze Abriss zeigt, wie die herrschenden Ambiguitäten und Zielkonflikte nicht normativ aufgelöst werden können, sondern ein ständiges Austarieren nötig machen. Soll es zum Beispiel ein Forcieren der Exzellenz- oder der Breitenförderungen geben, wie viele Marktmechanismen (auch in die Förderinstrumente eingeschrieben) sind zielführend, sollen Förderungen stärker an Institutionen oder Kunstschaffende gerichtet werden.

Entscheidend ist zu verstehen, dass es sich hierbei nicht um einfache kausale Wirkungsketten handelt, sondern um eine Momentaufnahme einer sich dynamisch veränderten Szene. Dies bedeutet zum einen, dass die Förderpolitik eine ständige gesellschaftliche und politische Verhandlung von Werten und Konzeptionen darstellt und zum anderen die Gestaltung bspw. einer Förderlandschaft kein endgültig abzuschließender Prozess sein kann, der im Sinne einer optimalen, dauerhaft so bestehenden Lösung angelegt ist. Vielmehr ist ein kontinuierliches transparentes Monitoring der Entwicklungen unabdingbar, wenn zukünftige Veränderungen zeitnah antizipiert werden sollen.

Ein ausgereiftes Fördersystem impliziert eine transparente und wertschätzende Kommunikation zwischen den Fördergebenden und den Kunstschaffenden, welche mit ihrer Kunst einen wertvollen Beitrag für die Gesellschaft erbringen. Dabei setzt das Fördersystem nicht auf ein „entweder oder", sondern hat stets ein „sowohl als auch" im Blick und orientiert sich an den jeweiligen Rahmenbedingungen der Zielgruppen, welche sie im Idealfall miteinbezieht.

In diesem komplexen System, in dem es beständig zu Interessensausgleichen kommt, ist es unumgänglich, dass auch Kritik geübt werden wird. Hier ist bei allen Beteiligten eine entsprechende Ambiguitätstoleranz unerlässlich. Zudem sollte nach den Beschreibungen durch die Befragten eine langfristigere Absicherung von existentiellen Risiken angedacht werden. Prekäre Lebens- und Erwerbsverhältnisse können sich negativ auf die Kunstproduktion und deren Qualität auswirken.

Sicherungssystem, die dies berücksichtigen und die Planungssicherheit (Alter, Krankheit, Familie, Kinder) erhöhen, würden die (psychischen) Belastungen senken und eine stärke Fokussierung für die Kunstproduktion ermöglichen. Um ökonomischen Erfolg zu erlangen, bedürfen Kunstschaffende Gelegenheiten, ihr Netzwerk zu erweitern und ihre Reichweite zu steigern, sowohl national als auch international. Die entsprechenden Formate und Orte, die entweder virtuell oder physisch stattfinden können und sowohl Veranstaltungscharakter als auch eine dauerhafte Präsenz haben können, sind entscheidend, um sich einem breiteren Publikum bekannt zu machen.

Literatur

ALLMANRITTER, Vera/RENZ, Thomas/TEWES-SCHÜNZEL, Thomas/JUHNKE, Sebastian (2020): *Kulturelle Teilhabe in Berlin 2019. Soziodemografie und Lebensstile. Ergebnisse einer repräsentativen Bevölkerungsbefragung*. Berlin.

ANHEIER, Helmut et al. (2016). *Cultural participation and inclusive societies. A thematic report based on the Indicator Framework on Culture and Democracy*. Strasbourg: Council of Europe.

CHRISTI, Clemens/GRIESSER, Markus (2017): *Unselbstständig selbstständig erwerblos: Studie zu Problemen von Kunstschaffenden in der sozialen Absicherung aus sozialwissenschaftlicher Sicht*. Wien: Kulturrat Österreich <https://kulturrat.at/studie-unselbstaendig-selbstaendig-erwerbslos> [16.01.2024].

CRESWELL, John W. (⁴2013): *Research Design. Qualitative, Quantitative, and Mixed Methods Approaches*. Thousand Oak, London, New Delhi: Sage.

DELEUZE, Gilles/GUATTARI, Félix. (1992): *Tausend Plateaus, Kapitalismus und Schizophrenie*. Berlin: Merve.

ECOPLAN (2021): *Soziale Absicherung von Kulturschaffenden. Auftraggeber: Suisseculture Sociale und Pro Helvetia*. Basel: Universität Basel <https://www.suisseculturesociale.ch/uploads/media/default/16/Absicherung_Kulturschaffende_Bericht_Schlussbericht_210624_de.pdf> [16.01.2024]

FOUCAULT, Michel (1974): *Die Ordnung der Dinge*. Frankfurt/M.: Suhrkamp.

FOUCAULT, Michel (1981): *Archäologie des Wissens*. Frankfurt/M.: Suhrkamp.

FUCHS, Tanja (2015): *Kunst in Zeiten der Kreativwirtschaft*. Kromsdorf: Jonas.

GEIßLER, Rainer (2014): Sozialer Wandel in Deutschland, Armut und Prekarität. – In: *Informationen zur politischen Bildung* 324, 30–30.

HIRSCHMAN, Albert O. (1970): Exit, Voice and Loyalty, Responses to Decline in Firms, Organizations and States. Cambridge/MA: Harvard University Press.

HENNING, Christof/SCHULTHEIS, Franz/THOMÄ, Dieter (2019): *Kreativität als Beruf. Soziologisch-Philosophische Erkundungen der Welt der Künste*. Bielefeld: transcript.

HUSSY, Walter/SCHREIER, Margrit/ECHTERHOFF Gerald (2010): *Forschungsmethoden in Psychologie und Sozialwissenschaften*. Berlin, Heidelberg, New York: Springer.

IBERT, Oliver/PFLANZ, Kai/SCHMIDT, Suntje (2012): *Spiel auf vielen Bühnen. Wie Musicaldarsteller ihre Vulnerabilität und Resilienz auf dem Arbeitsmarkt konstruieren.* Erkner: Leibniz-Institut für Regionalentwicklung und Strukturplanung <https://idw-online.de/de/attachmentdata19136.pdf> [24.04.2023].

KELLE, Udo (²2008): *Die Integration qualitativer und quantitativer Methoden in der empirischen Sozialforschung. Theoretische Grundlagen und methodologische Konzepte.* Wiesbaden: VS.

KNITTEL, Susanne (Hg.) (2011): *Artist-Management in Medienunternehmen: Lavieren zwischen Ökonomie und Kreativität.* Wiesbaden: Gabler.

LANDESREGIERUNG VORARLBERG (2019): *Unser Vorarlberg – chancenreich und nachhaltig, Arbeitsprogramm 2019 – 2024.* Bregenz: Abteilung Vermögensverwaltung, Hausdruckerei.

MICHEEL, *Heinz-Günter* (2010): *Quantitative empirische Sozialforschung.* München: Ernst Reinhardt.

MÜLLER-JENTSCH, Walther (2005): Künstler und Künstlergruppen. Soziologische Ansichten einer prekären Profession. – In: *Berliner Journal für Soziologie* 15(2), 159–177.

PRILLER, Eckhard (2016): *Die wirtschaftliche und soziale Situation Bildender Künstlerinnen und Künstler: Zusatzaspekte. Einkünfte aus Ausstellungsvergütungen, Engagement für Geflüchtete.* Berlin: Bundesverband Bildender Künstlerinnen und Künstler e.V. <https://internationalauthors.org/wp-content/uploads/2019/06/BB-KUmfrage_2016_24.10_print.pdf> [26.04.2023].

REBITZER, Fabian/ZABRODSKY, Thomas/KÜHNE, Sarah/ARNOLD, Lukas (2023): *Gesamtbericht: Lebens- und Einkommensverhältnisse Kunstschaffender in Vorarlberg* <https://vorarlberg.at/documents/302033/24334401/Bericht_PEVK_final.pdf> [16.01.2024].

STAUBMANN, Helmut (2001): Sozialsysteme als selbstreferentielle Systeme: Niklas Luhmann. – In: Morel, Julius (Hg.), *Soziologische Theorie: Abriß der Ansätze ihrer Hauptvertreter.* München, Wien, 218–239.

SPEICHER, Hannah/HAUNSCHILD, Axel (2022): *Systemcheck. Im freien Fall. Beschäftigungsformen, soziale Sicherungen, Selbstverständnisse und Bewältigungsstrategien in den freien darstellenden Künsten, Diskussionspapier zu ersten Ergebnissen der qualitativen Studien von Systemcheck.* Berlin: Bundesverband Freie Darstellende Künste e.V.

UZZI, Brian/SPIRO, Jarrett (2005): Collaboration and creativity: The small world problem. – In: *International Journal of Sociology* 111(2), 447–504

WEIGL, Aron/WIMMER, Michael/EHM, Veronika (2018): *Bericht zur Evaluation des Unterstützungsfonds im Rahmen des Künstler-Sozialversicherungsfonds.* Wien: EDUCULT <https://educult.at/wp-content/uploads/2020/11/EDUCULT_Politik-im-Freien-Theater_Evaluationsbericht_2020.pdf> [26.04.2023].

WETZEL, Petra unter Mitarbeit von DANZER, Lisa/RATZENBÖCK, Veronika/LUNGSTRAß, Anja/LANDSTEINER, Günther (2018): *Soziale Lage der Kunstschaffenden und Kunst- und Kulturvermittler/innen in Österreich: ein Update der Studie „Zur sozialen Lage der Künstler und Künstlerinnen in Österreich" 2008. LetR Sozialforschung.* <http://www.kulturdokumentation.org/download/EB_Soziale_Lage_Kunstschaffender_Kunst_Kulturvermittler_nb.pdf> [26.04.2023].

REPORTS

Introducing Urban Music Studies and Its Network

Einführung in die Urban Music Studies und ihr Netzwerk

ALENKA BARBER-KERSOVAN[A*], VOLKER KIRCHBERG[A**], TOBIAS LUTZE[B***]

[A] Leuphana Universität Lüneburg
[B] HAW Hamburg University of Applied Sciences

The first idea of initiating Urban Music Studies as a new field of social and cultural studies research dates to the year 2010 when Volker Kirchberg, Alenka Barber-Kersovan and Robin Kuchar, members of the Institute of Sociology and Cultural Organisation at Leuphana University of Lüneburg, organized a conference entitled *Music City Hamburg* (https://www.transcript-verlag.de/978-3-8376-1965-2/music-city/). This conference was inspired by theoretical works on creative industries and creative cities by authors such as Richard Florida and Charles Landry on one side and the controversial political dispute in Hamburg about a new and prestigious concert hall. At that time, the dispute erupted in connection with a large-scale construction project in the port of Hamburg, which, among other things, included the conversion of an old warehouse into the Elbe Philharmonic Hall as the designated landmark of the city.

Conference outcomes revealed that there are already some publications and research projects by Adam Krims, Sara Cohen and Andy Bennett, dealing with the relationship between the music and the city. However, they are located in different and mutually exclusive disciplines such as urban studies, human geography or music sociology, and thus lack a communal platform for a multidisciplinary scientific exchange. In order to improve this situation, an international workshop with the title *What is Urban Music Studies and what could it be?* was organized in Lüneburg in October 2017.

The main premises for this workshop were the following:

* Music is central to urban culture.
* The relationship between music and the city is dynamic and reciprocal.
* Music forms communities and acts as a symbolic resource for these communities.

[*]   alenka.barber-kersovan@leuphana.de
[**] volker.kirchberg@leuphana.de
[***] tobias.lutze@haw-hamburg.de

Journal of Cultural Management and Policy, 2024/2, pp. 159–162
doi 10.14361/zkmm-2024-0208

- Music scenes contribute to the self-awareness of its inhabitants as being urban.
- Music contributes to the cultural identity of a city.
- As the urban is an essential part of music also a number of musical compositions are shaped by the urban settings in which they are created.

On the organisational level the launch of an *Urban Music Studies Scholars Network* was proposed in order to

- establish Urban Music Studies as a new inter- and transdisciplinary field of research;
- provide a forum where individuals and institutions involved in Urban Music Studies can meet and share their work in workshops and conferences;
- collect and disseminate information about Urban Music Studies;
- document the work (researching, teaching, publishing) in this field.

To put these goals into practice, two international conferences were organized at Leuphana University in Lüneburg. The first one took place in November 2018 and was entitled, *Groove the City—Urban Music Policies between Informal Networks and Institutional Governance* (https://urbanmusicstudies.org/groove-the-city-urban-music-policies-between-informal-networks-and-institutional-governance/). Most contributions looked at the ways that cities precondition the emergence and flourishing of music scenes by providing the social, material, and cultural resources required and how they act as focal points of the production, distribution, and consumption of acoustic capital.

The second conference, which took place in February 2020, was entitled, *Groove the City 2020—Constructing and Deconstructing Urban Spaces through Music* (https://urbanmusicstudies.org/wp-content/uploads/2020/02/Book-Of-Abstracts_Groove-the-City-2020.pdf). It featured more than 90 presentations given by speakers from 32 countries. The individual streams dealt with music in material and social urban spaces; experiencing urban spaces through music; and the music and the political urban space.

Following the COVID induced pause, the third Groove the City event entitled, *Vienna Perspectives—Art, Urban Space and Social In/Equality* (https://muk.ac.at/fileadmin/mediafiles/documents/Programme_2022-23/PH_WienerPerspektiven.pdf) took place in

November 2022 at the Private University for Music and Art in Vienna. Drawing on the case of Vienna some 50 participants presented and discussed utopian (and dystopian) concepts of local urban politics and the organization of musical life before and after the pandemic. The next UMS conference with the title, *Groove the City—Move the Streets* will take place 17-19 September 2026 at the University of Music and Performing Arts in Vienna.

As an important communication platform, the Urban Music Studies Network (https://urbanmusicstudies.org/) was established. It has approximately 900 members from all five continents, including from countries in the Global South (India, Brazil, Mexico), and the previous Eastern Block (Czech Republic, Poland, and Ukraine) as well as East Asia—Japan, Hong Kong and Taiwan. Subscribers have free access to an Urban Music Studies blog and a Facebook channel.

Further, a book series, *Urban Music Studies* (Intellect Publisher, Bristol; https://www.intellectbooks.com/urban-music-studies) has been launched with series editors Alenka Barber-Kersovan, Lisa Gaupp, Andrea Glauser, Volker Kirchberg and Robin Kuchar. Editorial board members include Andy Bennett, Giacomo Bottá, Pranoo Deshraju, Murray Forman, Paula Guerra, Fabian Holt, Marek Jezinski, Will Straw and Susana Zapke.

Two books have already been published. *Sonic Signatures—Music, Migration and the City at Night* (Derek Pardue, Ailbhe Kenny and Katie Young, eds.) interprets contemporary migrant music as sonic signatures constitutive of the city at night. *Popular Music in Leeds—Histories, Heritage, People and Places"* (Brett Lashua, Karl Spracklen, Kitty Ross and Paul Thompson, eds.) offers the first academic compilation of the history, heritage, people and places of popular music in Leeds. Three more books are in preparation, and there is an ongoing open call for monographs, readers, and edited collections from, and for the field of Urban Music Studies. The series especially welcomes proposals by young researchers from a wide array of contents, methods, critical and analytical perspectives.

Urban Music Studies Scholars network deals with a broad range of topics and musical practices, current and historical, and focuses on countries and geographical regions that are normally excluded from the scientific discourse. The network is necessary in order to clarify the importance of music as a physical, mental, and politically formative factor in urban development within the framework of urban research, for example, among urban planners, urban sociologists and urban economists. Equally important is to make clear, to experts in musicology, that they too must abandon and break with monodisciplinary understandings of music in history and society in order to recognize the importance of music creation, music production, and music consumption for and in the city.

This lively platform, addresses scholars from a variety of disciplines, such as sociology, social geography, historical and systematic musicology, anthropology, architecture, and city planning, and offers a large range of activities, including regular conferences, publications and other means of academic exchange. Covering subjects as wide ranging as identity construction, city branding, musical heritage and cultural tourism, this international network provides an appealing arena for scholars of arts management studies and cultural policy studies interested in music in urban settings.

FROM OUR ARCHIVES

Socially Engaged Art, Post-Truth and the Monumentalising of Democracy

Sozial engagierte Kunst, Post-Truth und die Monumentalisierung der Demokratie

MARTIN LANG^A*, TOM GRIMWOOD^B**

^A School of Creative Arts, University of Lincoln

^B Centre for Research in Health and Society, University of Cumbria

Abstract

In 2021, for the first time, all the nominees for the Turner Prize were socially engaged art (SEA) collectives. The groups all democratised their practices by relinquishing their authorial control to non-artists. Framed by the prestige of the Turner Prize, this relinquishing of control, through collaborative actions with various communities, was lauded as ethically meritorious, because of its egalitarian and non-hierarchical nature. We argue that behind the growing institutional success of SEA lies a tension between its goodness as a necessity based on a model of authentic practice, and the context of post-truth that informs its rejection of artistic expertise in favour of egalitarian processes. However, we contend that it is not the processes themselves, but the *monumentalising* of democracy and equality that brings SEA into the domain of post-truth. We conclude that SEA must retain a dialectical tension between equality and the production of truth as a cultural value: a dialectic which involves the careful reinstatement of artistic authorship and a sincerer vision of its political ambitions and signification.

2021 waren erstmals ausschließlich Kunstkollektive für den Turner Prize nominiert. So wurde Autorschaft gleichsam 'demokratisiert´, indem die Kontrolle über die künstlerische Arbeit an Nicht-Künstler abgegeben hatten. Gerade bei einem derart prestigeträchtigen Preis wie dem Turner Prize wurde dieser erklärte Kontrollverzicht, den das kollektive Arbeiten mit unterschiedlichen Gruppierungen mit sich bringt, als ethisch wertvoll erachtet. Gilt der Kontrollverzicht doch als egalitär und nicht hierarchisch. Wir argumentieren dagegen, dass der wachsende institutionelle Erfolg von sozial engagierter Kunst ein Spannungsverhältnis erzeugt zwischen der Notwenigkeit ethisch Gutes zu tun, und zwar auf möglichst authentische Weise, und einer gewissen Unaufrichtigkeit, die Projekten innewohnt, die künstlerische Expertise angeblich zugunsten egalitärer Prozesse aufzugeben. Wir möchten zeigen, dass es nicht primär die kollektiven Prozesse selbst sind, die sozial engagierte Kunst in den Bereich des Postfaktischen drängen, verantwortlich hierfür ist vielmehr die allgemeine Überhöhung von Demokratie und Gleichheit. Dabei kommen wir zu dem Schluss, dass sozial engagierte Kunst eine dialektische Spannung zwischen Vorstellungen von Gleichheit und der Produktion von Wahrheit als kulturellem Wert beibehalten muss: eine Dialektik, die die behutsame Wiederherstellung künstlerischer Autorschaft und eine ehrlichere Vision politischer Ambitionen und Bedeutungen verbindet.

Keywords

Sozial engagierte Kunst/Socially engaged art, Postfaktische Politik/Post-truth politics, Monumentalisieren/Monumentalising, Demokratie/Democracy, Kuratieren/curating, Soziokultur/community arts, gesellschaftlicher Wandel/social change.

* MLang@lincoln.ac.uk

** tom.grimwood@cumbria.ac.uk

Journal of Cultural Management and Cultural Policy, 2024/2, pp. 165–182

doi 10.14361/zkmm-2024-0209

Introduction

In 2021, for the first time in its history, all the nominees for The Turner Prize (Britain's premier prize for contemporary art) were socially engaged art collectives. The jury lauded all five nominees for "their socially engaged artworks, and how they work closely and creatively with communities across the breadth of the UK" (TATE 2021). For example, Project Art Works run art workshops for people with complex support needs and then display the resulting work as a collaborative art practice at the intersection of art and care; Gentle/Radical are composed of "activists, conflict resolution trainers, faith ministers, equalities practitioners, youth workers, performers, writers, teachers—and [even] artists" (JANUSZCZAK 2021: 16) who create pop-up events including film screenings, walks, talks, meals and other actions that bring people together. The prize winners, the Array collective, campaign for women's rights, language rights and LGBT rights. These forms of socially engaged art are not new, of course, but the growing shift towards the institutional celebration of collectivised and communal practice (also prevalent in the British Art Show 2021 and documenta fifteen, 2022) is.

Before 2015, when Assemble won the Turner Prize, there had been no art collectives shortlisted for the prize. Although there had been some notable artist duos (Gilbert and George, Art & Language, the Wilson twins, the Chapman brothers, Langlands and Bell, the Otolith Group), they operated in the same cast as individual artists—that is, they were the sole creators of their artworks. All that changed after Assemble broke the mould. Gregory Sholette explains how the decision to award the prize to a collective "highlighted differences of opinion among artists" (2017: 131) and he argues that this showed that the so-called social turn, that Claire Bishop pronounced a decade before, had now reached the mainstream. In 2018, another high-profile collective was nominated (Forensic Architecture). In 2019 all four individual nominees declared themselves to be a collective and decided to share the prize equally between them. This might demonstrate that the current move towards collectivisation is broader than a trend directed by the Turner Prize. One could argue that the artists contested the competitive and implicitly individualist logic of prize-giving, indeed, going *against* the Turner Prize. Or maybe it demonstrated how artists are now expected to behave: the Turner Prize readily accepted their proposal to share the prize (and to much media pomp). There was no Turner Prize in 2020 because of the coronavirus pandemic. Instead, it was collectivised, by redistributing the prize money to ten artists in the form of Turner bursaries.

As perhaps a natural progression, the groups shortlisted for 2021 went beyond collectivising their practice or collaborating with other artists, to also relinquish their authorial control to non-artist participants—a move so common in contemporary forms of participatory and socially engaged art that it is usually considered unremarkable. Framed by the prestige of the Turner Prize, collaborative actions, such as working as a collective with various communities, are celebrated as egalitarian and non-hierarchical. As J.J. Charlesworth explains, "Social change through art, and artists working as collectives, have become pet interests for the Turner Prize and for the Tate as an institution, and this year's collective-fest suggests the prize is doubling down on the virtues of togetherness, anti-individualism and art as social activism" (CHARLESWORTH 2021). In such a context, it has become commonplace to view artists who insist on owning the authorship of their works, and in doing so aligning with an individual viewpoint or didactic position, as increasingly culturally aloof, somewhat antiquated or even modernist. "Collectivism after modernism", as Sholette (2017: 132) terms the phenomenon, appears to have become a prerequisite for art to be authentically engaged.

Is this collectivisation a success for art, a realisation of its radical potential to undermine the institutions of authority and challenge conventional perspectives on value and meaning? Perhaps. But there is also an unease with what Sholette terms "whatever collectivism" (2017:132). Social engagement has been framed by a particular way of seeing, where non-hierarchical collaboration with laypeople is seen as necessarily good. In this article, we argue that the success of social engagement in established art institutions often rests on a tension between, on the one hand, its benefits as a model of necessity, based on a model of authentic practice—which is to say, how art, social or not, engages with the world—and, on the other hand, the context of post-truth that feeds on the fragmentation of public and cultural spheres. We will argue that, at first sight, it seems that the necessity of goodness can easily become an example for, or performance of, the post-truth context by virtue of the relationship between democratising art, the celebration of everydayness, and subsequent critique of exceptionalism in artistic production. At a second look, however, we suggest that the tension is often complicated via a certain *monumentalising* of particular aspects of practice (such as democratic and egalitarian processes), and it is not the practices themselves but the monumentalising act that brings socially engaged art into the domain of post-truth. Indeed, a problem with post-truth itself may be rooted in this work of monumentalising and to address this, there is a need to consider what is at stake in the institutional validation of socially engaged art.

Post-Truth and the Ordinariness of Subversion

As a politico-epistemological context, post-truth is (perhaps purposefully) ill-defined (VOGELMANN 2018). While its symptoms include a disregard for objective fact and the shifting of arguments with little awareness of previous premises, the post-truth context provides a challenge to expertise precisely *because* it remains so elusive for experts to define. As Tom Grimwood argues:

> the 'era' of post-truth is effectively a fable, given its lack of any clear starting point, and its tendency to invoke rather worn 'enemies' at the core of its apparent structure: postmodernists, feminists, the irrational and the easily led. Nevertheless, it remains powerful as a fable, or, as I have termed it, an exercising in curating cultural memory in order to establish accounts that are not quite as complete as narratives or propositional arguments, but nevertheless retain a bank of stock figures and metaphors that are by now easily recognised (GRIMWOOD 2022: 43).

As such, the characteristics of post-truth provide an important context for the progress of, on the one hand, social activism (be it left wing, right wing or other), and on the other a dissatisfaction with traditional models and institutions of authority. Key to this is a tension between the artist as an expert in their practice and the potentially radical politics of collective production. Purveyors of socially engaged art have not been slow to pick up on this. The former half of this tension pertains to a history of artistic exceptionalism that runs up to Modernism. In this history, a particular expertise in the facilitation of art dominates. The tendency to collectivise and democratise artistic practice (by opening it up to non-artists outside the collective) that we see today in socially engaged art stems from a foundational problem for art since Modernism: that of a lack of stable criteria by which to assess art. Debates on deskilling, from Ian Burn's reflection on art of the Sixties (1981/1999) to John Roberts' *Intangibilities of Form* (2007), have all but eradicated the expectation that contemporary artists should display craft expertise, but the demise of the artist as expert in their practice goes beyond this. Successive waves of art have undermined any criteria for aesthetic assessment with the result that any notion of artistic expertise remains elusive and, in some cases, even manifested as a counter-authority pitched against conventional models of the expert.

The latter half of the tension is equally problematic. While such a contrast may be initially enticing, there is also reason to question how readily the radical nature of socially engaged art's subversive tendencies are. Indeed, after several decades of socially engaged practice, the Turner Prize's recognition may well be less an acknowledgement of artistic prowess, and more related to broader socio-cultural moves towards the democratisation of research. This is not just limited to the requirement of funded art practices to demonstrate their social value; co-production and shared decision-making in local cultural, social and economic activities has become the norm for funding bodies across health, social science and the humanities. In this way, far from subverting, socially engaged art can end up being complicit with the same institutions it was designed to challenge.

Far from creating spheres of public dialogue free from the assumed hierarchy and elitism of the gallery space, it can drive a dysfunctional model of cultural value and, consequently, contribute to, rather than challenge, instabilities around social identities, and fuel cultural tensions. This is what the Dutch research collective BAVO (founded 2001) termed "NGO-Art" (2007 : 23)). More recently, Marc James Léger has described socially engaged art as a kind of "unofficial official art" (2019: 16), a symptom of the political economy of global capitalism that has become synonymous with "victim politics" and "self-culpabilisation" (LÉGER 2019: 26).

Given that our focus is on the tensions inherent to the newfound institutional success of socially engaged art, we must explore the main components of this new context. The place of socially engaged art in the context of a post-truth narrative can be considered in terms of both content, with its suspicion of expertise, and form.

First, content. According to Boris Groys, philosophers and artists of yesteryear had something to say due the particular exceptionalism mentioned above. We might say that up to Modernism, when artists began to question what qualifies as skill or authorial expertise, artists believed they had artistic expertise (even if this included a rejection of dominant models of expertise). Today, Groys (2016) tells us, theorists and artists just want to be like everybody else—ordinary. This condition is not without its historical antecedents, of course. The exhibition *The Painting of Everyday Life*, curated by Ralph Rugoff at London's Hayward Gallery (2008) focussed on instances since 1960. In the same year, the Whitechapel Gallery added *The Everyday* (JOHNSTONE 2008) to its Documents of Contemporary Art series. This edited collection traces the origins of artists' fascination with the everyday to Surrealism, Situationism, Fluxus and conceptual and feminist artists of the 1960s and 1970s. We might add Pop Art to the list. Groys, however, uses the example of how Rirkrit Tiravanija cooked food (like everybody else does), as an illustration of the everyday as an ethically meritorious topic choice for artists, precisely because no expertise is required to participate. The relationship between the artist-facilitator and the non-artist participant is horizontal and egalitarian. Arguably unlike previous incarnations of creative challenges to institutional authority, the interest in the everyday is not so much a promotion of counter-cultural norms, or a deconstruction of the rituals of authority, as a simple enactment of the mundane: less a celebration of triviality than a trivialising of celebration.

While Tiravanija is usually considered in terms of relational aesthetics, the principle is also applicable to socially engaged art. Conflict Kitchen (2010-2017) only served food from countries that were in military or political conflict with America. It was conceived by artists Jon Rubin and Dawn Weleski. It is often discussed as a piece of socially engaged art and it was a finalist for the second International Award for Public Art. Sholette describes how it forced customers "into an intimate encounter with their alleged enemies" and this "mischievous, even ironic dimension" (2017:139) is what made the project as a work of art. Yet it was a kitchen that prepared and sold food: just like any restaurant does. As with Tiravanija's *Pad Thai* (Paula Allen Gallery, New York 1990), no special artistic training was needed to produce the work. Groys observes that these kinds of socially engaged art are a type of "activity in which everyone can participate, one that is all-inclusive and truly egalitarian" and that today the discussion of art is open to everybody precisely because "no one can be a specialist in art, only a dilettante" (2016: 39).

Groys' prognosis illustrates what Martin Lang terms the "democratisation of art" (LANG 2021: 25) where the most democratic forms of socially engaged art completely relinquish authority to non-artist participant-collaborators. Take Anthony Gormley's *One & Other* (2009). This artwork was a prestigious commission for Trafalgar Square's fourth plinth (London). The plinth had stood empty since 1841, when funds precluded erecting a statue on it, just as had been done with the three other plinths placed at each corner of the Square. Gormley invited volunteers to occupy the plinth for one hour and do whatever they liked. The work was so egalitarian that no criteria were used to select the applicants, who were randomly selected by a computer instead. Gormley himself applied, but his application was unsuccessful, seemingly proving the work's egalitarian credentials. Gormley (2018) himself has described *One & Other* as a kind of social sculpture. Indeed, it is no real stretch to understand the project as a socially engaged artwork where the artist gave up his voice and position of privilege so that others might speak (see Hans Ulrich Obrist in Gormley 2010, for example). The volunteers can be conceptualised as collaborators, or co-authors in the production of the work. It is not Gormley's fault if their contributions amount to nothing more than boring, tedious and uninspiring artwork, as he has delegated responsibility for the artwork to the community (to, mostly, non-artist volunteers). Furthermore, by doing so he takes an ethical stand, proving his moral worth and thereby creating a successful socially engaged artwork—one that cannot fail by any stuffy or authoritarian old aesthetic criteria: he has democratised the artwork and this is what counts.

On the other hand, if the volunteers produce some kind of profound statement or poetic gesture Gormley can claim their actions as his own. In this case Gormley acts as a sole artist-director, framing the actions of others, and the artwork ceases to be egalitarian or socially engaged. Paradoxically then, if the volunteers produce something interesting, the project fails as a work of socially engaged art, while if nothing interesting happens this is proof of its success on a social level. The greater the democratisation, the farther towards collaboration or co-authorship the work drifts, the more egalitarian, and therefore artistically worthy, the artwork is deemed to be.

There is a double edge to this distrust of artistic authorship. On the one hand, it drives the engagement of the socially engaged artists who eschew the elitism of the gallery. On the other, it displays an uncomfortable relationship with broader societal trends such as post-truth, as evidenced in the Brexit campaign, where (British Member of Parliament) Michael Gove infamously declared that Britain "has had enough of experts" (MANCE 2016). Whether this was hostility to expertise, or just to the expert as a figure or personality is still in some dispute (GRIMWOOD 2021). Indeed, the advent of post-truth is typically heralded as the ultimate threat to intellectual civilisation, embedded in the rise of the alt-right, left-wing populism, alternative facts, and fake news. Rather than take the reactive, scientistic position (seen in the work of, for example, Lee McIntyre or Matthew d'Ancona), which demands an unmitigated return to clear boundaries between the true and the false, the democratic principles of socially engaged art instead seek to renegotiate those boundaries. Bracketing the question of artistic expertise allows so-called truth to be released from the hierarchies of institutional elitism and prestige, and into the hands of collective and heterogeneous voices in the name of a new, reinvigorated authenticity.

How did we end up in this series of tensions between expertise and equality; subversion and institutional recognition that characterise socially engaged art in the post-truth world? Rather than present a metanarrative, it is important to consider this as something of a dialectical struggle between competing interpretations, both of which are embedded in particular institutional practices. First, the tensions can be understood in terms of foci of the artistic works themselves, which render socially engaged art complicit with the politics of post-truth. Second, the valorisation of objectivity and truth in the first narrative can be read as a form of monumentalising which drives a dysfunctional model of cultural value, and consequently contributes to instabilities around social identities and fuels cultural tensions. In the following two sections, we shall describe how this monumentalising drives the form of socially engaged art in the context of a post-truth narrative.

The Post-Truth Condition as a Driver for the Democratic Collectivisation of Socially Engaged Art

Writing in 2011, Grant Kester asserted that poststructuralist discourse had attained a canonical status in European, American and Latin American academia. He describes how it first becoming a popular strand within critical theory, before becoming essentially synonymous *with* critical theory, such that today it "constitutes a kind of globalized theoretical *lingua franca* in the arts and humanities" (KESTER 2011: 54—italics in original). While he uses the term poststructuralism, he takes a rather liberal approach to categorising a range of philosophers in doing so, lumping Agamben, Nancy, Rancière and Badiou in with Foucault, Derrida, Lyotard, and Deleuze. What links them, for Kester, is their shared set of characteristics, that includes:

> privileging dissensus over consensus, rupture and immediacy over continuity and duration, and distance over proximity, intimacy, or integration [...] extreme skepticism about organized political action and a hyper-vigilance regarding the dangers of co-option and compromise entailed by such action, the ethical normalization of desire and somatic or sensual experience, and the recoding of political transformation into a form of ontic disruption directed at any coherent system of belief, agency, or identity (KESTER 2011: 54).

Kester asserts that art criticism promulgated a hermeneutic system, based on the act of "reading" the image, which was largely drawn from the canon of structuralist and post-structuralist literary theory (KESTER 2011: 55). According to him, deconstruction of texts, images and meaning coupled with a postmodern tendency toward appropriation served to "undermine the status of the artist as author" (KESTER 2011: 55). We agree, but while for Kester the role of the artist came "to destabilize the viewer [...] through an essentially individual hermeneutic engagement" (KESTER 2011: 54), we contend that the demise of artistic authorship accounts for the contemporary popularity of art collectives: the *form* of socially engaged art.

If one consequence of democratically collectivised art is that artists lose their voices to assemblages of temporally passing collaborations and communities, another is that they are denigrated below the curator-star. Since artistic authority has been destabilised, it seems that artworks can be curated and used by others however they like. Claire Bishop argues that curators at the turn of the millennium (including Nicolas Bourriaud, Maria Lind, Hans Ulrich Obrist and others) encouraged art that was not only collaborative, participatory and interactive, but also open-ended and resistant to closure (all socially engaged traits). Hal Foster predicted this situation, writing in the mid-nineties that "the institution may shadow the work that it otherwise highlights: it becomes the spectacle, it collects the cultural capital, and the director-curator becomes the star" (FOSTER 1996: 198). Bishop notes how this trend seemed to "derive from a creative misreading of poststructuralist theory where, rather than the *interpretations* of a work of art being open to continual reassessment, the work of art *itself* is argued to be in perpetual flux" (BISHOP 2004: 52—Italics in original). This further undermined the status of the artist as author. If the artwork itself is in flux, it has no fixed meaning and so becomes an empty signifier onto which anybody can place any meaning. If meaning will be socially constructed by future publics, why not collaborate with the public to make the artwork in the first place, in the manner that Gormley did? Such creative misreadings of poststructuralism produce an assumption that the artist's intention does not matter, as experience is subjective and interpretation is relative. This explains why artists cede authorial control to become mere facilitators of collaboration with the general public (whose input is considered equally valid to that of trained artists). Indeed, one can suggest a correlation between this approach to artmaking and the shifts in journalistic practices towards user-generated content, if not the more recent use of focus groups to determine which political policy to pursue (WRING 2009).

Curators and artists almost seemed to have colluded to create a situation where poststructuralist theory—as a broadly construed term, rather than a clearly outlined position—became not only the inspiration behind contemporary art, but also the criteria by which to judge it, creating a kind of self-congratulatory feedback loop. Kester describes how such theorists became often-quoted in "catalog essays, artist's statements, reviews, course reading lists, and dissertations" (KESTER 2011: 54). Artists cited poststructuralists as their inspiration or even as the basis of their work (think of Thomas Hirschhorn's *Deleuze Monument*, 2000 and *24-Hour Foucault*, 2004; or Henry Bond's book *Lacan at the Scene*, 2009). These artworks were then selected by curators and praised by critics and theorists who themselves were inspired by and used poststructuralist thought as their standards for critique and judgement. This is part of the broader move towards artists relinquishing their status as distinct from the non-artist.

Artur Żmijewski's curation of the 7th Berlin Biennale (2012) is a clear example of a curator-star overshadowing artists. Żmijewski famously invited representatives from the Occupy and Indignados movements to use the main central space for activist planning and discussion. Critics felt that he had created a human zoo that was difficult not to read as an artwork, with the activists comprising the pieces of his composition (FOWKES/FOWKES 2012; LOEWE 2015; MCKEE 2016). The situation is further complicated because Żmijewski is not a curator, but an artist. Using his position as an artist-curator, he traded on the cultural capital in social movements by associating his work with their ethically meritorious political positions: these factors determined the form of the biennial.

In this interpretation, the institutional celebration of socially engaged art is not only the embodiment of a particular theoretical tradition's grip on artistic critique, but also a performance of post-truth. Art can reveal no truths, because truth itself is just a social construct and any notion of objective truth is equated with authoritarianism. What is post-truth if not the impossibility of truth claims? We have already argued that there are formal similarities between socially engaged art and the deep suspicion of expert elites associated with the post-truth era. After it establishes this moral code as aesthetic value, socially engaged art attempts to re-introduce these values back into society by collaborating with various publics. However, the ethically commendable position of recognising every person's moral worth becomes perverted into a situation where all opinions are viewed as having equal value. This conflates ethics with aesthetics, such that "the artworks created often [hold] equal or less importance to the collaborative act of creating them" (TATE n.d.).

Or the Monumentalising of Democracy, Equality and Collaboration as the Post-Truth Basis of Socially Engaged Art?

The problem with the first narrative is straightforward. While it helpfully explains the demise of expertise and the problems inherent to the authenticity seeking to fill its place, it also seems to lead us back to the starting point. If such a thesis simply returns us to singular truths held by institutional authorities, with the dominance of democratised art in the Turner Prize acting as a form of validation for success, then we are simply following the diluted responses to post-truth and their view of poststructuralism as a monolithic force for relativism. In doing so, it removes the significance of socially engaged art to the problematic context of post-truth.

To redress this, we can consider an alternative narrative that stands as an antithesis. Dave Beech rightly raised the problem of the way that many artworks aiming for collaborative and co-produced practice ended up "neutralising differences" (2008: 4) in the name of agreement. In other words, the principle of democratic art ends up as consensus, which leads to reproducing the same structures of authority that social engaged art was intended to dismantle. Beech's observation points us to the ways in which the democratisation of art involves an initial set of chance encounters: nobody knows, at first, who is going to enter the space of socially engaged art; nobody knows who is going to participate. If forms of communal creativity did not have these elements of chance, then there would be no point in conducting them—we would already know what we were aiming to produce. The problem that Beech alerts us to is the fact that such chance encounters, inherent to any democratic form of artistic practice, are all-too-often obscured by the artist's fixation on particular aspects of the work: namely, its success on the social level. This fixation on the success of the work, and its consequent social value, leads to a heavy emphasis on consensus and a lack of attention to the mechanisms by which participants are vetted and filtered: whether intentionally (by the artist or curator purposefully inviting them) or practically (by the fact that only certain types of audience will attend certain types of artistic performance).

This points us to the fault in the celebration of the ordinary and the egalitarian that Groys described earlier, which is not so much about the truth or authenticity of the content of socially engaged art, but rather the value attributed to it. For Groys, every cultural work—be it a book, a film, an artwork or even an act of protest—is an attempt to reassess values. This is done by engaging the concerns of what is excluded from the cultural archives (what Groys terms "the profane" (2014: 64)), and what is stored within them, and therefore maintained beyond their original use (the "sacred" (GROYS 2014: 116)). It follows that this distinction between the profane and the sacred is necessary for anything new to be created, because the new is defined as something that is different from what already exists in the archive. In this way, "cultural values are nothing more than archived memories of events in the history of the revaluation of values" (GROYS 2014: 70). The problem with the artistic turn to the ordinary emerges. It proposes a move away from the elite archives of the museum towards a more democratic and open access archiving system where the threshold is managed by users rather than traditional expert guardrails (think of the short-lived Occupy libraries, for example). However, the economy of value is still maintained: such that, while socially engaged art celebrates certain differences from more traditional works (such as its collaborative or democratic content), it overlooks the ways in which it potentially reproduces the same forms of value and meaning. The celebration of certain differences over others is not raised as a critique in and of itself here, though, but rather a key symptom of the post-truth age.

In his essay on 'The Paradoxes of Political Art', Jacques Rancière uses the term "monumentalising" (2012: 148) to describe a particular process in which artistic interventions in traditional exhibition spaces are judged as successfully subverting the social order. Monumentalising, Rancière suggests, involves a particular form of self-evident representation (a "sculptural presence" (RANCIERE 2012:148) combined with rhetorical demonstration) which anticipates and enables the effects of democratised art on the gallery or institution:

> The more art fills rooms of exhibitions with monumentalized reproductions of the objects and icons of everyday life and commodity culture, the more it goes into the streets and professes to be engaging in a form of social intervention, and the more anticipates and mimics its own efforts. Art thus risks becoming a parody of its alleged efficacy (RANCIÈRE 2012: 148).

Monumentalising is thus key to the relationship between the sacred space of the gallery (in Groys's terms) and the production of subversion. It is not limited to artistic performance, but to the circulation of key terms such as the collective, the democratic and the socially engaged. As Manuel DeLanda (2016) argues, material, human and theoretical assemblages—including the practices and democratic events inherent to socially engaged art—are typically described in terms of organismic metaphors: the body of the community, the voice of the people, and so on. This enables a line to be drawn between the gallery space and the real world, but such metaphors are also problematic precisely because they link together otherwise disparate entities that risk either reducing the whole to the sum of its parts (the art is simply an aggregate of the contributors involved), or the parts are effectively created by the whole (the art transforms everyday life into a work of art). Both instances, DeLanda argues, overlook the chance element of any collaborative or participatory encounter in the name of identifying it as a thing in and of itself, or at least a thing that can be adequately represented within the economy of the archive.

In the Marxist tradition of thought, and particularly the work of the Hungarian philosopher György Lukács (1885–1971), this might be termed reification: "the moment that a process or relation is generalised into an abstraction, and thereby turned into a thing" (BEWES 2002: 3). For Lukács, reification contributes to a problem of immediacy: focusing on the immediate world—the reified world—obscures the multiple mediations that enabled capitalist systems to manipulate its populations (LUKÁCS 1971).

In the case of democratised art, there is a double play here which Rancière alerts us to. For, in the assessment of the democratising of the Turner Prize, certain theories, names and approaches do appear set in stone, with a history and trajectory ascribed to them. Conversely, these are not simply lazy or reductive phraseology—as in the work of McIntyre or D'Ancona, for example—but rather an anticipatory aspect of the democratising activities. This, as Rancière points out, "short-circuits reflection on the powers of artistic practices" (2012: 148).

Take, for example, the unanimous decision to select the Jakarta-based ruangrupa (stylised uncapitalised) to curate documenta fifteen (2022). We argue that it was their reification of equality that led the organisers to choose the Indonesian collective. How radically egalitarian, they must have thought, to put a non-Western collective in curatorial control. ruangrupa curated the documenta around the theme of the *lumbung*—a store for collectively produced rice. According to the documenta website, "principles of collectivity, resource building and equitable distribution are pivotal to the curatorial work and impact the entire process—the structure, self-image and appearance of documenta fifteen" (DOCUMENTA 2022). The idea was to think of the exhibition as a resource pot from which visitors could take whatever they needed to heal "today's injuries, especially ones rooted in colonialism, capitalism, or patriarchal structures" (NGUYEN 2022: 24). This is precisely what we mean by how the monumentalising (might we say, reification?) of certain values (principles in ruangrupa's terminology) drive the form (the structure, or appearance in their terms) of socially engaged art.

Until 2022, documenta had been "the ultimate curator-led, thesis-driven exhibition" (FARAGO 2022), but in 2022 it collectivised curatorial decision-making by putting a collective in charge who invited dozens of other collectives to each invite yet more collectives. The reification of equality was supposed to guarantee ethically meritorious work. Unfortunately, ruangrupa's decision to include an unmistakably antisemitic mural (*People's Justice*, 2002) by fellow Indonesian collective Taring Padi (established in 1998 with inclusivity and a militant belief in art's potential for social change as their core values) dominated the discussions about the documenta. Then there were other controversies. A newly appointed advisory committee suggested to remove a set of Palestinian propaganda short films (the Tokyo Reels) from the show: so much for equality of opinion; when the ruangrupa 'got it wrong' they were overruled. In response, ruangrupa and many artists in the exhibition accused the press and the committee of racism and the *Tokyo Reels* remained on display.

The monumentalising of equality above authoritarian aesthetic criteria lies at the heart of a controversy that even led the *New York Times* to report that the debacle might signal the end for "the world's most prestigious art exhibition" (FARAGO 2022). In this sense, it might be possible to cast the narrative of post-truth as a problem of monumentalising. This problem of monumentalising is precisely what socially engaged art must address if it is to avoid perpetuating the fables of post-truth.

Monuments to Critique

We have already outlined how this monumentalising takes place within Kester's thesis on poststructuralism and its relationship to socially engaged art. Terms such as participation, or equality—so often associated with the critique of socially engaged art—(THOMPSON 2012) are necessarily temporary denominations that become rigid and consolidated through research papers, teaching curricula and references in public debate. This is precisely how they are embedded within the institutions of authority and expertise as much as they critique them. To paraphrase Rancière, the process of rigidifying anticipates their effect.

What if it is not the democratic collectivisation of socially engaged art *per se*, but this monumentalising process (which seems necessary for an engagement between radical critique and established practice) that forms the basis of post-truth? This would help to explain how the term post-truth has become, amid the genuine concerns over its political and cultural effects, a de facto victory of a positivistic certainty. Accompanying this victory is an industry of conferences, academic papers, and even research centres that have arisen in its wake. But within this response, post-truth rather too quickly becomes merely non-truth, and the complexity of the *post* prefix is lost. Too quickly, post-truth is shaped into a shorthand strawman figure to be bested by conservative epistemological mantra, a figure uncannily like older enemies of that same mantra, such as radical feminism, postmodernism, or the hermeneutics of suspicion (HAACK 2019). Too quickly, the complexities of post-truth become a cipher for nothing other than a yearning for an ideal model of academic institutions of truth and readily graspable—and reified—facts. Rather than displacing the monuments to hegemonic pasts, this simply leads to erecting more statues.

Socially engaged art would then stand in a particularly salient relationship to post-truth—not in terms of the truth or authenticity claims of its collaborators, but rather in its utilisation of reified or monumentalised figures. It is, in effect, a little too easy, or (channelling Lukács) a little too immediate, to celebrate artistic interventions as highlighting the mediations of the gallery or the institution as effective critical performances at work in settings such as the Turner Prize. The importance of artworks that incorporate public engagement lies not in the truth claims that they make—that they have changed the world, that they have brought down the gallery system and so on. Such claims are simply more monuments to defend and this overlooks the immediacies such celebrations are based on. The question should instead be how such claims are curated, stored, kept on display, and the institutions of power which enable this to be persuasive.

Similarly in this sense, post-truth is only the natural undoing of a society that loses touch with this curatorial aspect which is fundamental to culture itself. The motifs employed by those defending truth (in the context of post-truth) work well to pitch the expert against the foolish, and the intellectual against the masses, but only because they are too general, too clichéd, too monumentalised, to do justice to the micro-engagements which constitute new media. One need not look to poststructuralism to explain the rise of post-truth, and indeed the constant invocation as statues to be destroyed serves only to progress the process rather than halt it.

A Dialectical Tension Between Equality and the Production of Truth as a Cultural Value

What, then, are we to make of the institutional reception of democratic collectivisation of art evidenced in the Turner Prize 2021, The British Art Show 2022 and documenta fifteen? It is, for sure, tempting to see this as a success for subverting the expectations of artistic merit, allowing democratic principles to finally take root in the elite institutions. At the same time, conversely, it is equally plausible to see it as the final victory of a relativistic, anti-intellectual paradigm in contemporary art infecting the sacred halls of the gallery or the biennial (or quinquennial). Our analysis suggests that there is something more at work in the creation of value of the democratic and participatory aspects of socially engaged art practice that need to be attended to. Socially engaged art is concerned with art's relationship with the public (community, or society). More than that, it uses the public as an integral part of its practice, almost as the material of its practice. In doing so, it purports to place itself in stark contrast with more traditional forms of public art that include permanent murals, statues, memorials and monuments. However, we suggest that the varieties of socially engaged art that we have critiqued in this text are monumental in their reification of particular aspects of their practice, (democracy, equality and collaboration) which ironically remove their subversive value. It is this monumentalising process, rather than democratic collectivisation *per se*, that aligns socially engaged art with the hallmarks of post-truth, and in doing so produces, at best, forms of relativism, and at worst, cynicism.

Consequently, we call for art to retain a dialectical tension between equality and the production of truth as a cultural value; a dialectic which involves the careful reinstatement of artistic authorship and a more sincere vision of socially engaged art's political ambitions and signification. In doing so, the terms by which that authority and expertise is reinstated—including the chance assemblages it depends upon—need to be brought sharply into focus. Doing so would prove far more subversive to institutions such as the Turner Prize and documenta;

they would also subvert many of the assumptions of what allows art to call itself socially engaged.

References

BAVO (ed.) (2007): *Cultural activism today: the art of over-identification*. Rotterdam: Episode Publishers.

BEECH, Dave (2008): Include me out! – In: *Art Monthly* (315), 1–4.

BEWES, Timothy (2002): *Reification*. London: Verso.

BISHOP, Claire (2004): Antagonism and relational aesthetics. – In: *October* (110), 51–79.

BURN, Ian (1999): The sixties: crisis and aftermath (or the memories of an ex-conceptual artist). – In: Alberro, A./Stimson, B. (eds.), *Conceptual art: a critical anthology*. Cambridge MA; London: MIT Press, 392–408.

CHARLESWORTH, J.J. (2021): The Turner Prize's Radical Chic. – In: *ArtReview* (May) <https://artreview.com/the-turner-prize-radical-chic/> [11.10.21].

CURTIS, A. (2007, October 9). *The rise and fall of the TV journalist* [Documentary, Short]. BBC.

DELANDA, Manuel (2016): *Assemblage Theory*. Edinburgh: Edinburgh University Press.

DOCUMENTA (2022): *About* <https://documenta-fifteen.de/en/about/> [10.1.23].

FARAGO, Jason (2022): The World's Most Prestigious Art Exhibition Is Over. Maybe Forever. – In: *The New York Times* (23. September) <www.nytimes.com/2022/09/23/arts/design/documenta-15.html> [10.1.23].

FOSTER, Hal (1996): *The Return of the Real: The Avant-Garde at the End of the Century*. Cambridge, MA; London: MIT Press.

FOWKES, Maja/FOWKES, Rueben (2012):'#Occupy Art. – In: *Art Monthly* (359), 11–14.

GRIMWOOD, Tom (2021): *The Shock of the Same: An Anti-Philosophy of Clichés* London: Rowman & Littlefield Intl.

GRIMWOOD, Tom (2022): The Poetics of Rumour in the Age of Post-Truth. – In: *Janus Head* 20(1), 41-51.

GORMLEY, Anthony (2010): *One and Other*. London: Jonathan Cape.

GORMLEY, Anthony (2018): *In conversation with Hans Ulrich Obrist* <www.antonygormley.com/resources/texts/in-conversation-with-hans-ulrich-obrist> [10.1.23].

GROYS, Boris (2014): *On the New*. London: Verso.

GROYS, Boris (2016) *In the Flow*. London: Verso.

HAACK, Susan (2019): Post Post-Truth Are We There Yet. – In: *Theoria* (85), 258–275. DOI: 10.1111/theo.12198.

JANUSZCZAK, Waldemar (2021): Collective madness! The Turner is an insult to art. – In: *The Sunday Times* (3. October), 16f.

JOHNSTONE, Stephen. (ed.) (2008) *The everyday*. London: Cambridge MA: Whitechapel Gallery.

KESTER, Grant (2011): *The One and the Many: Contemporary Collaborative Art in a Global Context*. Durham NC; London: Duke University Press.

LANG, Martin (2021): Hazlitt on aesthetic democracy and artistic genius. – In: *The Hazlitt Review* 14, 25–36.

LÉGER, Marc James (2019): *Vanguardia: socially engaged art and theory.* Manchester: Manchester University Press.

LOEWE, Sebastian (2015): When protest becomes art: the contradictory transformations of the occupy movement at Documenta 13 and Berlin Biennale 7. – In: *FIELD: a journal of socially engaged art criticism*, (1), 185–203.

LUKÁCS Georg (1971): *History and Class Consciousness: Studies in Marxist Dialectics.* trans. Rodney Livingstone. Cambridge, MA: MIT Press.

MANCE, Henry (2016): Britain has had enough of experts, says Gove. – In: *Financial Times* [June 3, 2016] <www.ft.com/content/3be49734-29cb-11e6-83e4-abc22d5d108c> [10.1.23].

MCKEE, Yates (2016): Occupy and the end of socially engaged art. – In: *e-flux*, (72). <www.e-flux.com/journal/72/60504/occupy-and-the-end-of-socially-engaged-art/> [26.1.18].

NGUYEN, Minh (2022): Documenta 15. – In: *Art in America*, 110(5) 22–24.

RANCIÈRE, Jacques (2012): The paradoxes of political art. – In: *Dissensus: on the politics of aesthetics.* London: Bloomsbury, 142–159.

ROBERTS, John (2007): *The intangibilities of form: skill and deskilling in art after the readymade.* London: Verso.

SHOLETTE, Gregory (2017): *Delirium and resistance: activist art and the crisis of capitalism.* London: Pluto Press.

TATE (2021): *Array Collective Win Turner Prize 2021 – Press Release* <www.tate.org.uk/press/press-releases/array-collective-win-turner-prize-2021> [22.8.22].

TATE (n.d.): *Socially engaged practice – Art Term* <www.tate.org.uk/art/art-terms/s/socially-engaged-practice> [27.7.19].

THOMPSON, Nato (ed.) (2012): *Living as form: socially engaged art from 1991-2011.* New York; Cambridge MA: Creative Time Books; MIT Press.

VOGELMANN, Frieder (2018): The Problem of Post-Truth: Rethinking the Relationship between Truth and Politics. – In: *Behemoth: A Journal on Civilisation* 11(2), 18–37.

WRING, Dominic (2009): Focus Group Follies? Qualitative Research and British Labour Party Strategy. – In: *Journal of Political Marketing* 5(4), 71–97.

Performing Arts Organizations as Hybrid Organizations: Tensions and Responses to Competing Logics

Organisationen der darstellenden Künste als hybride Organisationen: Spannungen und Antworten auf konkurrierende Logiken

SALLY MOMETTI, KOEN VAN BOMMEL*
Vrije Universiteit Amsterdam

Abstracts

Performing arts organizations (PAOs) need to manage their artistic ambitions in the face of public sector reforms that promote cultural entrepreneurship, the commercializing, and marketization of art. This study uses an institutional logics lens to examine the tensions PAOs experience resulting from this need and their responses to and management of the complexities in their environment. This study draws on a qualitative analysis of nine PAOs in the Netherlands and finds that the main tensions experienced by PAOs stem mainly from stakeholder plurality and the identity of the individual organization. PAOs primarily employ the coping strategies of acquiescence, avoidance, and compromise, which they prioritize over stronger forms of resistance such as defiance and manipulation, and maintain separate logics of operation rather than working towards their synthesis. This leads to a dynamic process model which identifies both a vicious and a virtuous approach to managing tensions.

Organisationen der darstellenden Künste (PAOs) müssen ihre künstlerischen Ambitionen angesichts von Reformen des öffentlichen Sektors, die auf kulturelles Unternehmertum, Kommerzialisierung und Vermarktung von Kunst hinauslaufen, adaptieren. Diese Studie betrachtet aus der Perspektive institutioneller Logik Spannungen sowie Reaktionen auf diese veränderten Umfeldanforderungen. Die Studie stützt sich auf eine qualitative Analyse von neun PAOs in den Niederlanden und kommt zu dem Ergebnis, dass die wichtigsten Spannungen, denen PAOs ausgesetzt sind, hauptsächlich aus der Pluralität der Stakeholder und der Identität der einzelnen Organisation resultieren. PAOs verwenden in erster Linie Bewältigungsstrategien der Duldung, Vermeidung und des Kompromisses, die sie gegenüber stärkeren Formen des Widerstands wie eigensinniges Beharren und Manipulation bevorzugen und getrennte Handlungslogiken aufrechterhalten, anstatt auf deren Synthese hinzuarbeiten. Dies führt zu einem dynamischen Prozessmodell, in dem man sowohl einen ‚bösartigen' als auch einen ‚tugendhaften' Ansatz zum Umgang mit Spannungen identifizieren kann.

Keywords:

Arts organizations/cultural organizations/Kulturbetrieb, Arts administration/ Kulturverwaltung, arts management; Management/Management, Organization/ Organisation, Theatre/Theater

* Email: sally@sallymometti.nl; k.van.bommel@vu.nl

Journal of Cultural Management and Cultural Policy, 2024/2, pp. 183–216

doi 10.14361/zkmm-2024-0210

1. Introduction

Not-for-profit performing arts organizations (PAOs) operate in an environment that has changed significantly in the last 20 years (FÖHL/ WOLFRAM/PEPER 2016). In particular, in Western European countries public sector reforms have led to reduced public funding for the arts (LINDQVIST 2012; MARCO-SERRANO 2006). In 2014, such reforms included a substantial 22% decrease of national public funding in the performing arts sector as well as a categorical closing of 'production houses' which form a first step for young theatre makers after graduation to produce artistic work. Also, the reforms put more emphasis on income generation and announced deprivation of public funding in case a PAO would not be able to attract enough audience. Examples include the Nordic countries (LINDQVIST 2012), the United Kingdom (ZAN 2000), and Italy (BISES/PADOVANO 2004). As a consequence, PAOs need to increase other sources of income by deploying 'cultural entrepreneurship,' understood as engaging in entrepreneurial activities such as combining resources, mobilizing networks, building legitimacy, and introducing novelty in the cultural sector (BERGAMINI et al. 2018: 319), thereby blending cultural/artistic elements with market thinking. The effects of the Covid-19 pandemic have added another layer of (financial) complexity to the sector as income generation has become problematic if not impossible during lockdowns. PAOs are required to manage competing and potentially contradictory demands as they juggle their aim of offering art while sociopolitical demands are changing, and entrepreneurial thinking and greater effectiveness and efficiency is increasingly required.

Some of the extant research on PAOs addresses tensions arising from the complex environment in which PAOs operate. For instance, Amans, Mazars-Chapelon and Villesèque-Dubus (2015) examine how budgeting is affected by the institutional complexity that PAOs face. Barkela (2019) looks at the importance of strategic communication in managing conflicting organizational areas, and Bergamini et al. (2018) study the tensions related to entrepreneurship on the supply side of the performing arts sector in the Netherlands and Belgium. Lindqvist (2017) employs an institutional logics perspective and suggests that artistic ventures are hybrid organizations, i.e., organizations that combine multiple organizational forms or institutional logics (BATTILANA/DORADO 2010: 1419; BATTILANA/LEE 2014: 398), whose success depends on their ability to balance an art (art for art's sake) logic, a managerial (market) logic, and a political (public policy) logic. Lindqvist insightfully discusses how and why tensions arise in arts organizations. While to date, studies focus on the complexity of PAO environments, we know relatively little about the type of tensions PAOs experience as a result of this complexity, and the organizational responses they develop to manage these tensions and their effectiveness.

The study by Lindqvist (2017) offers an interesting starting point by arguing that the tensions PAOs experience result from a multiplicity of institutional logics, i.e., the different systems used by (individuals in) organizations to make sense of their everyday activities and organize those activities in time and space (THORNTON/OCASIO/LOUNSBURY 2012). Conceptualizing PAOs as operating in an environment characterized by institutional complexity, i.e., operating in a context of multiple logics, they face a challenging combination of oftentimes conflicting public and private (e.g., artistic, managerial, and political) logics which need to be managed for the PAO to be successful (AMANS et al. 2015; LINDQVIST 2017). How a PAO responds to political demands for market and managerial thinking can have crucial implications for the existence of the organization, since the balance between an artistic and a market logic influences external evaluations by decisive stakeholders such as peers and critics (SHYMKO/ROULET 2017) which subsequently influence the funding bodies that rely on these stakeholders' validation of the organization (BERGAMINI et al. 2018).

In a sector linked so intimately with, and dependent on politics, understanding how public sector reforms affect individual organizations is vital (FITZGIBBON 2019; LABARONNE/TRÖNDLE 2020; LINDQVIST 2012). Competing logics due to public sector reforms could leave PAOs in a 'lose-lose' situation. On the one hand, they are being required to embrace a stronger market logic. However, this can risk loss of a distinctive identity and the support of peers and critics which will affect the PAO's legitimacy and potentially result in decreased public funding. On the other hand, refusal to incorporate a market logic and retain the support of peers and critics could cause a reduction in public funding based on non-compliance with the norms of entrepreneurship and income generation. Is there a third scenario in which the PAO manages to become a truly hybrid organization which integrates both logics within a unified strategy? To explore this, we need to understand how PAOs manage conflicting logics. We address the following research question: What are the tensions that PAOs experience when dealing with multiple logics and what organizational responses do they deploy to manage these logics?

Based on a study of nine publicly funded PAOs, we show that all PAOs experience these tensions, and that performing (stakeholder conflicts) and belonging (identity conflicts) tensions are particularly salient. We find that PAOs' responses are only marginally resistant and include acquiescence, compromise, and avoidance strategies. Overall, there is a high level of inertia in the sector and a focus on adapting and executing what funding bodies require. PAOs try to satisfy all these demands to some extent and eschew strategies such as defiance and manipulation. PAOs seek also to maintain a separation of logics rather than to explore synthesis possibilities and the transition to a hybrid organization; most PAOs embody an art logic rather than a market logic.

Our study makes several contributions to both theory and practice. First, it extends earlier work which suggests exploitation of the theoretical lexicon of institutional logics to better understand the complexity of arts organizations and their environment (e.g., GLYNN/LOUNSBURY 2005; LINDQVIST 2017). In particular, we do so by combining logics with insights from paradox theory (e.g., LEWIS 2000; PRADIES et al. 2020; SMITH/LEWIS 2011) and propose a dynamic process model in which the currently dominant vicious response cycle is accompanied by a virtuous cycle showing the way towards a more hybrid organizational logic. Second, the analysis categorizes the various tensions PAOs experience, building on work on paradox theory, and extends the work around this theme (e.g., AMANS et al. 2015; BERGAMINI et al. 2018; LABARONNE/TRÖNDLE 2020; LINDQVIST 2017). Finally, from a more practical perspective, the findings have implications for how both practitioners and policy makers might best manage PAOs and create an environment conducive to long-term viability of the organization.

2. Theoretical Framework

2.1 Institutional Logics, Complexity and Arts Organizations

Institutional logics can be defined as "the socially constructed, historical patterns of material practices, assumptions, values, beliefs, and rules by which individuals produce and reproduce their material subsistence, organize time and space, and provide meaning to their social reality" (THORNTON/OCASIO 1999: 804). Logics explain the contradictory practices and beliefs inherent in institutions in modern western societies. Societal-level institutional logics including the market, the state, religion, the family, and democracy, "provide the master principles of society and guide social action" (GREENWOOD et al. 2010: 521) and constitute the "broad cultural beliefs and rules that structure cognition and fundamentally shape decision making and action" (MARQUIS/ LOUNSBURY 2007: 799).

In this article, the notion of arts organizations is used to denote organizations "within the arts and the creative field, having creative forms of expression with copyright linked to what is produced or distributed" (LINDQVIST 2017: 243).

These organizations operate within the market of symbolic goods (BOURDIEU 1985). Any cultural object, besides being a commodity that has commercial value, also is a symbolic good with cultural value (BOURDIEU 1985). In an arts context, Bourdieu (1985) distinguishes two sectors that are embedded in different institutional logics: the logic of organizations that operate in the field of restricted production (FRP), and the logic of organizations that operate in the field of large-scale production of symbolic goods (FLP). While economic profit is secondary to the cultural value of the symbolic good in FRP, it is primary in FLP, where products are rather short-lived and managed like other ordinary economic goods (BOURDIEU 1985). Producers who seek to take a position within FRP should make clear that, unlike producers in FLP, they are not responding to external demands (BOURDIEU 1985).

These organizations in the field of restricted production of symbolic goods (FRP, the primary focus of this study) face institutional complexity and need to balance utilitarian and normative identities (GOLDEN-BID-DLE/RAO 1997). To obtain public funding, PAOs also need to be in tune with public policy (FREY 2003; MCCARTHY et al. 2005). In particular, they face political and public pressure to adhere to a more market-based logic while their offerings tend not to be geared to an audience preference on a scale where ticket sales alone are sufficient to secure financial stability (HIRSCHMAN 1983). This shows the challenge for PAOs' performance management, namely attending to both a commercial and an artistic dimension (LABARONNE/TRÖNDLE 2020). As PAOs' services are usually performed by humans in front of an audience, compared to visual arts organizations such as exhibition spaces and museums, the business models are also more constrained by time and space (BERGA-MINI et al. 2018) and the limitations of the human body. In sum, PAOs are shaped by a plurality of logics and the resulting complexity gives rise to tensions that need to be managed in order to operate successfully.

In general, individuals and organizations, as part of the larger inter-institutional system, draw on logics when 'negotiating' their institutional context (FRIEDLAND/ALFORD 1991) and seeking legitimacy (DEEPHOUSE/SUCHMAN 2008). Organizational practices and structures are tangible manifestations of institutional logics (GREENWOOD et al. 2011: 321) and several authors have looked at the effect of (changing) logics on governance structures (FISS/ZAJAC 2004), executive succession (THORNTON/OCASIO 1999), and personnel management practices (BARON/DOBBIN/JENNINGS 1986). At the organizational level, Friedland and Alford (1991) argue that each organization, or collection of organizations, has a central logic which guides how it organizes itself and provides the individuals within it with a sense of self (i.e., identity). However, rather than being shaped by a dominant logic, increasingly organizations are facing demands from multiple institutional logics in an environment characterized by institutional complexity emerging from the competing demands from field-level actors (GREENWOOD et al. 2011; SMITH/TRACEY 2016). Institutional scholars have investigated organizational and individual approaches to dealing with the tensions arising from these competing demands (GREENWOOD et al. 2011). For instance, institutional complexity can give rise to a hybrid logic, new logics, new practices, and logic blending (LOUNSBURY 2008: 354).

In particular, a market logic has become a regular and sometimes dominant feature in many sectors including health care (SCOTT et al. 2000), finance (LOUNSBURY 2002), and public management (MEYER/HAMMERSCHMIDT 2006). Thornton and Ocasio (1999) describe how with the rise of a market logic, competition over resources is affecting the decisions and actions of organizations operating in the higher education publishing industry. With the shift to a market logic, the challenges around resource competition and resource dependency have become more salient and are receiving more attention.

The integration of a market logic within an existing logic is not always problematic; sometimes, conflicting logics can be made compatible (GREENWOOD et al. 2011). However, the introduction of a new logic often results in destruction of and disregard for the old logic, because it is incompatible with the new logic (THORNTON/OCASIO 1999; RAO/MONIN/DURAND 2003). In particular, when competing demands affect goals rather than means, tensions are likely to arise related to the requirement for "organizational members to overtly recognize the incompatibility of the demands on goals, which may, in turn, jeopardize institutional support" (PACHE/SANTOS 2010: 466). For PAOs, adopting a market logic promotes competition at the goal level, since the organization's purpose is built around creating or presenting intangible values (emotion, meaning, beauty) and not around making a profit (BAUMOL/ BOWEN 1965). Therefore, the addition of a market logic presents arts organizations with a situation where the organization's identity is being challenged by a market logic in a conflict between purpose and profit. The way the organization responds to these competing logics can threaten its legitimacy and the support it receives (e.g., funding), which eventually will endanger its existence (GREENWOOD et al. 2011; PACHE/ SANTOS 2010).

2.2 Managing Tensions

The tensions resulting from a plurality of logics come in various guises. We borrow from the burgeoning literature on paradox theory to categorize these tensions (LEWIS 2000; SMITH/LEWIS 2011). Paradox theory and institutional logics theory have developed independently (BATTILANA/LEE 2014; JAY 2013; SMITH/TRACEY 2016), but both research fields assume the coexistence of competing alternatives (SMITH/LEWIS 2011). However, whereas an institutional logic tends to focus on how to avoid, negotiate, or resolve tensions, paradox theory considers tensions inherent to organizations and seeks approaches that embrace them (SCHAD et al. 2016).

The four categories of tensions in the framework proposed by Lewis (2000) and Smith and Lewis (2011) represent organizations' core activities and elements: learning (knowledge), organizing (processes), belonging (identity), and performing (goals). Learning paradoxes are related to tensions between old and new, to the struggle between both building upon and destroying the past to create the future (O'REILLY/TUSHMAN 2008; SMITH/LEWIS 2011). Organizing paradoxes describe the tensions that arise as complex organizations create competing designs and processes to achieve desired outcomes. Organizing paradoxes include those between collaboration and competition, empowerment and direction, and routine and change (SMITH/LEWIS 2011). Belonging paradoxes or identity tensions are driven by complexity and plurality and are highlighted at an organizational level because of opposing yet coexisting roles, memberships, and values (SMITH/LEWIS 2011). Performing paradoxes originate from the plurality of stakeholders, and surface as the result of conflicting demands from external and internal stakeholders (DONALDSON/PRESTON 1995; SMITH/LEWIS 2011).

Work on the arts sector in relation to these tensions is scarce. In a study of the performing arts sector in the Nordic countries, Lindelof (2015) suggests audience development as a potential strategy which publicly funded arts institutions could deploy in response to their complex environment. However, the more general institutional logics literature shows that organizations may respond differently to the complexity of competing institutional logics. Greenwood et al. (2011) highlight how organizations' responses to competing demands affect organizational strategies and organizational structures, and Mair, Mayer, and Lutz (2015) discuss defiance, selective coupling, and innovation as potential strategies enabling organizations to balance conflicting logics.

Jay (2013) developed an extensive model which shows the various strategic and managerial responses of hybrid organizations which have tried to integrate both logics within one unified strategy to navigate conflicting demands and a pluralism of logics and identities. Drawing on Oliver (1991) and Pache and Santos (2010), the authors propose two mechanisms. First, an iterative process showing how conflicting external, institutional demands lead to the following strategic responses to external constituents (listed in increasing order of resistance to demands): acquiescence based on conscious incorporation of and compliance with demands, compromise based on finding a balance with or bargaining with external constituents, avoidance or decoupling based on concealment of nonconformity or avoiding rules and expectations, defiance based on dismissing, challenging or attacking demands and rules, and manipulation based on attempts to co-opt, influence, or control external pressure.

Second, a mechanism related to how "conflicting internal demands and identity claims" (JAY 2013: 140) lead to the following managerial responses: deletion based on getting rid of one or several logics or identities (PRATT/FOREMAN 2000), compartmentalization based on separating the different logics or identities within different organizational units (KRAATZ/BLOCK 2008), aggregation based on retention of all the logics and forcing links between them (PRATT/FOREMAN 2000), synthesis based on breaking down the barriers between logics to achieve one single logic (PRATT/FOREMAN 2000), and hiring and socialization policies to facilitate the integration of different logics within a hybrid organization (BATTILANA/DORADO 2010). Since the first mechanism concerns outward strategic responses to external demands and the second addresses these responses in the context of managing competing internal identities resulting from logic plurality, both may operate simultaneously within the organization.

Finding optimal responses to the necessity of balancing competing logics resembles discussions around paradox dynamics and vicious and virtuous cycles. That is, tensions can instigate creativity, opportunity, and change, but––with actors reacting defensively––can also inhibit change, thus leading to either negative (vicious) or positive (virtuous) reinforcing cycles (LEWIS 2000; SMITH/LEWIS 2011). Vicious cycles occur when actors suppress the "relatedness of contradictions and maintaining the false appearance of order" (LEWIS 2000: 763), which may at first relieve anxiety but eventually lead to continuation and aggravation of tensions (LEWIS 2000; SMITH/LEWIS 2011). Similarly, Battilana, and Dorado (2010) suggest that prioritizing one logic over another causes organizations to falter. On the other hand, virtuous cycles are based on exploring, accepting, and arguably even embracing competing demands simultaneously and seeing them as opportunities for synergy rather than obstacles. Smith (2014) suggests that organizations which engage with the tensions of multiple logics achieve both short-term improvements and long-term success. Moreover, it can lead to innovation, creativity, and learning (PRADIES et al. 2020).

Overall, a PAO's success arguably depends on the extent to which it is capable of integrating or synthesizing competing demands into one identity which strikes a balance between the various logics, and the tensions associated with this complexity, present in the organization (BATTILANA/DORADO 2010). In general, PAOs operate in a context characterized by a public logic, an art logic, and a market logic which results in tensions that require an adequate organizational response if the PAO is to thrive, yet we still know little about PAOs' responses to environmental complexities and whether these can in fact be expected to be similar to the responses of organizations studied to date (figure 1).

3. Methods

3.1 Research Design

The aim of the study is to identify and analyze the tensions experienced by PAOs, and their organizational responses to manage conflicting demands. This is an explorative, case-based qualitative study which tries to "illuminate a decision or set of decisions: why they were taken, how they were implemented and with what result" (SCHRAMM 1971 cited in YIN 2014: 15) based on semi-structured interviews with Dutch PAOs. We employ a maximum-variation case selection strategy to try to understand the various tensions and responses of PAOs in the Netherlands (PATTON 2014). Our strategy allows an examination of the whole range of PAOs in the Netherlands, and the identification of both common

Fig. 1: *PAOs' logics, tensions and responses (source: own illustration)*

patterns and particularities among cases. A multiple case study increases the generalizability of the findings and the relevance and credibility of the study (CRESWELL et al. 2007). Nine publicly funded PAOs were selected, a number deliberately kept between four and ten following Eisenhardt's (1989) recommendation.

3.2 Research Setting and Data Collection

A combination of convenience and snowball sampling resulted in a long list of 14 possible cases, all operating on the demand side of the performing arts sector, that is theatres. Since snowball sampling can influence design reliability and jeopardize generalization of the data collected (WALDORF/BIERNACKI 1981), the final selection was based on five comparable and objective criteria to achieve maximum variation (see table 1). Data was obtained from annual reports and annual accounts. Since we are interested also in those PAOs affected negatively by the 2014 reforms introduced above, we selected two cases which had closed during or soon after the reforms. All cases are Dutch not-for-profit foundations – which is a pre-condition for obtaining public funding from the cultural funding schemes of national and local governments. However, some of the PAOs created a structure involving an umbrella organization or foundation which can operate as either a non-profit or a for-profit limited company, making it possible to reallocate profit from the latter to the former. Four PAOs only presented artistic work of other theatre companies. Five PAOs also produced artistic work. This is relevant as the supply side (theatre companies that produce performances) is funded by the national government while the demand side (theatres that present performances) is funded mostly by local governments (municipalities). Theatres were located in either G4 cities (>250,000 inhabitants), G40 cities (100,000–250,000 inhabitants), or G100,000 cities (<100,000 inhabitants).

PAO	# visitors (2018 annual report)	total revenue in Euro (2018 annual accounting data)	% public funding 2018	legal structure	city size	producing artistic work
Theatre A closed since 2014	n/a	n/a	n/a	Foundation	G4	No
Theatre B	20,015	129,480	41%	Foundation	G100,000-	No
Theatre C	177,967	14,199,838	77%	Foundation	G4	Yes
Theatre D	210,000	3,874,000	19%	Limited Company + Foundation	G40	No
Theatre E	237,539	19,249,559	71%	Limited Company + Foundation	G4	Yes
Theatre F	45,174	2,289,627	66%	Foundation	G4	Yes
Theatre G closed since 2014	n/a	n/a	n/a	Foundation	G4	Yes
Theatre H	87,520	7,719,304	27%	Limited Company + Foundation	G40	No
Theatre I closed in 2015 and reopened in 2016	29,917	1,248,038	62%	Foundation	G40	Yes

Table 1: *Core characteristics of PAOs (source: own illustration)*

To achieve maximum variation among respondents, where possible, we interviewed people deemed to embody an art logic (i.e., artistic director, program director, theatre programmer) and individuals likely to embody a market logic (i.e., managing director, general manager). These cultural managers are likely to play an important role in shaping their institutions (FÖHL/WOLFRAM/PEPER 2016). However, in some theatres these functions were not strictly separated and as mentioned two had closed. Hence, in some cases we resorted to interviewing one informant per theatre instead of two (table 2).

Qualitative interviews were conducted with 12 respondents from the nine PAOs. The interviews were semi-structured and flexible but included some general themes such as the theatre's market-orientation, the tensions and challenges experienced, and the strategies employed to manage these issues. Respondents were selected based on their position (job title) in the organization. Respondents 1-4, cases A, B, and C were existing contacts. Respondents 5-12 were approached via e-mail. All 12 agreed to be interviewed. The interviews took place within a six-week timeframe during October to December 2019 which means that there was no effect of the Covid-19 pandemic which did not emerge in Europe until March 2020.

Respondent	Works at PAO	Position within the organization
1	A	Theatre programmer
2	B	Managing director
3	C	Managing director
4	C	Program director
5	D	Managing director
6	D	Theatre programmer
7	E	Managing director
8	E	Theatre programmer
9	F	Program director
10	G	Artistic director
11	H	Managing director
12	I	Managing director

Table 2: *Respondents (source: own illustration)*

The semi-structured interviews form the basis of this study and report the respondents' retrospective and immediate experience of how they embody various logics and try to cope with tensions and complexity. The interviews were conducted in Dutch and were recorded. They lasted between 35 and 85 minutes, with an average of 51 minutes.

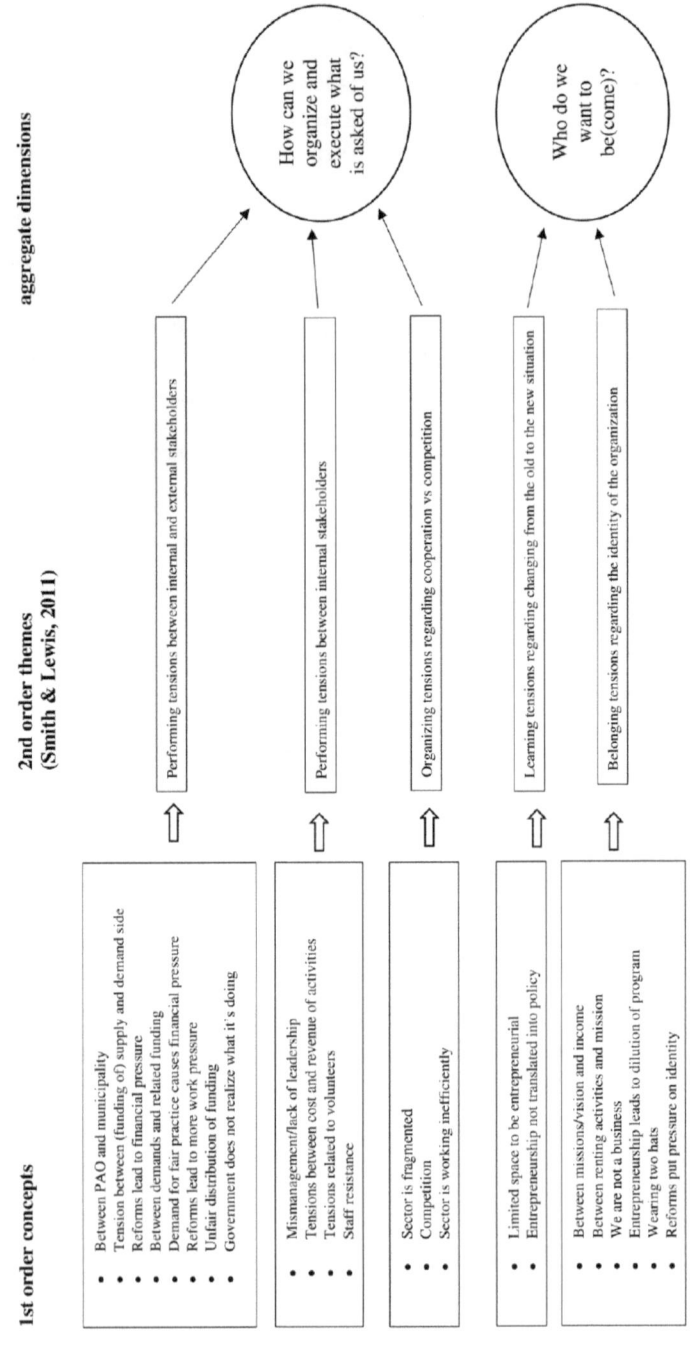

Fig. 2a: Tensions (source: own illustration)

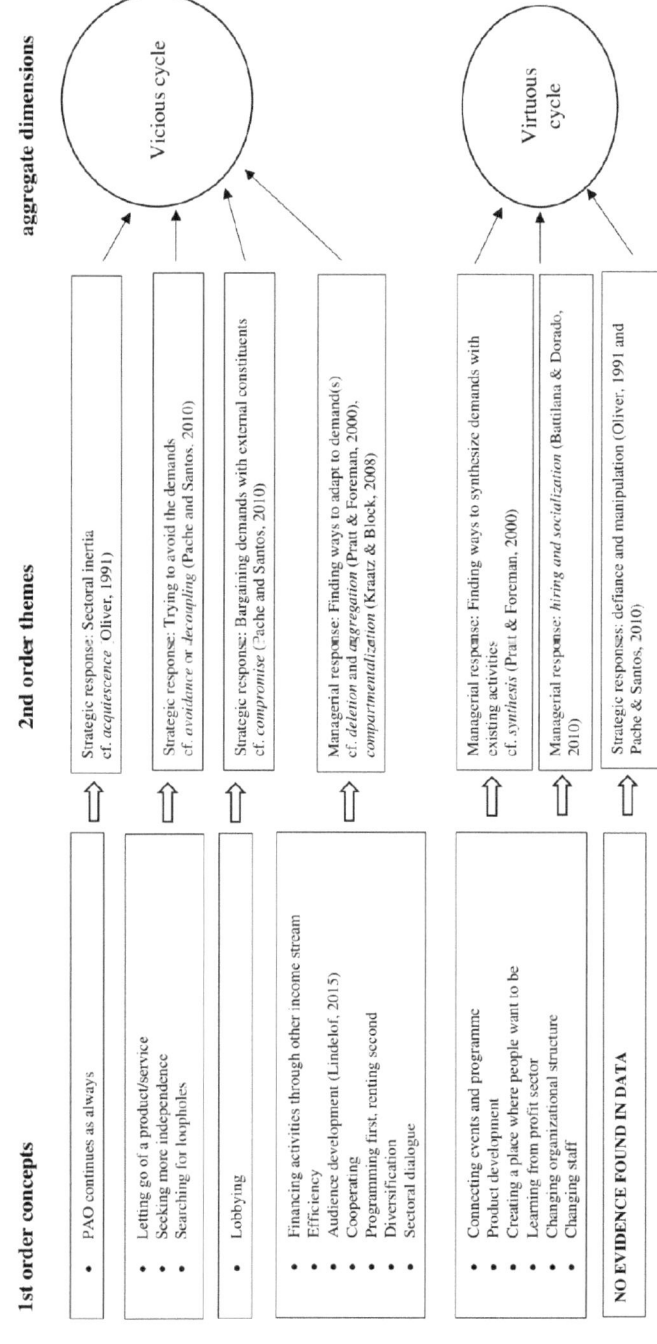

Fig. 2b: Organizational responses (source: own illustration)

3.3 Data Analysis

All the interviews were transcribed and were into Atlas.ti for coding. Coding was conducted in English and followed a three-step process. The first round of coding was based on respondent-centric terms and codes. This led to a total of 100 first order codes related to a variety of subjects, and these were reduced to 41 first order codes related specifically to tensions and organizational responses. The second round of coding used more researcher-centric terms and codes and resulted in ten second order codes. This inductive approach allows us to demonstrate the link between data and concepts in a systematic manner, using the voices of both respondents and researcher (GIOIA et al. 2012). This method of first and second order coding described by Gioia et al. (2012) is similar to what Strauss and Corbin (1998) refer to as "open" and "axial" coding. As a final step in the coding process five aggregate dimensions were defined: two regarding tensions and three regarding the organizational responses. The results were also compared across cases, but we found no significant differences in terms of tensions or responses based on the above-mentioned criteria. Figures 2a and 2b depict the data structure.

4. Findings

4.1 Institutional Complexity and Tensions

All the respondents referred to the competing demands they are faced with. In terms of identity, the art logic seems to prevail over the market logic. One PAO argued that, "It [artistic production] is why we are on earth" (Respondent 6), and another said that, "Even though we earn 70% of our own money, our intrinsic assignment is culture" (Respondent 11). However, the other demands are ever present: "We make art because we make art. In the awareness of an audience, in the awareness of justification of finances and in awareness of our surroundings. But we make art, we don't make soft rolls" (Respondent 4). The interviews provided ample evidence of the market and societal demands PAOs need to meet. Prominent examples of such demands are diversity, inclusiveness, entrepreneurship, fair practice, a financial mix to sustain the organization, and cooperation with other parties. This inevitably has led to tensions (see figure 3). In this figure, B refers to belonging tensions, L to learning tensions, O to organizing tensions, P1 to performing tensions between internal and external stakeholders, and P2 to performing tensions among internal stakeholders. The tensions differ slightly by position, with managing directors experiencing higher levels of performing tensions between internal and external stakeholders, and program directors experiencing higher levels of tension among internal stakeholders and higher levels of belonging tensions (LANDRY 2011; REYNOLDS/ TONKS/MACNEIL 2017).

4.1.1 Performing Tensions Between the PAO and External

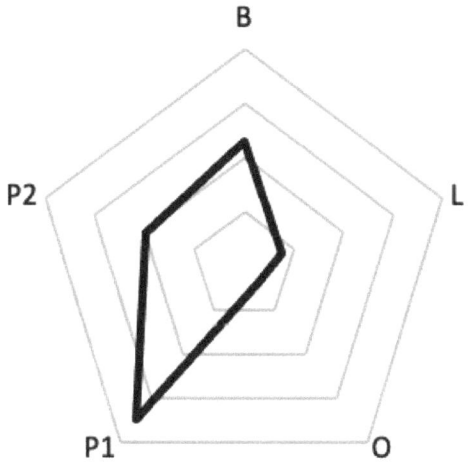

Fig. 3: Tensions within PAOs (source: own illustration)

Constituencies (P1)

Performing tensions were strongly felt between PAOs and external stakeholders or constituents. Ten respondents referred to problematic relationships with the municipality that was the PAOs' primary funding body. Respondent 2: "We were put under pressure by the municipality to merge with another theatre and that became a three-month drama on which we spent a lot of time and energy." Within the municipality, aldermen (members of the municipal executive council) seem to wield a great deal of power: "Until the last alderman came, who, out of nowhere, really out of nowhere... all these years we had fantastic assessments, you name it, all the annual accounts were approved, the whole 'shebang.' But he suddenly confronted us with a budget cut of 40%. To be implemented within one year" (Respondent 5).

In addition, there are discrepancies between the funding of the supply side (i.e., the theatre companies creating and performing performances) and demand side (i.e., the theatre venues that program these performances). In short, the national government subsidizes theatre companies to make and create performances, and the municipality subsidizes the "bricks," i.e., the physical theatre venues and the associated programming budget to actually show performances. Eight out of 12 respondents reported specific performing tensions related to this funding arrangement. Respondent 9 asked "Where is the responsibility for the demand side? Is it with the theatre? Then give the money to the theatres. Is it with the companies, then give the money to the companies" and Respondent 12, representing a theatre venue, told us that, "The theatre companies can offer or ask what they want, we just say 'no.' We'll come for free, they say. Free? That still means I have to pay technicians, so that's not possible. That market mechanism is totally out of balance." These examples show that the fragmented and disconnected funding causes tensions and frictions between theatre companies and theatre venues.

A third source of performing tensions is from discrepancy between societal demands and the related funding. The connection between societal demands (e.g., diversity, inclusion, fair practice) and the funding provided to meet these demands was identified as a financial tension by more than half of the respondents. Respondent 9: "I have to fulfil more demands while spending less budget on them, which of course is a very strange request. If you talk about market mechanisms, well in commercial businesses that would not be possible either." In addition, the societal demand for fair practice is set out in the Fair Practice Code (<https:// fairpracticecode.nl>), which aims at providing a normative framework for sustainable, fair, and transparent employment and enterprise practices in the arts, culture, and creative industries agreed upon by a broad number of cultural and creative professional representatives. The Fair Practice Code has put financial pressure on PAOs: "We are very much in favor of fair practice. But that means an average raise of 3% per year through the collective agreements. And there is only 1.2% price compensation. In our case, with a staffing budget of 10 million euro, that is undoable" (Respondent 7).

4.1.2 Performing Tensions Originating From Within the PAO (P2)

In the case of performing tensions within PAOs (P2), ten out of 12 respondents spontaneously referred to the discrepancy between the costs (imposed by the programming department) and the revenue (derived from the department responsible for renting out the theatre or organizing events) obtained from various activities: "You cannot keep programming no matter what, if the audience doesn't go for it or if the resources are not there, that would be stupid, so we are sort of stuck between a rock and a hard place" (Respondent 9), and "Programming activities and staffing, those are the only two buttons we can push if the income side decreases. So that is a real problem" (Respondent 5). In addition, nearly half of the cases (theatres A, C, G, and I) gave examples of the negative influence on the organization of mismanagement or lack of clear leadership direction: "They [the staff] don't have faith that there is a management that has an overview and that can make decisions" (Respondent 3).

4.1.3 Belonging Tensions (B)

Belonging tensions were also experienced by PAOs, and typically involve the dilemma between purpose and profit involving a choice between content and income. Respondent 11 describes "The tension [as being] two-sided. I'm always concerned about the artistic people in the organization understanding that we also need to make money. And on the other hand, I'm also concerned about the commercial staff in my organization understanding that we have artistic projects." This identity-focused dilemma between mission and income, or purpose and profit, was mentioned frequently in relation to renting activities: "For example, a big event from a Dutch bank like Rabobank, if you then have to choose between an international performance that costs 30,000 euros or 20,000 euros income, well, that international show will perish. And you just have to pay attention to that because if you always do that, well … in the end, we are here for the art" (Respondent 3). Overall, it highlights the tensions around the much-promoted concept of cultural entrepreneurship and the potentially negative influence on programming activity content: "If you want to be entrepreneurial in your programming, you will soon have a rather shallow program and while we strive to be accessible, we also want to have an interesting program" (Respondent 2).

Belonging tensions clearly are linked with the PAO's identity, an area where multiple logics collide. For example, some respondents mentioned that 'they are not a business' and explained how their theatre made decisions on the basis of and for the sake of art. Respondent 6: "I know this is going to cost a lot of money, but then I put on my other hat and think, yes, but we have to do this because this is what we are here for. Otherwise, I can just book a show, let the audience stream in, make money, and not think about it anymore. But where is the fun in that, right? Then you might as well not do it at all."

4.2 Organizational Responses

While institutional complexity and tensions were acknowledged by all the PAOs interviewed, their responses to both issues differed. Below we discuss these strategic and managerial responses.

4.2.1 Strategic Responses

The main strategies used to respond to conflicting demands from external constituents are avoidance, compromise, and acquiescence. In the first case, respondents referred to letting some activities go or outsourcing some activities to avoid these demands: "When the new director came, what he saw, there was only one thing to do in the middle of this economic malaise, which was to say, 'I'm sorry but I have to close the theatre department.' And that was that" (Respondent 1). Respondents 5 and 10 reported that their organization deployed actions that aimed at avoiding demands by becoming less dependent on funding. In one case this was achieved by exiting the funding system: "Out of fear you could say, we said 'maybe you're right, maybe we should go for the financial exit arrangement'" (Respondent 10).

In the case of the second strategy, lobbying was used by seven theatres as a way to signal to the government and municipality that they were resisting their demands but a solution in which the PAO tended to be 'the loser': "When the budget cuts were imposed, we said to the politicians, we cannot program seven days a week for the same budget, that is just not possible, because all costs are getting higher and you are asking more rent for the building, so our programming budget decreases and there is no extra money coming in. So, we will close two days a week, on Monday and Tuesday we don't program anymore" (Respondent 4) and "We could not change it. We pushed, we pulled, involved businesses, everything. But the council had that direction and the coalition supported it, so we had to pay the price" (Respondent 5).

The strategy of acquiescence refers less to inertia from individual theatres and more to passiveness among the sector as a whole: "Yeah, that is really weird, we just said to each other this week, it is strange that the sector is not able to also go to Malieveld [i.e. popular Dutch location for large protests] and strike" (Respondent 7), and "It seems like these things just happen to us, just as with the diversity discussion that is being dropped on us by the government" (Respondent 3).

Overall, these three strategic responses are illustrative of mild resistance to external constituents and highlight the focus of PAOs on trying to do what is asked of them. This seems to be preferred to trying to manipulate the playing field by using stronger forms of resistance, despite what is at stake and despite more active resistance perhaps being expected (PACHE/SANTOS 2010).

The data provided only some evidence of defiance and manipulation. An example of defiance (i.e., dismissing, challenging, or attacking demands and rules) can be seen in this case: "As of January 1, 2017, we got 20% less, so we just lost a lot of money. And that's when we agreed with the alderman that he'd just get fewer performances because of that" (Respondent 12). Rather than trying to do the same with less, this PAO had challenged the imposed budget cut by doing less. Finally, manipulation by attempting to co-opt, influence, or control external pressure had been practiced by only one PAO which had tried to alter the rules of the (funding) game with the city council around catering services and income. The PAO argued, "We lease it out to ourselves with a separate limited company. And we run all the risk, we're going to make the investments, they haven't made them, we agree on a rent for the property, it's commercial, you can determine that, we stick to it. And the moment money is earned, it's for us" (Respondent 5). The PAO gained from the catering income via a private limited company which allowed the profit to flow back as a gift to the PAO. The money flows were not considered transparent, and the municipality assumed that the hospitality and catering money profits had been based on community money. There was a legal case and eventually agreement was reached, and the PAO now operates successfully with only 17% of public funding (the lowest percentage among all the PAOs in our sample).

4.2.2 Managerial Responses

Among managerial responses, i.e., those focusing on "conflicting internal demands and identity claims" (JAY 2013: 140), compartmentalization, deletion, and aggregation dominated, with synthesis, hiring, and socialization policies being less prevalent.

Compartmentalization refers to adapting to the new demands as a separate logic, especially around the separation between the programming and rental departments: "Basically, at the beginning of the season, I can program everything. The program takes precedence. In April my program is ready and then, in principle, nothing can change. Then it goes to rental, and they can fill all the gaps with all the questions we get for rental" (Respondent 6). Deletion mostly involved dispensing one or more of the logics or identities. For instance, one PAO decided simply to close its entire theatre department and concentrate on the more lucrative popular music venue: "The first thing to be divested was visual art, and then it was theatre pretty quickly because we had three technicians on full time duty who didn't function in a room that was just too small to do anything at all, so at some point the theatre just stopped" (Respondent 1). Other theatres decided to forego the cultural rental (a substantial source of income) and to outsource the activities involved. The aggregation or logic retention and forcing links among logics without creating a real synthesis is exemplified by the PAO that allowed dance parties to take place because they generated a lot of money although these 'pill parties' added nothing to the artistic profile: "We earn 70% of our own money, but our intrinsic task is cultural. And if I stick to that, producing something from the commercial sector is not our core business. From a positioning point of view, I don't think we should want it. If I just look at it from a financial business point of view, we just have to do it" (Respondent 11).

While the above three responses maintained separate logics in PAOs that tried to 'add' the market logic to their priority art logic, some PAOs had tried to move towards a hybrid organization. First, a synthesis strategy aimed at an integrated way of working between programming and commercial activities: "I notice that we are doing more projects around an artistic performance [than before]. We put a pink bow around it, there is party, there are activities in the surrounding of the building, and you eat together. All the things that make the audience think, oh, this is nice, and where they almost get the performance as an extra" (Respondent 6). Linked to this, product development was mentioned specifically by seven respondents who referred to development of new products and services that combined both artistic content and a commercial approach, i.e., both purpose and profit: "The drinks and food became very important and also how to use those in a way that it supports the artistic content, became important" (Respondent 10). The move from event marketing to a more holistic approach of marketing the PAO as a place to stay and spend time seemed to be a change of direction: "The eye-opener was that we thought: we need to turn this around. We should not design a theatre, we should not design a cinema, we should design a place where people want to be" (Respondent 5).

Second, hiring and socialization were mentioned by seven theatres as approaches to organizational hybridity. Examples are changes in leadership, hiring staff with a more hybrid profile, and collaborating with independents: "It was a wish of our Board to have more of a businessperson in that position because we had grown, and also to approach things more like a business" (Respondent 9). In relation to this, five respondents gave examples of how they had adapted or wanted to adapt practices from commercial businesses: "All cinemas and amusement parks have self-service ticket booths. Except for the subsidized sector. There is always a person behind the ticket register. But if Pathé with more than 30 cinemas invented it, don't you think it's probably more efficient?" (Respondent 12).

Theory suggests that in order to be successful in the long-term, organizations need to create a common organizational identity which strikes a balance between the logics they combine (BATTILANA/DORADO 2010). Against this background, the current direction towards either separate logics or hybridity may not be optimal for PAOs. This would seem to be supported by the fact that during the course of this research, one of the most renowned Dutch theatres faced serious leadership and identity problems due to the failure to connect 'leadership and unified vision,' and was accused of not making enough effort to reach audiences and of being too 'l'art pour l'art' for a theatre in a big city. This crisis is a poignant reflection of the findings of this study. The implications of our findings are discussed below.

5. Discussion

5.1 A Dynamic Model of PAOs, Logics, Tensions and Responses

This study addressed the following questions: 1) What are the tensions that performing arts organizations (PAOs) experience as a result of multiple logics; 2) What organizational responses do they deploy to manage these competing logics?

Based on an analysis of nine Dutch PAOs, this study shows that the tensions related to competing logics are mostly performing tensions related to the question 'how can we better organize what is asked of us?', that is, executing and catering to diverse and shifting demands (environmental complexity), and only on a secondary level related to the question 'who do we actually want to be(come) in this new reality?' (identity). We found that performing tensions were the most salient for PAOs and originate from the plurality of stakeholders. These tensions emerge because of conflicting demands from external constituents or from factions within the PAO. We also identified belonging tensions, in particular when entrepreneurial activities clashed with the PAO's organizational identity. This echoes the work of Bergamini et al. (2018) and Amans et al. (2015) which hints at belonging tensions related to entrepreneurial activities versus the PAO's organizational identity.

The responses show a preference for avoidance, acquiescence, and compromise strategies. Avoidance occurs in conflicts over where a single logic (art logic) is represented internally (PACHE/SANTOS 2010). The nine PAOs reported extensive use of avoidance by concealing nonconformity or avoiding rules and expectations by separating the art and market logics within different departments, outsourcing or shutting down services, exploiting loopholes in the system, closing the theatre department, or closing the theatre entirely. The widespread use of avoidance might be explained by the fact that it is one of the least aggressive ways of resisting demands without jeopardizing legitimacy (PACHE/SANTOS 2010).

Acquiescence and sectoral inertia are also related to legitimacy. Several scholars predict that organizations are more likely to acquiesce to demands from powerful institutions on which they depend for legitimacy and resources (DIMAGGIO/POWELL 1983; OLIVER 1991). Although few references were made to sectoral obedience and inertia in relation to the own organization, many PAOs responded to the reforms by assuming business as usual and 'doing more work for less money.'

The success of acquiescence and sectoral inertia is ironic when viewed through an institutional public (government, municipality) logic lens. These institutions had praised the PAOs for finding more ways to be efficient than before. However, from the PAO perspective, the outcome was failure: the reforms they undertook as responses to public demands resulted in poorer quality programming and created tensions among those in the organization adhering to an art logic and those working in line with a market logic. This question of 'what is success?' is described in Jay (2013) as a paradoxical outcome which emerges when organizations are transforming from a business logic to a non-profit logic and have yet to truly synthesize. Although in our case, the transformation was undertaken in the opposite direction, that is, from a non-profit logic to a business logic, the transition process shows similarities.

Exploitation of compromise is not supported by previous research on this topic. The PAOs analyzed confronted the constituencies making the demands and lobbied widely to pass the message that what was being demanded by external constituents should be negotiated, balanced, or bargained. This is in line with the compromise response (JAY 2013; OLIVER 1991; PACHE/SANTOS 2010) in which organizations aim to partially satisfy all demands. However, a compromise strategy is generally used in the context of conflicts over means not goals (PACHE/ SANTOS 2010). In conflicts over goals, which we categorized earlier as competing demands over the PAO's identity, stronger responses such as defiance and manipulation to influence or control external pressure are more likely and arguably will be more successful (PACHE/SANTOS 2010). However, we found little evidence of these stronger responses. Although some strong terminology was used to describe lobbying, the power to defy or manipulate the government or the municipality appears very limited due possibly to the complex relationship with the funding body on which PAOs depend for legitimacy and resources (DIMAGGIO/ POWELL 1983; OLIVER 1991). In addition, since the sector is fragmented and therefore unable to organize itself efficiently, that might also limit PAOs' manipulating power.

In terms of how PAOs deal with external demands related to their internal identity, it seems that most responses aimed at integrating these demands as a separate logic rather than trying to incorporate them in the existing logics. PAOs tried to 'add' the market logic while retaining the art logic as their priority. This preference contradicts theories that suggest that in order to successfully deal with competing demands, the organization should accept the paradox between the not-for-profit status and the need for commercial activities, use it constructively (POOLE/ VAN DE VEN 1989), and finally synthesize these logics by combining organizational means and ends in new ways (JAY 2013). A useful example of this is Lloyd and Woodside (2015). They examined the values and identities of two religious non-profit organizations that were required to pursue a commercial entrepreneurial strategy and indicated that aligning their organizational identity with the commercial activities enabled the resolution of the competing logics paradox. PAOs could also learn from how for-profit businesses transition from purely commercial business models to sustainable business models, how they deal with the tensions that arise, and how they use the combination of multiple institutional logics to shape their business models around heterogeneous value logics (LAASCH 2018). Although PAOs are increasingly being required to actually integrate a commercial market logic, these examples could prove useful by showing that heterogeneous value logics can be based on the combination of commercial and non-commercial logics (LAASCH 2018).

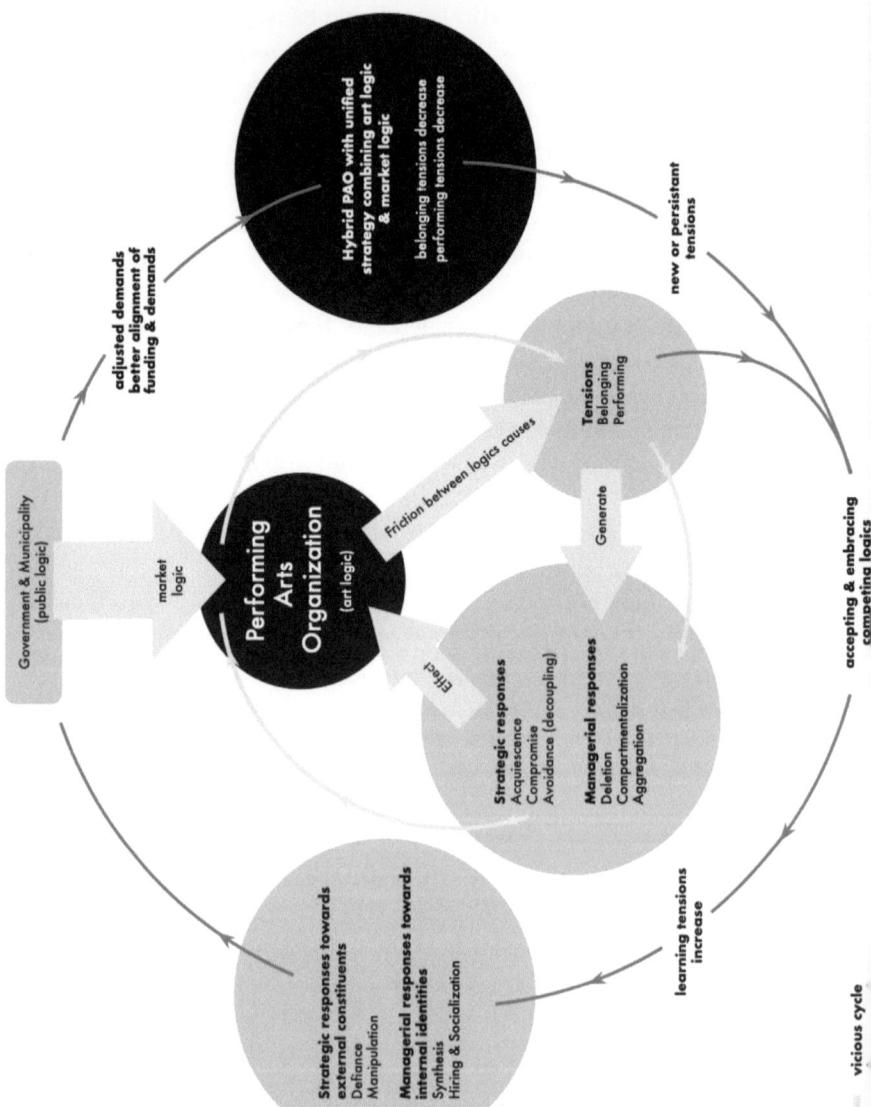

Fig. 4: PAOs, logics, tensions, and responses: a dynamic model
(source: own illustration)

Taken together, our model captures two types of responses (Figure 4), which link back to the vicious and virtuous responses explained in section 2.2. In the currently dominant response, PAOs put up mild resistance to external constituents (using acquiescence, compromise, and avoidance strategies) but focus mostly on doing what is asked of them and less on trying to manipulate the context using stronger forms of resistance. This suggests that PAOs are reactive. On a managerial level, although some PAOs are entrepreneurial, this takes the form mostly of diversification and not the development of new services with both economic and artistic value. Thus, the separation of logics persists. Synthesis of logics and transition to a hybrid organization are in their infancy in most PAOs which continue to primarily embody the art logic and prioritize it over a market logic which is related to generation of income. We consider this dominant approach a vicious cycle in arts management, since it risks the PAO becoming stuck in its current ways of working and failing to find a workable combination of the various logics operating in the contemporary environment which the theory suggests is required for long-term viability (BATTILANA/DORADO 2010).

An alternative but scarce approach involves a virtuous cycle aimed at achieving a hybrid state based on synthesis or integration of competing demands. This virtuous cycle is recommended for organizations dealing with competing logics. The first step is to accept and embrace the competing logics (SMITH/TRACEY 2016) which is likely to raise learning tensions. The emergence of a new logic requires the old logic to be revisited and made comparable with the new logic (RAO/MONIN/DURAND 2003; THORNTON/OCASIO 1999). Although most PAOs realize that the reforms have created a new environment, few are addressing the question of what they want to be in this new reality, and how they can recreate an organization that will be sustainable in the future. This likely explains the moderate levels of learning tensions experienced so far by PAOs. The next step is a strong strategic response based on defiance and manipulation to external constituents (municipalities, government) to dismiss, challenge, or attack the demands or rules being imposed on them and to attempt to influence or control these external pressures (PACHE/SANTOS 2010). If the sector were to resist reforms collectively this might result in adjustments to demands and/or a better alignment between demands and related funding. Adhering to a virtuous cycle would facilitate the creation of more hybrid PAOs that engage in activities which are both artistic and revenue generating which would reduce performing and belonging tensions. Working towards a hybrid state would not require PAO managers to choose between purpose and profit since both would be integrated in the same unified strategy (BAT-TILANA et al. 2012).

6. Implications

6.1 Implications for Theory

This study contributes to arts management scholarship by providing a better understanding of how arts organizations are affected by and are dealing with the competing logics resulting from public sector reforms (DEVERAUX 2009). First, it contributes on a general level to work on institutional logics within arts management. It provides a rich and useful perspective for arts management scholars on the case of PAOs (LINDQVIST 2017). These types of organizations operate in challenging and complex conditions and face a multitude of demands. This requires them to manage competing logics in a complex context characterized by artistic, financial-economic, and policy demands. Not only does an institutional logics perspective allow for a systematic analysis and a better understanding of this complexity, in our particular study it highlights also that PAOs typically prioritize an art logic instead of working to find a way to synthesize the various logics into a unified strategy. PAOs are working in a non-hybrid way which is problematic for long-term success (BATTILANA/DORADO 2010; JAY 2013; SMITH/TRACEY 2016) as suggested also by the virtuous-vicious nature of the proposed model. This non-hybrid approach towards competing demands shows that, ironically, PAOs are unable to do what many artists can do, namely, portraying the ambiguity, diversity, and complexity of perceptions (LEWIS 2000) which is the competence PAOs need to develop and apply.

Second, we categorize the tensions PAOs experience. While these tensions have been explored in previous works (AMANS et al. 2015; BERGAMINI et al. 2018; LABARONNE/TRÖNDLE 2020; LINDQVIST 2017), we add a structured and categorized perspective on the nature of these tensions. Drawing on paradox theory, we have proposed a framework to allow arts management scholars to investigate and categorize the tensions that arts organizations experience as a result of competing logics. A better understanding of the nature of these tensions, and the tensions PAOs are facing in particular, would improve their management in the long run.

6.2 Implications for Policy and Practice

This study has implications for both practitioners and policy makers. For PAOs, a shift towards a virtuous circle strategy which embraces tensions and multiple logics would be beneficial. Also, collectively PAOs could play a more active role in recomposing the sector by envisioning and reshaping the context and advocating for changes to public policy. PAOs could present a collective response to external constituents by outlining how their demands might be realized and the resources needed for a hybrid model. For policy makers, this study highlights the problematic imbalance between the funding of the supply and demand sides. Since the 1980s, the national government in the Netherlands bears responsibility for financing the supply side (theatre companies) and municipalities ensure that this supply is actually presented in theatres. This set-up has led to an imbalance and lack of alignment. For example, the Fair Practice Code, a code of conduct for the cultural sector, has been developed at the national level (see section 4.1.1), and aims to encourage theatres to contract performances at a fair price (without having very concrete measurements included for this), but most municipalities have no budget available to implement it.

This results in more expensive and a reduced number of productions per year which puts tension on the supply side to adhere to performance agreements with the national government (i.e., minimum number of performances a year). In addition, policy makers must realize that demand for a market logic could force PAOs to program more large-scale productions to compensate for artistically risky programming activities. The result is that less of the funding is used to finance niche productions and blockbuster productions are being funded by community money.

6.3 Limitations and Future Research

This study has some limitations which suggest directions for future research. The objective was to use a combination of paradox theory and an institutional logics lens to study (performing) arts organizations. The link between these bodies of literature and arts management is in its infancy and we mostly drew on studies that examine these tensions and logics in other contexts. This allowed a better understanding of how an art logic relates to and competes with other logics such as a market logic and a public logic. Still, future studies could look in greater detail at how the specific context of PAOs may differ from, or is in fact similar to, contexts previously studied. Also, the results of this study are based on the specific case of Dutch PAOs and a relatively small number of cases and interviews. While this is not unusual for qualitative studies, future work could include more countries, a broader range of arts organizations, and expand the number of cases and interviewees to further explore the generalizability of our explorative findings. Finally, this study highlights the potential of a hybrid virtuous approach to coping with complexity and its resulting tensions. However, this approach needs to be developed further and the way PAOs could create and manage a virtuous cycle approach requires more research.

Overall, the ability of PAOs or other cultural institutions to navigate complexity has been highlighted by the current Covid-19 pandemic. This has added another layer of complexity and left the cultural sector exposed and vulnerable as a continued period of closed doors has made income generation even more difficult and put many PAOs under financial pressure. In sum, it is crucial that the creativity and innovativeness, which PAOs demonstrate through their performances be demonstrated also in their management.

References

AMANS, Pascale/MAZARS-CHAPELON, Agnès/VILLESEQUE-DUBUS, Fabienne (2015): Budgeting in institutional complexity: The case of performing arts organizations. – In: *Management Accounting Research* 27, 47–47.

BARKELA, Berend (2019): Theatre leadership from a communication perspective. In: *Journal of Cultural Management / Zeitschrift für Kulturmanagement und Kulturpolitik* 2, 135–164.

BARON, James N./DOBBIN, Frank R./JENNINGS, P. Deveraux. (1986): War and peace: The evolution of modern personnel administration in US industry. – In: *American Journal of Sociology* 92(2), 350–383.

BATTILANA, Julie/DORADO, Silvia (2010): Building sustainable hybrid organizations: The case of commercial microfinance organizations. – In: *Academy of Management Journal* 53(6), 1419–1419.

BATTILANA, Julie/LEE, Matthew/WALKER, John/DORSEY, Cheryl (2012): In search of the hybrid ideal. – In: *Stanford Social Innovation Review* 10(3), 51–55.

BATTILANA, Julie/LEE, Matthew (2014): Advancing research on hybrid organizing: Insights from the study of social enterprises. – In: *Academy of Management Annals* 8(1), 397–441.

BAUMOL, William J./BOWEN, William G. (1965): On the performing arts: the anatomy of their economic problems. – In: *The American economic review* 55(1/2), 495–502.

BERGAMINI, Michela/VELDE, Ward van de/LOOY, Bart Van/VISSCHER, Klaasjan (2018): Organizing artistic activities in a recurrent manner: (on the nature of) entrepreneurship in the performing arts. – In: *Creativity and Innovation Management* 27(3), 319–334.

BISES, Bruno/PADOVANO, Fabio (2004): Government grants to private cultural institu-tions-the effects of a change in the Italian legislation. – In: *Journal of Cultural Econo-mics* 28(4), 303-315. <doi:10.1007/s10824-004-3973-3>

BOURDIEU, Pierre (1985): The market of symbolic goods. – In: *Poetics* 14(1/2),13–44.

CRESWELL, John W./HANSON, William E./CLARK PLANO, Vicky L./MORALES, Alejan-dro (2007): Qualitative Research Designs: Selection and Implementation. – In: *The Counseling Psychologist* 35(2), 236–264.

DEEPHOUSE, David L./SUCHMAN, Mark C. (2008): Legitimacy in organizational institu-tionalism. – In: Greenwood, Royston/Oliver, Christine/Sahlin, Kerstin/Suddaby, Roy (Eds.), *The Sage handbook of organizational institutionalism*. London: Sage, 49–77.

DEVEREAUX, Constance (2009): Practice versus a discourse of practice in cultural ma-nagement. – In: *The Journal of Arts Management, Law, and Society* 39(1), 65–72.

DIMAGGIO, Paul J./POWELL, Walter W. (1983): The Iron Cage Revisited: Institutional Isomorphism and Collective Rationality in Organizational Fields. – In: *American So-ciological Review* 48, 147–160.

DONALDSON, Thomas/PRESTON, Lee E. (1995): The stakeholder theory of the corpo-ration: Concepts, evidence, and implications. – In: *Academy of management Review* 20(1), 65–91.

EISENHARDT, Kathleen (1989): Building theory from case study research. – In: *Academy of Management Review* 14(4), 532–50.

FISS, Peer/ZAJAC, Edward J. (2004): The diffusion of ideas over contested terrain: The (non) adoption of a shareholder value orientation among German firms. In: *Adminis trative Science Quarterly* 49, 501–534.

FITZGIBBON, Ali (2019): Imposed Leadership in UK Funded Theatre and the Implica-tions for Risk and Innovation. – In: *Zeitschrift für Kulturmanagement* 5(1), 15–42 <doi:10.14361/zkmm-2019-0102>.

FÖHL, Patrick S./WOLFRAM, Gernot/PEPER, Robert (2016): Cultural Managers as 'Mas-ters of Interspaces' in Transformation Processes – a Network Theory Perspective. – In: *Zeitschrift für Kulturmanagement* 2(1), 17–49.

FREY, Bruno S. (2003): *Arts and Economics: Analysis and Cultural Policy*. Berlin: Spring-er.

FRIEDLAND, Roger/ALFORD, Robert (1991): Bringing society back in: Symbols, practices, and institutional contradictions. – In: Powell, Walter W./DiMaggio, Paul J. (Eds.), *New Institutionalism in Organizational Analysis*. Chicago: University of Chicago Press, 232–267.

GIOIA, Dennis A./CORLEY, Kevin G./HAMILTON, Aimee L. (2012): Seeking Qualitative Rigor in Inductive Research: Notes on the Gioia Methodology. – In: *Organizational Research Methods* 16(1), 15–31.

GLYNN, Mary Ann/LOUNSBURY, Michael (2005): From the Critics' Corner: Logic Blen-ding, Discursive Change and Authenticity in a Cultural Production System. – In: *Jour-nal of Management Studies* 42(5), 1031–1055.

GOLDEN-BIDDLE, Karen/RAO, Hayagreeva (1997): Breaches in the boardroom: Organi-zational identity and conflicts of commitment in a nonprofit organization. – In: *Orga-nization Science* 8(6), 593–611.

GREENWOOD, Royston/DIAZ, Amalia M./LI, Stan X./LORENTE, Jose C. (2010): The multiplicity of institutional logics and the heterogeneity of organizational responses. – In: *Organization Science* 21(2), 521–539.

GREENWOOD, Royston/RAYNARD, Mia/KODEIH, Farah/MICELOTTA, Evelyn R./ LOUNSBURY, Michael (2011): Institutional Complexity and Organizational Responses. – In: *The Academy of Management Annals* 5(1), 317–371.

HIRSCHMAN, Elizabeth C. (1983): Aesthetics, ideologies and the limits of the marketing concept. – In: *Journal of Marketing* 47(3), 45–45.

JAY, Jason (2013): Navigating paradox as a mechanism of change and innovation in hybrid organizations. – In: *Academy of Management Journal* 56(1), 137–137.

KRAATZ, Matt/BLOCK, Emily (2008): Organizational implications of institutional pluralism. – In: Greenwood, Royston/OliverR, Christine/Sahlin, Kerstin/Suddaby, Roy (Eds.), *The Sage handbook of organizational institutionalism*. London: Sage, 243–275.

LAASCH, Oliver (2018): Beyond the purely commercial business model: Organizational value logics and the heterogeneity of sustainability business models. – In: *Long Range Planning* 51(1), 158–183.

LABARONNE, Leticia/TRÖNDLE, Martin (2020): Managing and Evaluating the Performing Arts: Value Creation through Resource Transformation. – In: *Journal of Arts Management, Law and Society* 51(1), 3–18.

LANDRY, Pascale (2011): A Conceptual Framework for Studying Succession in Artistic and Administrative Leadership in the Cultural Sector. – In: *International Journal of Arts Management* 13(2), 44–58.

LEWIS, Marianne W. (2000): Exploring paradox: Toward a more comprehensive guide. – In: *Academy of Management Review* 25(4), 760–776.

LINDELOF, Anja M. (2015): Audience development and its blind spot: a quest for pleasure and play in the discussion of performing arts institutions. – In: *International Journal of Cultural Policy* 21(2), 200–218.

LINDQVIST, Katja (2012): Effects of public sector reforms on the management of cultural organizations in Europe. – In: *International Studies of Management & Organization*, 42(2), 9–28.

LINDQVIST, Katja (2017): Art ventures as hybrid organizations: Tensions and conflicts relating to organizational identity. – In: *International Journal of Entrepreneurial Venturing*, 9(3), 242–259.

LLOYD, Stephen/WOODSIDE, Arch G. (2015): Advancing paradox resolution theory for interpreting non-profit, commercial, entrepreneurial strategies. – In: *Journal of Strategic Marketing*, 23(1), 3–18.

LOUNSBURY, Michael (2002): Institutional Transformation and Status Mobility: The Professionalization of the Field of Finance. – In: *Academy of Management Journal* 45, 255–266.

LOUNSBURY, Michael (2008): Institutional rationality and practice variation: New directions in the institutional analysis of practice. – In: *Accounting, Organizations and Society* 33(4–5), 349–361.

MAIR, Johanna/MAYER, Judith/LUTZ, Eva (2015): Navigating institutional plurality: Organizational governance in hybrid organizations. – In: *Organization Studies* 36(6), 713–713.

MARCO-SERRANO, Francisco (2006): Monitoring managerial efficiency in the performing arts: A regional theatres network perspective. – In: *Annals of Operations Research* 145(1), 167–181.

MARQUIS, Christopher/LOUNSBURY, Michael (2007): Vive la résistance: Competing logics and the consolidation of US community banking. – In: *Academy of Management Journal* 50(4), 799–820.

MCCARTHY, Kevin F./ONDAATJE, Elizabeth H./BROOKS, Arthur/SZÁNTÓ, András (2005): *A Portrait of the Visual Arts: Meeting the Challenges of a New Era*. Santa Monica: Rand.

MEYER, Renate E./HAMMERSCHMID, Gerhard (2006): Changing Institutional Logics and Executive Identities: A Managerial Challenge to Public Administration in Austria. – In: *American Behavioral Scientist* 49(7), 1000–1014.

OLIVER, Christine (1991): Strategic responses to institutional processes. – In: *Academy of Management Review* 16, 145–179.

O'REILLY III, Charles A./TUSHMAN, Michael L. (2008): Ambidexterity as a dynamic capability: Resolving the innovator's dilemma. – In: *Research in organizational behavior* 28, 185–206.

PACHE, Anne-Claire/SANTOS, Filipe M. (2010): When worlds collide: The internal dynamics of organizational responses to conflicting institutional demands. – In: *Academy of Management Review* 35(3), 455–476.

PATTON, Michael Q. (2014): *Qualitative Research and Evaluation Methods*. Newbury Park/CA: Sage.

POOLE, Marshall S./VEN, Andrew H. van de (1989): Using paradox to build management and organization theories. – In: *Academy of management review* 14(4), 562–578.

PRADIES, Camille/TUNAROSA, Andrea/LEWIS, Marianne W./COURTOIS, Julie (2020). From Vicious to Virtuous Paradox Dynamics: The Social-symbolic Work of Supporting Actors. – In: *Organization Studies* <https://doi.org/10.1177/0170840620907200>.

PRATT, Michael G./FOREMAN, Peter O. (2000): Classifying managerial responses to multiple organizational identities. – In: *The Academy of Management Review* 25(1), 18–42.

RAO, Hayagreeva/MONIN, Pierre/DURAND, Rudolph (2003): Institutional Change in Toque Ville: Nouvelle Cuisine as an Identity Movement in French Gastronomy. – In: *American Journal of Sociology* 108(4), 795–843.

REYNOLDS, Sarah/TONKS, Ann/MACNEIL, Kate (2017): Collaborative Leadership in the Arts as a Unique Form of Dual Leadership. – In: *Journal of Arts Management Law and Society* 47(2), 89–104.

SCHAD, Jonatan/LEWIS, Marianne W./RAISCH, Sebastian/SMITH, Wendy K. (2016): Paradox research in management science: Looking back to move forward. – In: *The Academy of Management Annals* 10(1), 5–64.

SCOTT, W. Richard/RUEF, Martin/MENDEL, Peter J./CARONNA, Carol A. (2000): *Institutional Change and Health Care Organizations: From Professional Dominance to Managed Care*. Chicago: University of Chicago Press.

SCHRAMM, Wilbur (1971): *Notes on Case Studies of Instructional Media Projects*. Stanford University <https://files.eric.ed.gov/fulltext/ED092145.pdf> [July 23, 2021].

SHYMKO, Yulia/ROULET, Thomas (2017): When does Medici hurt da Vinci? Mitigating the signaling effect of extraneous stakeholder relationships in the field of cultural production. – In: *Academy of Management Journal* 60, 1307–1338.

SMITH, Wendy K./LEWIS, Marianne W. (2011): Toward a theory of paradox: A dynamic equilibrium model of organizing. – In: *Academy of management Review* 36(2), 381–403.

SMITH, Wendy K. (2014): Dynamic decision making: A model of senior leaders managing strategic paradoxes. – In: *Academy of Management Journal* 57(6), 1592–1623.

SMITH, Wendy K./TRACEY, Paul (2016): Institutional complexity and paradox theory: Complementarities of competing demands. – In: *Strategic Organization* 14(4), 455–466.

STRAUSS, Anselm/CORBIN, Juliet (1998): *Basics of qualitative research: Techniques and procedures for developing grounded theory*. Thousand Oaks: Sage.

THORNTON, Patricia/OCASIO, William (1999): Institutional Logics and the Historical Contingency of Power in Organizations: Executive Succession in the Higher Education Publishing Industry, 1958–1990. – In: *American Journal of Sociology* 105(3), 801–843.

THORNTON, Patricia/ OCASIO, William/LOUNSBURY, Michael (2012): *The institutional logics perspective: A new approach to culture, structure and process*. Oxford: Oxford University Press.

WALDORF, Dan/BIERNACKI, Patrick (1981): Snowball sampling: Problems and techniques of chain referral sampling. – In: *Sociological Methods & Research* 10(2), 141–163.

YIN, Robert K. (2014): *Case Study Research Design and Methods*. Thousand Oaks/CA: Sage.

ZAN, Luca (2000): Management and the British museum. – In: *Museum Management and Curatorship* 18(3), 221–270.

On digital artworks and their distribution and preservation infrastructures

Digitale Kunstwerke und ihre Vertriebs- und Bewahrungsinfrastrukturen

MILIA MATILDA WALLENIUS*
Aarhus University

Abstract
Digitalization offers new possibilities for cultural institutions but also challenges existing models. Looking at art institutions and their role as distributors and preservers of culture, this essay uses infrastructure theory and four case studies to discuss challenges that analog institutions face when they are dealing with digital art. The issues identified relate to resources, technical and financial, and knowledge about technological needs. The study also indicates that we hold on to old infrastructures and habits when it comes to preservation and distribution, but also when it comes to what an institution is and what it can be. Changing these habits takes time since they are often embedded in other systems. This suggests that the challenges institutions face in the cases of digital art are part of a larger infrastructural problem, which includes systems for funding, distribution of knowledge, educational programs, and habits.

Die Digitalisierung bietet neue Möglichkeiten für Kulturinstitutionen, stellt aber auch bestehende Modelle in Frage. Mit Blick auf Kunstinstitutionen und ihre Rolle als Vermittler und Bewahrer von Kultur werden in diesem Aufsatz anhand der Infrastrukturtheorie und vier Fallstudien Herausforderungen diskutiert, denen sich analoge operierende Institutionen gegenübersehen, wenn sie sich mit digitaler Kunst beschäftigen. Die identifizierten Probleme beziehen sich auf technische und finanzielle Ressourcen und auf das Wissen über technologische Bedürfnisse. Die Studie zeigt, dass wir an alten Infrastrukturen und Gewohnheiten festhalten, wenn es um Bewahrung und Vermittlung geht, aber auch im Hinblick auf das Selbstverständnis einer Institution. Diese Gewohnheiten zu ändern, braucht Zeit, da sie in andere Systeme eingebettet sind. Dies legt nahe, dass die Herausforderungen, denen sich Institutionen im Falle digitaler Kunst gegenübersehen, Teil eines größeren infrastrukturellen Problems sind, welches Systeme für die Finanzierung, die Verbreitung von Wissen, Bildungsprogramme und Gewohnheiten umfasst.

Keywords:
digitalization, museum, media, art

*   https://orcid.org/0000-0001-8787-4322

Journal of Cultural Management and Cultural Policy, 2024/2, pp. 217–234
doi 10.14361/zkmm-2024-0211

1. Introduction

Digitalization processes do not only change how art and culture are distributed, preserved, and consumed, but also how they are created. The fact that digital art forms are difficult for many art institutions to work with is not new and has numerous times been discussed by scholars such as Christiane Paul (PAUL 2015; PAUL 2007). Apart from apparent challenges concerning technical solutions, resources, and conceptual problems, this essay discusses the possibility of a larger infrastructural dilemma related to the distribution and preservation of digital art in an institutional context. This essay aims to open up a discussion on a conceptual level, which in the future could lead to more practical solutions.[1]

Using infrastructure theory (PARKS 2017; PARKS/STAROSIELSKI 2015; STAR/RUHLEDER 1996; STAR 1999) this essay looks at the art world and its institutions (DICKIE 1997: 83–92) as an infrastructure for how art is organized, reached, experienced and understood in society. Infrastructures are embedded systems, structures for fundamental functions to operate in our society (PARKS 2017: 106; PARKS/STAROSIELSKI 2015: 6). Roads, railways, water pipes, airports, and telecommunication networks are examples of such structures. Apart from these material systems the term infrastructure also includes non-material constructions, so-called soft systems. Such infrastructures are for example systems for producing and organizing knowledge in society (PARKS/STAROSIELSKI 2015: 9). This includes political, technological, philosophical, communicative, epistemological, and social infrastructures. Social infrastructures include social institutions, among them institutions of art and culture (HOWE et al. 2016: 548–558).

Some characteristics of infrastructures are that they remain invisible while being part of our everyday lives and that they involve and are connected to other infrastructures and systems (STAR/RUHLEDER 1996: 113; STAR 1999: 381–382). Infrastructures maintain structures while being structures in themselves (HOWE et al. 2016: 558). The art world is thus not just an infrastructure in itself but also includes other infrastructures. These infrastructures can be material, like museums and galleries, or non-material, like conventions and organizational models, which for example include how exhibitions are being produced or how artworks

---

1   This essay is based on research, which was conducted for my MA thesis in aesthetics and culture at Aarhus University in 2019. The thesis was supervised by Nanna Bonde Thylstrup.

are being collected and preserved (DICKIE 1997: 83–92). These infrastructures in turn also relate to other infrastructures, such as political and financial infrastructures, outside the art world.

The discussion in this essay follows case studies of four platforms created for digital art. These platforms are *Net.Specifc*, *Ars17+ Online Art*, *Digital Museum of Digital Art* and *New New Wight*. Two of the cases were created by physically existing art institutions, two by artists working with digital art. In this essay, the cases are used as examples of solutions for distributing and preserving digital art in an institutional context. The examples have been chosen because they represent different approaches to the distribution and preservation of digital art. When studying the examples attention has particularly been paid to what has been done, why, how, and what happened next.

While these cases by themselves cannot give a full picture of how digital art is being presented and preserved, they can be used to fuel the discussion on the challenges that analog art institutions face when they work with digital art. At the same time, these examples can help us identify some of the reasons, methods, ideas, and concepts which are present when digital art is being distributed and preserved.

2. Digital art

Although there is no clear definition of what digital art is or what it can be, many of the works that today are understood as 'digital art' are digitally born works that are created, sorted, and distributed through digital channels, using different digital technologies from production to presentation (PAUL 2015: 7–25, 67). This means that digital artworks are part of a media infrastructure within which and through which they are created and distributed. At the same time, as artworks, they are also part of the infrastructure of art.

From an art-historical point of view, digital art is closely related to movements such as Dada and Fluxus along with conceptual art, all of which have embraced participation, happening, formal instructions, and a focus on concept rather than material objects (PAUL 2015: 7–25). Digital art is thus part of a history of artistic experiments involving process, systems, and interactivity (SHANKEN 2007: 43–70). Additionally, as it often plays with different contexts, it also relates to site-specific practices. Digital art is however difficult to place in a periodical or stylistic category (SØNDERGAARD 2016: 87).

While an overall characterization of 'digital art' indeed is lacking, suggesting that earlier forms of classification have become outdated, there are some features that are common for many of the artworks usually labeled 'digital art'. Although applicable in various degrees depending on the work, digital art is an interactive, performative and generative art form that is multi-, inter-, and transdisciplinary as well as event-based, time-based, or process-based (DIAZ 2016: 238; PAUL 2007: 251–274). It often plays with themes directly related to the digital or explores its possibilities (PAUL 2015: 7–25, 67). Such themes are for example artificial life and intelligence, body and identity, database aesthetics and data visualization, narrative environments, games, tactical media, activism, hacktivism, future technologies, augmented and mixed realities, social media, and web 2.0 (PAUL 2015:139–259). In this essay 'digital art' is used in a wide sense and refers to such artworks that relate to the digital.

Why then is it challenging for physical institutions to work with digital art forms? One of the often-presented arguments is that physical intuitions were created for art forms that are object-oriented, material, and static. Analog institutions are therefore not flexible enough to meet the requirements of digital artworks (PAUL 2015: 7–25).

Institutions have often been criticized for not meeting the contextual needs of digital artworks (PAUL 2015: 7–25, 67). The institutions create a certain context governed by certain traditions and behavioral norms and can therefore be limiting, extracting the artwork from its natural digital context (BENNETT 1997: 17–105; SCHUBERT 2000: 17). This especially applies to internet art, which natural habitat is the internet and should therefore be experienced whenever, wherever, and by whomever as long as there is an internet connection. This means that digital artworks do not only require new technical solutions but also create conceptual dilemmas (ANDERSEN/POLD 2015: 29–30; PAUL 2015: 7–25; PAUL 2007: 251–274).

How then can institutions work with these art forms without killing crucial parts of what makes them important in the first place? As an attempt to explore this question I have looked at four case studies.

3. The webpage and the game – some examples

In 2012 the *Museum of Contemporary Art* in Roskilde, Denmark, launched an online exhibition space or platform for digital art called *Net. Specific* <http://netspecific.net/>. The platform is a webpage where the museum, between 2012 and 2015, opened two exhibitions showcasing internet art with artworks commissioned by the museum for the platform. The museum specializes in contemporary art and focuses largely on new media, including sound art, video art, and net art. According to Sanne Kofod Olsen, who was the director of the museum at the time of the launch of *Net.Specific*, the platform was created as part of the museum's work with contemporary time-based and performative art forms. It is the result of a research-based project and the desire to extend the museum's practice online to include internet art, which back then had not received much attention in an institutional context in Denmark (OLSEN 2019).

Net.Specific is independent of the museum's webpage but the museum logo indicates the origin of the page. The works presented on the platform are not hosted on the page, instead, the site links to artworks that exist or existed elsewhere on the internet. Explanatory texts are used to communicate the concept of the platform and the artworks. The works are only shown online and none of the exhibitions or works were installed in the physical museum, but there was an on-site computer through which the platform could be reached. Although at the time it was launched, the platform was supposed to be an ongoing project, the page has not been maintained since 2015 (OLSEN 2019). The page still exists, but some of the works can no longer be accessed. The works are not included in the permanent collection of the museum.

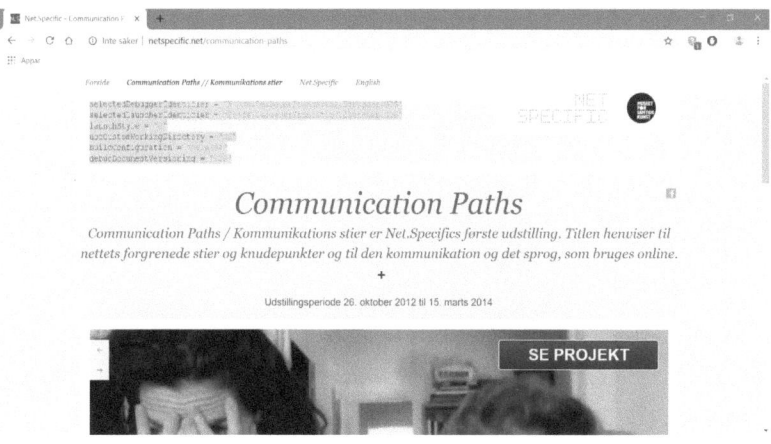

Fig. 1: *Net.Specific (source: screenshot, August 30, 2019)*

Similarly, in 2017, *Kiasma Museum of Contemporary Art* in Helsinki, Finland, launched its *Ars17+ Online Art* platform for a new collection of digital art <http://arsplus.kiasma.fi/en/>. The platform is a webpage that showcases digital artworks of various forms, including video, net art, gifs, apps, games, and software. It was created as a result of the museum's wish to include digital art in their collection and exhibition program (MILLER/LIIMATAINEN 2017), which engages with contemporary art. The platform was curated by Arja Miller and Milja Liimatainen from *Kiasma* and guest curator Attilia Fattori Franchini. It was originally launched in connection with the physical exhibition *Ars17: Hello World*, an exhibition about the digital revolution in art, which was exhibited at the museum in 2017. Although the physical exhibition has run its course, the online extension is still available.

Most of the works on the platform were commissioned for the platform and exhibition, and they have been included in the permanent museum collection (MILLER/LIIMATAINEN 2017). Most of the works are hosted on the platform together with explanatory texts and artist descriptions. The platform is a subdomain of the official museum page and shares its visual identity. During the run of the physical exhibition at the museum, the platform was accessible in the physical museum building through a tablet placed in the museum library.

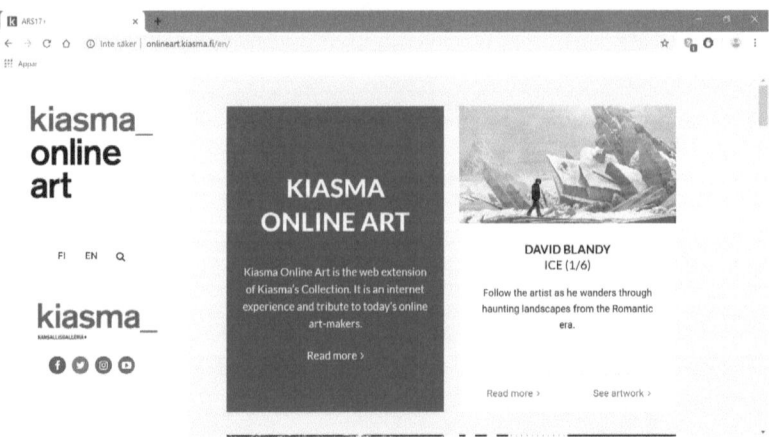

Fig. 2: *Ars17+ Online Art (source: screenshot, August 30, 2019)*

A slightly different approach was used by artists Alfredo Salazar-Caro and William Robertson (who both work with digital art) when they in 2015 launched their *Digital Museum of Digital Art* <https://dimoda. art/>. This platform is a software application developed in the game-engine *Unity* and made available for download through a webpage. Once downloaded it can be accessed from a personal device. The platform is a virtual interactive computer game-like space with a 3D model of a neo-classical museum building in which works by different artists are show-cased. The works are built into the platform and are part of the infra-structure. Mostly focusing on VR art, the *Digital Museum of Digital Art* has to this date produced three exhibitions, all available for download on their webpage. This webpage also includes texts explaining the concept. The main idea with the *Digital Museum of Digital Art* was to create a new platform, a new museum, where digital artworks and VR art could be presented in their intended context: the digital (FABBULA 2019).

Although the *Digital Museum of Digital Art* is an independent vir-tual space, they have organized launches in collaboration with physical institutions such as *Transfer Gallery* in New York. They have also been using the concept of pop-up exhibitions to collaborate with other institu-tions, events, organizations, and festivals taking place in physical spaces.

Fig. 3: Digital Museum of Digital Art
(source: screenshot, August 30, 2019)

Using the game infrastructure to create art spaces for digital artworks is also something artists Theo Triantafyllidis and Julieta Gil did when they, in 2015, created the *New New Wight*, a virtual copy of the New Wight Gallery at the University of California, Los Angeles (UCLA) <http:// dma.ucla.edu/exhibitions/newnewwight/thegalleryisnaked/index. html>. The platform was launched together with the opening exhibition The *Gallery is Naked*, where digital works by 14 artists selected from an open call were presented. Like the *Digital Museum of Digital Art*, the *New New Wight* is an interactive digital space, created using the *Unity* game-engine, where the artworks are built into the platform itself.

Triantafyllidis and Gil both work with digital art and new media and have studied at UCLA. When they created the space they were interested in audience experience and exploring the boundaries between space, artwork, and authorship (TRIANTAFYLLIDIS 2019). The platform was made available through download from UCLA's webpage and online using the browser plug-in *Unity Web Player*. As the plug-in is no longer supported the space is no longer accessible online, but can still be downloaded and then accessed from a personal device. After the first exhibition presented in the virtual space, no other exhibitions have taken place. Documentation of the first exhibition is available as a video on YouTube (THEOTRIAN 2020).

Fig. 4: *New New Wight*
(source: screenshot from YouTube, August 30, 2019)

4. Challenges – what can be learned

In an interview about *New New Wight*, Triantafyllidis points out that the main challenges with the space were technical and related to the implementation of the artworks in a game-engine (TRIANTAFYLLIDIS 2019). Birgitte Kirkhoff Eriksen, the current director of the *Museum of Contemporary Art* in Roskilde, has also in an interview mentioned technical difficulties in the case of *Net.Specific* (ERIKSEN 2019). The same goes for *Ars+ Online Art* and *Kiasma* in which case curators Miller and Liimatainen have expressed how the regular museum staff had to deal with technical challenges they necessarily were not trained or equipped to work with (MILLER/LIIMATAINEN 2017).

According to Susan Leigh Star's and Karen Ruhleder's studies on collaborative systems across different communities, what may seem easy for one group might appear difficult for another and the reason for this is a gap between different user contexts (STAR/RUHLEDER 1996: 127f.). Such a gap could for example be identified in the development process of *Ars17+ Online Art* where the curators, with knowledge about art, had limited experience of working with digital technologies, and the IT-department, who built the platform, had no experience of working with art (MILLER/LIIMATAINEN 2017). In other words, lacking knowledge about technical solutions related to digital art in an institutional context can also be seen as an infrastructural problem. This calls for a closer look at, for example, recruiting processes, but also on how education is structured, to allow interdisciplinary studies and tighten the professional gap between art and IT.

One of the major challenges with *Net.Specific* was financial, and the lack of external financial resources was in the end what closed the project down (OLSEN 2019). Limited financial resources were also mentioned in the case of *Ars17+ Online Art*, where it affected the overall outcome and design of the platform (MILLER/LIIMATAINEN 2017).

This is interesting from the point of view of financial infrastructures that make funding cultural projects and art possible. For example, to what extent do digital artworks or projects centering on digital art gain funding? Is the funding continuous and what aspects affect the possibilities of funding? Digital artworks are often for example dependent on material components, hardware, to be experienced (PAUL 2007: 251–274). Even if the archived codes of the digital space and artworks could be kept as such, the hardware is part of ongoing development and changing fast, which means that older digital works might not exist in formats that can be processed by later technology (LENOIR 2007: 364f.). As digital technologies are continuously advancing they also require constant maintenance. This requires a constant flow of financial resources. How this is taken into account in the funding processes could refer to another infrastructural issue, namely a cultural-political one.

When it comes to the preservation of digital artworks, their often process- and time-based interactive nature challenges existing models of preserving, commonly developed for more static art forms. Documentation through video or photography, often used in the cases of performance art, is one method also used for preserving digital art (PAUL 2015: 25). This we have seen in the case of *New New Wight*. This of course does not preserve the artwork itself, but can be used to study aspects of the artworks later.

In the case of *Ars17+ Online Art*, the artworks presented on the platform are part of *Kiasma*'s collection. Practically this means that the museum owns the source code. Traditionally this means that the museum is responsible for the works. Possible preservation strategies were discussed with the artists while the platform was being built, and attempts were made to include these in the contracts. However, the museum has expressed an understanding of the fact that they might not be able to preserve the platform and the works (MILLER/LIIMATAINEN 2017). *Net.Specific* was never supposed to be a permanent collection nor a space for preserving the works exhibited on the platform (OLSEN 2019). Rather it seems to be an experiment on how to work with internet art in an institutional context.

As for the *Digital Museum of Digital Art* and the *New New Wight*, preserving the artworks means preserving the space. The downloadable version of the *New New Wight* was made for archiving purposes (TRIANTAFYLLIDIS 2019). The *Digital Museum of Digital Art* was developed with the vision of a permanent collection and archive of the digital works presented on the platform. Part of the preservation strategy in this case included the copies of the museum that would be created and spread out when visitors would download the files containing the space on the webpage (BORS 2015). Both *New New Wight* and the *Digital Museum of Digital Art* are, however, apart from the hardware, also dependent on software (*Unity*) to be experienced.

According to Tina Mariane Krogh Madsen, who curated *Net.Specific*, traditional preservation strategies need to be reinvented focusing more on process, concept, and performativity. One such strategy is to more closely include the artists in the discussion and development process of a preservation method for their work and, through contracts and databases, state the future of each artwork (MADSEN 2015: 313–320). This was the case with *Ars17+ Online Art*. Depending on the artwork and its needs, the preservation methods could, apart from documentation, also involve permissions to recreate artworks or update them following technological developments (MADSEN 2015: 313–320).

This means that the artwork would change over time and it would also question institutional ideas about originality, authenticity, and the concept of a unique artwork that should be conserved for future generations. Digital art therefore does not only challenge traditional ideas of exhibiting and presenting (distribution) but the concept of preservation as a whole. This in turn challenges the role of the intuition as a caretaker (preserver) of culture.

5. Digital imaginaries

Looking at the examples discussed above it is interesting to see how they all, although digital, seem to simulate an analog reality in various degrees. *New New Wight* is a virtual copy of a physically existing gallery within which artworks are shown. The white cube model and the fact that it relates to an actual institution, create a clear institutional framework around the space. The *Digital Museum of Digital Art* is in itself already called a museum and the platform is a virtual building that with its neoclassical style looks like a traditional museum. While *Net.Specific* and *Ars17+ Online Art* both are webpages, they are framed by their mother institutions through museum logos and exhibition texts. Why is it that the digital platforms seem to replicate elements of physical exhibition spaces and institutions when the possibilities of the digital space are different from an analog one? To explore this question I have looked into whether this has something to do with how 'the digital' is imagined or understood.

When we examine the cases we can see that there are different ideas of what digital art is and what the digital space can be. The *Digital Museum of Digital Art* and *New New Wight* are for example focusing on a certain type of digital art that can be exhibited in the virtual space created. *Net.Specific* focused on internet art and *Ars17+ Online Art* is a collection of various types and forms of digital artworks.

All of the cases mentioned have in one way or another involved the internet in their infrastructure. As Christiane Paul points out, what often happens when we think of the digital or the internet is that we imagine it as immaterial, or as the invisible cloud accessible by whomever, whenever and wherever (PAUL 2007: 251–274). The idea of this accessibility is for example something *Kiasma* found attractive in the case of *Ars17+ Online Art* (MILLER/LIIMATAINEN 2017). The digital is however not immaterial, it just involves another kind of materiality, which consists of all those infrastructural components that make it possible to transport information and audiovisual content (PAUL 2007: 251–274). This materiality is crucial to whether one has access and it is affected by other systems, among them political, financial, and social (CHUN 2016: 4–19; STAR 1999: 389; THYLSTRUP 2019: 133). The digital space is thus not neutral but governed by its power structures while simultaneously relating to others.

According to media theorist Lisa Parks, how we understand or imagine infrastructures (what we think of them, where they are, who controls them, and what they do) is also an infrastructure (PARKS 2015: 355). The infrastructure of art institutions, therefore, includes, apart from buildings and people (material components), ideas and conventions (soft systems), also our ways of thinking about and being around art and institutions. The same goes for media infrastructures, which apart from cables and satellites also consist of our idea of them. This is what Parks calls infrastructural imaginaries, and as imaginaries, they might not always represent the full truth (PARKS 2015: 355).

When a cultural institution presents art online, the online space (platform) becomes an extension of the institution and its infrastructure but is also part of the digital and that infrastructure. Looking at how institutions understand the digital can help us understand their relationship to the digital, how they treat it, and work with it in an institutional context. It could also explain why the digital platforms discussed seem to mirror analog setups. This suggests another infrastructural dilemma related to infrastructural imaginaries, namely to how we imagine institutions and the digital.

6. Broken infrastructures

According to Wendy Chun, our understanding of the digital is based on habits. Like infrastructures, habits exist by being invisible, automatized, and unconscious (CHUN 2016: 6, 13). Infrastructures are both forming and formed by social conventions (STAR/RUHLEDER 1996: 113; STAR 1999: 381f.). Like habits, they have been learned from somewhere. Institutions are what maintain certain ideas about art and art institutions, which in turn affect our understanding of them (DICKIE 1997: 83–92). If our understanding of the digital, as Chun says, is based on habits, then it is possible that also our understanding of the art institution is based on habits (that which we are used to).

According to Star and Ruhleder, infrastructures remain invisible due to their quality of connecting to other infrastructures and systems in a standardized way. Since infrastructures are constantly built on older, already existing systems, they inherit the strengths and weaknesses of those older structures (STAR/RUHLEDER 1996: 113; STAR 1999: 381f.). It then seems possible that the digital spaces for art, at least when it comes to the cases discussed, are built on older institutional systems, which are, in turn, based on habits. The platforms thus echo the infrastructures and logic of these analog systems, which include models of (re)presentation and the concept of preservation.

When it comes to the digital, break down and glitches are an inevitable part of its logic. This also means that digital artworks are not necessarily made to last. As mentioned above this possible outcome was discussed in the case of *Ars17+ Online Art*, although nothing permanent was decided, and it is evident in the case of *Net.Specific*, that still links to works (pages) that no longer work.

As Cymene Howe et al. writes in the article *Paradoxical Infrastructures: Ruins, Retrofit and Risk* we constantly live among broken infrastructures, ruins of earlier projects, which no longer hold the same optimism they once did (HOWE et al. 2016: 550). According to Star and Ruhleder infrastructures become visible when they break and no longer do what they are supposed to do (STAR/RUHLEDER 1996: 113; STAR 1999: 381f.). When it comes to digital art, it has become clear that traditional analog art institutions find it challenging to do what they are supposed to do (used to do), including distributing and preserving. This in turn suggests a broken infrastructure.

7. The update

According to Chun, the digital is bound to the update. That which is no longer updated becomes unusable (broken) and is no longer cared for (CHUN 2016: 2). This constant updating relates to hardware and software, but it can also relate to the institution as a sort of 'hardware' for art. One of the reasons behind *Kiamsa* creating *Ars17+ Online Art* was for example the wish to stay 'up to date' regarding new art forms (MILLER/LIIMATAINEN 2017).

As digital art is challenging traditional and habitual ways of thinking about institutions, distribution, and preservation, it offers us a chance to rethink these concepts when it comes to digital art. In the case of the update Chun indicates that "to delete is not to forget, but to make possible other ways to remember" (CHUN 2016: 19). In the same way, by moving away from previous infrastructural arrangements and habits we can think of other possible infrastructures. What then is the updated institution?

To explore this question I talked to artists working with digital art. When it comes to preservation, artists Nora Al-Badri and Michael Takeo Magruder both agree with rethinking the whole concept (AL-BADRI 2019; MAGRUDER 2019). As digital art is more about keeping the artwork alive and accessible, it becomes more a question of maintenance rather than dead preservation (MAGRUDER 2019). And then not only a question of what should be maintained but also of longevity – for how long shall it be preserved? (AL-BADRI 2019) As Andreas Broeckmann has pointed out, the process of erosion and perishability (dying and disappearing) can be an important aspect of the aesthetic of digital artworks (BROECKMANN 2007: 201). In regards to preservation, this means they cannot be preserved in the traditional sense, that is, kept in original condition, when there is no one original condition.

Triantafyllidis agrees with Al-Badri and Magruder. What he and the artists involved with the *New New Wight* learned from the project was knowledge and experience, which lives on (is preserved) in future projects by these artists (TRIANTAFYLLIDIS 2019). Instead of preserving works, more focus could be put on preserving concepts, ideas, and knowledge. This is where intuitions have an important role to play, and not only as preservers but by actively allowing projects, concepts, ideas, and knowledge to be generated. And it is curious to see that while preservation indeed has been discussed in all cases mentioned, no solid plans were made in regards to the future of these platforms at the time of their launch. This can of course relate to the financial or technical resources discussed earlier, but it can also suggest that the question of preservation has been less important, and more significance has been placed on the experiment.

When it comes to distribution, Al-Badri and Magruder talk about the advantages of a distributed system. Working with festivals and other public, less formal contexts outside of the institution, has the potential of providing wider contexts for presenting and experiencing digital art forms (AL-BADRI 2019). This would also enable random encounters, chance, and unexpectedness, and generate new audiences (MAGRUDER 2019). The *Digital Museum of Digital Art* also works through a distributed system. The museum itself only exists digitally, but through various pop-up events, collaborations with physical institutions, and festivals, the platform, and the art it presents become distributed and are made available in different analog contexts. Also here, in the case of distribution, institutions have a significant part to play in taking the initiative to allow new collaborative and distributed practices.

New ways of thinking about the institution, preservation, and distribution are needed when it comes to digital art. And when trying to figure out how these new strategies could look like, old infrastructural models might come in handy. Salazar-Caro addressed this in an interview about the *Digital Museum of Digital Art*. According to him, although the idea with the digital museum was to move as far away as possible from the physical reality and embrace the possibilities of the virtual, the use of traditional concepts and traditional architecture anchors the visitor in familiar surroundings (BORS 2015). Even if concepts such as 'museum', 'institution' or 'gallery' reflect an earlier system, because we are used to them, they might help us navigate the complex reality in which digitalization has placed us. And this is where cultural institutions have an important communicative task in helping us make sense of this reality and its implications.

Changing that which we are used to (habits) is difficult and takes time. Infrastructures are large and complex, exist in different layers, and are connected to other infrastructures. No one is therefore fully responsible for an infrastructure, and changing one might require other parts of the system or other systems to be changed (STAR/RUHLEDER 1996: 113; STAR 1999; 381f.). This means that to overcome some of the challenges institutions are facing when dealing with digital art, it is not enough to only change or 'update' the institution. Instead, other systems might have to be changed or updated as well. As discussed above, such systems include financial and educational structures, but also our habits around and ways of thinking about art, culture, and institutions and what they do.

8. Conclusion

In the context of mass digitalization I have, by focusing on the concepts of distribution and preservation, in this essay discussed the challenges art institutions face when they are dealing with digital art. To do so, I have looked at four case studies that serve as examples of digital platforms for digital art. The studies show that the immediate issues, when it comes to these examples, were technical and financial. Using infrastructure theory I have been able to argue that these issues can be related to larger infrastructural arrangements, concerning funding, education, and recruiting processes.

Further, I have been able to argue that how digital art is treated in an institutional context is based on how we imagine and understand institutions and digital art, which is based on habits. These habits, which include organizational models and concepts such as preservation, live on in how institutions work with digital art, which can be limiting. As digital art challenges these habits, it has become difficult for institutions to do what they are supposed to do, which, in infrastructural terms, suggests an infrastructural breakdown. The difficulty in fixing this breakdown is that changing habits is challenging and takes time. At the same time infrastructures are large, intertwined, and complex systems, which means that changing one (in this case the institution and our habits around it) needs other infrastructures to change as well. This all suggests that an overall challenge when it comes to institutions working with digital art is an infrastructural one.

We need new ways of thinking about the digital, but also art, institutions, distribution, and preservation. Cultural institutions have an important role here, not just as communicators but also by allowing more experimental practices to take place and accepting that there is no universal way of working with digital art in an institutional context. Working with digital culture is in itself a process, constantly developing, breaking down, and changing and it can therefore never be definite nor flawless.

For further research, I would suggest looking more deeply into funding possibilities and structures for digital art projects. I would also suggest studying how knowledge of art and digital technologies is distributed in an institutional context, along with how educational programs for institutional staff are structured. Last but not least I would also suggest a closer look into how the digital is understood in an institutional context. As this essay has discussed the topics at hand on a conceptual level, I believe the outcome of studying the suggested would bring forth more practical solutions.

References

AL-BADRI, Nora (2019): interview, Skype, July 5, 2019.

ANDERSEN, Christian Ulrik/POLD, Søren Bro (2015): Manifest for Kunstmuseet i den Digitale tidsalder. – In: Hejlskov, Ane (Ed.), *Cybermuseologi. Kunst, museer og formidling i et digitalt perspektiv*. Aarhus: Aarhus Universitetsforl., 27–45.

BENNETT, Tony (1997): *The Birth of the Museum: History, Theory, Politics*, London, New York: Routledge.

BORS, Sabin (2015): *DiMoDA: The Digital Museum of Digital Art. A Virtual Institution* <https://anti-utopias.com/newswire/dimoda-digital-museum-digital-art/> [November 22, 2020].

BROECKMANN, Andreas (2007): Image, Process, Performance, Machine: Aspects of an Aesthetic of the Machinic. – In: Grau, Oliver (Ed.), *Media Art Histories*. Cambridge/MA, London: MIT Press, 193–205.

CHUN, Wendy (2016): *Updating to Remain the Same. Habitual new media*. Cambridge/MA, London: MIT Press.

DIAZ, Lily (2016): Media Art. – In: Ekman, Ulrik/Bolter, Jay David/Diaz, Lily/Søndergaard, Morten/Engberg, Maria (Eds.), *Ubiquitous Computing, Complexity, and Culture*. London, New York: Routledge, 237–239.

DICKIE, George (1997): *Introduction to Aesthetics*, New York.

ERIKSEN, Birgitte Kirkhoff (2019): interview, Copenhagen, May 13, 2019.

FABBULA (2019 [2016]): *DiMoDA, the Making of a VR Counter Culture* <https://fabbula.com/dimoda-vrindieart/> [23 August 2019].

HOWE, Cymene/LOCKREM, Jessica/APPEL, Hannah/HACKETT, Edward/BOYER, Dominic/HALL, Randal/SCHNEIDER-MAYERSON, Matthew/POPE, Albert/GUPTA Akhil/RODWELL, Elizabeth/BALLESTERO, Andrea/DURBIN, Trevor/EL-DAHDAH, Farès/LONG, Elizabeth/MODY, Cyrus (2016): *Paradoxical Infrastructures: Ruins, Retrofit, and Risk*. – In: *Sience, Technology & Human Values* 43 (3), 547–565.

LENOIR, Timothy (2007): Making Studies in New Media Critical. – In: Grau, Oliver (Ed.), *Media Art Histories*. Cambridge/MA, London: MIT Press, 355–380.

MADSEN, Tina Mariane Krogh (2015): At Holde Flygtigheden i Live – Netkunst, Processualitet og Bevaring. – In: Hejlskov, Ane (Ed.), *Cybermuseologi. Kunst, museer og formidling i et digitalt perspektiv*. Aarhus: Aarhus Universitetsforl., 313–326.

MAGRUDER, Michael Takeo (2019): interview, Skype, July 19, 2019.

MILLER, Arja/LIIMATAINEN, Milja (2017): Interview. – Available at: Finnish National Gallery, Archives, AV-archive, Helsinki, Finland.

OLSEN, Sanne Kofod (2019): interview, e-mail, June 5, 2019.

PARKS, Lisa (2017): Infrastructure. – In: Ouellette, Laurie/Gray, Jonathan, *Keywords for media studies*. New York: University Press, 106–108.

PARKS, Lisa (2015): Stuff You Can Kick: Toward a Theory of Media Infrastructures. – In: Svensson, Patrik/Goldberg, David Theo, *Between Humanities and the Digital*, MIT Press, 355–373.

PARKS, Lisa/STAROSIELISKI, Nicole (2015): Introduction. – In: *Signal Traffic*. Chicago, 1–28.

PAUL, Christiane (2015): *A Companion to Digital Art*. Chichester/UK: Wiley Blackwell.

PAUL, Christiane (2007): The Myth of Immateriality: Presenting and Preserving New Media. – In: Grau, Oliver, *Media Art Histories*. Cambridge/MA, London: MIT Press, 251–274.

SCHUBERT, Karsten (2000): *The Curator's Egg: The Evolution of the Museum Concept from French Revolution to Present Day*. London : One-Off Press.

SHANKEN, Edward A. (2007): Historicizing Art and Technology: Forging a Method and Firing a Canon. – In: Grau, Oliver, *Media Art Histories*. Cambridge/MA, London: MIT Press, 43–70.

STAR, Susan Leigh/RUHLEDER, Karen (1996): Steps Toward an Ecology of Infrastructure: Design and Access for Large Information Spaces. – In: *Information Systems Research* 7 (1), 111–134.

STAR, Susan Leigh (1999): The Etnography of Infrastructure. – In: *The American Behavioral Scientist* 43 (3), 377–391.

SØNDERGAARD, Morten (2016): Media Art. In – Ekman, Ulrik/Bolter, Jay David/Diaz, Lily/Søndergaard, Morten/Engberg, Maria (Eds.), *Ubiquitous Computing, Complexity, and Culture*. London, New York: Routledge, 85–88.

THYLSTRUP, Nanna Bonde (2019): *The Politics of Mass Digitization*. Cambridge/MA, London: The MIT Press.

TRIANTAFYLLIDIS, Theo (2019): interview, e-mail, July 6, 2019.

THEOTRIAN (2020): *New New Wight: The Gallery is Naked – Walkthrough* (20 May 2016) <https://www.youtube.com/watch?v=r4I7dF62OYM> [22 November 2020].

Smart City Cluj, from Provincial Hotspot to Transnational Hub: The Adventures of a Would-Be Post-Industrial City in Romania

Smart City Cluj, vom provinziellen Hotspot zum transnationalen Knotenpunkt: Die Abenteuer einer rumänischen Möchtegern- Post-Industriestadt

STEFAN-SEBASTIAN MAFTEI*

Department of Philosophy, Cluj-Napoca, Romania

Abstract

The focus of this essay is, first, to see if the Transylvanian city of Cluj can really be counted amongst post-industrial cities—or, at least, if its strategies of development would really allow it to be listed as a post-industrial city in the foreseeable future. Secondly, the essay will try to find the set of factors that determines the city's current—as it will unfold—ambitious development and, future—no less ambitious—projects. Thirdly, the link between the post-industrial spin and the emergence of an important creative industries scene will be considered, as the essay will try to explain the role of creative industries in the new post-industrial economic dynamic of the city.

Dieser Essay analysiert zunächst, ob die transsilvanische Stadt Cluj tatsächlich als „post-industrielle" Stadt charakterisiert werden kann, oder ob ihre Weiterentwicklungsstrategien eine solche Einordnung zumindest in absehbarer Zukunft erlauben. Anschließend werden einige Faktoren herausgestellt, die aktuellen ambitionierten und zukünftigen, nicht weniger ambitionierten Stadtentwicklungsprojekten zugrunde liegen. Zuletzt wird der Zusammenhang zwischen Post-industrialismus und der Entstehung relevanter Kreativindustrien erläutert, um die Rolle der Kreativindustrien in der neuen post-industriellen Wirtschaftsdynamik von Cluj zu erklären.

Keywords

creativity studies, diversity, internet creativity

As the title indicates, the intention of this essay is not to simply analyze the digitization of the city of Cluj-Napoca (or, by its shorter name, Cluj), or the transformation of Cluj into a smart city *stricto sensu*, by this, meaning the use of information and communication technologies in order to improve, to optimize the functioning of a city and the life of its citizens. That is because our intention is to employ the phrase smart city as a synecdoche for a larger process, which is the multifaceted process of

* Babeş-Bolyai@University

stepping into the post-industrial age as described by Daniel Bell's semi-nal work *The Coming of Post-Industrial Society*, first published in 1973 (BELL 1999). This, of course, does not mean that the phenomenon of turning Cluj into a smart city *stricto sensu* will not be illustrated. At the same time, the essay intends to foray into the life of the creative indus-tries of Cluj-Napoca. Important phenomena of creative industries sig-nificant for the life of the city will be identified, described, and analyzed. Also, the connection of these industries to a bigger picture, that of the smart city dynamic, will be commented upon. The suggestion is that these creative industries are part of the network of activities involved in the current shaping of the city as a future post-industrial hub.

Smart City Cluj: description

Smart City Cluj is a new trend (SMART 2017a; SMART 2017b). I am re-ferring at this point to the efforts of transforming Cluj into a smart city. Cluj is now dubbed the Silicon Valley of Transylvania—the historical province of the former Austro-Hungarian Empire and the North-Western region of present day Romania. According to a 2018 Vegacomp Report (VEGACOMP 2018), entitled *Smart City Romania*, Cluj-Napoca, or, by its shorter name, Cluj (also the county town of Cluj County), is the "sec-ond most important city" in Romania following Bucharest (PETROVICI 2014: 2), and the fastest in terms of economic growth. At least according to some indicators (BENEDEK/CRISTEA 2014: 131), Cluj is listed third, following Alba Iulia and Oradea (two other middle-size Transylvanian cities), in a competition regarding smart city implemented projects. This smart city project competition took six aspects into account, all referring to the informational transformation of a city's life: economy, mobility, environment, people, living, governance (VEGACOMP 2018). As for the creative industries, they are already organized (TCIC 2020; CREAT 2020) into what has been named the Transylvania Creative Industries Cluster, located in Cluj. One of the initial objectives of this cluster, set up in 2016, was the

> increasing [of the] competitiveness of enterprises in the field of creative industries, based on the intensive use of knowledge, as well as [the] supporting and promoting [of] projects of common interest, including big projects, cross-border, through the creation of collaborative mechanisms. (TCIC 2020)

In *Colliers International Romania Research & Forecast Report 2019* (COLLIERS 2019), Cluj was mentioned amongst other regional cities in

Romania (with Timişoara, Iaşi and Braşov) where the business environment becomes more and more favourable to internal and external economic migration, due to "the increased living standards [...], alongside wages not too far below (or at all) to those in Bucharest" (COLLIERS 2019).

The report also cites a World Bank study where Cluj is mentioned as the "number one town in the country Romanians would move to [...], even ahead of Bucharest" (COLLIERS 2019). In addition to this, Cluj possesses a very lively creative class comprising artists, media artists, architects, curators, IT experts, advertisers, and a wide range of creative industry offerings. I will analyze this in the second part of the essay.

In terms of the so-called tertiary economy, represented by "call centres, accounting, marketing, audit, consultancy, judicial services and so on" (COLLIERS 2019), which has the highest rate of growth, especially due to outsourcing, the capital, Bucharest is the "absolute leader." However, the next on the list is "Cluj-Napoca and the entire Cluj county," as this city and its county "have become a case study about the development of the business, investments, hiring activity, office and residential spaces and about the general market growth" (COLLIERS 2019). According to the same report, Cluj is listed as being the second city in the country in terms of net wages. With this expansion, the office development business is also high, with Cluj situated as the second biggest in terms of modern office stock.

Transportation, meaning passenger air traffic, alone, has increased almost doubling its size in four years, at Cluj airport—from 1.48 million passengers in 2015 to 2.78 million in 2018 (COLLIERS 2019). Cluj is also placed third amongst Romanian cities in terms of foreign capital investments (FORBES 2019). There are strong investments in creative industries as well, with foreign and local capital, primarily in software development industries, as I will illustrate. In addition to that, the gaming industry is present with a set of companies that base much of their business models not just on games, but on a combination of services. Evozon is the best example of a multiservicing business, but there are others listed as well: Zynk Software, Idea Studios, Oves Enterprise. Indie companies such as Firebyte Games, Tractor Set GO, Stuck in Attic, Rikodu, are mostly focused on game and interactive media development. One only has to take a look at several hiring sites that list the profile of software and gaming companies in Cluj to realize that there is a lot going on in these small companies in terms of their services: for example, one company put "full cycle game development, mobile games, AR/VR, interactive apps, serious games, 3D modeling, animations, VFX, sound and music production, level design" (TRACTOR 2020)—on its list of services.

CEE Investment Report 2019 – Thriving Metropolitan Cities (CEE 2019) lists Cluj as the 7 on a list of the "20 fastest growing cities in the European Union" (CEE 2019: 8). This ranking had three main factors in view: "productivity growth," "connectivity growth," "human capital growth" (CEE 2019: 9). Wheels are in motion. A 2019 report announcing a Smart Transformation Forum held last year in Bucharest and bringing together the most important, governmental as well as private, actors involved in the "Smart City" initiative (PURICE 2019) began its argument by stating that

> major metropolitan areas are expected to implement technologies that could bring urban living into the digital age. Successful and sustainable Smart Cities are not built solely upon the technology mainframe, but on the support and engagement of the broader community, by prioritizing and practicing people-centered urban design and providing multi-modal pathways for all citizens to join-in and meaningfully participate in the co-creation of their Smart City. By meaningfully and continuously engaging the public in all Smart City planning processes, city leadership, urban & private sector partners are ensuring the systems, projects & plans they create are grounded in real community needs. It's time for our community to start turning towards smart technologies. (PURICE 2019)

The Forum considered implementation of four major strategies, all of them considering the link between community and technology, with an emphasis on involving the city communities as partners in the fashioning of these smart cities. These strategies were: *Smart energy, Smart mobility, Smart infrastructure,* and *Smart public services* (PURICE 2019). The current mayor of Cluj-Napoca, Emil Boc, addressed this issue in 2019, when speaking of the future strategies for a Smart City Cluj (CĂTĂLIN 2019). Amongst other projects—free wifi, smart parking, EV charging stations, online payment for taxes, electric buses, Boc spoke about the most important one, in his view: *Cluj Innovation City,* a 500 million Euro future investment. He then added: "Our goal is to shift from 'made in Cluj' to 'invented in Cluj'" (CĂTĂLIN 2019). On the site dedicated to the project, this investment is described as,

> a planned high technology business area to be built in and around Cluj [...]. The site aims to be a highly modern complex created to encourage companies that are part of the recently established Cluj IT Innovation Cluster and also other science and technology companies from Romania and abroad to establish their base of operations and research here. (CIC 2020)

This is not out of the blue, however. Cluj already hosts powerful IT, as well as IT-related and engineering industries run by giants such as Google, Emerson, Endava, Bosch, Siemens, and Microsoft. Cluj also founded the *Cluj IT Cluster* in 2012, a conglomerate of

> 16 gold members, 6 regional universities, 23 silver members, and 10 catalyst organizations, including the Regional Development Agency, the City Hall of Cluj-Napoca and county-level institutions in Cluj, as well as Steinbeis Europa-Zentrum in Stuttgart (CLUSTER 2020),

as promoted by the site of the European Commission.

A lot of IT businesses in Cluj are dependent on outsourcing on a very competitive, global, market, as "the prevailing segment remains for the time being in the software outsourcing service area" (DRAGAN 2018). Yet this outsourcing is constantly growing and, at the same time, a constant source of economic boom. So much so that, according to some of the latest data, provided by the site of the software development company Softech,

> one out of eleven employees works in the IT sector in Cluj-Napoca ... there are 1235 IT companies in Cluj-Napoca, employing about 14,000 persons—that is the equivalent of 8.7 % of the city's total employees. When counting the total number of free-lance and start-ups, the number of people professionally involved in IT reaches over 20,000 persons. (SOFTECH 2017)

Softech also emphasizes that 20,000 out of the total of 100,000 IT professionals in Romania work in Cluj. Szélyes Levente, the Hungarian speaking CEO of the Cluj company Codespring, quoted by Softech, states that the advantage of Cluj, in comparison to Bucharest, is that Cluj, as it lacks the necessary business connections to work with the internal, national, IT clients, is mostly oriented towards the global market. Cluj is thus more global-oriented than the capital city of Romania in terms of establishing long-term business connections with major clients (SOFTECH 2017).

The high-tech and IT industry in Cluj therefore contributes heavily to the growth of a more cosmopolitan city. Global business connections mean more foreigners working or doing business in the city. This sparks a thriving social life hosted by a growing number of chic cafés, restaurants, so-called creative bars, such as Joben Bistro, Enigma, Insomnia, Booha Bar, and other pubs and clubs. A 2020 article in the *Guardian* (2020) lists these as part of the main attractions of the city. The inflow of tourists also contributes to this cosmopolitanizing trend, leading to an increase in the number of hotels, hostels, and other accommodations. The IT industry also has a very good relationship with the municipality of Cluj. The article has already noted the support of the Smart City Cluj project provided by the mayor. In support of the idea of IT connected with urban development in Cluj the municipality created an Innovation and IT Consultative Council, its task being the development of the Innovation and Information Technology Strategy for 2014-2020 (SOFTECH 2017).

Besides IT, there are other investments currently running in high-tech and engineering. The Tetarom Industrial Park, built at Jucu, near Cluj, has the mission, according to the Industry Section of the European Commission's page on Internal Market, Industry, Entrepreneurship & SMEs, to

> build and to develop high tech industries that are in need of qualified work force such as information technology, electronics & telecommunication industry, automation, robotics; to stimulate research activities in high tech department; to set up, at a fast pace, new available jobs especially for the graduates from Cluj Napoca Universities; to bring non pollutant technologies in accordance with the environmental legislation; and to set up specific industrial park infrastructures, local and regional expansion 'engines'. (TETAROM 2020)

According to the data previously shown, it is by now obvious that new capital flows have unleashed the force of local businesses and initiatives, with major cities (Cluj, Timişoara, Iaşi, Braşov) as major competitors on the external and internal markets against the hegemony of the capital city, Bucharest.

In the new office development business, there is constant and substantial growth, with big office buildings being raised in the areas formerly occupied by Socialist-era warehouses and factories. In Cluj, there is Liberty Technology Park, The Office, Mainstream Office, and other venues. All are new, inspiring locations, populated mostly by high-tech and IT companies occupying the new business environment in Cluj (OFFICE 2020). The banking business is also well personified by the Cluj-based *Banca Transilvania* (Transylvania Bank), currently running as the largest bank in Romania.

As others areas of high-tech & IT industries have already experienced, the working life of these professionals is generally driven by a "centrality of work" ethos, "entrepreneurialism," "extreme individualism," "aggressive competition" spirit, but also "technostress" diffused by "compensatory consumption" generated by high incomes, which determines "affluence" and a certain lifestyle (CASTELLS/HALL 1994: 21–24). This consumption is hosted in Cluj by a large network of malls, restaurants, clubs, cafés, pubs, bars, and clubs which have become a part of the local culture. Of the creative bars already mentioned, Casa TIFF, is unique: it has been directly linked to one local cultural event happening each year in the city from 2002 onwards, the TIFF (Transylvania International Film Festival). Casa TIFF is the venue that hosts the TIFF offices, not just during the festival, but throughout the year. Located in the city centre, the bar also hosts numerous other cultural events, a lot of them related to film. Another bar, "Insomnia," is a venue very familiar to literati, artists, and especially poets, as it hosts a well-known local independent poetry club, called *Nepotul lui Thoreau* [*Thoreau's Nephew*]. However, in terms of creative industries networking and organizing, there is more than the independent niche. There is also mainstream organizing. The *Transylvania Creative Industries Cluster* (TCIC) mentioned above is an important alliance of institutions such as the University of Art and Design (whose former rector is also the cluster's president), The Technical University of Cluj-Napoca, and business actors such as Aries Transylvania, Cluj Innovation Park, Vitrina Advertising, and Transylvania Bank. The cluster also enjoys support from the mayor's office. The TCIC is, according to its site, Romania's first Creative Industries Cluster (TCIC 2020). There is also the *The Regional Center of Excellence for Creative Industries,* an initiative started and implemented by the mu- nicipality in 2013, with support from the European Regional Development Fund. The building which hosts the Centre, covering an area of over 13,000 sqm, which is already up and running and located near Cluj Innovation Park, offers services to all kinds of creative industries, such as office space for creative businesses and working space for creative workshops and audio-video productions , for example, a film studio. The Centre also provides operational space for various events such as conferences, exhibitions and shows. The Centre includes a Green Amphitheater, an outdoor amphitheater providing location for open-air events (CREICa 2020). According to the description of the venue,

> CREIC is a building with four different units—A, B, C and D, three underground levels, ground floor and four stories. There are more than 2,300 sqm dedicated to office and coworking spaces, 966 sqm for the micro production spaces, 1,056 sqm for the event spaces and 629 sqm for the film studio. Our outdoor amphitheater and green terraces of CREIC are dedicated to formal and informal, artistic, social or business events. (CREICb 2020)

It is, indeed, a real, life-size, factory dedicated to creative industries.

Another initiative, which is NGO-level and dedicated to the support of creative industries in Cluj, is the *Cluj Cultural Centre*, a "non-governmental organization for culture and urban development" (CCC 2020), according to its online description. The projects of this centre focus on

> contemporary art, well-being, cultural and artistic education, urban re- generation, community connection, social inclusion, cultural industries, rural development, ethnography of imagined worlds, cultural sector's capacity-building, social and urban innovation, international cooperation, research, and policies. (CCC 2020)

The Centre struggles to promote the development of "the city of Cluj as a strategic European city in the field of art and culture" (CCC 2020). Its mission is "to mobilize culture, in partnership with other sectors, in order to contribute to the social transformation and urban development" (CCC 2020).

Sporting events and entertainment (of all sorts) are well represented, with classical music festivals, countless smaller-scale events, big summer music festivals (Untold, Electric Castle, Form Days, Jazz in the Park), as well as important film festivals (TIFF). There is also a newly built sports infrastructure area located in the city centre comprising a new stadium (Cluj Arena) and a new sports hall nearby that is already functioning. This entertainment industry attracts a lot of internal and external tourism (espe- cially in the summer, during the major festivals). As a result, there is also a booming tourist industry.

Another two important elements in this highly complex puzzle—besides IT and high-tech companies, air travel, office development, industrial parks, technological parks, banking industry, entertainment and sports industry, retail, smart city, and community projects—are, first, the new urban and extra-urban transport infrastructure developed or upgraded or waiting to be developed and upgraded. And, second, the new residential areas built in the city and in its vicinities, creating a large metropolitan residential area adding roughly 100.000 to the already 325.000 people living in Cluj. This also encouraged the real estate business and the insurance business. The municipality is looking to upgrade the existing transport infrastructure with new major investments such as a city beltway, a Cluj Metropolitan Train, a Cluj Metro Line in order to make possible a demographic boom of up to 1,000,000 people in the Cluj Metropolitan Area in the next 15 years (CĂTĂLIN 2019). A lot has been invested in new public transportation vehicles as well. A bike rental system and a smart parking system have been implemented. Also, an investment in upgrading the airport infrastructure is partially functional; more is underway.

Last, but not least are the universities and their connection to the creative industries—the latter comprising nine sectors, such as arts and culture, IT, software and computer services included, according to a British DCMP analysis from 2015 (DCMP 2015: 10). University life in

Cluj, counting on almost 100,000 students from all the higher education institutions in the city, is the biggest and most important human capital provider, a capital which is the most precious resource for the IT, high-tech, engineering, and other informational industries.

These university graduates are the most valuable current and future workforce for these industries. The creative industries, on the other hand, are also well represented due to the presence of institutions providing the education necessary to develop special skills for jobs in the sector: an independent University of Art and Design, an independent Music Academy, and other specializations offered by other institutions, necessary for these kinds of jobs.

An interesting case is the Paintbrush Factory project. Located on the site and in the buildings of a former paintbrush factory, its presence helped forge a stronger sense of community among the different artists and artists' cohorts in the city.

Art Cities of the Future: 21st Century Avant-Gardes (BYRD et al. 2013: 64–83) published by Phaidon Press, analyzed twelve prospective cities that would influence the art world in the 21st century. Cluj was included on a short-list of cities, along with Beirut, Bogotá, Lagos, New Delhi, Istanbul, and others relevant to the contemporary art world. The "Cluj" section is authored by Jane Neal. The author notes, right from the start, the multi-cultural history of the city and also its high cosmopolitan potential, including the struggle of local artists to become more internationally acknowledged. This quest for international acknowledgement was, and is, higher in the Cluj artist community for two reasons, she argues: first, because of the simple fact that Cluj is the "provincial" (BYRD et al. 2013: 64) element or center, less important politically or administratively, in comparison to the capital, the metropolis, and, therefore, the chance for the artist acquiring a "national recognition" (BYRD et al. 2013: 64) is less palpable than in Bucharest; second, because—due to its centuries-old historical and symbolic ties to Western Europe, especially through its Habsburg imperial history—Cluj was constantly driven towards Western Europe. Western, particularly German, art influences are the result of direct historical liaisons with Vienna and Budapest (BYRD et al. 2013: 64).

The Paintbrush Factory is significant to the artistic development of Cluj. Several art galleries, such as Plan B, Bazis and Sabot, were quick to locate, and to exhibit on the site of the former factory, which became a "centre for the arts, with artists' studios, workshops and galleries on site" (BYRD et al. 2013: 65). The activities fostered by the Paintbrush Factory project only helped catalyze the image of what international newspapers called the "Cluj Scene" (BYRD et al. 2013: 67). The Phaidon Press publication includes mention of several artists from Cluj who are part of its art scene, and who have achieved global recognition and fame: Marius Bercea, Mihuț Boşcu Kafchin, Răzvan Botiş, Adrian Ghenie, Victor Man, Alex Mirutziu, Ciprian Mureşan, Serban Savu. In addition to these, Mircea Cantor, another world-famous Romanian con- temporary artist, now living in Paris, but who continues to collaborate with the Cluj art world, was himself a graduate of the Cluj Art School.

According to BRANIŞTE (2019), the Paintbrush Factory projects the city of Cluj into the post-industrial age, yet on a somewhat different path: the creative/artistic path. In other words, the Paintbrush Factory, which was a project managed by artists and creative industries entrepreneurs, a project that changed a former Socialist factory into a post-Socialist and post-industrial arts enterprise, putting the spotlight on Cluj as a new world-class site of artistic production and community-focused creative industries, marked a crossing into the "post-industrial age" through the shift from "industrial production" to "symbolic production" (BRANIŞTE 2019: 76). Thus, "cultural provincialism" (BRANIŞTE 2019: 76) alchemized into global cultural/artistic fame through a symbolic maneuver operated by the efforts of an entire "creative class" (RAȚIU 2013: 126ff.) of artists from Cluj, Bucharest, and elsewhere, for that matter. The local was miraculously alchemized into the global. This is a perfect example of a crossing from an industrial to a post-industrial age by the hand of artistic creativity:

> Cluj-Napoca joins the pattern of the post-industrial town that is eager to establish a new narrative to rid itself from a haunting past failure of economical anonymity and cultural provincialism. (BRANIŞTE 2019: 76)

Smart City Cluj: analysis

Before going into the analysis, I would like to emphasize some of the economic and cultural history of this city. Cluj has always been a part of Transylvania, the centuries-old historical province populated by various ethnic groups, such as Germans, Romanians, Hungarians, Jews, Roma, and others. This multi-ethnic and multi-cultural atmosphere has left its mark on the culture and history of its cities and territories. Although a lot of this multi-ethnicity has been lost, the province still remains multi-ethnic and multi-cultural. Nowadays, there are two major ethnic groups living in Transylvania: Romanians and Hungarians. Cluj/ Kolószvár/ Klausenburg are the three names (Romanian, Hungarian, German) of this city. Cluj has always been, since the Middle Ages, a flourishing city of trade and crafts. It was also inhabited for centuries by the Hungarian nobility. There is a long tradition first of craftsmanship, then of various industries, with the arrival of the Modern Age. The post-war arrival of Communism and then the Ceauşescu era turned Cluj into an industrialized city. The regime built large residential areas around the old city of Cluj to host the new workforce needed for industrial work. After the 1989 collapse of the regime, the old Communist economy collapsed as well, and the industrial workforce became economically disenfranchised. In the 1990's, working-class anger towards the economic debacle was channeled into a rhetoric of "neo-nationalism" by a populist mayor (PETRO-VICI 2011). On the other hand, "everyday practice" showed that "multi-cultural life simply went on [...] as if little had happened" (PETROVICI 2011: 59). This period, from 1992 to 2004, was marked by a sort of "protectionism" towards the local economy (PETROVICI/SIMIONCA 2011: 140). Cluj remained a provincial, albeit still historically important and culturally effervescent city. After 2004, with the election of a new mayor, Cluj emerged as a "regional center for the transnationalization of the Romanian economy" (PETROVICI 2011: 72).

Now, looking over the scheme sketched by Bell (1999: lxxxv) in his 1973 *opus*, we may consider the basic elements by which he defined the

> "post-industrial": the "mode of production"—of the "post-industrial"—is "processing, information;" the "economic sector" is "services;" the "transforming resource" is basically "information;" the "strategic resource" is "human capital"(in comparison to the "financial capital" of the "industrial age"); its "technology" is "intellectual;" its "skilled base" is the "professional," in comparison to the "engineer" or "semi-skilled worker" from the "industrial age;" its "mode of work" is "networking;" its "time perspective" is the "future;" its "design" is the "game between persons" and not "game against nature," as in the earlier ages; finally, its "axial principle" is not "productivity," but the "codification of theoretical knowledge". (Bell 1999: lxxxv)

Examining the economic sectors of the post-industrial economy reveals at least some of the aforementioned elements identified in the description of the new investments in Cluj reflected by Bell's distribution of services:

(BELL 1999: lxxxv)	(BELL 1999: lxxxv)	(BELL 1999: lxxxv)
Tertiary (economic sector) Transportation Utilities	*Quaternary* (economic sector) Trade Finance Insurance Real estate	*Quinary* (economic sector) Health, education Research, government Recreation, entertainment
Cluj major investments	Cluj major investments	Cluj major investments
Upgrading transport infrastructure "Smart" vehicles	Retail Insurance business Real estate business Banking industry	Universities Creative industries Industrial parks Technological parks Entertainment & sports industry Tourism industry

Table 1: Comparison between the post-industrial economic development sketched by Bell (1999: lxxxv) and major post-industrial investments in Cluj and in Cluj metropolitan area from 2004 onwards.

The answer to the question whether Cluj can really be counted amongst post-industrial cities is that there are many post-industrial investments recently made by the private sector or by the government. However, Cluj is, at this point, neither a fully-fledged post-industrial city as it has a lot of catching up to do with respect to urban planning, both in the city and in its surrounding areas. Nor is it a technopole, an actual Silicon Valley, futuristic global hub of creativity, cutting-edge engineering, and innovation, as these purebred "technopoles" are rather rare (CASTELLS/HALL 1994: 10ff.). At the same time Castells and Hall argue that for a city or a location to become a technopole, it has to produce self-standing innovation, and also, that innovation must be absorbed into the societal and infrastructural schemes of the city. This is why so few locations or areas can truly be labeled technopoles.

Nevertheless, portraying Cluj as a Silicon Valley means good "image

> making," as this "has become a central basis for successful competition in our latter-day economy and culture" (CASTELLS/HALL 1994: 8). The post-industrial economy also favours the local above the national—at the same time turning towards the global, precisely because of its "transforming resource," information, and of its tendency to expand: "regions and cities are more flexible in adapting to the changing conditions of markets, technology and culture" (CASTELLS/HALL 1994: 7).

The post-industrial local trend, however, will improve in the future, as new developments will follow. One can observe a tendency of the new Cluj industries to value human capital at least equally to the financial one. Also, one may remark that the focus is on favoring intellectual technology over machine technology in terms of production, innovation over industrial era production. The most desired and advertised jobs on the market are not engineering or semi-skilled jobs. The most favored is the IT professional. The IT profession becomes a source of productivity. His division of labor is the network. He works in data, information, knowledge, which are also the transforming resource—the basic source of productivity. The IT class seems to be also very close to, if not the epitome of the "creative class" (FLORIDA 2012: 38–83). He is the "creative" individual *par excellence*. This has, apparently, already been made clear by Richard Florida, who talks about "creative capital" (FLORIDA 2012: 120) including engineering and data management, and not in a metaphorical sense: "creativity—the ability to create meaningful new forms [...]—is now the decisive source of competitive advantage" (Florida, quoted in RAȚIU 2013: 126). The "new growth theory" is also very close to the idea that, as knowledge is the "transforming source," it is also "sustainable," as it is virtually infinite in terms of productivity (RAȚIU 2013: 126).

Of course, there are downsides to this "creativity" spin, and these downsides include the well-documented emergence of new social and labor divisions through the rise of this new, elitist, so-called creative, superclass. This almost makes the creative class narrative a mark of the ideological or, at best, of the imaginary. In addition to that, there are intrinsic, conceptual difficulties with the operationalizing of the idea of creative class. This is why phrases such as *creative city* are very difficult to grasp as well. Thus, the creative industries are well represented in the new economic and cultural life of the city as part of the cluster of elements involved in the current development of Cluj as a would-be, post-industrial hub.

Finally, with respect to the reasons behind the favoring of Cluj over other cities in this high-tech, IT, and engineering investment competition, I would propose a few, and list them into two major sets of advantages: obvious and discrete. Amongst the obvious advantages, are: the location (situated near the West of Romania, rather close to the border with Hungary), the road and aerial connections (an expanding city international airport, connection to a highway that leads directly to the border), the size (a medium-size city), the educated, highly-skilled workforce; the city's developed and developing infrastructure. Amongst the discrete advantages, which tilt the balance a lot in favor of the city, in my view, one counts: the city's major historical significance to both communities, Romanian and Hungarian, which creates a powerful sense of local identity in these communities; the city's economic tradition of trade, manufacturing and industries, which also feeds into the local business ethos, creating a sense of local economic identity; the city's embedded multiculturalism and multilingualism, which is more discrete and more pervasive than usually expected—the cultural contact between two communities always creates an advantage; and, finally, as observed by Petrovici and Simionca (2011), the discrete, informal business ties amongst powerful actors on the local business scene, a thing which forges a very powerful competitive advantage.

References

BELL, Daniel (1999 [1973]): *The Coming of Post-Industrial Society. A Venture in Social Forecasting*. With a New Foreword by the Author. NY: Basic Books.

BENEDEK, J./CRISTEA, M. (2014): Growth Pole Development and 'Metropolization' in Post-Socialist Romania. – In: *Studia UBB Geographia* (LIX.2), 125–138.

BYRD, Antawan I. et al. (2013): *Art Cities of the Future: 21st-Century Avant-Gardes*: Phaidon Press.

BRANIȘTE, Miki (2019): Transforming Narratives: Reaction, Context and the Emerging (Im)-Possibilities of Social Discourse on Art in Cluj-Napoca. – In: *Studia UBB Sociologia* (64.2), 63–84 <doi: 10.2478/subbs-2019-0010>.

CASTELLS, M./HALL, P. (1994): *Technopoles of the World: The Making of 21st Century Industrial Complexes*, London: Routledge.

CĂTĂLIN, Raluca (2019): Proiecte Smart City noi anunțate în Caravana Smart City [New Smart City Projects Announced at the 'Smart City Caravan']. – In: *Smart City Magazine* <https://smartcitymagazine.ro/2019/07/03/proiecte-smart-city/> [27.4.2020].

CCC (2020): *Cluj Cultural Centre* [Centrul Cultural Clujean] <https://cccluj.ro/about-us/> [27.4.2020].

CEE (2019): *CEE Investment Report 2019 – Thriving Metropolitan Cities* <www.skanska.pl/CEEinvestmentreport2019> [27.4.2020].

CIC (2020): *Cluj Innovation City* <https://www.clujit.ro/cluj-innovaton-city/> [27.4.2020].

Cluster (2020): *Cluj IT Cluster* <https://ec.europa.eu/growth/tools-databases/regional-innovation-monitor/organisation/cluj-it-cluster> [27.4.2020].

COLLIERS (2019): *Colliers International Romania Research & Forecast Report 2019* <https://www2.colliers.com/en-RO/Research/Colliers-Research-and-Forecast-Report-2019> [27.4.2020].

CREAT (2020): *Transylvania Creative Industries Cluster* <http://creativetransilvania.ro/en/about-us/> [27.4.2020].

CREICa (2020): *Centrul Regional de Excelență pentru Industrii Creative* [The Regional Center of Excellence for Creative Industries] <https://storage.primariaclujnapoca.ro/userfiles/files/creic.pdf> [27.4.2020].

CREICb (2020): *Centrul Regional de Excelență pentru Industrii Creative* [The Regional Center of Excellence for Creative Industries] <https://clujbusiness.ro/market-overview/business-support/creic-the-regional-center-of-excellence-for-creative-industries/> [27.4.2020].

DCMP (2015): *Creative Industries Economic Estimates January 2015* (UK Department for Culture, Media & Sport), 1–46 <https://assets.publishing.service.gov.uk/government/uploads/system/uploads/attachment_data/file/394668/Creative_Industries_Eco nomic_Estimates_-_January_2015.pdf> [27.4.2020].

DRAGAN, Aurel (2018): Calin Vaduva, Fortech: The outsourcing business will dominate the IT industry for the next decade. – In: *Business Review* 30(10) <https://business-review. eu/br-exclusive/br-exclusive-calin-vaduva-fortech-the-outsourcing-business-will- dominate-the-it-industry-for-the-next-decade-189039> [27.4.2020].

FLORIDA, Richard (2012), *The Rise of the Creative Class, Revisited*. New York: Basic Books.

Forbes (2019): Cluj-Napoca, în dezvoltare permanentă [Cluj-Napoca, in perpetual de- velopment]. – In: *Forbes Romania* (04.06.2019) <www.forbes.ro/articles/forbes-best-cities-2019-locul-3-cluj-napoca-dezvoltare-permanenta-140455> [27.4.2020].

Guardian (2020): 10 of the best things to do in Cluj-Napoca, Romania: a local's guide. – In: *The Guardian* (27 Jan.) <www.theguardian.com/travel/2020/jan/27/cluj-napoca-romania-city-break-locals-guide> [27.4.2020].

Office (2020): *Why is Cluj-Napoca the leader in office building development outside Bucharest* <www.officerentinfo.ro/article/officemarket-news/why-is-cluj-napoca-the-leader-in-office-building-development-outside-bucharest> [27.4.2020].

PETROVICI, Norbert (2011): Articulating the Right to the City: Working Class Neo-Nationalism in Postsocialist Cluj, Romania. – In: *Headlines of Nationalism, Subtexts of Class*. Edited by D. Kalb and G Halmai. New York, Oxford: Berghahn Books, 57-77.

PETROVICI, Norbert (2014), *Personal Development and the Flexible Contracts: Depoliticized Class Struggles between Highly Skilled Workers and Manual Workers in Cluj (Working paper)*, 1-20, <http://issuu-download.tiny-tools.com/doc/erste-foundation/petrovici/> [27.4.2020].

PETROVICI, Norbert/SIMIONCA, Anca (2011): Productive Informality and Economic Ties in Emerging Economies: The Case of Cluj Business Networks. – In: Bhambry T./Griffin C. (eds.), *Transformation andTransition in Central and Eastern Europe & Russia*. London: University College London, 134–144.

PURICE, Magda (2019): Smart Transformation Forum to take place on September,26 at Bucharest. – In: *Oursourcing Today* (Sept. 30.) <https://outsourcing-today.ro/?p=343> [27.4.2020].

RAȚIU, Dan-Eugen (2013): Creative cities and/or sustainable cities: Discourses and practices. – In: *City, Culture and Society* 4(3), 125–135 <http://dx.doi.org/10.1016/j.ccs.2013.04.002>. [27.4.2020].

SMART (2017a): *'Silicon Valley'-ul din Transilvania transformă orașul Cluj în primul smart-city din România* [The Transylvanian 'Silicon Valley' Transforms the City of Cluj into the First Smart City of Romania] <https://romaniansmartcity.ro/cluj-smart- city-2/> [27.4.2020].

SMART (2017b): *Cluj-Napoca, un viitor smart city?* [Cluj-Napoca, a Future Smart City?] <https://romaniansmartcity.ro/cluj-napoca-smart-city/> [27.4.2020].

SOFTECH (2017): *Cluj-Napoca IT sector is growing fast* <https://softech.ro/cluj-napoca-it-sector-is-growing-fast/> [27.4.2020].

TCIC (2020): *Transylvania Creative Industries Cluster* <www.clustercollaboration.eu/cluster-organisations/transilvania-creative-industries-cluster> [27.4.2020].

TETAROM (2020): *TETAROM Industrial Park I, II, III* <https://ec.europa.eu/growth/tools-databases/regional-innovation-monitor/organisation/tetarom-industrial-park-i-ii-iii> [27.4.2020].

TRACTOR (2020), *Tractor Set GO* <https://tractorsetgo.com/supplier/> [27.4.2020].

VEGACOMP (2018): *Radiografia Smart City Romania. Raport Pilot* [Smart City Romania Review]. By Vega Comp Consulting <https://vegacomp.ro/wpr/wp-content/uploads/2018/03/radiografia-smart-city_2018.03.14.pdf> [27.4.2020].

REVIEWS

Axel Petri-Preis und Johannes Voit: *Handbuch Musikvermittlung – Studium, Lehre, Berufspraxis*. Bielefeld (transcript) 2024, 522 Seiten.

Was ist Musikvermittlung? Wer sind die Musikvermittlerinnen und Musikvermittler und wie arbeiten sie heute? Und welche Diskurse und Spannungsfelder existieren rund um dieses Praxisfeld?

Mit dem *Handbuch Musikvermittlung* legen die beiden Musikpädagogen und Musikvermittler Axel Petri-Preis und Johannes Voit einen umfangreichen Sammelband vor, der den Anspruch erhebt, die „zentrale Ressource für die universitäre Lehre" (S. 13) in dem seit Jahren stetig wachsenden Praxisfeld der Musikvermittlung zu sein. Auch verstehen die Herausgeber die Sammlung von insgesamt 69 Einzelbeiträgen als Dokumentation des Status quo der Musikvermittlung im deutschsprachigen Raum, denn hier legt die Anthologie ihren Schwerpunkt. Die beiden Herausgeber sind seit vielen Jahren als Musikwissenschaftler als auch als Praktiker im Feld der Musikpädagogik und Musikvermittlung tätig. Petri-Preis (Universität für Musik und darstellende Künste Wien) und Voit (Universität Bielefeld) verfolgen dabei in Zusammenarbeit mit den insgesamt 57 Autorinnen und Autoren aus Wissenschaft und Praxis einen praxistheoretischen Ansatz, der musikpädagogische Wissenschaft und musikvermittelnde Berufspraxis als Einheit denkt. Die einzelnen Beiträge der Anthologie umfassen meist nicht mehr als sechs Seiten und wurden einer Begutachtung unterzogen.

Der Logik eines Grundlagenwerks entsprechend, werden im ersten Kapitel zunächst Definitionen gegeben, dann wird das Feld abgesteckt und die historische Entwicklung aufgezeigt (I. *Grundlagen*). Anschließend stehen die Akteure der Musikvermittlung im Zentrum, unterteilt in Personen, Institutionen und Dialoggruppen (II. *Akteur_innen*). Im dritten Kapitel werden systematisch Spannungsfelder aufgemacht und in den einzelnen Beiträgen näher verhandelt (III. *Spannungsfelder und Diskurse*). Und schließlich werden *Praxen der Vermittlung* (IV.), einerseits hinsichtlich verwandter Praxisfelder und andererseits in einer Auswahl konkreter Musikvermittlungsformate vorgestellt.

Im ersten Kapitel wird Musikvermittlung als Praxis beschrieben, die sich vor allem in diesem und letztem Jahrhundert im deutschsprachigen Raum zwischen Musikpädagogik und Konzertwesen herausgebildet hat, um kulturinstitutionellen, sozialpolitischen und kulturpolitischen Problemstellungen vorranging im Bereich der klassischen Musik zu begegnen. Dabei wird Musikvermittlung vor allem terminologisch, historisch und als berufliche Tätigkeit beleuchtet und verortet. Im Zuge dessen wird deutlich, dass sich im Begriff der Musikvermittlung eine Vielzahl von pädagogischen und künstlerischen Handlungsweisen kreuzen, die sich kaum in einer einzigen Definition festhalten lassen. Mit einer praxistheoretischen Herleitung führt Sarah Chaker die Praxis der Musikvermittlung schließlich als Forschungsgegenstand wissenschaftlicher Beobachtungen und Analysen ein, womit eine theoretische Ausgangslage für die folgenden Abhandlungen gelegt wird, die sich wie ein roter Faden durch den gesamten Band durchzieht. Ein Überblick über bisherige Forschung und das wachsende Arbeitsgebiet rundet dies ab (Hendrikje Mautner-Obst), bevor kurze historische Einordnungen über Musikvermittlung in den verschiedenen deutschsprachigen Ländern und Regionen das Einleitungskapitel beschließen.

Das zweite Kapitel arbeitet die unterschiedlichen Akteursgruppen im Feld der Musikvermittlung heraus. Dabei werden zunächst empirische Untersuchungen zur Soziodemografie und Bildungsstruktur von in der Musikvermittlung tätigen Personen, Ausbildungsmöglichkeiten und schließlich machtkritische Perspektiven auf das Berufsfeld vorgestellt (Nina Stoffers). Anschließend werden 14 verschiedene Kategorien von institutionellen Akteuren kurz hinsichtlich ihrer Rollen und Strukturen skizziert (z.B. gegliedert nach Tätigkeitsfeldern im Umfeld von Orchestern, Festivals, Stiftungen usw.). Unter der Überschrift *Dialoggruppen* setzen die Beiträge dann verschiedene Kommunikationsverhältnisse im Kontext von Musikvermittlungsaktivitäten in Beziehung, wobei ein Schwerpunkt auf die Grundproblematik der kulturellen Teilhabe gelegt wird. In diesem Sinne zeigen die Beitragenden verschiedene Differenzierungsmerkmale auf, problematisieren Gruppenbegriffe (Lisa Gaupp) und diskutieren Machthierarchien und migrationspädagogische Perspektiven (Paul Mecheril). Mit den Kapiteln zu *Audience Engagement* und *Community Outreach* werden außerdem Vermittlungsstrategien thematisiert, die auf die Überwindung von Barrieren zwischen Publikums- und Akteursgruppen reagieren.

Das dritte Kapitel bildet den diskursiven Hauptteil des Sammelbands. Hier wird die künstlerische und musikpädagogische Praxis der Musikvermittlung in unterschiedlichen Spannungsfeldern zum Thema gemacht. Das „Dazwischen" der Vermittlungspraxis steht hier im Mittelpunkt. Gegensatzpaare wie *Rezeption und Partizipation, Tradition und Innovation* oder *urbaner und ländlicher Raum* zeigen einerseits die Herausforderungen und andererseits die Potentiale und gelebten Praxen einer reflektierten Arbeitsweise im Feld auf. Herausforderungen liegen beispielsweise im Gegensatz zwischen einer objekt- gegenüber einer subjektorientierten Vermittlungspraxis (Joshua Schippling & Johannes Voit) oder im Verstehen gegenüber dem Erleben von Musik (Christoph Stange). Potentiale liegen in transformativen (Irena Müller-Brozović) und partizipativen Vermittlungsansätzen (Cornelia Wild). Meist werden dafür die Gegensatzpaare durch einen theoretischen Ansatz eingeführt und anschließend in praktischen Beispielen und Beobachtungen aus dem Feld vertieft.

Im vierten und letzten Kapitel werden anfangs verwandte Praxisfelder behandelt, die in einer gewissen Nähe zur Musikvermittlung stehen. Hier sind die Autoren der Überzeugung, dass „in deren fruchtbarem Zwischen Neues entstehen kann" (S. 313). Community Music, Musikgeragogik oder Soziokultur sind dabei nur einige Beispielfelder, deren Überschneidungen mit Musikvermittlung augenscheinlich sind. Diese werden in den Beiträgen kurz und überblicksartig skizziert. In der Folge präsentieren die Textbeiträge dann ausgewählte Praxen im Sinne konkreter musikvermittelnder Tätigkeiten und Projekte. Dabei wird erneut ein historischer und terminologischer Überblick über die jeweiligen Praxen gegeben (z.B. inszenierte Konzerte, Kompositionsprojekte, Partizipative Musiktheaterprojekte). Von hier aus werden diverse idealtypische Beispiele aus der Praxis beschrieben.

Den Herausgebern Axel Petri-Preis und Johannes Voit und den zahlreichen Beitragenden ist es gelungen mit dem *Handbuch Musikvermittlung* ein Schlüsselstück der Lehr- und Praxisliteratur der Musikvermittlung vorzulegen. Die vielfältigen Perspektiven auf die Geschichte, die Handlungsweisen und Herausforderungen des „Dazwischens", die die Musikvermittlung ausmachen, werden durch den praxistheoretischen und gleichzeitig immer wieder machtkritischen Ansatz des Buches gekonnt verknüpft. Dies führt zwar einerseits zwangsläufig zu Redundanzen, diese helfen jedoch andererseits auch die Grundprinzipien und Denkweisen der Praxis der Musikvermittlung zu verinnerlichen. Besonders für Studierende, an die die Publikation vor allem auch gerichtet ist, bietet sie deshalb eine geeignete Grundlage für das Studium der Musikvermittlung oder Musikpädagogik.

Doch nicht nur im Lehrkontext, sondern letztlich für alle, die beruflich oder privat mit Musikvermittlung zu tun haben, bildet dieses neue Standardwerk in seiner Fülle umfassende und in den einzelnen Beiträgen kurzweilige Einblicke ins Feld. Der Band profitiert davon, dass die Autorinnen und Autoren qua ihrer Professionen aus der Innenperspektive der Vermittlungspraxis schreiben, was eine sehr angewandte und tageaktuelle Abhandlung ermöglicht. Dadurch fehlt, möchte man etwas kritisieren, allerdings eine Außenperspektive, die Musikvermittlung und ihre aktuellen Praxen aus der Beobachtung heraus hinterfragt und damit ganz neue Denkanstöße setzten könnte. Beiträge aus verwandten Disziplinen wie der Musikpsychologie oder der empirischen Ästhetik einerseits und der Kultursoziologie andererseits, könnten hier spiegeln und reflektieren, ebenso wie internationale Perspektiven. Hinsichtlich seiner eigenen Zielstellung übertrifft der Sammelband die Erwartungen und wird ohne Zweifel als wissenschaftlich angereicherter Praxisband in der universitären Lehre nutzbringend zum Einsatz kommen. Für das Kulturmanagement kann der Sammelband sowohl als Überblick über das Feld der Musikvermittlung dienen, als auch eine Inspiration für weiterführende Forschung sein. Vor allem für machtkritische Themen im Musikbereich sowie hinsichtlich der praxistheoretischen Analyse des Kulturbetriebs liefert er zahlreiche Anregungen.

CHRISTIAN WEINING[*]

Lepa, Steffen/Müller-Lindenberg, Ruth/Egermann, Hauke (Hgg.) (2023): Classical Music and Opera during and after the COVID-19 Pandemic. Empirical Research on the Digital Transformation of Socio-cultural Institutions and Aesthetic Forms. Cham: Springer, 151 pages and 19 fig.

Dass die Covid-Pandemie gravierende Auswirkungen auf Kunst und Kultur hatte, muss wohl nicht eigens betont werden. Auch das eine Rückkehr zu Vor-Covid-Zeiten nicht unbedingt zu erwarten war oder mindestens längere Zeit in Anspruch nehmen dürfte, konnte man eigentlich voraussetzen, auch wenn zumindest einige der aktuell erfolgreichen Kulturinstitutionen an diese Zeiten anknüpfen können.

Das Ziel des Bandes besteht demgegenüber eher darin, empirische Erkenntnisse aus aktueller Forschung zu versammeln, die auf mögliche positive langfristige Konsequenzen und Lernprozesse aus den Erfahrungen mit der Pandemie weisen. Die Beiträge befassen sich mit Künstlern und Institutionen und diskutieren mögliche künftige Krisen in Gebiet der klassischen Musik und betrachten den durch die Pandemie ausgelösten Digitalisierungsschub.

[*]   Christian.Weining@zu.de

doi 10.14361/zkmm-2024-0213

Alenka Barber-Kersovan (*Quo Vadis Classical Music? Remarks on the Post-pandemic Condition*, 1–15) fragt zunächst nach der Zukunft der klassischen Musik und stellt unterschiedliche digitale Formate vor: Streaming-Plattformen, bspw. die Digital Concert Hall der Berliner Philharmoniker, ohne allerdings darauf hinzuweisen, dass ungeachtet aller Zuwächse (ein Plus von 2.5 Millionen gestreamter Stunden) das Angebot sich bis heute nicht selbst trägt. Als weitere Beispiele führt die Verfasserin virtuelle Orchester und Chöre an, ferner Kinoproduktionen sowie neue Live-Angebote wie Drive-in-Opern, um dann auf einige weitere Perspektiven einzugehen.

Die Pandemie als ein Experiment im sozialen Feld untersuchen Steffen Lepa und Ruth Müller-Lindenberg (*The Pandemic as a Peephole into the Ongoing Digital Transformation of Opera*, 29–50). Ausgehend von der These einer Stimulierung zur Digitalisierung geht es mit Hilfe von Experteninterviews darum, Herausforderungen und Vorbehalte, aber auch Chancen und Vorteile einer digitalen Transformation im Hinblick auf die Oper als soziale Institution, als Format bzw. als ästhetische Form zu untersuchen. In den Blick genommen werden dabei die drei Berliner Opernhäuser. Ausgehend von einer Reflexion des Forschungsstandes geht es in der Untersuchung um Aspekte der Produktion und Dramaturgie von Inszenierungen, um die öffentliche Kommunikation und um Aspekte der Medialisierung, charakterisiert durch Re-Medialisierung und transmediales Storytelling, eingebettet in Aspekte von Präsenz und Liveness sowie der partizipatorischen Logik von sozialen Medien (S. 33f.).Hierzu wurden Interviews mit Vertretern der künstlerischen Leitung, der Dramaturgie sowie den Abteilungen für Marketing und Kommunikation geführt. Einige der Ergebnisse weisen auf gewisse Vorbehalte gegen Digitalisierung aus künstlerischer Perspektive und richten sich insbesondere auf die mangelnde Rückkopplung zum bzw. Interaktion mit dem Publikum, die nur das Live-Erlebnis bieten könne. Ferner werden die mangelnde Atmosphäre bzw. Aura genannt sowie eine fehlende Emotionalisierung bei digitalen Angeboten. Bei den Chancen der Digitalisierung werden Möglichkeiten eines breiteren Repertoires genannt, ferner die Ansprache unterschiedlicher, auch neuer sozialer Gruppen sowie Altersklassen. Und letztlich scheint die Digitalisierung bei der Demokratisierung einer als elitär betrachteten Institution wie der Oper helfen zu können. Letztlich werden also positive Effekte vor allem in der Angebotspolitik und im Audience Development erkannt. Weitere Aspekte nennen die Vertreter aus dem Marketing und der Kommunikation. Hier wird, verwiesen wird auf das sogenannte Ungeduldsargument, eine mangelnde Kompetenz seitens des Publikums erkannt, eine Oper komplett gestreamt anzuschauen. Der Opernbesuch sei eine komplexe sozialer Handlung, die im Stream entfalle. Ferner wird auf die ökonomischen Herausforderungen bzw. Defizite im technologischen Know how auf Mitarbeiterseite verwiesen bzw. auf die fehlende Expertise und damit die Notwendigkeit, zusätzlich Mitarbeiter zu engagieren. Letztlich verweist man auf die Grenzen der vorhandenen Budgets (S. 40f.) und damit auch auf Einschränkungen bei der technischen Qualität (S. 45). Als weitere strategische Vorbehalte gegen Digitalisierung werden mögliche Kannibalisierungseffekte mit Präsenzangeboten, eine unzureichende Monetarisierung, das Fehlen eines unmittelbaren Feedbacks und schließlich die Notwendigkeit einer vollkommen neuen Organisationsform genannt, die mit der bisherigen analogen Institution kaum zu vereinbaren sei (S. 41f.). Andererseits erkennen die Interviewpartner durchaus Chancen: so erhöhe sich die Sichtbarkeit des Hauses durch Angebot eines sehr viel größeren Repertoires (Showcase-Effekt). Ferner bot die Digitalisierung die Möglichkeit, während des Lockdowns mit dem Publikum in Kontakt zu bleiben. Künftig erkennt man Potentiale im Audience Development z. B. bei Benachteiligten oder Behinderten. Und man sieht neue Möglichkeiten für die Ansprache in Schulen (S. 42f.). Nachfragen nach einer Medialisierung jenseits von Streaming ergaben Einschätzungen bzgl. Chancen durch eine weitgehende Digitalisierung der Information und des Ticketing, ferner im Hinblick auf die Durchsetzung neuer audiovisueller Kurzformate, die bereits in der Pandemie entwickelt wurden sowie eine digitale Verwertung der von der Oper angebotenen kulturellen Werte. Für die erfolgreiche Umsetzung einer Digitalstrategie nennen die Experten verbesserte liveness-Erfahrungen, ausreichende Inhalte und deren Einbettung in professionelle Streaming-Plattformen (S. 44).

Die Ergebnisse dieses Beitrags werden von einem weiterer Text des Bandes bestätigt, in dem es im Rahmen einer online-Erhebung um die Erfassung von Konzertteilnahme und Mediengewohnheiten ging (Lepa, Steffen/Weinzierl, Stefan: *Did Lockdowns Stimulate Digital Cultural Participation? Mapping the Post-pandemic Berlin Classical Concert Audience and Its Adoption of Audiovisual Concert Streams*, 113–144). U. a. kann auch hier die Kannibalisierungsthese widerlegt werden, nach der Konzert-Streaming zu einem Rückgang bei Live-Konzerten führe.

Die Zuschauerperspektive nimmt der Beitrag von Ann-Kristin Zoike in den Blick (Streaming Opera: *Compromise Solution or Future-Oriented Reception Form?* 75–93). Hierzu wurden Interviews mit sieben Rezipienten von *OperaVision* aus Deutschland, Großbritannien, Irland und den USA geführt, wobei sich zeigt, dass die digitale Rezeption von Oper den Besuch von Präsenzveranstaltungen ergänzt und diese nicht ersetzt (was in dem vorigen Beitrag seites einiger Probanden ja befürchtet worden war). Vorteile des Streamings von Opern, so die Respondenten, liegen in der zeitlichen Flexibilität und dem breiteren Angebot, aber auch in offeneren Rezeptionspraktiken, man spricht von einem veränderten Rezeptionsstil. Hierzu gehören interaktive Formen (z. B. Kommentierung des Gesehenen), aber eben auch eine geringere emotionale Involvierung. Im Hinblick auf die Streaming-Situation und den Rezeptionsmodus werden genannt: häufig abends, in komfortabler Atmosphäre und ohne Begleitung, mal mit, mal ohne Nebentätigkeiten, mal mit, mal ohne Unterbrechungen. Ein wichtiges Argument für Streaming bilden offenbar die geringeren Kosten neben der individuellen Nutzung (Lautstärke, Playback, Kommentierung mit anderen Usern). Das Streaming von Opern scheint somit etwas für Opern-Enthusiasten zu sein, eine Ergänzung zur Live-Performance.

Das Digital Concert Experience einer Forschergruppe um Melanie Wald-Fuhrmann und Martin Tröndle geht von der Krise des Konzerts für klassische Musik aus, wobei bisher nicht ganz klar sei, ob es sich dabei um eine generelle Krise klassischer Musik oder um eine ihrer (überkommenen?) Präsentationsformen und Angebote handelt (*Digital Concert Experience: an Online Research Project on Live Streaming During the Pandemic*, 95–112). Geht es also um pädagogische Aktivitäten oder um eine grundsätzliche Reform des Formates Konzert? Das Projekt untersucht daher das Konzert-Setting mit den individuellen Komponenten, welche die musikalische Erfahrung beeinflussen (S. 96). Das Konzert wird dabei verstanden als ein streng choreographiertes Ereignis mit ritualisierten Prozeduren und sozialen, internalisierten Konventionen, kombiniert mit einem festen Repertoire und einem stabilen Format. Bisherige Innovationsversuche seien eher punktuell erfolgt, es fehlt insgesamt eine valide wissenschaftliche Erforschung. Bezogen auf Möglichkeiten des Streaming von klassischer Musik, das seit der Pandemie eine Neubewertung erfuhr, werden in dem Projekt drei unterschiedliche Zuhörer-Segmente identifiziert, jeweils abhängig von den Präferenzen und Sozialisationen: Enthusiasten, was digitale Formate betrifft; Puristen, die traditionelle Angebote bevorzugen; Unentschiedene bzw. geringer engagierte Hörer. Damit stellt sich die Frage, wodurch das traditionelle Live-Konzert so besonders wird bzw. welches die damit verbundenen spezifischen und einzigartigen

Erfahrungen sind. Ausgehend von diesen Fragen konnte die Forschergruppe einige zentrale Dimensionen ableiten:

> Seven main dimensions of concert experience were derived from the domain-speci-
> fic, post-concert measures via exploratory factor analyses: (1) immersion and being
> moved; (2) appreciation; (3) intellectual stimulation; (4) analytical listening; (5)
> social experience, (6) concentration, and (7) understanding. (S. 104)

Im Ergebnis eröffnen sich damit Möglichkeiten, eine hohe Zustimmung
für digitale Angebote zu erzielen bei allerdings geringerer emotionaler
bzw. immersiver Einbindung. Wichtige wäre daher, die soziale Interaktion
während des Streams, ein Gefühl sozialer Einbindung zu verstärken, was
mit den Befunden der anderen Beiträge übereinstimmt. Zusatzinforma-
tionen zur Musik haben zudem einen stärkeren Effekt auf das Verständnis des Gehörten.

Weitere Beiträge befassen sich mit Musikfestivals (Martina Kal-
ser-Gruber: *The Role of Artistic Directors of Classical Music Festivals in
COVID-19 Crisis communication*, 51–73) oder werfen Aspekte auf Fragen der Weiterbildung (Hermiston, Nancy et al.: *Opera – Training-Re-
search During Lockdown*, 29–50). Abgeschlossen wird der Band mit einem ‚post-pandemischen' Interview (*Combining Two Differenz Worlds*,
145–151) mit den beiden Intendanten Merle Fahrholz (Aalto-Musikthe-
ater Essen) und Ulrich Lenz (Oper Graz), die zu Beginn der Pandemie
an der Oper Dortmund bzw. an der Komischen Oper Berlin tätig waren.

Den Beiträge des Bandes gelingt damit eine überzeugende erste Bestandsaufnahme zur Situation der klassischen Musik nach der Pandemie
sowie eine Skizzierung weiterer Perspektiven insbesondere im Hinblick
auf Aspekte der Digitalisierung.

STEFFEN HÖHNE‍˙

**Grant H. KESTER, *Beyond the sovereign self: Artistic auto-
nomy from the avant-garde to socially engaged art*, Durham
and London, Duke University Press 2024. 283 pp.**

Grant Kester, professor of art history at the University of California San
Diego, has made a noteworthy contribution to the discussion about the
relation between art and society with an impressive set of two interrelat-
ed monographs published in as many years. The second of these, *Beyond*

˙   steffen.hoehne@hfm-weimar.de

Journal of Cultural Management and Policy, 2024/2, pp. 256–260
doi 10.14361/zkmm-2024-0214

the Sovereign Self, is the subject of this review but the first instalment, *The Sovereign Self: Aesthetic Autonomy from the Enlightenment to the Avant-garde* (2023), which the author sees as an independent work, will not be left entirely unattended to. As clearly indicated by the titles (and subtitles) of the books, their pivotal point is the notion of sovereignty, primarily with regard to its application to beings possessing a self—for Kester, this means humans—but also in relation to the phenomenon referred to as art. In essence, Kester's thesis comes down to a claim about the notion of sovereignty descended from the (primarily German) Enlightenment, having impinged rather too heavily upon artistic practice, not least in the twentieth century through conceptions of art manifested in avant-garde movements. Kester's claim, in other words, is that the avant-garde in particular, and even modernist art in general, over-emphasizes the notion of the autonomous artist. Such an over-emphasis, for Kester, recycles romantic notions of genius, intuition and transcendence in a contemporary context where an individualistic paradigm of this mold cannot but fall prey to capitalist appropriation with its all-consuming commodification of (the products of) any type of freedom-seeking activity (KESTER 2023). A prime example is, of course, artistic creation. Thereby, art's socio-critical edge is blunted or even obliterated.

The introduction to *Beyond the Sovereign Self* clearly and helpfully elucidates the author's concerns as well as his manner of dealing with the issues, also providing the reader with a concise summary of the discussion found in the companion volume, *The Sovereign Self.* Thus, we learn that whereas the first book mainly deals with the historical emergence of autonomy in art—or aesthetic autonomy, which is Kester's preferred term— the second volume sets out to explore the way the notion "relates to contemporary activist art practices and to the broader processes of social transformation with which they are engaged" (1). This, for Kester, is bound to appear "counterintuitive" to the reader, "given the conventional association of aesthetic autonomy with a radical separation between art and political action" (1). As it turns out, the convention that the author has in mind primarily finds its representatives, in the two volumes, in a line of thinkers that includes Schiller, Kant, Hegel and Adorno, but also Chantal Mouffe, Claire Bishop, Alain Badiou, Slavoj Žižek, Jacques Rancière and John Roberts.

To be sure, Kester wants to extract evidence from recent examples of socially engaged artistic practices to the effect that "a paradigm shift" is underway towards a "dialogical understanding of aesthetic experience" which, we learn, essentially revolves around the issue of "how we come to resist" (3). This notion of the possibility of resistance is a major theme in Kester's line of thinking, and the problem he sees with avant-garde approaches to artistic theory and practice comes down to their being precisely, and even purposefully, dismissive of any such attempts. Accordingly, Kester wants to pinpoint a

> central tension within the history of modernism between a concept of art that must remain inviolable and pure and a concept of art that gains its power precisely through its active engagement with the impure actuality of the world as it is (6).

This latter, impure concept, Kester wants us to understand, is precisely what socially engaged art has brought home to us, thereby expressly going against what he sees as the kernel of avant-garde practices: If the avant-garde schema is predicated on the assumption that decisive political change is foreclosed in the current moment, engaged art assumes that its potential here and now is not yet exhausted.

Kester carries out his analysis in seven chapters. The first two take their cue in an interview with Jacques Rancière where he (according to Kester) subscribes to a revived notion of aesthetic autonomy which essentially involves a reference to "a degraded cultural other" (34). This latter term is then further discussed in relation to the so-called *escrache* actions in Argentina in the first years of the 21st century which consisted in peaceful activist resistance-cum-art projects directed towards the government's past and present injustices. In a word, Kester sees Rancière as turning his back to the emancipatory potential harbored by the masses. This analysis is then further developed in Chapter 3 through exploration of Adrian Piper's performance-based work aimed at "de-transcendentalisation" (11). Kester sees de-transcendentalisation as having to do with "forms of critical insight generated in the interstices between self and other" (11). Chapter 4 brings more art projects to the table, such as the Tamms Year Ten project in the US and the Lava la Bandera actions in Peru, with a focus on their tactical, critical and prefigurative aspects. Chapter 5, in turn, moves towards a more theoretical analysis inasmuch as it primarily discusses Marx's notion of social labor, seen as representing "the latent aesthetic potential at the heart of the Marxist tradition" (158). In Chapter 6, nonetheless, Kester moves towards critiquing this Marxist notion, which he sees as overly reliant on "a conventional model of autonomous subjectivity" (13) and proposes to replace it with Mikhail Bakhtin's conception of a dialogical exchange. Indeed, the reader quickly discovers that the author holds Bakhtin in such high regard that he also gets a fair share of the spotlight in Chapter 7. Kester attempts to synthesize the previous discussion and formulate his new, and dialogical, aesthetic paradigm, referring in the process to de Sousa Santos's notion of a "rear-guard theory" that "seeks to establish a dialogical, rather than regulatory, relationship with praxis" (13-14).

As can be gathered from this brief summary, Kester's ambition in *Beyond the Sovereign Self*, and by implication, in the entire two-volume work, is quite extraordinary. On the whole, he achieves what he sets out to do, even if some of the argumentation, conceptual usage and historical discussion contains minor discrepancies that have to do with conciseness, accuracy and overall clarity. To name just a few such issues, one may, first of all, wonder whether the notion of autonomy that he wants to criticize isn't rather too uniform and strong, and whether any of the thinkers that he associates with it would ever have seen it in such stark terms. To name but one example, Kester at one point advises us not to conceive of one-to-one relationships in terms of "two fixed selves, each seeking to defend its a priori autonomy," affirming instead "modes of self-transformation that are reciprocal rather than unilateral" (125). Frankly, one would be hard pressed to find any examples of thinkers who would seriously entertain such a fixed, unilateral view—barring, perhaps, the most radical and self-contradictory adherents of an individualistic-libertarian viewpoint of the mold that Marx liked to trace back to the literary character Robinson Crusoe. In the current situation, thankfully, such a non-relational ethics seems destined for the proverbial garbage heap of history. But in any case, as Kester himself is manifestly aware such a view is not altogether new, running, for example, back to *The German Ideology* (1932) where Marx observes that "the changing of oneself coincides with the changing of circumstances" (<marxists.org>). Such a remark, however, would seem to fly rather directly in the face of Kester's critical stance towards Marx in his Chapter 6. To follow up on that point, one would also be tempted to counter Kester's reading of Hegel—which relies heavily on Habermas—with a more nuanced sense of the way that Hegel would never have "abandoned" the idea of "a concrete other, in relationship to which truth could be reciprocally disclosed" (143). Rather, as Klaus Vieweg has recently shown in his massive biography of Hegel (2020), the German philosopher consistently adhered to a conception of freedom which remains, of course, in any concrete situation, essentially reciprocal, or, in other words, dialectical. In such a way, therefore, one would be more inclined to follow art philosopher John Roberts in his assessment that, regarding the question of art and society, "Hegel's position is essentially a critique of the autonomy of the aesthetic" (2015: 9). These, however, are mostly negligible nuances and academic niceties.

In sum, Kester's ambitious work serves as a timely and substantial appreciation of socially engaged art, bearing witness to an exemplary understanding of its radically democratic essence in all its complexity. Thus, his work contributes weightily to the theoretical reserve needed by those who want to engage in radical social transformation without adhering to what Kester happily terms the "incapacity of the masses thesis" (128) which entails viewing one's "collaborators as cognitively deficient" (119), be they defined as "women, colonized subjects, [...] the European working class" (16) or as something else. Instead, we should acknowledge that "new forms of knowledge emerge through the art of resistance" (170) and realize that this knowledge cannot arise anywhere else than among those who do the resisting.

References

KESTER, Grant H. (2023): *The sovereign self: Aesthetic autonomy from the enlightenment to the avant-garde*. Durham and London: Duke University Press.

MARX, Karl (1932): *The German Ideology*. https://www.marxists.org/archive/marx/works/ 1845/german-ideology

ROBERTS, John (2015): *Revolutionary time and the avant-garde*. London: Verso.

VIEWEG, Klaus (2020): *Hegel: Der Philosoph der Freiheit*. München: C.H. Beck.

BJÖRN BORSTEINSSON˙

Patrick Lo. et al.: Inside Hong Kong's Arts and Cultural Scene: Conversations with Hong Kong's Leading Arts and Cultural Administrators, Educators, Producers, and Presenters. New York (Nova Science Publishers) 2023, 379 pp.

Authored by five specialists with balanced expertise in arts and culture, *Inside Hong Kong's Arts and Cultural Scene* is an insightful guide to the city's thriving sector. In its twenty-eight chapters, Lo and his co-authors Okpoti, Hsu, Anghelescu, and Chiu reflect about the city's unique blend of global cultures seen through an arts management lens.

˙   bjorntho@hi.is

Journal of Cultural Management and Policy, 2024/2, pp. 260–264
doi 10.14361/zkmm-2024-0215

In the conversations with leading industry professionals, Lo et al. trace the socio-economic impacts of arts festivals and fairs in Hong Kong, examine the city's position as the Asian centre for arts and culture, and investigate the direction the industry is heading. The inside knowledge, abundant experiences, and varied perspectives documented cover key areas in the fields of arts management and cultural policy research including arts infrastructure, funding, leadership, censorship, entrepreneurship, and technology.

In the Introduction, the overall analysis of arts and culture including the art market in Hong Kong as an international and geographical hub, provides a useful background. Importantly, Lo et al. introduce the West Kowloon Cultural District (WKCD). Led by the Hong Kong Special Administrative Region Government since 1998, WKCD is expected to be completed in 2026 with seventeen venues for music, performing arts, and visual art. The brief overview of the long term planning and establishment of the world-class cultural district in Hong Kong offers a glimpse into the complexities of a contemporary arts and cultural scene in progress.

Opened in July 2022, the Hong Kong Palace Museum (HKPM) is one of the key WKCD venues. In Chapter 3, Daisy Yiyou Wang (Deputy Director of HKPM) introduces the museum's mission and discusses its collaboration with local artists. In Chapters 22 and 23, the interviews with Paul Tam (Executive Director of Performing Arts Division of West Kowloon Cultural District Authority) and Scarlett Jie Chen (Former Head of Development for Performing Arts of West Kowloon Cultural District) provide a broader perspective of WKCD.

For M+ Museum, a museum of contemporary visual culture in WKCD, the way Lo et al. shed light on the new prestigious cultural organisation's presence in Hong Kong's socio-political context stands out. Instead of including a designated chapter, the authors invite some of the interviewees to discuss censorship issues at M+ Museum. In Chapter 5, for example, Frank Vigneron (Professor and Chair of Fine Arts Department of The Chinese University of Hong Kong) outlines a controversy triggered by a pro-Beijing politician. According to Vigneron, the politician interpreted contemporary Chinese artist and activist "Ai Weiwei's photo of his hand giving the finger to Chairman Mao's portrait on Tiananmen Square" (75) as an insult to China. Pointing out the politician's insufficient understanding of the series of artworks, where the artist also gives "the finger to many other symbols of power around the world" (75–6), professor Vigneron diagnoses the controversy as an overreaction that is likely to recur in the context of Hong Kong's national security law, which was introduced in 2020.

In Chapter 4, in an interview with Laurence James Wood (Associate Head of Department of Cultural & Creative Arts, The Education University of Hong Kong), Lo et al. further address the removal of "three politically engaged works by Chinese contemporary artists" (47) at M+ Museum and enquire about Wood's view on the controversies. While Wood, an academic and artist, acknowledges the likelihood of "cautious pragmatic self-censorship by artists, curators, galleries, and museums", he assuredly reminds the reader that "radical, subversive, provocative or politicised art is only one field of art practice" (47).

Compared to the views of the two scholars above, interestingly, Sandy Angus (Chairman of Angus Montgomery Arts) cautiously shares an optimistic outlook in Chapter 9. With the introduction of the law, some may be concerned that "there will now be a degree of censorship" (117). Angus, however, believes that "Hong Kong will settle back into the role it has played all along" (117). In this way, the documented conversations cover diverse perspectives on current and sensitive issues, such as the newly introduced national security law and its impact on arts and culture in Hong Kong.

Lo et al.'s conversations further capture the wide spectrum of cultural and artistic leadership, as well as leadership principles, across the sector in Hong Kong. Unlike Cho-Liang Lin (Music Director of Hong Kong International Chamber Music Festival, Chapter 14), Michelle Kim (Founder & Artistic Director of Hong Kong Generation Next Arts, Chapter 18) and Louis Nixon (Former Director of Academy of Visual Arts, Hong Kong Baptist University, Chapter 7), who are also musicians and visual artists, other leaders, including Benedikt Fohr (Chief Executive of Hong Kong Philharmonic Orchestra, Chapter 11) and Andrew Strachan (General Manager (Asia) of Art Basel (2011-22), Chapter 28), have non-arts-related educational backgrounds. Representing the diverse backgrounds and career paths of arts managers, their clear leadership and management principles point the reader towards core leadership values. While Flora Yu (Executive Director of Hong Kong Arts Festival Society Ltd., Chapter 1) foregrounds the value of offering trust, respect, empowerment, and autonomy, Anna Kwong (Programme Director of Centre for the Arts, The Hong Kong University of Science and Technology, Chapter 6) considers being democratic with team members a key characteristic of their management and leadership style. Paul Tam (Chapter 22) and Scarlett Jie Chen's (Chapter 23) point on avoiding micromanagement also offers useful advice to the reader, who might be a current or future cultural leader. That said, the adequate application of leadership theories, such as Path-Goal Theory, would have provided sufficient analytical depth.

The conversations also cover the varying challenges creative entrepreneurs face. In the 1990s, Lindsey McAlister (Founder of Hong Kong Youth Arts Foundation, HKYAF, Chapter 19), with HKD $500 in her bank account and little understanding of Cantonese culture and language, struggled to attract investment to turn her idea into an actual project. The non-quitter, however, finally managed to persuade a bank manager to lend her HKD $200,000. This hard-won money then led to further investment, disproving the previous mistrust of the investors. Compared to HKYAF, a charity that offers children and young people access to arts experiences, the Collective HK, founded in 2013, is a for-profit organisation. Interestingly, the Collective HK, introduced in Chapter 25, created a non-profit technology platform. Using technology to create interactive art installations, they aim to bring positive impacts on society and our planet. Through these (dis)similar cases, Lo et al. highlight creative entrepreneurs' determination and passion for their work in a challenging and changing environment.

Throughout the chapters, Lo et al. deliver the interviewees' answers faithfully. Contrary to my expectation, additional examination is not pursued in each chapter. Instead, the authors provide an analytical summary of the interviews in the Conclusion. The critical comment on the result-oriented focus in cultural programmes and the question of how arts in Hong Kong should differ from those in New York, London or Paris lead the reader to contemplate the possibilities and challenges addressed in the chapters. Even with the exclusive focus on Hong Kong, the enthusiasm, strategies and visions of the cultural leaders discussed in this book will certainly benefit arts managers worldwide.

In some of the interviews, Lo et al. invite the interviewees to share their views on the contrasting perceptions of Hong Kong as a cultural desert and one of the top international art markets. While some may find this characterisation of Hong Kong unacceptable, the ongoing development of the much-needed arts infrastructure in WKCD lends credence to the blunt metaphor. Indeed, it is undeniable that Hong Kong is still primarily known for its global reputation as an economic hub, its iconic skyscrapers, and its Cantonese cuisine, such as dim sum, rather than for its artistic attractions. When presented with the view that Hong Kong is a cultural desert, however, the interviewees disagree without hesitation, offering various explanations for that. The cultural pride and confidence evident in their answers intrigue the reader to see the potential growing inside Hong Kong's vibrant arts and cultural scene.

BOMI CHOI*

*   b.choi@bbk.ac.uk

Journal of Cultural Management and Policy, 2024/2, pp. 264–268
doi 10.14361/zkmm-2024-0216

Journal of Cultural Management and Cultural Policy

Aims and Scopes

The *Journal of Cultural Management and Cultural Policy* is dedicated to international perspectives that address a wide range of issues in cultural management and cultural policy research and practice. We invite articles that reflect on organizational structures of creative enterprises, economic and managerial issues in the arts, cultural policy in all its dimensions, as well as creative and aesthetic processes in cultural production, distribution and perception.

The journal aims to present multifaceted analysis and rich discourse on current issues in cultural management and cultural policy and to promote the development of research designs and methods relating to both new and established practices in these fields. The journal is open to any theoretical and methodological approach, as long as authors adhere to scholarly rigor.

To strengthen the inter- and transdisciplinary character of research in the arts and culture, the journal publishes **research articles** (6.000 to 10.000 words), exploratory **essays** (about 6.000 words), and **case studies** (about 4.000 words) from disciplines such as sociology and psychology (of the arts), (cultural) politics, economics, history, cultural theory, philosophy, theatre studies, musicology, and arts education, or the interdisciplinary integration of these.
Research articles must fulfill the highest standards in methodological and theoretical approaches; whereas essays give the opportunity to develop a more personal perspective on topics. Case studies offer insights into particular questions and methods applied in a specific research context.
Reviews of books and conferences (850 to 1.000 words) related to the topic of the special issue complement each issue. Reviews of events organized by the authors themselves will not be published.

Submissions

The peer-reviewed journal is published twice a year with a thematic section focusing on a special issue and an open section with contributions on varied topics. Contributions should be clearly written, well-structured, novel and interesting for our audience. Only original, unpublished manuscripts can be submitted. Submissions are welcome in English or German.

Peer Review Process

For quality assurance purposes all submitted research articles and essays are reviewed in a double-blind peer review procedure. The editors-in-chief and managing editor evaluate every submitted manuscript. If a manuscript does not meet the required formal or academic criteria or if the topic and content of an article clearly do not fit in with the Journal it can be directly rejected instead of being submitted to a review. Authors are informed of this approximately four weeks after submission of the manuscript.

Three experts review each manuscript. Two reviewers are selected by the editors-in-chief, one is suggested by the author. The two reviewers are selected according to the methodological scope and the topic of the manuscripts. The reviewing follows a standardized procedure, including quantitative and qualitative aspects.

The results of the reviews will be sent to the author in the editorial decision letter. Manuscripts might be accepted, subjected to revisions, or rejected. This process can take up to four months.

The revised manuscripts are then resubmitted to the reviewers. The second reviewing should not take longer than four weeks. The authors are informed about the decision on the definitive acceptance of the manuscript; last small changes may be requested.

Review criteria are:

- conceptual quality of the manuscript
- soundness of methodology
- precision of objectives
- academic importance of the topic
- significance of research approach
- relevancy to arts management practices
- readability (presentation, stylistic form)

Submission Guidelines

You can find more information on the formal guidelines for submissions here <https://jcmcp.org/submission-guidelines>.

Upon submitting the manuscript, the authors consent to the JCMPC publication and malpractice statement.

Please send your submission to submissions [at] jcmcp [dot] org